QUARTER LIB

D1756691

LEEDS BECKETT UNIVERSITY
LIBRARY
DISCARDED

Leeds Metropolitan University

17 0503643 2

CRISIS MANAGEMENT PLANNING AND EXECUTION

OTHER INFORMATION SECURITY BOOKS FROM AUERBACH

Assessing and Managing Security Risk in IT Systems: A Structured Methodology
John McCumber
ISBN: 0-8493-2232-4

Audit and Trace Log Management: Consolidation and Analysis
Phillip Q Maier
ISBN: 0-8493-2725-3

Building and Implementing Security Certification and Accreditation Program
Patrick D Howard
ISBN: 0-8493-2062-3

The CISO Handbook: A Practical Guide to Securing Your Company
Michael Gentile; Ronald D Collette; Thomas D August
ISBN: 0-8493-1952-8

The Complete Guide for CPP Examination Preparation
James P Muuss; David Rabern
ISBN: 0-8493-2896-9

Curing the Patch Management Headache
Felicia M Nicastro
ISBN: 0-8493-2854-3

Cyber Crime Investigator's Field Guide, Second Edition
Bruce Middleton
ISBN: 0-8493-2768-7

Database and Applications Security: Integrating Information Security and Data Management
Bhavani Thuraisingham
ISBN: 0-8493-2224-3

The Ethical Hack: A Framework for Business Value Penetration Testing
James S Tiller
ISBN: 0-8493-1609-X

Guide to Optimal Operational Risk and Basel II
Ioannis S Akkizidis; Vivianne Bouchereau
ISBN: 0-8493-3813-1

The Hacker's Handbook: The Strategy Behind Breaking into and Defending Networks
Susan Young; Dave Aitel
ISBN: 0-8493-0888-7

The HIPAA Program Reference Handbook
Ross Leo
ISBN: 0-8493-2211-1

Information Security Architecture: An Integrated Approach to Security in the Organization, Second Edition
Jan Killmeyer Tudor
ISBN: 0-8493-1549-2

Information Security Fundamentals
Thomas R Peltier; Justin Peltier; John A Blackley
ISBN: 0-8493-1957-9

Information Security Management Handbook, Sixth Edition
Harold F Tipton; Micki Krause
ISBN: 0-8493-7495-2

Information Security Policies and Procedures: A Practitioner's Reference, Second Edition
Thomas R Peltier
ISBN: 0-8493-1958-7

Information Security Risk Analysis, Second Edition
Thomas R Peltier
ISBN: 0-8493-3346-6

Information Technology Control and Audit, Second Edition
Frederick Gallegos; Daniel P Manson; Sandra Senft; Carol Gonzales
ISBN: 0-8493-2032-1

Intelligence Support Systems: Technologies for Lawful Intercepts
Kornel Terplan; Paul Hoffmann
ISBN: 0-8493-2855-1

Managing an Information Security and Privacy Awareness and Training Program
Rebecca Herold
ISBN: 0-8493-2963-9

Network Security Technologies, Second Edition
Kwok T Fung
ISBN: 0-8493-3027-0

The Practical Guide to HIPAA Privacy and Security Compliance
Kevin Beaver; Rebecca Herold
ISBN: 0-8493-1953-6

A Practical Guide to Security Assessments
Sudhanshu Kairab
ISBN: 0-8493-1706-1

Practical Hacking Techniques and Countermeasures
Mark D. Spivey
ISBN: 0-8493-7057-4

The Security Risk Assessment Handbook: A Complete Guide for Performing Security Risk Assessments
Douglas J Landoll
ISBN: 0-8493-2998-1

Strategic Information Security
John Wylder
ISBN: 0-8493-2041-0

Surviving Security: How to Integrate People, Process, and Technology, Second Edition
Amanda Andress
ISBN: 0-8493-2042-9

Wireless Security Handbook
Aaron E Earle
ISBN: 0-8493-3378-4

AUERBACH PUBLICATIONS
www.auerbach-publications.com
To Order Call: 1-800-272-7737 • Fax: 1-800-374-3401
E-mail: orders@crcpress.com

CRISIS
MANAGEMENT
PLANNING AND
EXECUTION

EDWARD S. DEVLIN

FOREWORD BY RICHARD L. ARNOLD

Auerbach Publications
Taylor & Francis Group
Boca Raton   New York

Auerbach Publications is an imprint of the
Taylor & Francis Group, an informa business

LEEDS METROPOLITAN
UNIVERSITY
LIBRARY

1705036432
BV-B
BP-96670
8.7.08
658.4056 DEV

Auerbach Publications
Taylor & Francis Group
6000 Broken Sound Parkway NW, Suite 300
Boca Raton, FL 33487-2742

© 2007 by Taylor & Francis Group, LLC
Auerbach is an imprint of Taylor & Francis Group, an Informa business

No claim to original U.S. Government works
Printed in the United States of America on acid-free paper
10 9 8 7 6 5 4 3 2 1

International Standard Book Number-10: 0-8493-2244-8 (Hardcover)
International Standard Book Number-13: 978-0-8493-2244-0 (Hardcover)

This book contains information obtained from authentic and highly regarded sources. Reprinted material is quoted with permission, and sources are indicated. A wide variety of references are listed. Reasonable efforts have been made to publish reliable data and information, but the author and the publisher cannot assume responsibility for the validity of all materials or for the consequences of their use.

No part of this book may be reprinted, reproduced, transmitted, or utilized in any form by any electronic, mechanical, or other means, now known or hereafter invented, including photocopying, microfilming, and recording, or in any information storage or retrieval system, without written permission from the publishers.

For permission to photocopy or use material electronically from this work, please access www.copyright.com (http://www.copyright.com/) or contact the Copyright Clearance Center, Inc. (CCC) 222 Rosewood Drive, Danvers, MA 01923, 978-750-8400. CCC is a not-for-profit organization that provides licenses and registration for a variety of users. For organizations that have been granted a photocopy license by the CCC, a separate system of payment has been arranged.

Trademark Notice: Product or corporate names may be trademarks or registered trademarks, and are used only for identification and explanation without intent to infringe.

Library of Congress Cataloging-in-Publication Data

Devlin, Edward S.
  Crisis management planning and execution / Edward S. Devlin.
     p. cm.
  Includes bibliographical references and index.
  ISBN 0-8493-2244-8 (alk. paper)
  1. Crisis management. I. Title.

HD49.D483 2006
658.4'056--dc22   2006048419

Visit the Taylor & Francis Web site at
http://www.taylorandfrancis.com

and the Auerbach Web site at
http://www.auerbach-publications.com

CONTENTS

FOREWORD

When asked to write a foreword for Ed Devlin's latest book, I was honored. His previous book, *Business Resumption Planning*, has served as a standard in this industry. It has stood the test of time and contains must-read information for anyone interested in resuming business operations following a disaster. In this evolving industry, it is rare to find advice and information that remains a constant throughout the years.

Devlin's newest book focuses on *crisis management planning and execution*. It is a subject that has often been overlooked and misunderstood in our industry. As you will learn in this book, the term "crisis management planning" is sometimes used in relation to a disaster recovery plan, a security plan, an emergency response plan, a corporate communication plan, and more. With all these uses, it is no surprise that practitioners and executives are confused as to what it means.

Devlin defines crisis management planning as the role of senior executives to effectively manage a crisis when one strikes. It sounds like a simple, straightforward process. But as those in the business continuity industry know, a simple definition does not mean a simple process.

Devlin provides a clear, concise, and complete look at crisis management planning. He imparts his years of experience and knowledge to give us a look at the entire process. He provides us with the "how's," the "why's" and the "why not's." In true Ed Devlin fashion, he tells it like it is.

I have been blessed to know Devlin for more than 20 years. We have had a wonderful working relationship and a long-standing friendship. I have always admired his tenacity, his longevity, and his willingness to do anything for the good of the contingency planning industry.

Although he is often referred to as "the father of the industry," I like to think of him as more than that. During his 30 years of service to our industry, he pioneered much of the terminology and technology we still use today. He also introduced the first conference dedicated to business continuity and disaster recovery planning, beginning in 1977 and continuing it through 1992.

But he has done so much more. He is more than a "father" to our industry. He is a leader, a mentor, an educator, and a friend. Some 15 years ago, I suffered a stroke that affected my speaking abilities. Devlin helped me through some very tough times and continues to serve as an announcer at *Disaster Recovery Journal* annual conferences. He has been the voice that has welcomed our attendees and introduced our speakers. And he has served as the voice of reason in many other industry projects.

Like his first book, *Business Resumption Planning*, Devlin serves as a standard in our industry. From his early days in data processing through his years as co-founder of Devlin Associates and into the present day, Devlin has been known for his reliability, his knowledge, and his innovativeness.

With this book, Devlin has again forged new ground by daring to define an often-misunderstood term. One of the key complaints I have heard throughout the years is the misuse and misguided use of industry terminology. In a conference workshop Devlin co-conducts, he does an excellent job of explaining how and why the terms have evolved to keep up with the changes in the planning industry. There are not many people who could manage this task.

In this book, Devlin gives us not only a clear definition of crisis management planning terminology, but also solid, clear-cut examples of its importance. He uses his extensive industry history to provide details on the types of crises an organization might face, the actions to take when a crisis occurs, and he shares examples of organizations that have thorough plans in place.

Devlin's years of experience allow him to not only explain what has happened, but also provide personal insight into a variety of crises. He has spent years working in our industry — as a consultant, a manager, a speaker, an author, and a conference presenter. During that time, he has witnessed, worked with, and written about numerous disasters, recoveries, and emergency response events. I can think of no one better to help us understand the crisis management planning process.

I plan to add this book as a staple in my business continuity library. I know I will refer to it often. I think of this book in the same terms that I have used to describe Devlin: reliable, informative, insightful, and enlightening. I hope the readers enjoy it as much as I have.

Richard L. Arnold, CBCP
Publisher/Owner of the Disaster Recovery Journal

PREFACE

This book has been written to share my thoughts and ideas with the many Business Continuity Planning professionals who are attempting to more actively involve senior management in their organization's Business Continuity Plan.

In my 30+ years of experience in the Business Continuity Planning (BCP) or Disaster Recovery Planning industry, I have found that the best BCP programs are those in which the organization's executive management has an active role to play. By this I mean that as part of the BCP, senior management has included the actions they expect they will take when faced with a critical situation (i.e., a disaster or crisis). This is what I refer to as the Crisis Management Plan (CMP).

I have been very fortunate to be able to work with CEOs and their key executives during my years with Devlin Associates Inc. and then with organizations such as Sungard Planning Solutions, Strohl Systems, and Peak Associates.

With this book, I am attempting to share with other BCP professionals how I have worked with the senior management of organizations to encourage them to participate in the BCP — by documenting the actions they anticipate using when faced with a situation.

By combining the research I have accumulated over the years I have been in the business, with the experiences I have enjoyed with CEOs and their top executives, I believe this book will provide BCP professionals with numerous ideas that will assist them in incorporating the Crisis Management Plan into their organization's Business Continuity Plan.

OVERVIEW OF CHAPTERS

Chapter 1 defines the term "Crisis Management Plan." It defines the terms "crisis" and "disaster" and gives numerous examples of both. Section 1.6

answers the question frequently asked: Why do companies need a Crisis Management Plan?

Chapter 2 gives a detailed explanation of the Business Continuity Plan, and how it comprises the Prevention, Emergency Response, and Business Resumption Plans. It also provides an interesting "history" of the Business Continuity Plan, starting with the original name "Contingency Plan." The history explains different incidents that occurred and resulted in the modification of the name used to describe what we now call the "Business Continuity Plan." (By the way, shortly after this book is published, I expect that the industry will have changed Business Continuity to a new name.)

Chapter 3 explains the stages of a crisis. It goes into detail on the Pre-Crisis stage, then on the Acute-Crisis stage, and finishes with the Post-Crisis stage.

Chapter 4 discusses the four steps needed to manage a crisis. The chapter discusses each step; that is, Take Charge Quickly, Establish the Facts, Tell Your Story, and finally Fix the Problem.

Chapter 5 provides detailed information on the Executive Management Team (EMT) section of the Crisis Management Plan. It discusses the types of executives that would normally be represented on the EMT, their role during the Pre-Crisis stage, and the importance for them to recognize the Pre-Crisis "warning." It explains why they activate and empower the Crisis Management Team to take charge during the Acute-Crisis stage. Finally, it explains why it is important for the EMT to apologize, or make changes to recoup losses sustained during the crisis or disaster.

Chapter 6 provides detailed information on the Crisis Management Team (CMT). It discusses the types of executives that would normally be represented on the CMT and how they would carry out the four steps needed in managing a crisis from Chapter 4. It also mentions how the CMT would carry out their responsibilities if their offices were affected by the same disaster that affected key business units of the organization. Chapter 6 also provides examples of Service Level Agreements from each of the CMT members discussed in the chapter, i.e., Facility Issues, Security Issues, Public Relations Issues, Human Resources Issues, Legal Issues, Insurance Issues, and Finance Issues.

Chapter 7 deals exclusively with the Crisis Communications Plan (CCP) and the Crisis Communications Team (CCT). This element of the Crisis Management Plan is so important that it deserves a chapter of its own. The chapter explains why an organization needs to have a CCP at the ready before a crisis strikes. It discusses the importance of having a clearly defined policy; who could, or who should, be on the CCT; and the importance of having members of the team trained to deal with the media.

Chapter 8 discusses developing the Crisis Management Plan. It points out the role of the BCP professional in the development of the plan and presents a couple of methodologies that can be used in finalizing the CMP.

Chapter 9 details information relating to the Command Center, its functions, considerations, location(s), and resources needed.

Chapter 10 discusses the importance of exercising the Crisis Management Plan. It covers the Exercise Responsibilities of the Crisis Management Administrator, the planning involved before attempting to exercise the CMT, and the value of the exercises (using actual examples).

In summary, with the information presented in the book, especially the roles of the EMT and CMT during a crisis, the Business Continuity professional, or any reader, should be able to craft a Crisis Management Plan that the executives of an organization will actively support.

ABOUT THE AUTHOR

Edward S. Devlin is a leading consultant, author, instructor, and speaker in the field of Business Continuity and Business Resumption Planning. He co-founded Devlin Associates Inc. in 1973, the first company in the U.S. to specialize in Disaster Recovery Planning consulting services. From 1973 to the present, Devlin has assisted well over a thousand companies worldwide in the development or enhancement of their Business Continuity programs. During his 29 years in the industry, he has pioneered much of the philosophy, procedures, and nomenclature used in the industry today. Ed Devlin is often referred to as the "Father of Disaster Recovery Planning."

Currently, Devlin is the principal of Edward S. Devlin & Associates, where he provides BCP presentations for Business Continuity Planning professionals and executives of organizations.

Chapter 1

THE CRISIS MANAGEMENT PLAN — WHAT IS IT?

1.1 INTRODUCTION

According to various crisis management experts, the term "crisis management" could be defined as "special measures taken to solve problems caused by a crisis."

"To confine or minimize any damage to the organization's reputation or image," was another definition offered by executives when asked by Julia Gabis*. Gabis pointed out in the article entitled "Crisis: Danger or Opportunity" that good crisis management accomplishes more. Good crisis management should involve more than simply trying to minimize danger to an organization; it should also seek to maximize every possible opportunity. Good crisis managers achieve both. Gabis used as examples the Tylenol incident and the Exxon-Alaska incident.

> "A classic case of excellent crisis management is Johnson & Johnson's handling of the Tylenol poisoning incident a few years back. The situation was every corporate executive's worst nightmare come true; it could have put Tylenol (and perhaps Johnson & Johnson itself) out of business. Instead, the company not only retained consumer confidence, but today Tylenol has a larger share of the market than it did before the scare."

> "On the other hand, an example of how NOT to manage a crisis is Exxon's mishandling of the oil spill in Alaska. It's a perfect case of a company doing everything wrong from not

---

* Julia E. Gabis is an attorney specializing in health care law and crisis management with the Philadelphia law firm of Gollatz, Griffin, Ewing McCarthy.

> being prepared for a spill of such mammoth proportions to the media's portrayal of Exxon's chief executive, sitting passively in his New York home waiting by the telephone for reports of the situation."

Crisis management planning is not a science; it is more of an art.

> Science is "knowledge covering general truths" or the operation of general laws, as obtained and tested through scientific methods.
>
> Art is "skill acquired by experience, study or observation."
>
> —**Steven Fink,** *Crisis Management: Planning for the Inevitable*

Therefore, when referring to the members of the Crisis Management Team throughout the book, we are referring to a group of executives who have the expertise (skill acquired by experience, study, or observation) to carry out the successful management of a crisis situation.

The Crisis Management Plan (CMP) is a documented plan detailing the actions the executives want to be taken when a crisis strikes the organization. It is designed to put order into confusion. After a crisis has surfaced, the executives who have been selected to serve on the Crisis Management Team (CMT) will work together to achieve control of the crisis in order to minimize the impacts of the crisis. When a crisis has reached the acute stage, the team will employ the following steps:

1. Take charge quickly.
2. Determine the facts.
3. Tell your story.
4. Fix the problem.

Adhering to these steps will enable your organization to achieve control of the crisis. Remember that the key to successfully managing a crisis is *to Be Prepared*. A number of organizations are not prepared.

1.1.1 Plan Should Be Inclusive

The plan cannot limit itself to disasters, or to one or two types of crises (non-physical crises.) Organizations are exposed to more than one type of crisis, so the plan must identify actions to be taken based on a number of different crisis scenarios. The plan will identify these actions based on the specific "type" of crisis. The actions needed for a product safety problem will probably differ from the actions that need to be taken when the organization experiences an incident that is threatening the organization's reputation, or a financial crisis.

Throughout the book there will be a number of examples of organizations that have experienced a crisis. The information was obtained from articles in newspapers or magazines. The objective is not to cast aspersions on these organizations, or their management; rather, the objective is to share information acquired over the past three decades that will explain how a crisis started, its cause, and how an organization managed it. The aim in this book is similar to the course a professor has been teaching at Dartmouth. Let me share an article I recently read in *Business Week* magazine (June 9, 2003), entitled "Why Smart Executives Fail."

> "Professor Sydney Finkelstein of Dartmouth College's Tuck School of Business teaches a class entitled, 'The ABC's of Failure.' Casting off standard management fare about how to copy what companies do right, Professor Finkelstein presents his unconventional research on worst practices and corporate mistakes. The course is a twist on the hundreds of case studies churned out each year at other School's of Business, which mostly prompt students to dissect successes. Prof. Finkelstein's approach is "Some of the best learning comes from studying the things that go wrong." His theory is that troubled companies are more interesting than happy [companies].

> His interest is not so much about pointing out flaws, as it is about identifying the decisions that lead to mistakes in the first place. He starts at the source of the problem rather than conduct the more typical examination of just the negative result.

> And because he focuses mainly on otherwise intelligent managers who were respected in business, the lessons are more profound, say students. Professor Finkelstein has published a book entitled *Why Smart Executives Fail.*"

1.1.2   Plan Viability

People often ask me, "What does the plan need to be viable?" Unlike most other plans in the organization, the Crisis Management Plan *needs the participation of executive management*. What I mean by the participation of the executives is they have to do more than give the Crisis Management Plan "lip-service." They also need to do more than just provide a budget. As discussed in Chapter 5, they must participate in developing the plan. They should identify the people they feel would be in the best position to answer the key questions of What, When, Why, Where, Who, and How. This is the group consisting of the members of the Crisis Management Team (CMT).

Also, to be a viable, workable plan, the Crisis Management Plan must be developed with *the participation of the members of the CMT*. Without their participation, the plan lacks context, the interrelated conditions in which something exists or occurs. Without their participation, there is no guarantee that they are committed to it. The members of the CMT will not feel they own the plan because they were not involved in preparing it.

1.1.3   When Did the Concept Start?

In books and articles by Steven Fink, Gerry Meyers, and Ian Mitroff, it appears that the concept of managing a crisis evolved from the incident at Three Mile Island. That experience, in 1979, demonstrated that in an era of aggressive news media, and an evolving sophisticated public, organizations cannot avoid a crisis. During the Three Mile Island incident, people wanted answers — and they wanted them then, and not in a couple of days. This was true for the nearby residents of the nuclear plant, government officials of the Commonwealth of Pennsylvania, as well as people throughout the United States. The news media acted as the voice of the people. The organization responsible for Three Mile Island was negligent in its actions because it tried to put a different spin on the story.

For example, because it provided more misinformation than information, it caused confusion, anger, and fear. This situation has become a legendary example of how "not to manage" a crisis. As Steven Fink (President of Lexicon Communications Corp., Los Angeles, California, 1986) said, "The term Crisis Management was literally born as the nuclear reactor was dying. Five years after the Three Mile Island crisis event, the first-ever graduate school program in crisis management was started by Carnegie Mellon University in Pittsburgh.

1.2   WHAT IS A CRISIS?

In discussing the development of a Crisis Management Plan, one should start by clarifying what a crisis is. A crisis is defined in *Webster's New Collegiate Dictionary* as "a time of decision," an unstable or crucial time whose outcome will make a decisive difference for better or worse.

> When written in Chinese, the word crisis is composed of two characters: one represents danger and the other represents opportunity.

> **—John F. Kennedy**
> *President of United States*

For the purpose of this book, a "crisis" is an unstable time for an organization, with a distinct possibility for an undesirable outcome. This undesirable outcome could interfere with the normal operations of the organization, it could damage the bottom line, it could jeopardize the positive public image, or it could cause close media or government scrutiny.

Obviously, the full gamut of disasters comes to mind; that is, fires, floods, tornadoes, earthquakes, bombings, etc. In addition, examples of a crisis can include when an organization experiences a product failure, a product safety issue, product tampering, a product market-shift, an incident that results in a poor image or negative reputation, an international incident that negatively affects the organization, and a financial problem — especially a fuzzy accounting problem. (***Author Note:*** The "fuzzy accounting" problem is difficult to prepare for because you will be working with the culprit when developing the Crisis Management Team's plan.)

Keep in mind that crisis does not only mean danger. It also means an opportunity.

1.2.1 The American Red Cross

An example of an incident that was an unstable time with a distinct possibility for undesirable outcome occurred in 2001 when the American Red Cross came under fire for its planned use of money raised after the terrorist attacks of 9-11 at the World Trade Center. The reason for choosing this case study is because it depicts so many of the lessons that can be learned from a crisis. It shows how a small problem grows into the acute-crisis stage. It shows some of the steps that should be used in managing a crisis. It also shows what actions organizations can take during the post-crisis stage to change some of the negative effects the crisis has caused.

Soon after the attacks, the American Red Cross created the Liberty Fund, a special fund designated for terrorism relief efforts. (This was considered an unusual step because typically donations to the Red Cross go into its Disaster Relief Fund, which is a general account designed to meet emergencies of all types.) But soon after the September 11 attacks, Red Cross President Bernadine Healy created the Liberty Fund as a special account targeted for victims of the attacks on the World Trade Center.

Families across the nation gave the Red Cross their hard-earned dollars and their trust that the donations would go directly to September 11 relief efforts. Eventually, donors found out that all of the donations made to the Liberty Fund were not going directly to September 11 relief efforts.

In an article entitled "Red Cross may triple aid to victims," published in *USA Today* (November 6, 2001), the American Red Cross said it has spent about $143 million of the $550 million pledged. That money went chiefly to families of the dead and to the injured and displaced. The relief agency said it had set aside an additional $180 million for immediate and long-term relief efforts. It said it would reserve the remaining $240 million to help victims of future terrorist attacks on the United States.

This created quite an outcry from the donors. Many donors made it perfectly clear that their donations were targeted for the victims of attacks.

In an effort to minimize the controversy, Bill Blaul, a Red Cross Senior Vice President, said, "Our mission is not to burn through $500 million as fast as we can and walk away. Our mission is getting as much assistance to people affected by this disaster as quickly as possible and over the longest term possible."

The American Red Cross organization was faced with a crisis — "credibility" crisis. The donors said they felt they no longer could trust the Red Cross. The probable result would be the loss of future donations. For an organization that depends on donations to meet its obligations, this translated into a "financial" crisis as well. The Red Cross had to decide how it was going to deal with the negative image being projected to many of its donors.

One of the steps an organization uses to help manage a crisis effectively is to "fix the problem." In many crises that we all research and study, we find that as part of the "fix the problem" decisions, a change in either the operation or the management is required. So it was in the Red Cross case. High-profile former President Bernadine Healy was forced from her $450,000-a-year post. On October 26, Bernadine Healy announced that she would resign on December 31.

Some Red Cross board members were unhappy that Healy created the Liberty Fund without their approval, and that much of the money would not go directly to victims. The Red Cross "overdid it and acted opportunistically, raising money for other programs that were not on the minds of donors when they gave them money," says Daniel Borochoff, President of the American Institute of Philanthropy, a watchdog group based in Bethesda, Maryland. For her part, Healy came to recognize that perhaps she and the Red Cross just were not the right fit. "Despite the many successes," she wrote to the board in a farewell note, "what you really wanted was a different personality ... maybe ... more of a Mary Poppins and less of a Jack Welch."

After the Red Cross admitted it planned to keep some of the money for other future disasters, the spotlight was on the organization. (***Author's Note:*** On the positive side, the American Red Cross serves disaster victims in over 65,000 disasters a year — everything from house fires to regional disasters, such as quakes, floods, tornadoes, etc.)

Once the spotlight is on, it is not easy to turn it off. In the same article in *USA Today,* it pointed out that:

> Typically, the Red Cross has not been in a position of publicly explaining itself to Congress. But there are limits to the charity's independence. Some lawmakers in a congressional oversight committee accused the Red Cross of taking advantage of the tragedy to bolster its budget. It is chartered by Congress and required to operate according to terms outlined by the federal government. Rep. Bart Stupak, a Michigan Democrat on the oversight panel, says the Red Cross should expect either a written reprimand from Congress or another Capitol Hill hearing to discuss possible redress.

> —*USA Today*
> *November 6, 2001*

1.2.2 "Opens the Door" Effect

Another problem developed over the Liberty Fund donation distribution. I tend to call this phenomenon the "opens the door" effect. When an organization gets itself into the spotlight, good investigative reporters start to do research on the organization. Lo and behold, they find prior crises the organization experienced. (Obviously, the organization would rather put the prior crises behind it, and not have people reminded of them.) But when the current crisis is similar to a prior crisis, bingo! The investigative journalist finds that the organization has "done it again." (*Author's Note:* I will refer to this term, "Opens the Door," on many occasions throughout the book.)

An article published in the *Philadelphia Inquirer* (November 21, 2001), entitled "A string of Red Cross fund fights," pointed out that in at least a half-dozen disasters over the last decade, local officials have had to pressure the American Red Cross to give victims the donations the public intended for them. The article went on to identify the following:

■ *Oklahoma City, 1995.* The Red Cross came under criticism months after the 1995 Oklahoma City federal building bombing for spending only one-fourth of the $13 million it had collected for victims and their families.

■ *North Dakota Flood, 1997.* When the Red River flooded parts of Minnesota and North Dakota in 1997, nearly $16 million was donated, yet the Minnesota attorney general had to resort to stinging public hearings and a 40-page report to prod the release of nearly $4 million in unspent funds for the victims.

■ *San Diego.* In the San Diego area, a recent audit of collections for victims of a January wildfire found money improperly used for vehicles and a telephone system's upgrade while burned-out families waited for money earmarked for them. "They went out and raised money on the backs of fire victims here and put it to other uses," said Dianne Jacob, a San Diego County supervisor who has been battling the Red Cross over its handling of the disaster in Alpine, about 20 miles east of downtown San Diego. "They got caught big-time in New York because it was big-time money, but it was the same pattern."

As one can see, this crisis did result in an undesirable outcome; it could damage the bottom line because it threatened future donations, it did jeopardize the positive public image, and it did cause close media and government scrutiny.

1.2.3 Cook County Administration Building, Chicago, Illinois

Another example of an unstable time for an organization with a distinct possibility for an undesirable outcome occurred on October 17, 2003, when Cook County suffered a fire on the 12th floor of its 35-story building in downtown Chicago. Questions raised about the fire department's response is of an undesirable outcome.

The building can accommodate as many as 2500 people during business hours, including employees from the public defender's office, county prosecutors, the secretary of state's office, and other local and state government agencies. Fortunately, the building was not full when the fire started at the close of the business day. People obeyed an announcement to evacuate.

Only after the blaze had been put out did firefighters find more than a dozen people in the stairwell and on the 22nd floor, fire officials said. Six were dead. The dead were overcome by smoke. They were not found until after the fire was brought under control Friday evening and firefighters started searching the building floor by floor, authorities said. The people who died appeared to be from one stairwell around the 22nd floor, ten stories above the source of the fire. Most of the injured were found in the stairways and hallways from the 16th to the 22nd floors.

The Fire Commissioner, James Joyce, explained that, "Searching for all those people, at the same time fighting the fire, is more complicated than it looks from the outside." A comprehensive search of the building was completed about five hours after the fire was first reported, he said.

Firefighters escorted some workers down stairways and evacuated a daycare center without incident, fire officials said.

First of all, the Fire Commissioner said the building had an alarm system but no sprinklers. When the County of Chicago acquired the building in 1996, they spent $40 million on extensive "remodeling" to the 35-story building.

The question being asked now is: how could they spend all that money and not put in a sprinkler system?

Public officials and employees who worked in the 35-story building have also raised questions about the thoroughness of the Fire Department's response and the system that has doors that will not open back into the building from the stairwell when fire alarms are activated. Several government workers who escaped the blaze said they tried to exit a stairwell as it became filled with smoke but found that doors on several floors allowed people into the stairwell but not out. And how can you have a system that has doors that open but won't let you back in?

This is another example of an incident that created an undesirable outcome. It could jeopardize the positive public image of Cook County and of the Fire Department, and it has caused close media scrutiny.

These examples are not to say that a crisis must result in a negative. As mentioned previously, a crisis also offers an opportunity. Some organizations have taken the opportunity that a crisis has presented and used it to their advantage:

> Gerald Meyers, former head of American Motors, author, and crisis management expert, pointed out during a Ford Co. recall that "the recall could provide Ford the opportunity to forge stronger relationships with customers. He reminded people that in 1994, Saturn recalled 322,000 cars because of a wiring harness problem. When customers came in for replacements, dealers held picnics, washed their cars, and provided entertainment. The customers left the dealerships with a positive attitude, rather than a worried concern."

> —*USA Today*
> *April 26, 1996*

1.3 TYPES OF CRISES

An organization can face a number of different *types of crises*. The list below contains some of the incidents that can evolve into a crisis. It is by no means an all-inclusive list. There are other incidents that are not identified here, yet could be considered a crisis situation by a particular company.

Examples of incidents that can escalate into an *acute crisis* include:

- A product issue: for example, a product does not work as promised (credibility), is injuring people (safety), has been tampered with; a market shift (sudden change, or over a long period of time).
- A negative public perception of your organization (e.g., your organization has a problem, and it appears it does not care about the problem).
- A financial problem (cash problem, fraud, or fuzzy accounting).
- An industrial relations problem (e.g., worker strike problem, employee lawsuits).
- An adverse international event (e.g., disaster at their location has jeopardized your product or service).
- Workplace violence (e.g., employees have been violently attacked while working on your organization's property).
- Senior executives have died or been killed (i.e., executive succession problem).

Other examples of incidents that can escalate into an acute crisis include:

- A disaster at one of your organization's locations, including acts of nature (e.g., earthquake, tornado, flood, etc.); accidents (e.g., fire, leak, lengthy power outages, etc.); or intentional acts (e.g., bomb or arson).

Let us further define the types of crises by sharing an example of each. The discussion begins with nonphysical types of crises, followed by physical types of disasters.

1.3.1 Nonphysical Damage Crises: Definition and Examples

1.3.1.1 Product Issue: Credibility

This type of crisis occurs when a manufacturer of a product finds that there are questions regarding the product's effectiveness, credibility, or satisfaction. A recent example of a product credibility crisis is Mercedes Auto (2003).

> Product satisfaction: on July 8, 2003, the world's most esteemed luxury auto maker suffered the humiliation of seeing its ranking in the annual J.D. Power & Associates Inc. survey of car dependability plunge to No. 26 from No. 16 last year, eight slots below the industry average, trailing Chrysler, Ford, and Plymouth.

In 1990, Mercedes-Benz proudly ranked No. 1. "Once it was the nameplate of envy. It may be losing some of that shine," says Brian Walters, J.D. Power's research director.

Problems cited by consumers in the 962-page report included handling, braking, shocks and struts, electronic window controls, and inaccurate fuel gauges.

Mercedes' famed engineering prowess is hardly kaput. The problems cited in the survey affect three specific models from the year 2000. One of them, the midsize E-Class sedan — Mercedes' big money-maker — already has been replaced by a newer version that is winning raves from critics. And the M-Class sport-utility vehicle received an extensive overhaul in September 2001, including the replacement of 1100 parts. Mercedes officials insist that the quality problems highlighted in the J.D. Power survey are history, and that cost-cutting does not affect quality at Mercedes.

—*Business Week*
July 21, 2003

1.3.1.2   *Product Issue: Defective*

This type of crisis occurs when a manufacturer of a product finds that there are questions regarding the product's effectiveness or credibility. A recent example of a product defective crisis is Tyco International–Grinnell (2002):

Tyco's Grinnell Fire Protection subsidiary is liable for $20.5 million because of a fire that destroyed 152,000 boxes of documents owned by Wachovia Corp., a Pennsylvania jury ruled. The bank accused Grinnell, a maker of sprinkler systems, with building a defective fire-protection product for Diversified Information Technologies Inc., which stored the documents for Wachovia.

—*Philadelphia Inquirer*
December 20, 2002

1.3.1.3   *Product Issue: Safety*

This type of crisis occurs when a manufacturer of a product finds that one of its products is being accused of injuring or killing customers. A recent example of a product safety crisis is Firestone Tire Company (2000):

Federal investigators are examining deaths that they think could be linked to faulty Firestone tires. Complaints suggesting that the tread of the Firestone models peel off. Recall: Firestone said it would give credit toward new tires for customers who wanted to exchange their current tires. Several major tire retailers have announced they will stop carrying the tires until the investigation is complete: Sears, Montgomery Ward, Tire Discounters. [Ford has replaced Firestone tires for free on vehicles sold in Venezuela, Ecuador, Thailand, Malaysia, Columbia, and Saudi Arabia.]

—Philadelphia Inquirer
August 8, 2000

1.3.1.4 Product Issue: Tampering

This type of crisis occurs when a manufacturer of a product finds that one of its products is being accused of injuring or killing customers. Product tampering is one of the biggest threats to a manufacturing organization. For this reason, most manufacturing organizations have a plan to respond to a tampering incident. History will show that organizations lose their reputation in a matter of days if they fail to act adequately during this type of crisis. An example of a product tampering crisis is Burroughs Wellcome of Triangle Park, North Carolina (1991).

The manufacturer of Sudafed 12-hour cold capsules issued a nationwide recall after two people who had taken the medication died of cyanide poisoning and a third became seriously ill. The company recalled all Sudafed 12-hour cold capsules after a capsule packed with cyanide powder sent a 28-year-old woman of Tumwater, WA, into seizures. The woman lapsed into a coma but (fortunately) survived. Within three weeks of the woman's poisoning, a 40-year-old woman of Tacoma, WA, died on February 11, and a 44-year-old man of Lacey, WA, died on February 18 after taking tainted Sudafed capsules.

"We are moving rapidly to alert the public and retrieve all Sudafed 12-hour capsules from the retail stores. Our sympathies go to the families of the individuals involved, and they have our assurance that the company will investigate these incidents quickly and thoroughly," [Philip R. Tracy, president and chief executive officer of the company]. Burroughs Wellcome offered a $100,000 reward for information leading to a conviction in the cyanide tampering case.

—USA Today
March 3, 1991

1.3.1.5 Negative Public Perception of Your Organization

This type of crisis occurs when an incident occurs that can cause a negative reaction toward the organization. A recent example of a negative public perception crisis is Greyhound Bus Co. (1997).

> A Greyhound's bus driver ordered an 80-year-old woman off the company's bus at a rural truck stop at 3:00 a.m. in the morning. The bus stop was 80 miles from the woman's home in Tampa. She was ordered off the bus because she had a dog on the bus, and that was against the company's rules — a tiny Pekinese puppy, her birthday present.

> The woman, who uses a crutch and has trouble both hearing and seeing, had boarded the bus in Panama City, FL, after visiting her daughters. Police from several jurisdictions teamed up to ferry the woman from the Ocala area to her home, using five patrol cars. Greyhound's bus driver, a 20-year veteran, was suspended pending an investigation. Greyhound apologized and gave her a refund on Saturday.

—Philadelphia Inquirer
November 24, 1997

1.3.1.6 Market Shift

This type of crisis occurs when a manufacturer of a product finds that one of its products is no longer selling as anticipated. A recent example of a market shift crisis is Packard Bell NEC (1999).

> The Packard Bell name and 1600 jobs will cease to exist in the USA by the end of the year. The company failed to meet performance goals set by its Tokyo-based parent, NEC. Packard Bell was once the largest U.S. maker of PCs for consumers, had fallen to No. 6 by last summer. It lost $650 million last year.

—USA Today
November 4, 1999

1.3.1.7 Financial or Cash Problem

This type of crisis occurs when an organization experiences a cash problem, a difficulty meeting its obligations, or an accusation of fuzzy accounting. An example of a financial or cash crisis is Executive Life (1991).

> The warnings that Executive Life was teetering toward insolvency began a year before the State of California placed the insurer in state-controlled conservatorship. Executive Life had 245,000 clients and was holding $40.5 billion of life insurance and annuities when the California state insurance commissioner announced that his agents were seizing control of Executive Life.
>
> Executive Life's failure — the industry's largest yet — comes when many insurers are burdened with large investments in mortgages and junk bonds that have gone south. Fred Carr, CEO, disdained the slow, steady process of writing policies and building reserves through careful investments to cover eventual payouts. Instead he built the company with sizzle and flash, turning in the 1980s to the high-yield junk bonds. Of Executive Life's $10.1 billion in assets, $6.4 billion is junk. As the junk-bond market fizzled in 1989, First Executive reported a stunning $859 million write-down in its portfolio. In announcing his takeover last week, the California state insurance commissioner assured policy-holders that medical claims and death benefits will continue to be paid while the state manages the company.
>
> *—Newsweek*
> *April 4, 1991*

1.3.1.8 Industrial Relations Problem

This type of crisis occurs when a manufacturer of a product finds that one of its products is being accused of injuring or killing customers. Here are two good examples of an industrial relations crisis: one negative and the other is counter to that.

The first example is Coastal Oil Co. (1995):

> Margaret Graziano, while keeping a vigil at the hospital bedside of her comatose 10-year-old son, was told by her boss that she was being laid off. She was a credit analyst who had worked for the company for six years. Her son had been hit by a car October 29 in Queens. She took unpaid leave to stay close to

her comatose 10-year-old son in the intensive care unit at New York Hospital – Cornell Medical Center in Manhattan. She was keeping a vigil at the hospital bedside of her son when her boss showed up — not for support or comfort. Instead, he told her she had been laid off because the company was restructuring and had to cut 18 jobs.

(CMT-H.R.) Coastal knows it was "horrible timing for everybody concerned," the Coastal spokesperson said. He said Graziano knew before her son's accident that the company was restructuring and that jobs were being eliminated. He conceded that she had no way of knowing that hers was one of them. "They should have waited for a better moment, when they knew my son was out of danger, or they could have contacted me somewhere else other than here."

—Philadelphia Inquirer
November 12, 1995

A second example of an industrial relations crisis (which was handled differently) is Safety Kleen Corp. (2000):

Mark Hamlin, a sales representative for Safety Kleen Corp. in Fairless Hills, has spent nearly all his time with Megan Hamlin, 16, since the June 20 accident, with his employer's blessing. Megan Hamlin is one of two girls critically injured when a red Toyota 4Runner ran over their heads as they sunbathed at the Anastasia State Recreation Area beach in St. Augustine, Fla. Megan remains comatose at Brooks Rehabilitation Center in Jacksonville, where she was transferred after a two-month hospitalization. She is now breathing on her own but has been mostly non-responsive; her father said she had shown some progress, reacting to commands, before a recent regression.

—Philadelphia Inquirer
September 8, 2000

1.3.1.9 Adverse International Event

This type of crisis occurs when an organization is disrupted by an international incident. An example of an adverse international crisis is Drexel Furniture Co. (1989):

The largest mass-disaster case ever litigated to a jury verdict ended when a jury found that Drexel Heritage Furnishings (North Carolina) and four other defendants had no responsibility for the loss of life or injuries that resulted from the tragic fire at the Dupont Plaza Hotel on December 31, 1986. Killed 97; injured 140. A disgruntled hotel employee set the fire by using cooking fuel to ignite several packaged Drexel Heritage dressers that had been delivered to the hotel the day before and were being stored in an unsprinklered ballroom on the hotel's ground floor. (CMT-Legal) More than 2300 plaintiffs filed claims for more than $3 billion against more than 200 defendants. The plaintiffs alleged that the furnishings were unreasonably dangerous because of their alleged ease of ignition and undue flammability. Drexel maintained that its wood dressers were made of non-hazardous materials commonly used by all furniture manufacturers. The company defended the lawsuit for almost three years. In the course of the suit, the law firm representing Drexel established an office in San Juan and developed its own computer system to track the millions of documents and the more than 2000 depositions in the case. Following a 15-month trial in the federal district court in San Juan, the jury reached its verdict after one week of deliberations, finding Drexel had no liability for any damages sustained by the plaintiffs. By the time the jury began its deliberations, all but nine of Drexel's co-defendants had reached out-of-court settlements that totaled between $190 and $200 million (November 2, 1992). The hotel, closed after an '86 fire, will reopen in '94 after a $131 million renovation. New name: San Juan Marriott Hotel.

—NFPA Journal
January 2, 1991

1.3.1.10 Workplace Violence

This type of crisis occurs when an organization experiences an assault on its employees or management personnel by another employee on the organization's premises. A typical example of this type of crisis is Windy City Core Supply (2003):

A man who was fired from an auto-parts warehouse six months ago came back with a gun and killed six employees before being shot to death by police. Salvador Tapia, 36, lost his job at Windy City Core Supply for causing trouble at work and frequently showing up late or not at all.

When police arrived shortly after 8:30 a.m., they tried to get in the building but were driven back by gunfire. Then an assault team entered the building, but it had trouble maneuvering through all the auto parts. Tapia died in a gun battle he waged with police inside and outside the building. The dead included two brothers who owned the business, and one of their sons. The other victims were all of Chicago. "From the scene, it appears that he went throughout the supply warehouse shooting them," a police official said. "They weren't all in one section." Tapia had at least one previous conviction for unlawful use of a weapon, officials said. It was the nation's deadliest workplace shooting since July 8, when Doug Williams shot 14 coworkers, killing five, at a Lockheed Martin plant in Meridian, Miss., before taking his own life.

—Philadelphia Inquirer
August 28, 2003

1.3.2   Physical Damage Disasters: Examples

Other examples of incidents that can escalate into an acute-crisis include a physical disaster at one of your organization's locations:

- Acts of nature (e.g., earthquake, tornado, flood, etc.)
- Accidents (a fire, leak, lengthy power outage, etc.)
- Intentional acts (e.g., a bomb or arson)

1.3.2.1   Earthquake

A recent example of an earthquake causing an undesirable outcome is The Puget Sound, Washington, Quake (2001):

The strongest temblor to hit the Pacific Northwest in 52 years — deep beneath Puget Sound — sent Seattle's high-rise office towers swaying. More than 250 people were injured but only one person died. The temblor's epicenter was buried in solid rock 30 miles underground. It was felt as far away as Salt Lake City and British Columbia. Began at 10:54 a.m. and lasted nearly 45 seconds — long enough to send old brick building facades crashing down onto cars, trigger a landslide that blocked a major river in Seattle's eastern suburbs, open fissures in roads and puncture gas and water lines. Washington state's two largest previous quakes — the 7.1 temblor in 1949 that killed eight people and a 6.5 quake in 1965 that killed seven

— both occurred in the same zone and relatively near where this quake occurred.

Property/casualty insurers will pay $330 million to homeowners and businesses for insured property damage from the earthquake that struck Seattle and adjoining areas in Washington and Oregon, according to preliminary estimates by Insurance Services Offices Inc.'s Property Claim Services unit. The February 28 catastrophic earthquake, which measured 6.8 on the Richter scale, generated 13,550 claims for insured damage to personal and commercial property and automobiles. Earlier damage estimates had exceeded $1 billion, but many earthquake-policy endorsements provide for deductibles, and that coverage may only apply to less than a quarter of the buildings in areas affected by the earthquake.

—Los Angeles Tmes
March 1, 2001

1.3.2.2 Tornado

A recent example of a tornado causing an undesirable outcome is The Missouri Tornadoes (2003):

"Tornado ends year for some Missouri schools" — The tornado wrecked school buildings in De Soto, forcing officials to cancel classes for the rest of the year and send students home for an unexpectedly early summer. Three schools in De Soto, about 40-miles southwest of St. Louis, were heavily damaged by the storm. The early summer break is hardly cause for celebration in the town of 6400, one of many in Missouri banged around by a series of tornadoes and thunder storms that killed more than 45 in the Midwest. In Carl Junction, the school year is over for all students except those in high school. Two grade schools, a junior high, and an intermediate school were damaged by tornadoes. Classes were also canceled last week in tornado-damaged Stockton and Pierce City. School officials there are still deciding if and when classes will resume. In De Soto, the tornado blew the roofs off the high school and an elementary school, leaving both with significant water damage. Graduation for the high school's seniors will still go on May 31. But for class work, there was simply no place to go, superintendent Terry Noble said. "We have extensive damage not only to our facilities but to other buildings that might normally be alternatives."

Many workers in the affected areas had to make arrangements to have their children taken care of before they could return to work.

—Philadelphia Inquirer
May 13, 2003

1.3.2.3 Flood

An excellent example of a flood causing an undesirable outcome is The City of Grand Forks, North Dakota, Flood (1997):

> The Red River crested at 54 feet on April 21, 26 feet above flood stage. It overflowed its 60-yard channel and at one point stretched 40 miles across the valley. Roughly 4.5 million acres in ND and MN were under temporary lakes. The mayor of Grand Forks imposed a 24-hour curfew on the evacuated area and said police would arrest anyone still in the zone who was not attempting to leave.

> During the worst of the flooding, the downtown area was struck with a fire that destroyed three city blocks. Firefighters were unable to get into the area with their fire trucks because of the 6 ft. deep water that flooded the area. Airplanes normally used to fight forest fires dive-bombed the buildings with a smoky red chemical. The retardant left a reddish film on the buildings. Firefighters also used a helicopter with a bucket, able to hold 2200 pounds of water, to scoop up floodwater and dump the water on the fire. Two fire department pumpers were ferried in on big-wheeled flatbed trucks to fight the fire. Also a specialized Air Force fire truck, able to operate in 8 ft. of water, got close enough to fight the fire from the ground.

> A federal relief agency paid an estimated $23 million for 376 structures in Fargo and Grand Forks. The homes and buildings will be removed to avoid future flood damage.

—Philadelphia Inquirer
April 22, 1997

1.3.2.4 Hurricane

An excellent example of a hurricane causing an undesirable outcome is Hurricane Floyd (1999):

> Hurricane "Floyd" slammed into North Carolina, causing that state's costliest natural disaster, and then moved up the East

Coast, dumping heavy rain as it went. Once deemed a Category 4 storm with winds of 155 miles per hour, Hurricane Floyd hit the Carolina coast on September 16 with winds of 115 miles per hour. The storm then proceeded through Virginia, New Jersey and parts of New York dumping up to 20 inches of rain on the region, causing "500-year" floods in some areas. Altogether, "Floyd" killed at least 69 people from the Bahamas to New England.

"Floyd" was massive in size — at one point it covered more than 700 miles. After the storm passed through the Bahamas, it was feared it would head toward the Florida or Georgia coast, but these states felt little more than light rain and winds as the hurricane took a turn to the north. Overall, hundreds of thousands of residents were evacuated from the coasts of Florida, Georgia, South Carolina and North Carolina. Eventually, the hurricane's eye hit landfall near Cape Fear, North Carolina. With damage in that state expected to surpass the $6 billion caused by Hurricane Fran in 1996, President Clinton declared the eastern two-thirds of North Carolina a disaster area. The Tar River at Tarboro rose to a record high of 43 feet. The old record was 34 feet, set in 1919. North Carolina's Neuse River rose more than 12 feet above flood level. North Carolina agricultural officials estimated that more than 1 million poultry and 110,000 hogs were killed by flooding. Health risks were one of the greatest fears as thousands of decaying animals and waste floated through the flood waters. Many cities along the East Coast lost power and had water supplies cut off because of the flooding. In Rochelle Park, New Jersey, an AT&T switching center was destroyed by flood waters, making communications difficult until accounts could be moved to a different switching center. Across North Carolina, about 300 roads, including parts of Interstates 95 and 40, were closed for several days. As the storm moved toward the New England states, Floyd was downgraded to a tropical storm, packing winds of less than 74 miles per hour. Many businesses closed early and airports along the East Coast canceled hundreds of flights. Amtrak suspended all train service south of Washington. The storm dropped up to 12 inches of rain in Philadelphia and 11 inches in Annapolis, MD.

—Disaster Recovery Journal
Fall 1999

1.3.2.5 Fire

A recent example of a fire causing an undesirable outcome is The Comfort Inn, Greenville, South Carolina, Fire (2004):

> Fire broke out in a five-story motel around 4 a.m. while guests were asleep, killing six and forcing others to leap from windows or climb down bed sheets to safety. At least a dozen people were injured, including at least five in critical condition at a burn unit in Augusta, Ga. The Comfort Inn had standpipes and wall-mounted hoses in the hallways and stairwells, but none had been activated and no fire extinguishers were used before emergency crews arrived, said Wade Hampton Fire Chief.

> (Sprinklers – No) He did not know the last time the building was inspected but said it was not required to have sprinklers. "If there had been sprinkler systems in the hallways, probably the fatalities and injuries would not have been near what they were," the Fire Chief said.

> (Evacuations) Greenville County deputies ran into the building to evacuate people, but they could not get past the second floor because of smoke. Some people on upper floors lowered themselves to the ground using bed sheets and others jumped from the windows.

> —***Philadelphia Inquirer***
> *January 25, 2004*

1.3.2.6 Leak

An excellent example of a leak causing an undesirable outcome is The Chicago River Flood caused by a leak into the tunnel system (1992):

> A hole developed in a branch of the tunnel beneath the Chicago River on April 13, 1992. River water poured through the aging tunnel system beneath a 12-square block area of Chicago's Loop, paralyzing the downtown area. An estimated 250 million gallons of river water rushed through car-size hole flooding basements at a rate of 2 feet per hour. Power was cut off to the area at 10:48 AM CDT and as much as 30 feet of water flowed into skyscraper basements. Eighteen (18) companies went to Comdisco's computer backup site to resume critical operations during the outage caused by the leak. Seven (7) companies went to other backup sites. The business units moved local computer equipment to temporary locations.

One month after a service-tunnel flood interrupted business in the downtown area, some establishments remained closed, and officials said some will never reopen. The Chamber of Commerce said at least 75 of the 8000 offices, stores and restaurants never reopened

In the aftermath of the flood, the city made major repairs in the tunnel and started new inspection routines. Old buildings in the Loop got mechanical and wiring renovations. Some are talking about the need to repair bridges, roads and the rest of Chicago's infrastructure. Some businesses in the loop were closed for up to a month.

Ironically, on Jan. 14, 1992, the Chicago Cable Company, which uses the tunnels for its cable, discovered the leak. River silt and water appeared to be coming through the wall beneath the river. But when it notified a city worker, he took a week to inspect. He took an additional five days to take pictures. Then the worker sent the film to an Osco drugstore, a regional chain. He waited a week to pick up the photos.

Another city worker briefly considered fixing the leak, but decided that the $75,000 bid to do the work was too high. His resignation has been accepted. The Chicagoland Chamber of Commerce now estimates the flood will cost up to $1.5 billion in direct clean-up costs and lost business. This week, an abashed mayor labeled the bureaucrats as "paper-shufflers" who "dropped the ball," and apologized to citizens. "The people of Chicago have experienced an understandable loss of confidence in their government," he said, "and that's something we can't fix with cement trucks, or with federal disaster funds, or with all the experts in the world."

"Chicago flood a wash with worker fumbles"
—USA Today
April 1, 1992

1.3.2.7 Power Outage

A good example of a power outage causing an undesirable outcome is The San Francisco Blackout (1998):

At 8:17 a.m. — the power went out for about 940,000 people across a 49-square mile area. Across San Francisco, office workers in high rise buildings were trapped in elevators. The cause — a construction crew forgot to remove the ground wire after completing maintenance on a substation switchboard, causing a blowout and triggering a chain reaction that knocked two generators off line. The outage was caused accidentally by a four-person crew upgrading a substation in San Mateo. The crew forgot to remove two grounding rods, causing a blowout and triggering a chain reaction that knocked generator's offline.

Retailers and city departments spent much of the day figuring out the financial toll. And within 24 hours of the outage, more than 600 customers had called PG&E requesting claim forms for potential reimbursement. The utility set up a hotline for claims, and made claim forms available on its Website. The company said it expected to have thousands of customers file claims. PG&E said that the outage was more widespread than first thought, affecting 435,000 customers rather than the 375,000 estimated a day earlier.

—USA Today
December 17, 1998

The San Francisco blackout on 12-08-1998 that affected more than 1 million residents was triggered by a mechanical failure and human error. PG&E workers performing system upgrades at the substation neglected to remove six of 18 ground wires when they re-energized the lines.

—Philadelphia Inquirer
December 9, 1998

1.3.2.8 Bombing

An excellent example of a bombing causing an undesirable outcome is The Murrah Federal Building bombing in Oklahoma City, Oklahoma (1995):

A bomb, planted in a yellow Ryder rental truck parked at a meter on Fifth Street, exploded at 9:04 a.m., destroying the Alfred P. Murrah Federal Building. The entire north side of the 9-story building was blown off.

The bombing killed 169 people; injured more than 500. 25 buildings in the blocks surrounding the site have been rendered unfit for occupancy. 350 businesses affected; 14 collapsed buildings, 30 with severe structural damage; and $650 million property and business loss.

Long-distance phone calls to Oklahoma rose sharply as news of the blast spread, causing overloaded circuits and delays. Priority was given to Oklahoma City callers who were dialing out.

Teams coordinated triage, performed first aid and surgery, counseled survivors and their families. The first night, three surgeons laid on their stomachs in 18 inches of sewer water with flashlights and cutting tools so they could amputate the right leg of young woman in order to free her.

Survivors of the Oklahoma City terrorist bombing may carry long-term emotional scars, even if they escaped physical injury, according to mental health experts. The emotional shock will be far-flung and long-lasting. People were calling the hot lines crying. The explosion just triggered something. They said they can't stop crying. Post traumatic stress counseling will be required for years.

—Boston Globe
November 13, 1997

1.3.2.9 Arson

A good example of arson causing an undesirable outcome is The Seton Hall University fire (2000):

The Boland Hall dormitory was set on fire around 4:30 a.m. The fire killed three students and injured 62. The building had no sprinklers because it was built before such devices were required.

The fire immediately set off fire alarms in the 640-student freshman dorm — but most students simply rolled over and went back to bed. There have been 18 false alarms in the dorm since the school year began in September, and students have become accustomed to ignoring them.

The fire alarms sounded. Unfortunately, because the students experienced 18 false alarms in the prior 4 months, most students simply rolled over and went back to sleep. They had become accustomed to ignoring the alarms. South Orange firefighters extinguished the third-floor fire quickly.

One student said, "I just thought it was another false alarm. I just laid there, kind of ignoring it, until I heard someone running down the hall. They were screaming, 'This is real, this is a real fire! Get out!'"

The state fire code governing dormitories requires a multitude of fire-safety devices, including twice-yearly drills and various alert systems. University officials acknowledged they have not held any fire drills at Boland since September. A spokeswoman from Seton Hall said false alarms provided enough practice. "There were no called fire drills because we were evacuating students at a rate of more than two times a week with fire alarms," she said.

—*USA Today*
January 25, 2000

Two students were arrested for setting the fire.

—*Philadelphia Inquirer*
June 6, 2003

As you can see, there are many different types of crises that can strike your organization.

Fact 1: *You cannot prevent all crises from striking your organization.* Therefore, you need to be prepared.

Opinion 1: *The best way of managing the crisis so that it does the least damage is to be prepared.* A Crisis Management Plan is a resource that prepares an organization to manage a crisis successfully.

Opinion 2: *Just because an organization has developed a Crisis Management Plan, does not ensure that the executives will manage it successfully.* Remember that the hammer does not make the carpenter. It takes a skill — acquired by experience. That experience is gained during the tests and the exercises performed by the organization throughout the year..

1.4 HOW TO DETERMINE WHICH CRISES COULD STRIKE YOUR COMPANY

Part of the Crisis Management Planning process is to evaluate if a crisis could occur in an organization and the type of crisis with which the organization could be faced.

Then the organization needs to develop a strategy on how it will handle the crisis, or each of the crises if there is more than one. (***Author Note:*** Having been involved as a consultant with many organizations during this process, I can say that there is always more than one type of crisis that can threaten most organizations. When performing this step, I used my crises/disaster database to select all of the crises and disasters that have struck other organizations in the same industry. That usually provided the information I needed to present to my client.)

Every organization should perform a risk analysis that will identify the most likely types of crises that could occur to their organization. This allows them to concentrate initially on building a plan to respond to the more probable crises.

Even after this risk evaluation step has been completed, many organizations have been faced with a crisis that was either not identified as having a high probability, or one or more that was not identified at all.

1.4.1 Analyze the Threats

Make a list of all the crises that could strike your organization. Here are some that I keep in my database — crises caused by:

- A product issue (e.g., product is defective, product is not dependable, product is polluted, product is unsafe, product is in short supply, product has been tampered with, or a product/services market shift)
- An organization's image/reputation problem, caused by deceptive practices, fraud, "fuzzy accounting," or scandal
- A financial problem
- Industrial relations or strike
- Disasters (e.g., acts of nature, accidents, or intentional acts)

1.4.2 Predictability

This is where the study of history comes in handy. Studying what happened to other organizations that have experienced a crisis, or a disaster, puts one in a better position to explain the potential that the threat could become a reality. Do some research, and find out if this type of disaster has occurred in the area. Determine if this type of crisis has occurred in another organization, especially one in the same industry.

1.4.3 Frequency

As part of the research, determine the frequency of occurrence. If the disaster, or crisis, happens on occasion, include it in your thinking. If, on the other hand, it has only occurred on one occasion, I would not advise to spend a lot of time or money responding to it. Executives are not interested in spending potential profits on something that is not likely to occur. (**Author's Note:** In most cases when providing examples, I have given you more than one example. On the other hand, I did not want to overwhelm you with too many, but I will include a list of examples in the appendix.)

1.4.4   Crises That Could Be Missed

Some rare crises can be missed when preparing the list; for example, a crisis caused by:

- A supplier/vendor
- A bad exercise
- The actions of your employee
- Actions of your human resources department
- Actions of the news media
- An owner liability issue
- An industrial espionage situation
- The sudden death of the CEO, or of a number of senior executives

A problem that business continuity professionals have is justifying that the threat can actually become a reality. Because they are not common crises, let me share some examples I have in my database with you so you can justify using an actual case.

1.4.4.1   Crisis Caused by a Supplier or Vendor: Examples

- *Play-Doh Co., Central Falls, Rhode Island.* Play Doh was forced to lay off 80 employees because a vendor in Illinois was unable to supply flour for the modeling dough. The vendor facility was under water from the Midwest flooding. (The Great '93 Flood.) The workers will be recalled when a new supplier is found.
- *Prudential Insurance Co.* Prudential said a warehouse fire in May destroyed about 4600 boxes of documents the company was ordered to keep for a class-action suit over the insurer's admittedly deceptive sales practices. Fire in the Diversified Records Services, Inc., records-storage facility in West Pittston, Pennsylvania, burned for several days and destroyed about 50,000 boxes of records, including customer complaints and some agents' disciplinary records relating to the national settlement. The fire destroyed 4653 boxes of documents the company was under court order to preserve in a class-action suit.

1.4.4.2 Crisis Caused by a Bad Exercise: Examples

- *The Federal Reserve Bank of San Francisco.* The bank learned a key lesson in disaster recovery in 1992: Do not test your disaster recovery system at a time when it is likely to cause a disaster. During such a test, the West Coast arm of the Fed's mainframe in Los Angeles froze for 12 hours, leaving thousands of consumers in California and Arizona stranded without automatic payroll deposits. Although the Fed would not release specific figures regarding the funds affected, about $2 billion is processed per day through its Los Angeles office. Banks were still assessing the impact of the accident last week and assuring customers they would be covered for any resulting over draft charges. About 15 banking institutions were affected. The Fed blamed human error. (From *Information Week,* April 9, 1992.)

- *TCI Cable Co. in Tulsa, Oklahoma.* TCI Cable learned a lesson when they tested their plan. Two strangers burst into the TCI's lobby, cursing and aiming guns at terrified employees demanding money. Some of the 25 workers were shaken and physically ill as the robbers fled with the cash. Managers then revealed the break-in was fake; the robbers were actors. The purpose, according to a memo three days after, was "to prepare the possible victims to be alert and to take action to help make them a less desirable target should a real robbery occur." (CMT – Legal) Five women at the simulated robbery quit their jobs and sued, saying the faked event amounted to a vicious assault and outrageous conduct. The trial begins April 7, 1997. In depositions among the 6 volumes of documents in the case: one woman said she couldn't sleep and her hair fell out. Another said she cried a lot and was depressed, and a third said she began vomiting the day she returned to work. Each seeks in excess of $10,000 in damages from the Englewood, CO-based Tele-Communications Inc.; its Tulsa subsidiary, and Elite Protective and Security Services Inc., contracted to run the seminar. (From *The New York Times,* February 17, 1997.)

- *Memorial Hospital in Martinsville, Virginia.* This hospital also learned a lesson when they tested a test. Five masked men burst into the emergency room of the Memorial Hospital in Martinsville, Virginia, in 1996, waving guns and demanding drugs. Real, unloaded guns were pointed at the nurses during the 5-minute drill, which was arranged by the hospital's security staff. Police are looking into a mock assault at the hospital that left several emergency room nurses and patients badly shaken. (CMT-Legal) "I don't think you can point a gun at someone's head and get away with it," said lawyer James Shortt, who represents 3 of the nurses. Physician Phillip Levin said at least 2 patients were put in danger — a boy suffering an asthma attack and an elderly patient whose heart started racing. (From *USA Today,* January 25, 1996.)

1.4.4.3 Crisis Caused by the Action of an Employee: Examples

■ *Rite Aid Corp., Rock Hill, South Carolina, store, 1995.* An elderly pharmacist who was finishing a 12-hour shift, made a terrible error and gave the mother of a little girl the wrong medicine. Gabrielle Hundley was in school and became sick. She was rushed to the hospital, where she went into a deep coma. After 12 hours in the coma, Gabrielle awoke. She had brain damage that left her mentally retarded. At the hospital, a teacher showed the parents the oblong yellow pills the couple had sent to school for Gabrielle. They were supposed to be Ritalin, a drug widely used to treat attention-deficit hyperactivity disorder. But Ritalin tablets are round, not oblong. Since it was Gabrielle's first prescription, the family didn't know that.

The Rite Aid pharmacist gave Gabrielle a diabetes medicine, called Glynase, that had drained her blood sugar. Doctors said the child's life was saved only by a sugary snack her mother had packed in her lunch, which the little girl had eaten about the same time she took the medication.

The family sued Rite Aid and the pharmacist. (Reason Why) — It was alleged that the Rite Aid store was short-staffed and employed retirement-age pharmacists who worked 12-hour shifts and were paid less than younger peers in South Carolina. The 65-year-old pharmacist who was finishing his shift the night Mrs. Hundley went into the drugstore, was working 12-hour days, five days a week. (Pre-Crisis Warning) The pharmacist had been warned by the state Board of Pharmacy after misfiling a prescription in 1989, and he admitted in testimony that there had been other incidents involving incorrect dosages. A jury awarded the Hundley's compensatory and punitive damages totaling $16 million, believed to be the largest personal-injury award ever in South Carolina. (From *Philadelphia Inquirer,* November 25, 1996.)

■ *Sloan-Kettering Cancer Center, New York, New York.* New York health officials fined Sloan-Kettering $12,000 after a surgeon operated on the wrong side of the brain. State officials said medical staff at the famed cancer center failed to review the patient's history and medical reports before the operation. The neurosurgeon was later fired. Officials didn't say if the patient suffered lasting damage. She is the mother of Indian actress Sridevi Ayyappan. (From *Philadelphia Inquirer,* March 11, 1996.)

1.4.4.4 Crisis Caused by the Action of the Human Resources Department: Examples

■ *General Dynamics.* Dean Farness of Santee, California, was fired by General Dynamics when he returned to work from bereavement leave after 6-year-old son Brent died in a car accident. Firing was on March 15, the day Brent would have turned 7. Farness said, "They just called me in and said, 'It's hard for us to do this, but we've got to do it.'" (CMT – HR) General Dynamics spokeswoman Julie Andrews said the plant was laying off 40 percent of its 4200 workers. Farness worked 10 years with General Dynamics. On the other hand, the family's pastor said: "Holding off a bit would not have made a significant dent in their profit-loss margin, but it would have been compassionate."

 (*Newsweek,* July 19, 1993) This is especially striking because it was at General Dynamics a year earlier that former employee Robert Earl Mack shot and killed a supervisor, after he was fired while on forced leave he believed was temporary. General Dynamics admitted that the layoff was mishandled.

■ *Structural Dynamics Research in Cincinnati, Ohio.* Bill Means (42) took his daughter Marisa (8) to his office on 'Take Our Daughters to Work Day.' She was two hours into the special day when the company vice president told Bill Means that he was being fired. The computer software company had laid off 140 employees (12 percent of its worldwide workforce) since disclosing financial problems in Sept. of 1994. The company V.P. said he did not know Mean's daughter was in the office. While he said the company would not reconsider the firing, he conceded the "timing was truly regrettable." Means has worked in computer systems for 20 years, and was recruited by Structural from General Electric Co. two years ago.

1.4.4.5 Crisis Caused by the Actions of the News Media: Examples

■ *AirTran Airlines versus Plain Dealer of Cleveland (1998).* (Rumor) The FAA has found serious safety-related violations at the airline according to documents obtained by the Plain Dealer of Cleveland. Violations included falsified documents and faulty repairs. The documents, based on a 3-week inspection that ended Nov. 7, show the airline had more serious violations than the 1996 report that recommended that ValuJet be grounded. AirTran officials said they "understand that the outcome (of the probe) was excellent." (From *USA Today*, January 12, 1998.)

(Negative Rumors Hurt) Federal aviation officials say a special inspection found no systemic safety problems at AirTran despite a published report indicating widespread trouble at the discount airline. FAA managers said action already would have been taken against the airline if serious problems had been found. (From *USA Today*, January 14, 1998.)

■ *GM Truck — NBC.* The network faked crash-test results on a GM pickup truck, on a November 17, 1992, *Dateline NBC* program. After GM sued, NBC admitted that it had misrepresented key details in the crash staged for the cameras. It acknowledged that it had (aided the crash by) attaching model rocket engines to the truck, (allowing) gasoline had leaked from an ill-fitting cap and that the resulting fire lasted only 15 seconds. In that scandal, the network was forced into an apology Feb. 9 to settle a defamation lawsuit. (*USA Today*, March 3, 1993); (Executive's Account) NBC News president Michael Gartner announced he was resigning. Gartner's mistake was to call the broadcast "fair and accurate." Staffers said that Gartner's ill-considered reaction to GM's challenge was the final straw. Gartner (54), a distinguished newspaper editor before he took over NBC News almost five years ago, acknowledged that the now-infamous *Dateline NBC* story contributed to the timing of his departure. (From *USA Today*, March 22, 1993.) NBC yesterday fired three top staff members on its *Dateline NBC* program over the staging of the fiery crash involving a General Motors truck: Jeff Diamond, executive producer of *Dateline NBC*, David Rummel, the program's senior producer, and Robert Read, who produced the segment. The decision was made after NBC President Robert Wright reviewed a report from outside attorneys hired by NBC to look into the GM fiasco.

1.4.4.6 Crisis Caused by an Owner Liability Issue: Examples

■ *Bloomingdale's Department Store, Stamford, Connecticut,* must pay $1.5 million to the estate of a woman who was stabbed to death in its dim and lightly patrolled parking garage, the state Supreme Court ruled. (Pre-Crisis) Bloomingdale's was warned years earlier that better security was needed. (From *USA Today*, August 1, 1995.)

■ *Wal-Mart and Mall, Memphis, Tennessee.* Dorothy McClung (37) was kidnapped from the mall's parking lot in 1990. The family filed suit, claiming security was inadequate. The state Supreme Court reinstated a $20 million lawsuit. (From *USA Today*, October 31, 1996.)

■ *Merrymead Farm, Worcester, Pennsylvania.* Eileen Sweeney, the mother of two small children sickened after a visit to a Montgomery County farm that health officials suspect is the source of an *E. coli* outbreak, sued the farm and its operators. Claim is that the operators of Merrymead Farm, Worcester, PA, were negligent in allowing Sweeney and her 2-year-old son, and 1-year-old daughter to be exposed to the *E. coli* bacteria when they visited as part of an Easter Seal Society field trip Oct. 16. The son has suffered a condition known as hemolytic uremic syndrome, which is a complication of *E. coli* infection that can lead to kidney failure. The daughter also suffered *E. coli*-related symptoms. The lawsuit is the second filed against the dairy farm since the *E. coli* outbreak. There are 16 confirmed cases of *E. coli* linked to the farm — most of them children — and as many as 61 people may have been infected, according to the Montgomery County Health Department. (From *Philadelphia Inquirer,* November 25, 2001.)

1.4.4.7 Crisis Caused by an Industrial Espionage Incident: Examples

■ *Perdue Farms, Salisbury, Maryland, 1999.* A Tampa, Florida, jury awarded $27 million to a man who said Perdue Farms betrayed a confidentiality agreement and stole his secret method of preparing roasted chicken. It is now up to a judge to decide how much the nation's third-largest poultry company must pay to Dennis P. Hook in punitive damages. The jury awarded the compensatory damages on Friday. (From *Philadelphia Inquirer,* April 12, 1999.)

Perdue has been ordered to pay an entrepreneur nearly $49 million for stealing his cook-in-a-bag method of roasting chicken. In addition to a jury award, a judge Thursday ordered Perdue to pay $6.75 million in punitive damages and $15 million in interest. Perdue said it would appeal. The judge did not immediately rule on Hook's request to stop Perdue's marketing of TenderReady. Forbes magazine has estimated Perdue's annual revenues at $2.2 billion. (From *Philadelphia Inquirer,* April 24, 1999.)

■ *Lucent Technologies, New Jersey, 2001.* Two Lucent Technologies scientists and a third man were arrested and charged with stealing trade secrets from Lucent to share with a firm majority-owned by the Chinese government (two Chinese nationals, Hai Lin and Kai Xu, and a U.S. citizen, Yong-Qing Cheng). The men allegedly conspired to steal software associated with Lucent's Path-Star Access Server, which switches data and voice over networks. Federal authorities allege that the trio had been conspiring since July to take the technology from Lucent for a partnership with the

Chinese firm Datang Telecom Technology, one of China's largest telecom equipment sellers. Until their arrests, Lin and Xu were regarded as "distinguished members" of Lucent's staff. Their intent court documents say, was to build a networking powerhouse akin to "the Cisco of China," referring to the U.S.-based Cisco Systems. They face a maximum 5 years in prison and a $250,000 fine. (From *USA Today,* May 4, 2001.)

1.4.4.8 Crisis Caused by the Unexpected Death of CEO, or of a Number of Senior Executives: Examples

Organizations have lost CEOs and other key employees on the same airplane. Here are a couple of examples:

- *Swire Coca-Cola; Salt Lake City, Utah, 1996.* Airplane crashed. Wiped out the top management of the company — the CEO, the CFO and the V.P. of marketing. (Policy) People whose decisions can have a dramatic effect on a company should not fly together.
- *Bruno's Inc., Rome, Georgia, 1998.* A corporate jet taking executives on a Christmas good-will tour of their grocery store chain crashed into Lavendar Mountain yesterday. Killed the seven passengers and two crew members on board. Killed were chairman Angelo J. Bruno, his brother vice chairman Lee J. Bruno, and three company vice presidents. Bruno's Inc. operates more than 240 stores in Alabama, Georgia, Florida, Tennessee, Mississippi, and South Carolina.

In the terrorist attacks on 9-11, a number of employees were killed inside the towers, as well as on the airplanes. A few examples where CEOs were killed because they were inside the building include:

- *Keefe Bruyette & Woods; New York City, 2001.* Securities firm. (Executive Succession) Keefe's casualties include Joseph Berry, the co-CEO, and David Berry, the director of research. The firm also lost five of its nine board members.
- *Fred Alger Management Co., New York, New York, 2001.* David Alger, CEO, was killed on September 11. So were 37 of his 55 employees who worked in the North Tower. Within 24 hours, Fred Alger announced that he would return from retirement and lead the firm to recovery.
- *Cantor Fitzgerald Co., New York City, 2001.* The bond trading firm lost about 700 employees in the attack. (Executive Succession) Howard Lutnick, the CEO, lost his brother, Gary, and his best friend, Douglas Gardner, in the incident.

1.5 WHY COMPANIES NEED A CRISIS MANAGEMENT PLAN

Executives often ask why they need to have a Crisis Management Plan (CMP). After all, crises have been occurring forever. In fact, one of the first crisis managers was said to be Noah. He built the ark before the flood. In all seriousness, crises have been occurring as far back as I can remember, and senior executives have been able to manage the effects successfully. Many of the executives I have spoken with have experienced a crisis, or two, with their present organization. They point out that they did not have a documented CMP then, and they do not see why they need one now. They feel that during a crisis, they are perfectly competent to manage it — no matter which type of crisis comes along.

When this question is raised to me, I use a comparison of the Crisis Management Plan with the organization's Emergency Response Plan (ERP): the objective of the ERP is to safeguard employees.

The ERP (which is discussed in more detail in the next chapter) tells employees what they should do when an emergency arises. What are employees expected to do during and immediately after an earthquake? A tornado? A flood? A hurricane? A bombing? A fire?

The ERP is documented. Copies of the plan are distributed to employees or posted in various locations throughout the facility. As part of the policy to keep the ERP current and ready for use, the alarms are tested frequently. Periodically throughout the year, the documented procedures in the ERP are exercised to ensure that employees are familiar with its content. The objective is that the constant training (exercises) will cause the employee to respond automatically when the alarms sound. The longer it takes for them to respond, the greater the potential for injury to the employees.

This is the same concept behind the Crisis Management Plan. When a situation moves to the Acute-Crisis stage, and it has become visible outside the organization, the Crisis Management Team (CMT) must take charge quickly. The organization is in the spotlight. Time is of the essence. (We will discuss "time" and its importance during a crisis throughout the book.)

Without a plan, executives may be forced to make split-second decisions in an effort to answer questions from the news media. Split-second decisions are dangerous.

> "When the wrong split-second decision can cost a company millions in negative publicity, not being prepared isn't worth the risk."

—**Steven Wilson, President**
Wilson Group Communications, Inc.
Crisis Magazine, Jan./Feb. 1990

A plan — a plan that has been tested and exercised — affords the executives an opportunity to manage the crisis successfully with little or no damage to the organization.

Executives must be prepared — because the news media is prepared. They are prepared to write (or speak) about your crisis. And they will continue to write and speak about the crisis until your organization gets it under control.

As soon as it moves to the acute stage, and the media knows about it, they are prepared to announce "breaking news."

One of the major reasons an organization should have a viable CMP is the speed with which a crisis becomes visible to the outside world. Today the news media have the technological resources to announce your crisis throughout the world in nearly real-time. Remember the CNN channel on television had a live broadcast shortly after the Iraq War in 1991? That was the first time in my experience that something like this happened.

Remember that, not too long ago, we did not have instant communications, the cable television, with its 24-hour news programs, telecommunications satellites, etc. It was a lot easier to manage the crisis communications part of the CMP. Organizations had a little time before they had to be managing a crisis. Not so today. With stories being reported in real-time, Crisis Management Teams must respond quickly. There is no longer an opportunity to say, "The situation is under review. We'll get back to you as soon as we have the facts." Reporters will not accept that any longer.

Organizations, and their executives, need to be prepared with a Crisis Communications section of the Crisis Management Plan. The Crisis Communications plan contains the public relations strategy. It will be documented in the plan. To ensure it the proper strategy, it should be exercised multiple times a year using different scenarios each time. (This is discussed in more detail in Chapter 6.) The crisis communications spokesperson will have to have been trained, tested, and exercised to cope with the news media.

A second consideration organizations must be aware of when the news media move into "breaking news" mode of operation is their ability to research your organization quickly. After the news breaks, the media will research everything they can about your organization. It will only take minutes before many news items become known that were not even considered news before the crisis broke.

Within a day, the media will be reporting on new stories that can negatively influence the reputation of your organization. I call this offshoot the "opens the door" crisis. What I mean by this is that the first crisis, if it goes unchecked for a while, allows investigative journalists the opportunity to uncover another situation that can be even more harmful to the stability of your organization than the original crisis. Let me show you what I mean:

Coca-Cola Co., Belgium, 1999. After the episode in Europe where Coca-Cola was accused of causing school children to be sick (Belgium), and after Europeans felt Coke, as an organization, did not take the problem seriously the "Opens the Door" crisis occurred (discussed in 1.2.3.).

A few months later, European Commission officials seized internal company records in four European nations, looking to see if the beverage giant had violated competition rules. A company spokesman said authorities raided its offices in Britain, Germany, Austria, and Denmark and also seized records from three Coca-Cola bottlers. The action comes just weeks after millions of cases of Coca-Cola products were recalled in Europe after dozens of people became sick after drinking Coke products. The authorities said, "We suspect that Coca-Cola has … offered three types of incentives, all of which are unlawful for dominant companies m any market." Under EU rules, a dominant company is restricted in its use of incentives to get retailers to raise sales, carry more of its products or drop a rival.

The New York Times – Jayson Blair incident, 2003. The scandal that broke when the *New York Times* acknowledged repeated outright fakery by reporter Jayson Blair has left *Times* staffers, their press colleagues and their readers anxious, angry and appalled — and given a measure of vindication or satisfaction to many *Times* and media critics.

Blair, a *Times* reporter for nearly four years, was fired after the *San Antonio Express-News* complained to the *Times* that much of a Blair story about the mother of a missing soldier — a story ostensibly reported and written from Texas — was substantially identical to one published by the *Express-News*. The *Times* later discovered that for months, and perhaps longer, Blair had been stealing material from other papers or simply making up people quoted in his stories. Although a number of his stories carried date-lines indicating they had been filed from West Virginia, Ohio, or other places outside New York, it appeared he had rarely left his apartment in Brooklyn. The *Times* bared all of Blair's deceptions it could uncover in a four-page self-expose.

And with this the "Opens the Door" crisis occurred. "Reporting and editing procedures are being examined and tightened at other outlets. The scandal threatened to cast a shadow on all news media," says Arlene Morgan, assistant dean at the Columbia University Graduate School of Journalism. "The *Times* is considered the most credible source of news in the world. When something like this happens there, it really confirms to people who do not trust the press that we're only in this business to sell papers and to sensationalize stories," says Morgan. (From *USA Today,* June 6, 2003.)

1.5.1 News Media Can Make or Break You

Another issue with the news media is there ability to "make or break you." As an example, when John Hancock Insurance Co. experienced a fire in its corporate headquarters building in September 1992, the *Boston Globe* had reporters out interviewing some of the 3000 people who had to evacuate the building. I am sure the newspaper did not have a bias against Hancock, but the article read like it did. Instead of talking about the 2900+ people who successfully evacuated the smoky building, the article dwelled on the anomalies. For example:

> *One person* interviewed was from Marsh McLennan, and said, "There was no direction and no contingency plan. We have a great concern about the lack of communications. It's something that needs to be addressed very strongly," according to a spokesperson for Marsh.

> *Another person* interviewed was from Hill Holiday Conners Cosmopulos and said, "The communication was unbelievably bad, and the lack of backup is very bothersome. We still had people in the agency about 2:00 p.m. who didn't know about the fire until the firemen showed up and kicked them out," according to a senior production manager.

> *A third person* interviewed was a temporary employee working his first day on the 42nd floor. When he evacuated, he left on an elevator. It began jerking. He got off at the next floor down. When interviewed by the reporter, the temporary employee said he did not think the building had an adequate evacuation plan.

(Apparently the reporter did not ask the temporary employee why he entered an elevator to exit the building while the fire alarms were sounding. The building had signs in the elevator lobby instructing people not to get on elevators when fire alarms were sounding, Very few Emergency Response Plans do work, anywhere in the country, if the people do not follow directions.)

On the other hand, there are organizations that have been struck by disasters or crises and have seemed to manage the crisis communications rather well. The determining factor I use to determine if the organization has managed the communications well is if the news media choose to allow the story to "quietly fade away" rather than keep the articles going for days and weeks until it is deemed "under control." For example, the Meridian Bank fire at One Meridian Plaza Philadelphia, Pennsylvania, on February 23, 1991.

"An $11.1 billion, multi-bank financial holding company headquartered in Reading, Pa., Meridian leased space on the concourse level and on floors 1, 3, 4, 5, 7, 36, and 37 — both above and below the fire floor in the building. About 300 administrative employees worked at One Meridian Plaza, the home of the bank's Delaware Valley division. Meridian didn't have a data center on site, but it did have a vault full of negotiable and non-negotiable securities on the concourse level of the building."

"We set up our command post outside the fire department's van," said Ken Maher, Meridian Bancorp's Vice President for Corporate Risk and Insurance Management. "My divisional security manager and our property manager met me there. The three of us were in downtown Philadelphia on cellular phones communicating with a group at our headquarters in Reading headed by Philip Toll, the president of our facilities company. He and two of his managers were notified early on. At that point, we had no idea how big a fire we had to really contend with."

"I told them, 'We have a contingency situation. I would suggest that we have an activation meeting at 10:00 a.m. Sunday morning in Reading. Let's get our Business Resumption Support Team (BRST) notified and get them there promptly at 10 a.m.'" Maher headed Meridian's Business Resumption Support Team. (Another name for the Crisis Management Team. It included key officers from property management, security, risk management, human resources, legal, purchasing, media and internal communications, voice and data equipment, data processing, PC support, and other groups.)

Maher and the other members of Meridian's Business Resumption Support Team met in Reading. They all took their copies of the plan and went to work. By Sunday evening, all business units affected had new locations to report to on Monday. The business units involved worked on laying out how they would resume operations at their new sites. The BRST (Crisis Management Team) provided their expertise to get the organization back to normal operations as soon as possible.

"They mobilized their BRST, which had fortuitously gone through a test of a mock blaze only a few months earlier. We figured that if we had an exposure, it would be a fire," said Ken Maher, Vice President, Corporate Risk Management & Insurance. So when Maher declared a disaster, the 25-member team … knew exactly what to do. "The question is not whether you can afford to plan, the question is whether you can afford not to plan. The fire proved that planning has to be part of every organization. It's far easier to respond to a loss if you've done some planning than try to handle a crisis in crisis situation," Maher said. (From *Contingency Journal*, July/August 1991.)

Four days after the fire, the only stories written in the newspaper about the fire had to do with the lawsuits being filed against the owners of the building by tenants and surrounding store owners. (The owners were a U.S. insurance organization (50 percent) and a European financial organization (50 percent).) Meridian appeared only in stories about how rapidly they resumed their banking operations following the fire.

1.6   PREVENTING A CRISIS FROM OCCURRING

Preventing a crisis is the least costly and the simplest way to control a potential crisis. Unfortunately, preventing crises or disasters from striking your organization is difficult.

This idea of preventing a crisis reminds me of some of the early seminars I conducted on Disaster Recovery Planning for Data Centers in the 1970s. Invariably, one of the attendees at the seminar would indicate that he would rather spend his organization's budget money on preventing a disaster from occurring — rather than on preparing a plan that would enable them to recover the computer after a disaster occurred.

When we began to discuss the steps we could take to prevent each type of disaster that was threatening data processing at that time, and we put a cost to each step, it quickly became apparent that it would cost many times more to secure the data processing department than it would to implement a viable Disaster Recovery Plan.

I was just one of many consultants who, at that time, had the opinion that "absolute security is unattainable."

As I said, preventing a crisis or disaster is difficult, if not impossible. Why? One reason is that most organizations are threatened by a large number of crises. Second, each type of crisis or disaster is difficult to prevent. Let me explain what I mean.

- *Acts of nature.* As far as disasters are concerned, "acts of nature" cannot be prevented. The best planning an organization can do for acts of nature is to avoid locating business operations in areas that experience acts of nature. Now tell me, where in this country can you locate your operations and be free from all acts of nature?
- Intentional acts. As it relates to preventing "intentional acts," many of those acts are caused by employees, or ex-employees. Despite excellent security controls and (security) policies, organizations have experienced intentional disasters: vandalism, sabotage, arson, or workplace violence.
- *Accidents.* Accidents are accidents. They are not expected to happen, but they do.
- *Product crises.* Preventing a "product" crisis from occurring is extremely difficult. Why? I cannot believe that all of the organizations cited in this book that have suffered product crises, wanted those crises to occur. I feel confident that for nearly all of them, it was a surprise. And I also feel that organizations would prefer to avoid financial problems and incidents that cause a negative public perception problems.

Now do not misunderstand my motives. I feel that all organizations should put plans and procedures in place in an attempt to minimize the potential that a disaster, or crisis, will occur. However, I would not guarantee the organization that a disaster, or crisis, would never occur.

Crises are an unavoidable occurrence for an organization. In fact, executives believe that their organizations will experience a crisis. As Steven Fink wrote,

> "While 89 percent of corporate executives believed a crisis was inevitable, half admitted that they had no plan to deal with it."

> **—Stephen Fink**
> *Crisis Management: Planning for the Inevitable*

Another thought to consider was presented by Norman Augustine in an article entitled "Managing the Crisis You Tried to Prevent":

> "It is useful to point out that General Motors has about the same number of employees as San Francisco has citizens; that AT&T is about the same size as Buffalo, New York; and that Lockheed Martin is the size of Spokane, Washington. Executives must keep in mind that almost any one of thousands of employees can

plunge an entire corporation into a crisis through either misdeed or oversight."

—Norman R. Augustine
Crisis Management Review

I agree with Norm Augustine. Almost any one of your employees can cause a crisis for your organization. Even in a small company, it only takes one employee to cause the crisis. Imagine the problem with large organizations the size of General Electric, Boeing, Citicorp, etc.

> Speaking of Boeing Co. and an employee causing a crisis for an organization, in July of 2003, the U.S. Air Force stripped Boeing of seven rocket-launch contracts. Also suspended by The Air Force were three former Boeing employees allegedly involved in the scandal. All worked on Boeing's rocket contracts. Last month, a federal grand jury in Los Angeles indicted two of them for misusing trade secrets during the 1998 bidding for the rocket contracts. The problem started when a Boeing employee recruited a former Lockheed engineer in 1996 to bring proprietary Lockheed documents to Boeing in exchange for a high-salary job. The penalties cap a year-long Air Force probe into allegations that Boeing, the nation's No. 2 defense contractor after Lockheed Martin, used thousands of pages of stolen Lockheed documents in 1998 to beat its rival for contracts to build a military satellite-launch rocket. Boeing, which had won 14 military contracts to build the Delta IV satellite rocket system, must hand over seven of the contracts, worth about $700 million, to Lockheed, the Air Force said. (From *USA Today,* July 25, 2003.)

Let us move to Chapter 2, "The Business Continuity Plan," which will explain how the CMP fits into the BCP.

LEEDS METROPOLITAN
UNIVERSITY
LIBRARY

Chapter 2

BUSINESS CONTINUITY PLANNING: WHAT IS IT?

2.1 HOW DOES THE CRISIS MANAGEMENT PLAN FIT INTO THE BUSINESS CONTINUITY PLAN?

This chapter provides an overview of the Business Continuity Plan (BCP) to show that the Crisis Management Plan (CMP) is one of the major elements of the plan.

The BCP consists of three major elements:

1. The *Prevention Plan* is developed to minimize the potential for a disaster (or crisis) to occur. The plan consists of policies and procedures that employees should adhere to before a disaster (or crisis) strikes. It consists of planning elements such as the Risk Analyses, Security Plans, and Facility (Building Engineering) Plans.

2. The *Emergency Response Plan* is developed to ensure employees know how to respond when they discover a potential disaster, or when and how to evacuate the building if necessary and who and how to assess the damage. The plan consists of policies and procedures for employees to follow during a disaster (or crisis). It consists of planning elements such as Incident Response, Life Safety, and Damage Assessment.

3. The *Business Resumption Plan* is developed to minimize the impact on the organization — by minimizing the length of time a business interruption lasts and providing procedures to use in resuming business operations. This plan consists of policies and procedures for employees to follow after a disaster (or crisis) is contained. It consists of planning elements such as the Information Technology Plan, the Business Units (throughout the organization) Plans, and the Crisis Management Plan.

See Figure 2.1 for the elements of a Business Continuity Plan.

While this chapter does introduce all the elements of the Business Continuity Plan, it does not provide extensive detail on them. (There have been numerous books written on the topics of Prevention Plans, Emergency Response Plans, and Business Resumption Plans that provide extensive coverage of these elements.)

With that being the case, let us now introduce the first element of the Business Continuity Plan: the Prevention Plan (or Program).

2.1.1   The Prevention Element: Introduction

The first of the three fundamental principles of the Business Continuity Plan discussed is the Prevention Plan. (See the Business Continuity Plan diagram in Appendix.)

The Prevention Plan consists of policies, procedures, and controls employed to minimize the potential for a disaster (crisis) to occur. For the purpose of this book, it comprises three types of planning processes: (1) the Risk Management/Risk Analysis Planning, (2) the Security Plan, and the (3) Facility/Building Engineering Plan.

The Risk Management/Risk Analysis Planning process is an ongoing process designed to identify the potential threats to the organization and the possibility for a threat to become a reality. The process includes:

■ Identifying potential threats
■ Estimating the potential that the threat will become a reality
■ Reviewing and evaluating existing security and contingency controls
■ Recommending improvements to the security and contingency controls

The Security Plan is an ongoing program designed to protect the assets of the organization from intentional damage or loss. Security planning includes restricting access into the building (during working hours as well as during non-working hours) and controlling access throughout the building. Controls, such as access control systems, and security policies are designed to protect against intentional acts such as arson, bombing, and other forms of terrorism.

The Facilities/Building Engineering Plan is an ongoing program designed to protect the assets of the organization from accidental damage or loss, and to minimize the potential of a lengthy business interruption. The elements include ensuring that the building has been constructed to resist acts of nature (e.g., earthquakes, wind storms, or floods), ensuring that the fire prevention controls are adequate, and ensuring that there are adequate plans to resume operation during a power outage.

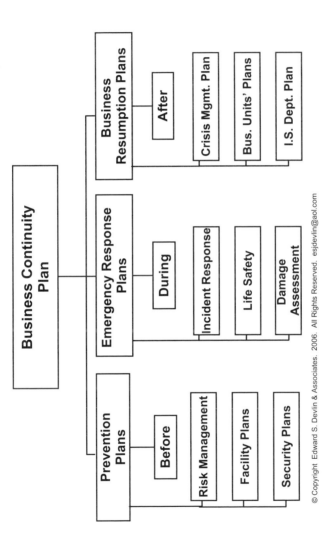

© Copyright Edward S. Devlin & Associates. 2006. All Rights Reserved. esjdevlin@aol.com

Figure 2.1 Business Continuity Plan.

Now let us look at an overview of the first type of planning process of the BCP's Prevention Plan, that is, the Risk Management/Risk Analysis Planning process.

2.1.1.1 The Risk Management/Risk Analysis Process

The Risk Management/Risk Analysis process consists of a risk analysis performed to determine the potential threats an organization might experience and the potential for each threat to occur. The Risk Analysis process must be performed at any location where the organization houses operations or assets.

This subsection focuses on the processes involved in determining the potential for a disaster or crisis to occur.

2.1.1.1.1 Risk Analysis: Determine Threats from Disasters

The first step is to determine the threats. If we are looking at performing a "risk analysis" to determine the potential for a disaster to occur, the process will establish which types of disaster could strike the organization. Examples of incidents that can develop into a disaster include:

- Acts of nature:
  - Earthquake, flood or rising water, hurricane, tornado, other (e.g., volcano)
- Acts of man — accidental:
  - Airplane, explosion, falling water, fire, nuclear accident, power outage, other (e.g., Hazmat)
- Acts of man — intentional:
  - Arson, bombing, sabotage, terrorism, vandalism, other (e.g., civil disturbance/riot)

The second step is to analyze the available information on the *predictability,* the *frequency,* and the *statistics* of actual occurrences. (A good source for this information is a knowledgeable risk manager. Be sure to work with your Risk Management personnel.) The predictability, frequency, and statistics will be measured against the current Security and Facilities/Building Engineering Department's controls, policies, and procedures.

2.1.1.1.2 Risk Analysis: Determine the Potential for a Disaster to Strike

Suppose that an organization has its headquarters in New York City and offices in a number of cities throughout the country (i.e., Los Angeles and

San Francisco, California; Dallas/Ft. Worth and Houston, Texas; Miami and Orlando, Florida; St. Louis and Kansas City, Missouri; and Oklahoma City, Oklahoma). When performing a risk analysis, risk management department professionals will start with acts of nature. They will evaluate the potential threats for each location and the potential for the threat to occur. They will determine the predictability of the threat to occur, the statistics of when it has actually occurred, and the frequency of occurrence.

Predictability. For Los Angeles or San Francisco, California, the threat is from an earthquake.

Statistics. There are statistics that will validate that an earthquake could occur. These statistics are based on earlier events that show when earthquakes have occurred (e.g., Northridge, Whittier Narrows, and Sylmar in the Los Angeles area, and Loma Prieta and Hollister in the San Francisco area). (The statistics do not indicate when the next earthquake might occur.)

Frequency. Based on the statistics, the frequency is low because earthquakes do not occur often. In general, there are a number of years between earthquakes in the same vicinity.

Level of Damage. Based on the results of recent earthquakes, the damage caused by Northridge and Loma Prieta was extensive. So, while the frequency is low, the potential impact is high.

Now take a look at two other office locations.

Predictability. For Miami and Orlando, Florida, the threat is from a hurricane or tropical storm.

Statistics. There are statistics that will validate that a hurricane can occur. These statistics are based on earlier events that show when hurricanes have occurred (e.g., Hurricane Andrew and Hurricane Charley). (The statistics do not indicate when the next hurricane could occur.)

Frequency. Based on statistics, hurricanes occur somewhere on a coastline in the United States every year. While risk management professionals feel comfortable saying that a hurricane will strike the U.S. coastline every year, they cannot accurately predict that Florida, or North Carolina, or Texas will be hit with a hurricane next year. A risk management professional in Miami cannot predict if, or when, Miami will experience another "Hurricane Andrew."

Level of Damage. Based on the results of Hurricanes Andrew and Charley, the damage caused was extensive. So, while the frequency is questionable, the potential impact is high.

If we were to perform a risk analysis on the other offices (i.e., Dallas/ Ft. Worth and Houston, Texas; St. Louis and Kansas City, Missouri; and Oklahoma City and Tulsa, Oklahoma), the results would be similar. The risk management or business continuity professional would find that there were real threats from acts of nature based on statistics from recent events. The Ft. Worth tornado, the Houston floods, the St. Louis and Kansas City floods, and the Oklahoma City tornado threats are real.

2.1.1.1.3 Risk Analysis: Determine Threats from a Crisis

If we are looking at performing a "risk analysis" to determine the potential for a crisis to occur, the first step will be to determine which types of crises could strike the organization. Examples of incidents that can escalate into a crisis include:

- A product issue (where a product does not work as promised [credibility], is injuring people [safety], or has been tampered with; a market-shift (sudden change, or over a long period of time)
- A negative public perception of your organization (e.g., your organization has a problem, and it appears it does not care about the problem)
- A financial problem (e.g., cash problem, or fuzzy accounting)
- An industrial relations problem (e.g., worker strike problem, employee lawsuit)
- An adverse international event (e.g., disaster at their location has jeopardized your product or service)
- A workplace violence incident (e.g., employees have been violently attacked while working on your organization's property)
- Senior executives have died or been killed (executive succession problem)

The second step is to analyze information on the predictability, the frequency, and the statistics of actual occurrences. Business continuity professionals will have to research information based on the history of organizations within the industry as an example. The predictability, frequency, and statistics will be measured against the policies and procedures established by the Executive Management Team to minimize the potential for a crisis to become acute.

2.1.1.1.4 Risk Analysis: Determine the Potential for a Crisis to Occur

If you perform a *risk analysis* of your organization, there is a good chance that your organization may face the threat that a crisis could occur that will cause a negative public perception of your organization. All types of organizations have faced this type of crisis at one time or another in the past decade.

The risk analysis could also find that your organization is threatened by a financial problem, an industrial relations problem (e.g., worker strike problem, employee lawsuits), a workplace violence incident, or an adverse international event that could affect your organization's product or service. Again, these are common crises that organizations have faced at one time or another during the past few years.

If your organization is a manufacturing organization, the risk analysis could find that your organization is threatened by a product problem (e.g., product does not work as promised [credibility], is injuring people [safety], or has been tampered with; or a market-shift (e.g., sudden change, or over a long period of time). Because most manufacturing companies have experienced a product problem of one sort or another in the past few years, they have developed and implemented plans to manage product problem crises when they occur.

Statistics: the best source of crisis statistics would be from various industry organizations that keep track of the instances where "crises" have affected an organization in that industry. However, these statistics are not always available to organizations and people outside the industry. Also, there are some statistics on crises available from government agencies.

Frequency: statistics from various industry organizations within your type of industry will indicate how often this type of crisis occurs. Some industries seem to receive more media coverage than others do when it comes to product problems. For example, it appears that auto manufacturers have had to recall some of their cars, or trucks, quite frequently. As an overall industry, statistics (and history) indicate that auto manufacturers seem to have had recalls every year. This does not mean that every auto manufacturer has had a recall every year.

In fact, one automaker did not have a recall for several years. This statistic was mentioned by a number of vehicle owners of that car manufacturer, as to why they bought that manufacturer's product. But when the organization is found to be hiding its defects, as Mitsubishi Motors Corporation did, they create an acute crisis relating to their integrity and reputation. A story published in the *Wall Street Journal* on August 23, 2000, indicated that:

> For years, employees at Mitsubishi tucked consumer complaints about auto defects away by the dozens in a special place. That was the file known to workers as "H," for the Japanese word for "secret" or "defer." The complaints by Japanese consumers were never reported to authorities; they stayed filed, awaiting

clarification, explanation or documentation that usually never came. The defects, including failing brakes, fuel leaks, malfunctioning clutches, and fuel tanks prone to falling off, were fixed on a case-by-case basis to avoid any humiliating recalls. Mitsubishi acknowledged that the cover-ups, which dated back to 1977, were carried out with the full knowledge of workers, managers, and one current board member. The revelation is a blow to the struggling automaker, which is likely to face an uphill battle to regain consumers' shattered faith in its ethics and the quality of its vehicles.

Three months after revealing that Mitsubishi never reported the defects to authorities, the *Wall Street Journal* published this in their November 14, 2000 edition:

Mitsubishi, hit hard by a vehicle-defects scandal as well as a shortfall in its employee pension reserve, reported the largest first-half net loss in its history. The automaker also doubled projections for its full-year loss, underscoring the deep problems that 34%-owner DaimlerChrysler AG faces in turning the company around. The company admitted in July that it systematically hid customer complaints about vehicle defects from government regulators for two decades. Mitsubishi's vehicle sales in Japan have fallen sharply since the disclosure. Mitsubishi said it would post an 11.5 billion yen special loss in the year ending in March to cover the cost of recalling and repairing some 620,000 cars and trucks. It also said it would take a one-time, 129 billion yen charge to cover the shortfall in its reserve for retirement benefits.

2.1.1.1.5 Other Threat Considerations

Internal Threats — from organizations inside the same building. In addition to the steps above, business continuity professionals should also pay attention to other tenants located inside buildings housing your business units.

- Who is on the floor above?
- Who is on the floor below?
- Who is located on the same floor?

What is the potential that they will cause a disaster to occur, such as an explosion or a leak?

■ Are there any high-profile organizations located inside the buildings housing some of your business units (e.g., political organizations, embassies, abortion centers)?

■ Is there a cafeteria or restaurant in the building? There have been numerous reports of fires starting in restaurants and cafeterias and spreading through the building. Some examples include:

  ■ A fire at the MGM Grand Hotel/Casino in Las Vegas, Nevada, in 1980 started in the kitchen of the restaurant on the first floor. Flames quickly spread to the nearby casino. It moved rapidly, assisted by thick carpets, plastic furnishings, and a large electronic keno board that exploded. The fire never went above the second floor, but the smoke and toxic gases did. It killed 84 people. Most of the 84 victims were trapped between the 19th and 24th floors. Eighteen found dead on one staircase, overcome by smoke and fumes before they could open a jammed door. Six others died in the elevators.

  ■ A fire in the TGI Fridays restaurant on the ground floor of the Time Warner building in New York City's Rockefeller Center in 1997 shot through ducts in the 33-story building and caused an explosion on the roof.

  ■ Cooking gas exploded in the ground-floor cafeteria of the Royal Jomtien Resort Hotel, in Pattaya, Thailand, in 1997. The fire and smoke spread up into the 16-story building, killing 84 and injuring more than 70 people.

External Threats — from organizations outside the building, but in close proximity.   Business continuity professionals should also pay attention to other organizations located in close proximity to those housing your business units.

■ An explosion at Pacific Engineering & Production Co. in Henderson, Nevada, in 1988 gutted the rocket fuel plant. It killed nine and injured hundreds. The explosion destroyed or severely damaged 12 buildings at the site. A nearby plant operated by Kidd & Co., the second-largest producer of marshmallows in the United States, was flattened. The force of the explosions also broke windows all over town, peeled off roofs, upended cars, and even rocked an America West jetliner flying over the area. The fire and explosions resulted in a direct loss to the facility of $27 million and a direct loss to exposure properties of $76 million.

The question is: how many of the other plants in the industrial complex had determined the risk from Pacific Engineering's manufacture of ammonium perchlorate?

■ An explosion at Concept Sciences in Allentown, Pennsylvania, in February 1999 destroyed the building, killed five, and injured fourteen. Nearby buildings and property were damaged. The blast at Concept Sciences hurled chunks of debris hundreds of yards in all directions and sent a foul-smelling chemical cloud and a fine white powder high into the frigid night air. The industrial park is adjacent to Lehigh Valley International Airport. The Roadway Packaging System building across the street looked like it had been moved by the concussion. It will have to be demolished.

Again, the question is: how many of the other plants in the industrial park had determined the risk from an explosion at Concept Sciences?

In summary, the Risk Analysis Process includes the following steps:

1. Identify the potential threat(s) that could interrupt operations at a company location.
2. Research and analyze the following information about each threat:
   a. Predictability
   b. Frequency
   c. Statistics
3. Review existing prevention and disaster mitigation controls.
4. Estimate the potential for the threat to become a reality.
5. Make recommendations to reduce the exposures.
6. Build contingency plans.

To repeat the statement given in the beginning of the chapter, while this chapter introduces the Risk Analysis element of the Prevention Plan, it presents an overview but no extensive details.

Now take a look at the next type of planning process in the BCP Prevention Plan — The Security Plan.

2.1.1.2 The Security Plan

From the business continuity planning point of view, the goal of the Security Plan is to protect the assets of the organization from an intentional disaster (e.g., sabotage, vandalism, or terrorism in the form of a bomb or arson). The plan concentrates on protecting an organization's assets, that is, people (employees), facilities and contents, vital records (and other critical data), and the intellectual properties.

The elements in the Security Plan deal with establishing security policies and procedures for employees, controlling access into the building, controlling access throughout the interior of the building, and providing a secure perimeter around the outside of the building.

2.1.1.2.1 Policies and Procedures

During working hours, the Security Plan policies and procedures include that:

- All employees are issued identification badges.
- Guards will verify the person entering the building is the person identified on the identification badge.
- All employees wear identification badges while working.
- All visitors will sign in at the guard desk where they will be issued "visitor badges."
- All visitors must wear the "visitor badges" at all times while in the organization's facilities.
- All visitors must be escorted while working on-site.

Many years ago, a couple financial organizations related to me that they had very tight security policies and procedures. They hired my organization to provide an outside evaluation of their security. Invariably, the policy required visitors to wear badges at all times while on-site. The problem was that they did not require the employees to wear their identification badges at all times. I am sure you can see where this is going. I either removed my badge at lunch, or on my first trip to the men's room. After removing my badge, I was just like an employee. I was never challenged by anyone in the organization.

The moral of this story is: the policy and procedures were good, but carrying them out was very poor.

Question: What has your organization done to minimize the potential for the threats from intentional acts such as bombings, arson, sabotage, etc. to become a reality?

2.1.1.2.2 Controls

Many organizations have implemented solid security controls and procedures to minimize just such a threat. In addition to security guards, they have installed sophisticated access control systems that will allow employees to enter and exit the building.

The value of having an access control system implemented in a building is that it:

- Minimizes traffic in high-profile areas. This protects against vandalism; sabotage; bombing; terrorism; and theft.
- Regulates employee and visitor access. This protects valuable assets and minimizes potential losses.

■ Provides a secure environment. This helps employees feel more secure. There is nothing more destabilizing than to have a workplace violence incident occur inside your organization.

During regular working hours, the Security Plan can include the use of security guards, closed-circuit TV, card and badge readers, and bio-metric systems. And during the after-work hours as well as weekend and holiday hours, the Security Plan will include all the controls used during regular working hours, and can also include motion, sound and/or vibration detectors.

There are a variety of types of systems that can be used to allow employees into the building while restricting them from high-profile areas. In addition to card key locks, organizations have implemented biometric access control systems. There are several basic biometric characteristics presently used to identify and authenticate the identity of individuals, including Fingerprint verification, hand geometry, voice verification, retinal scanning, iris scanning, signature verification, and facial recognition. (***Author Note:*** For more details on the specifics of these biometric systems, go to an article entitled "Biometrics" written by David Hochman and published in *Contingency Planning & Management* magazine in March 2002.)

Because terrorism has become a major concern during the past few years, changes have been made to the Prevention Plans. Some of the changes implemented include:

■ Facilities/Building Engineering Plans:
  ■ Wrap columns with steel to reinforce and protect against "pancaking."
  ■ Erect concrete planters or other large buffers to stop vehicles from ramming the building.
  ■ Move outdoor parking away from the building. Funnel deliveries through a central checkpoint; and log all arrivals and departures. (At the World Trade Center, trucks must go through three checkpoints and drivers are photographed.)
  ■ Paint with shatter-resistant coating and install heavy curtains or blinds to stop flying glass.
  ■ Install video cameras and public address systems in the stairwells. (The WTC installed battery-powered lighting and stairs with phosphorescent paint that glows in the dark.)

In summary, the Security Plan includes the policies and procedures dealing with employee's responsibilities while working on-site and rules visitors must adhere to while working on-site.

The Security Plan includes the following controls used to permit or deny access to the building, and to certain high-profile areas in the building — during working hours as well as during after-work hours, weekends, and holidays.

To repeat the statement given at the beginning of the chapter, while this chapter introduces the Security Planning element of the Prevention Plan, it only presents an overview and not extensive detail.

Now take a look at the overview of the next type of planning process of the BCP Prevention Plan — The Facilities/Building Engineering Plan.

2.1.1.3 The Facilities/Building Engineering Plans

From a business continuity point of view, the goal of the Facilities/Building Engineering Plan is to protect the assets of the organization from an act of nature (e.g., an earthquake, storm [tornado, hurricane, rain, snow], flood, etc.) or an accidental disaster (e.g., a fire, leak or falling water, power outage, etc.).

Similar to the Security Plan, the Facilities/Building Engineering Plan concentrates on protecting the organization's assets — that is, the people (employees), the facilities, and the contents.

The elements of the Facilities/Building Engineering Plan deal with: ensuring that (1) the building has been constructed to resist acts of nature, (2) the fire prevention controls are adequate, and (3) there are adequate plans to resume operation during a power outage.

Question: What has your organization done to minimize the potential for the threats from acts of nature or accidents to become a reality?

2.1.1.3.1 Building Construction — Acts of Nature

Buildings that house the organization's business units should be built to minimize damage from an act of nature (e.g., earthquake, tornado, flood, etc.). Due to space limitations, let us just look at one type of act of nature — an earthquake.

Earthquake-Resistant Construction. If you have business units located in an earthquake threat zone, the building should be built to earthquake-resistant standards. Earthquake-resistant construction includes:

- Steel frame buildings — experience has shown steel frame buildings will not collapse.
- Reinforced concrete buildings — have a more checkered experience record.
- Older brick buildings — without reinforced steel are considered to be collapse hazard buildings and may be total losses.

Earthquake-Nonresistant Construction.

■ *San Fernando Valley/Sylmar 1971 Quake.* A Richter magnitude 6.6 earthquake damaged 180 schools, 2 hospitals, 22,000 single-family homes, 62 apartment houses, and 370 commercial buildings. The Veterans Administration Hospital presented a classic picture of inadequate-versus-modern earthquake-resistant building techniques. The structures built in 1926 collapsed. The structures built after earthquake-resistant designs were included in building codes in 1937 and 1947 escaped without any significant structural damage. The death toll at the hospital was 46, and would have been higher if the quake had struck during normal business hours.

■ *Coalinga 1983 Quake.* Most of Coalinga's buildings are one- or two-story, turn-of-the-century structures. Approximately 70 percent of the 2700 homes and businesses in Coalinga sustained serious damage.

■ *Loma Prieta 1989 Quake.* The Bluxome Street Office Building, across from the Highway 280 off-ramp at Sixth Street, housed several companies, including Major League Services and de Vries & Co., an insurance firm. The entire fourth-floor wall and cornice along the west side of the half-block-long structure collapsed. Huge chunks of wall smashed about a dozen cars and blocked the street, killing six people in their cars.

■ *Northridge 1994 Quake.* A Richter magnitude 6.6 earthquake killed 57 and injured 9000 people. It damaged 60,000 structures. One of the many companies affected was Baker & Taylor Software. A wall and part of the roof at Baker's automated warehouse collapsed.

2.1.1.3.2 The Value of the Earthquake-Resistant Building

The goal of an earthquake-resistant building is to prevent the collapse of the building and the associated injuries to people a collapse would cause. Examples include:

■ *El Centro, California.* The Imperial County Services Center, a six-story building in El Centro, housed the Welfare, Planning, Agriculture, and Public Works departments. It suffered a 6.4 Richter quake. The building, built to survive an 8.0 earthquake, was damaged beyond repair by a 6.4 quake. Was this poor construction? Not really. The earthquake-resistant building did what it was supposed to do. It stayed up — it did not collapse. In fact, Governor Edmund Brown said that "those earthquake standards may have been what saved a tremendous loss of life."

■ *Seattle, Washington.* Seattle's regularly updated building code, including the provisions for seismic retrofitting, limited the extent of the city's overall damage from the 6.8 Richter magnitude earthquake on February 28, 2001, according to Kenneth Carper, an architecture professor who teaches seismic design at Washington State University in Pullman. The Seattle area also has invested millions in retrofitting schools and other public buildings. In November, 2000, voters approved spending $193 million to renovate and seismically retrofit Harborview Medical Center, the state's only top-level trauma center.

2.1.1.3.3 Type of Soil

While the type of construction is key, a complicating factor is the soil on which the building was built. Loosely compacted, water-saturated sediments, especially in landfills, can lose their strength, causing major subsidence, fracturing, and horizontal sliding of the ground surface. Liquefaction occurs when sandy soil and a high water table shake so violently that the solid particles separate from the liquid and a gooey lake of mud forms. Buildings are often thrown off their foundations. Some will sink into the mud.

Building Collapses.

■ *Anchorage, Alaska, 1964.* An area 80 miles to the north and west of the epicenter suffered the greatest damage. This was caused by liquefaction. Some 30 blocks of residential and commercial buildings were completely destroyed, including a new five-story J.C. Penney's store, the six-story Four Seasons apartment complex, and two twin 14-story apartment buildings. In Turnagain Heights, an 8600-foot-long section of the bluff collapsed, destroying 75 homes. It resulted in the death of an estimated 131 people.
■ *"Loma Prieta" 1989 Quake.* The Marina District, a former lagoon filled for the 1915 Panama-Pacific International Exposition. The major damage was caused by locally amplified shaking and by permanent deformation of the ground due to liquefaction of the sands and debris used to fill the former lagoon.

2.1.1.3.4 Earthquake Resistance: Seismic Base Isolation Systems

Earthquake-resistant construction includes shock absorbers. The concept is that earthquake motions at the ground-floor level of high-rise buildings are amplified in the upper floors. The use of shock absorbers mitigates this effect. (Each building has its own vibrational characteristics based on stiffness.) Shock absorbers are appropriate for buildings up to about 12 stories. Taller buildings vibrate more slowly and would not require the absorbers, in fact, the fear is that the absorbers on taller buildings could make a skyscraper tip over. (Shock absorbers do add an additional cost to the construction of a new building, but not that much (estimated at 5 percent).)

I can speak to the concept of shock absorbers in a building first-hand. Back in 1984–1985, my organization was assisting the American Express (AE) organization in developing and implementing of its IT plans. After working with the three key locations in the United States, we began assisting American Express' locations in Mexico, Brazil, and Argentina. While working with AE Mexico, I was told that the building was new, and because of the threat of quakes, it was built with shock absorbers. Then in September 1985, a massive earthquake destroyed one third of Mexico City. The new AE building survived with little damage. The building that they had previously occupied collapsed. The morale: good planning pays off.

2.1.1.3.5 Earthquake Hazard: Stress on Glass

A study at the Naval Civil Engineering Laboratory (Port Hueneme, California) found that earthquake-induced stress on window glass in buildings is a potential hazard to building occupants and personnel in close external proximity to buildings during and after an earthquake. Extensive breakage is expected if measures to prevent or minimize its occurrence are not taken. Heat-treated, annealed, and tempered and semi-tempered glasses are subject to explosive fragmentation during earthquake-induced stress.

The hazard potential from earthquake-induced glass breakage is nearly eliminated when a film of 2- to 4-mil-thick polyester is bonded to the inner surface of window glass. The polyester film's adhesive holds the fragments of the broken glass together, preventing explosive propulsion of dangerous glass fragments into an interior space. The holding property of the film/adhesive combination prevents glass fragments from becoming hazardous free-falling missiles.

There are several spin-off benefits to the fragment-retaining film for building windows. When clear film covers the interior surface of a building's windows, it acts as an effective thermal barrier, which contributes to improved interior environmental control. When tinted, the film reduces the amount of solar radiation passing through the window. The strength of the polyester film with its fragment retention characteristic provides an additional measure of entry security and reduced vandalism opportunity.

Given more space (which would take the size of an entire book), we could perform the same analysis for hurricanes, tornadoes, and floods. We could spend time on what Facilities/Building Engineering needs to do for the heavy spring rainstorms as well as the heavy winter snowstorms. However, this chapter is designed to provide only a very brief overview of the other plans that interface with the Crisis Management Plan.

2.1.1.3.6 Building Construction: Accidents

Buildings that house an organization's business units should be built to minimize damage from an accident (e.g., fire, leak or falling water, power outage, etc.). Again, due to space limitations, let us just look at one type — fire.

Fire-Resistant Construction. Fire-resistant construction is classified based on the combustibility of structures as:

- Type I — fire resistive
- Type II — noncombustible
- Type III — ordinary
- Type IV — heavy timber
- Type V — wood frame

Type I construction has the least amount of combustible material, and Type V has the most. Each of the five basic groups of building construction has a fire-resistive weakness, which results in a recurring fire spread throughout the structure.

When evaluating the potential for a fire inside a building, you must look at its construction and its contents. Materials stored inside a building, as well as the materials the structure was built with, add fuel to the fire.

Combustibility of Structures.

- *Type I — fire resistive.* Concrete and steel structure, called fire resistive when first built at the early 1900s, was supposed to confine the fire by its construction. Today, that is not true. Fire does spread several floors in a modern fire-resistive building, — by air conditioning ducts and by auto-exposure (when flames extend vertically from window to window).
- *Type II — noncombustible.* A Type II constructed building has steel or concrete walls, floors, and structural framework; however, the roof covering is combustible, burns, and spreads fire. (During a fire, the flames rise to the underside of the steel roof deck. They may conduct heat through the metal and ignite the combustible roof covering above.)

- *Type III — ordinary construction.* A brick and joist structure. It has masonry-bearing walls but the floors, structural framework, and roof are made of wood or other combustible material. Firefighters call Type III buildings "a lumberyard enclosed by four brick walls." A fire inside Type III buildings spreads by convection (the transfer of heat by fluid motion, such as by a liquid or gas). Heated fire gases and flame in a concealed space can travel upward several floors and break out in the roof space above the top-floor ceiling and below the roof deck.

- *Type IV — heavy timber.* Heavy timber is sometimes called "mill construction" because it was the type of structure used at the turn of the century to house textile mills. Have masonry walls, but the interior wood consists of large timbers. The floor and roof are plank board. The exposed wood timber girders, columns, floor beams, and decks, if ignited in a fire, create large, radiated heat waves. Floors will collapse and walls will push outward until they fall into the street.

- *Type V — wood frame.* A wood-frame building is the only one of the five types of construction that has combustible exterior walls. Flames can spread out a window and then along the outside wood walls.

(***Author Note:*** The above information was obtained from *Firehouse* magazine, June 1996.)

2.1.1.3.7 How to Reduce Fire Losses

Fire suppression systems. When properly installed and maintained, automatic sprinkler systems are the most effective means of limiting the spread of fire. There are a number of cases in my database that substantiate the value of automatic sprinkler systems in containing and controlling a fire. In fact, there are so many that I cannot even list them in the appendix due to space limitations.

While everyone agrees that automatic sprinkler systems are the most effective means of limiting fire spread, it does not mean that the fire will not burn down a building. There are examples where buildings with sprinklers installed have been seriously damaged by a fire. But in most such cases, the sprinklers had not been properly installed and maintained. In other cases, it was because the fire load inside the building overwhelmed the sprinklers. One of the recommendations made by fire departments when visiting organizations is to reduce the amount of combustible materials available to burn.

Good housekeeping. Standard office procedures should require employees to remove work papers from desktops before leaving the work area. Clutter in and around offices and in stairwells should be removed.

> A fire started in the Cash Processing Center of a life insurance company in Chicago, Illinois, a number of years ago. Within minutes, firefighters were on the scene and the fire was extinguished. While it was contained to a 2500-square-foot area, there was considerable smoke damage to the second floor. The fire caused an estimated $200,000 of structural damage and destroyed nearly $300,000 of equipment. Several factors were credited with preventing greater damage. The organization participated in a program where firefighters familiarize themselves with the floor plans and changes in structure on a monthly basis. This ongoing relationship enabled the firefighters to respond quickly and to promptly extinguish the fire. Standard office procedures required employees to remove work papers from desktops before leaving work. There was nothing on top of the desks to allow the fire to spread.

In summary, the Facilities/Building Engineering Plan includes controls used in building construction to protect the assets of the organization from acts of nature (e.g., earthquakes, tornadoes, floods, etc.) or accidents (fire, falling water, etc.). It also includes policies and procedures on day-to-day operating environment issues such as good housekeeping.

Now we present an overview of the second fundamental principle of the BCP — The Emergency Response Plan and its three type of planning processes: incident response, life safety, and damage assessment.

2.1.2 The Emergency Response Plan

The second of the three elements of the Business Continuity Plan (BCP) is the Emergency Response Plan (see the Business Continuity Plan diagram in Appendix).

The Emergency Response Plan consists of policies, procedures, and controls employed to assist employees in responding to a disaster (crisis) when it occurs. For the purpose of this book, it is composed of three types of plans:

1. *Incident Response Plan* consists of incident discovery reporting procedures and identifying actions personnel should take during the discovery of a disaster.
2. *Life Safety Plan* includes personnel evacuation, protecting the company's assets, obtaining medical care for the injured, and

personnel policies for employees to follow if they are at work. It also contains policies and procedures for employees to follow if they are at home when the incident occurs, or if they are traveling to or from a work location.

3. *Damage Assessment Plan* consists of policies and procedures to use to determine the amount of damage sustained from a disaster after it has been contained.

And now for an overview of the first type of planning process of the BCP's Life Safety Plan — The Incident Response Plan.

2.1.2.1 The Incident Response Plan

The incident response plan is developed and implemented to provide instructions for employees to follow during and immediately after a disaster (crisis). It is documented to ensure that employees have a resource to reference if needed.

The Incident Response Plan identifies whom employees should notify if they are the first to discover a disaster during normal working hours. It also identifies information on those the employee should call if they are the first to discover a disaster after normal working hours, or on weekends or holidays. After-hours emergency notifications are often different from those identified to be called during normal working hours.

2.1.2.1.1   Incident Response: Incident Notification during Normal Working Hours

If the employee discovers a potential disaster (e.g., fire flood, leak, etc.), he should notify the person who will be responsible for managing the crisis. The phone call will be made to the emergency number identified in the Emergency Response Plan, which might be the:

- Emergency telephone number identified on the telephone
- Security Department telephone number
- Facilities Department telephone number
- Switchboard
- Local authorities, such as the police or fire department

2.1.2.1.2   Incident Response: Incident Notification After Normal Working Hours, on Weekends and Holidays

If the employee discovers a potential disaster (e.g., fire flood, leak, etc.) after normal working hours, or on weekends and holidays, the telephone call will be made to the emergency number identified in the Emergency Response Plan, which could be the:

- Number on the telephone (will there be anyone to answer this call if it is 2:00 a.m., on a Sunday, or a holiday?)
- Security Department (will there be anyone from the Security Department on-site if it is 2:00 a.m., on a Sunday, or a holiday?)
- Facilities Department (will there be anyone from the Facilities Department on-site?)
- Switchboard (if your organization still has a switchboard, will there be anyone monitoring the switchboard?)
- Local authorities (i.e., the police or fire department)

2.1.2.1.3 Incident Response Plans Do Not Always Work as Documented

Do you have a plan if an employee discovers a disaster after normal working hours or on weekends or holidays and the phone system is not working? On occasion "the best-laid plans of mice and men aft gang aglee."

An example of when the phone system cannot be used to call the fire department follows:

> *Illinois Bell, Hinsdale, Illinois.* A 4:00 p.m. fire at the Illinois Bell central office and switching station in Hinsdale, one of the largest switching stations in the Illinois Bell system, damaged the phone lines. This central office and switching station handled long-distance telephone service routing for several local offices, and was considered a "gateway hub" station. This location:
>
> Processed an estimated 3.5 million calls every day
> Provided local switching service for approximately 38,000 customers
> Operated 118,000 trunk lines for local and long-distance call routing
> Performed switching for 13,000 special-service lines such as data transmission lines
> Provided "800" and WATS service and links to AT&T, MCI, and other interexchange carriers, as well as to cellular phone carriers
>
> When the fire was discovered, a local Bell supervisor tried to call the Hinsdale Fire Department. The supervisor was unable to notify the fire department because the fire damaged the lines. The office was a victim of its own outage.

Another example of the inability to call out to the fire department:

The New York Telephone Company. The NY Telephone Co. Main Switching Center was on the corner of 2nd Avenue and 13th Street in New York City. For nearly a half century, the 11-story building served as the Main Switching Center for the Lower East Side. It served a 300-square-block area and was equipped to handle 100,000 calls per hour. Its customers included hospitals, universities, almost all units in the Fire Department's First Division, as well as 92,000 residential phones.

At approximately 4:00 p.m. on February 26, 1975, an internal fire alarm rang in the lobby of the New York Telephone Co. Main Switching Center. A foreman discovered that the glass in the alarm box on the first floor stair landing had been broken, apparently by accident. He manually reset the alarm and the fan system that had automatically shut down. At about 10:00 p.m., lights over three public telephone booths in the lobby went out. The guard called the foreman, who reset circuit breakers and the lights went back on. At 12:13 a.m., an employee saw heavy smoke coming from the switching center's frame.

When the employee tried to phone in an alarm, the telephones were dead. The fire had taken out the phone lines. Eventually, the guard in the lobby dispatched a man to pull the alarm box at the corner (at 12:25 a.m.).

2.1.2.1.4   Incident Response: Actions to Take during an Incident

When an incident occurs, the employee assigned in the Emergency Response Plan should establish crowd control. This employee assigned to establish crowd control should:

- Post security personnel on perimeter areas to prevent the "inquisitive" from coming too close to the disaster site. Be prepared to direct emergency vehicles to the site.
- If necessary, assist in clearing access to parking areas for emergency vehicles.
- Provide a list of employees believed to be in the building, or those who have not yet been accounted for.

Contingency planning. If the primary person is not available, his alternate will be responsible for establishing crowd control. (All employees assigned a primary assignment in the Business Continuity Plan should have an assigned alternate identified. In some organizations, a tertiary person has also been assigned.)

In summary, the Incident Response Plan identifies "who" employees should notify — if they discover the disaster, both during normal working hours as well as after hours, on weekends, etc. The Plan also presents crowd-control actions to be taken.

Now let us look at an overview of the second type of planning process of the BCP's Emergency Response Plan — the Life Safety Plan.

2.1.2.2   The Life Safety Plan

The Life Safety Planning element is developed and implemented to provide instructions for employees to follow during a disaster (crisis) and includes personnel evacuation, the protection of the company's assets, obtaining medical care for injured, etc. It also contains policies and procedures for employees to follow if they are at work, as well as if they are at home when the incident occurs, or if they are traveling to or from the work location.

2.1.2.2.1   Life Safety Plan for Disasters

Question: Do your employees know what to do when the alarms sound? What has your organization told employees to do in case an earthquake occurs, or a tornado is threatening, or a fire is taking place, or a bomb threat has been received? As we know, there is no standard answer, such as "evacuate the building." When threatened by each type of disaster, the employee will have a unique response.

Standard answers to this question include:

- An earthquake: "Do not evacuate; get under a desk, table, etc., or in a doorway."
- A tornado: "Do not evacuate; go to an interior section of the building; preferably on lower floors."
- A fire: "Evacuate the building; report to a predesignated area so you can be accounted for. If that area is not usable, go to the secondary location that has been identified."
- A bomb: "Do not evacuate until you are told by management. Then evacuate to a predesignated area." (In some cases, you will be asked to look for the bomb. Follow the instructions prepared by your company.)

The Emergency Response Plan is designed to ensure that employees know how to respond during *and* immediately after a disaster. If they are the first to discover a disaster, they should notify the assigned personnel.

They then must decide whether they have time to protect the assets of the organization without risking their own safety, or the safety of other employees. (If the business units have documented and implemented their plan properly, there is little or no reason or need to protect the assets of the organization because they are stored off-premises or can be replaced.) As part of the Life Safety Plan, the employees should know when and how to evacuate the building. "When" generally depends on the type of disaster (see evacuation suggestions above). "How" means the stairwells, not the elevators. There is, and has been, a cardinal rule for the use of elevators when evacuating a building during a fire, and that is "Never use elevators during a fire."

2.1.2.2.2 Evacuation Options during a Fire

When an alarm sounds, or the public address system announces the need to evacuate, employees should use the stairwells. They should move in an orderly fashion down the stairwells to ground level. (All employees should remain calm.) They should never panic. (Panic begets more panic, which begets more panic.) The employees should respond in the same way they did during the last fire drill evacuation of the building.

I am sure that most organizations run a fire drill at least once a year. Fire drills provide the training experience all employees will need to use, and fall back on, when there is a real emergency. The National Fire Protection Association recommends conducting fire drills once a month, placing the emphasis on orderly evacuation rather than on speed.

If personnel find that the stairwell is blocked and cannot be used for exiting the building, they should:

- Move to one of the other stairwells in the building and attempt to move down to the ground-floor exit. They should not use the elevators to evacuate a high-rise building, especially when the fire is on a floor below the one they are on.
- Consider going up away from the fire. Can personnel go up to the roof? Is there a roof exit? Does the roof exit open from the inside (crash bars), or are they locked?

If employees can reach the roof, they could be rescued by helicopters. A few examples of helicopter rescues from the roofs of high-rise buildings include:

MGM Grand Hotel Fire, Las Vegas, Nevada, 1980: Nearby Nellis Air Force Base rushed in helicopters to help those who had made their way to the roof. Cables were dropped from the helicopters to rescue approximately 100 people. This operation was stopped however, because the draft created by the aircraft was fanning the fire.

Las Vegas Hilton Hotel, Las Vegas, Nevada, 1981: The hotel had to evacuate the 4000 guests in a fire. Some guests were rescued by helicopters, which helped airlift them to safety. The fire killed 8 and injured more than 190.

First Interstate Bank Fire, Los Angeles, California, 1988: During a fire that damaged four floors of the high-rise building, some employees were unable to evacuate the building via the stair-wells. At 2:30 a.m., firefighters reached a man on the 50th floor. He was taken to the roof for evacuation by helicopter.

World Trade Center Bombing, New York City, 1993: Twenty-eight people were rescued by helicopters from the roof, including one pregnant woman and eight disabled people who had been trapped on the 94th floor for nine hours.

Boston, Massachusetts, high-rise, 1996: In 1996, a fire started on the 5th floor of a 10-story office building in Boston's down-town financial district. Approximately 100 people were in the building. Helicopters were standing by to rescue people who fled to the roof, but were not needed.

Despite these examples, I need to recommend that safety officers of organizations that consider this as an alternative — if stairwells are blocked — read the story in the *Wall Street Journal* published on October 23, 2001, entitled "Could Helicopters Have Saved People from Trade Center." This story, about the helicopter's inability to rescue workers from the World Trade Center North tower on 9-11, worries me. It is the reason I suggest that the safety officer, or the person responsible in your organization for the Emergency Response Plan, contact the fire and police departments to determine if there are any local problems that would prevent helicopters from landing on the building housing the organization's business units.

This article led me to question the accuracy of the writer, or the motives of the emergency response personnel. The author pointed out that heli-copters were unable to land because the doors to the roof were locked. It goes on to suggest that the doors were locked because the firefighters suggested that the Port of NY/NJ keep them locked. The article suggests that the rescue of 28 people from the roof of the World Trade Center

North Tower after the 1993 bombing did not reinforce the life-saving potential of rooftop rescues.

> "But rather than reinforce the life-saving potential of rooftop rescues, the police department's daring helicopter operation in 1993 had had the opposite effect. After the 1993 garage bombing, the Port Authority of New York and New Jersey and the fire department made a deliberate decision not to plan for future helicopter rescues."

According to the article,

> "The agencies rejected recommendations from police pilots that an area of the north tower's roof be kept clear for helicopter landings. The antennas were put back up. And mostly for security reasons, the Port Authority kept the two sets of heavy metal doors leading to the building's only roof exit tightly locked — as they would be on the morning of Sept. 11. ... Part of the explanation for this decision in the wake of the 1993 blast was an intense feud then raging between the city's fire and police departments over who had control at emergencies. The fire department, which has no helicopters of its own, dismissed the 1993 rooftop rescue as grandstanding. Fire commanders said the mission was dangerous and unnecessary. And they said any future evacuations should be carried out by fire personnel from the ground."

Furthermore the article went to say,

> "On Sept. 11, a rescue from the north tower would have been difficult but possible, Mr. Semendinger and other veteran helicopter-rescue pilots say. The first building hit by a hijacked plane, at 8:48 a.m., the north tower was the second to collapse, one hour and 45 minutes later. Records of calls to 911 operators, first reported by the *New York Daily News*, show that people on the top floors were seeking help at least until 10:12 a.m., one hour and 24 minutes after the strike. With fire raging on the floors below them, they had no hope of walking down to safety."

Based on this article, I again suggest that you check with the local authorities to determine if rooftop rescues are suggested. (***Author Note:*** If I were trapped in a high-rise building, on a floor above a fire, and unable to go down the stairwell, I would want the opportunity to go up to the roof (with the hope that a helicopter could rescue me). Since reading this article, I have felt very uncomfortable because I have always included going up to the roof as one of my options for evacuation in a high-rise fire. Now I have to worry about if I am in a city that uses helicopters for rescue, such as Los Angeles, or in one that does not use helicopters, such as New York.)

2.1.2.2.3 Evacuation Options

If personnel cannot go down the stairwells and cannot go up to the roof, then they should stay on their floor. They should attempt to block all spaces around doors and vents using towels, clothes, etc. They should move to a room with the least amount of combustibles (bath/rest room). They should avoid breaking windows to get fresh air. The smoke from below will funnel in through the windows that have been broken, making it difficult to breathe.

2.1.2.2.4 Evacuation Planning

Develop guidelines that includes primary and secondary exits. Give each employee a copy of the plan. Also post the plan in public areas. Establish meeting places outside the building and tell the employees where they should report. Establish a method of accounting for employees and assign the task to floor wardens. The floor wardens should make a head count of employees outside the building at the meeting places.

Conduct fire drills regularly, requiring all building occupants to participate and respond as if there were actual fires. Why? All employees should be acquainted with the sound and locations of the fire alarms and with the emergency communications systems.

Instruct employees to respond immediately to the sound of the alarm or emergency communication system. In high-rise buildings, evacuation may only be required from the fire floor.

Make sure all employees understand the fire emergency plan. Involve employees who have hearing, vision, or physical impairments in evacuation planning. If your organization has hearing-impaired employees, ensure that there are fire alarms with lights that will get the attention of those individuals. Another consideration when the public address system is used: what language is being used? Is any other language being used? In a high-rise office building fire a couple of years ago, the majority of people in the building were the cleaning crew. Many of the crew spoke Spanish, not English. Organizations must consider all these issues in their Life Safety Plan.

2.1.2.2.5 Evacuating the Handicapped

In an emergency, how do you evacuate the handicapped or disabled? With the Americans with Disabilities Act in place, there is an increasing opportunity for the disabled in the workplace. Over the years a lot of attention was given to a means of access for the disabled. The Emergency Response Plan must address plans to help evacuate disabled people during an emergency such as a fire.

- If an evacuation vehicle will be used, where will it be located?
  - How does it work, and who will be responsible?
  - Can the unit be stored in a place that is easily accessible?
  - How many people will be required to operate the evacuation vehicle?
  - What training have they received to ensure the safety of both themselves and the passenger?
  - How much strength is required of the person operating the device in relation to the weight of the passenger?
- How many people who are in the building on a daily basis would need assistance?

In summary, the Life Safety Plan includes the policies for employees to follow during and after an earthquake, a tornado, a fire, or a bomb threat. The plan deals with evacuation options during a fire, the use of stairwells, or rooftop helicopter rescue in high-rise buildings. The plan stresses that employees must not use elevators to evacuate in a high-rise fire. The plan should remind employees what they should do if they decide to stay on their floor because they cannot evacuate via the stairwell. The plan also covers evacuation policies for the handicapped employees.

Now let us look at an overview of the third type of planning process of the BCP's Life Safety Plan — the Damage Assessment Plan.

2.1.2.3 The Damage Assessment Plan

The Damage Assessment Plan was developed and implemented to provide employees with instructions to follow immediately after a disaster is contained. This plan identifies "who" will enter the building, the safety precautions they must take, and the information they are to gather.

Usually, the Damage Assessment Team consists of employees from the Facilities/Engineering Department, the Security Department, and employees from the affected departments (if they have specific technical knowledge needed during the assessment effort).

The first step the damage assessment team should do after a disaster is to get approvals to gain access to the building. If your organization owns the building, your Damage Assessment Team will be negotiating with local authorities to obtain access to your building.

Why do you have to negotiate? First of all, the building may be unsafe. If the building has suffered a fire, there is the possibility that people entering could be injured. How many times have you heard about firefighters being injured in the building? The floor collapses, the ceiling collapses, fluorescent lights fall from the ceiling. If your organization has not experienced a fire before, you will find that firefighters have the authority to delay access of civilians to the building. Another reason is that smoke pockets have been found as far away as 15 floors from the site of the fire. If employees enter an area with these smoke pockets, they could be overcome by the carbon monoxide in the smoke. Firefighters do not want civilians injured during, or after, a fire.

> *Precision Assembly Co., New Hampshire, August 1996:* People who worked there requested entrance to assess the damage and recover items that were not damaged. Officials refused because of the dangerous gases that were still inside the building.

Another reason for delayed access occurs when the cause of the disaster is a bombing or arson. In either case, a felony crime has been committed. The police and ATF authorities will seal the building while they do an investigation. They do not want anyone in the building who is not properly trained as a bomb or arson investigator. One reason for this is that you could accidentally remove evidence from the scene (e.g., on the bottom of your shoes). A second reason is that if they find the perpetrator of the crime, they will prosecute that person. If the perpetrator's lawyer finds out that you were in the building (an untrained, unauthorized person), they will bring this to the attention of the judge and jury. Their presentation will accuse you of planting the evidence found in the building, because for some reason, you did not like their client, or something to that effect. At any rate, it is unlikely that the perpetrator will be found guilty in that instance.

If your organization does not own the building, the owner now presents another potential delay in getting into the building. The owner's insurance company will probably suggest that no one enters the building until the insurance company's adjuster checks it and until the building is shored up — to prevent injuries to people doing damage assessment or salvage.

After obtaining authorization to enter the building, the team should check for safety hazards.

2.1.2.3.1 Initial Damage Assessment

In the initial damage assessment, there are three basic questions that need answers:

1. Have there been any employees injured in the disaster? Who?
2. Has there been physical damage to the building? Was it structural damage, or damage to the building's utilities (e.g., heating, ventilating and air conditioning systems)?
3. Has there been any physical damage to the equipment?

If there is a lot of water damage, from ruptured overhead pipes, look to see if the source of the water flow can be stopped.

Some damage assessment tips from ServPro ("Emergency Water Tips") include:

- Do not use electrical outlets or fixtures that were affected by the water.
- Protect electronic equipment.
- Locate electrical fuse panel and disconnect breaker.
- Disconnect backup batteries (only employees who are trained).
- Remove moisture from equipment as soon as possible.
- If there is water dripping from the ceiling, cover equipment with water-resistant covers to minimize further damage.
- Remove as much water from furniture as possible.
- Do not apply corrosion-inhibiting lubricants to electronic equipment.
- Remove all assets from the area: cash, checkbooks, securities, etc.
- Place dehumidification equipment in the room to quicken the drying process.
- Identify wet documents, files, or books.

In later damage assessments, other issues will come into play, such as:

1. Are there any negotiable instruments missing?
2. Who will account for missing negotiable instruments?

Damage Assessment after a flood. Because water after a flood may be contaminated, employees on the Damage Assessment Team should wear protective clothing. In addition, the organization should consider providing voluntary typhoid and tetanus inoculations.

In summary, the Damage Assessment Plan includes the policies for employees to follow in performing an initial damage assessment following a disaster. The Plan includes who will enter the building, the safety precautions they should take, and the information they are to gather. The plan explains why there might be delays in getting into the building (e.g., authorities such as firefighters, police, bomb squad, etc.). It also explains that an owner of a building may delay your access due to their insurance company's requirements. The plan identifies the three main questions members of the team should try to answer: (1) injuries to employees,

(2) damage to building, and (3) damage to equipment. Departmental personnel will perform detailed damage assessments after the building is shored up and it is safe to go into damaged areas.

Now let us look at an "overview" of the third fundamental principle of the BCP — the Business Resumption Plan and its three types of planning processes (The IT Disaster Recovery Plan, the business unit's Business Resumption Plan, and the Crisis Management Plan.

2.1.3   The Business Resumption Plan

The third of the three elements of the Business Continuity Plan is the Business Resumption Plan. (See the Business Continuity Plan diagram in Appendix.)

The Business Resumption Plan consists of policies and procedures employed to assist employees in resuming business operations after an interruption caused by a disaster or crisis. For the purpose of this book, it is composed of three types of plans:

1. *The Information Technology (IT) Disaster Recovery Plan (DRP).* These plans were documented as early as the 1960s but have evolved over the years. This evolution is discussed later in this chapter.
2. *The Business Unit — Business Resumption Plan (BRP).* These plans began in the late 1970s and gained momentum after some high-profile disasters occurred to revenue-generating departments of organizations in the early 1980s. This evolution is also discussed later in this chapter.
3. *The Crisis Management Plan.* While many organizations have the IT plans and the Business Unit BRPs in place, the Crisis Management Plan is often the missing piece.

Key BRP objectives include:

■ Ensure employee safety and well-being.
■ Respond swiftly and effectively to minimize business interruption and financial loss.
■ Resume time-sensitive operations immediately to maintain shareholder value and confidence.
■ Recover operations quickly and accurately to retain public goodwill and protect the corporate image.
■ Restore the company to "business as usual."

Now let us look at an overview of the first type of planning process of the BCPs Business Resumption Plan — the Information Technology (IT) Disaster Recovery Plan.

2.1.3.1 The Information Technology-Disaster Recovery Plan

The IT Disaster Recovery Plan consists of procedures that will enable IT employees to respond swiftly and effectively to minimize business interruption and financial loss, to resume time-sensitive operations immediately to maintain shareholder value and confidence, and to recover operations quickly and accurately to retain public goodwill and protect the corporate image.

IT Disaster Recovery Planning includes the Computer Operations Recovery team, the Disaster Site recovery team, and the Recovery Headquarters team, as well as a number of processes, such as the Applications Impact Analysis, the Data Protection Strategy, and the Alternate Operating Strategy.

2.1.3.1.1 The Computer Operations Recovery Team

The Computer Operations Recovery Team is responsible for performing the recovery activities that take place at the computer backup site. This team consists of experts in systems and applications software, tape operations, databases, and communications. Its responsibilities are to return services to end users on a timely basis. Team members perform such actions as recovery of systems and applications software, recovery of databases, and retrieval of backup data from the off-premises storage facility.

The DRP must describe the actions to be followed in notifying team members of a disaster, transporting the team to the backup site, managing and performing all critical recovery operations, and completing the shutdown of the backup site. Each team leader has a unique set of responsibilities that must be clearly defined in the plan.

2.1.3.1.2 The Disaster Site Recovery Team

The Disaster Site Recovery Team is responsible for performing recovery activities at the site of the disaster. This team consists of specialists in facility damage assessment and restoration, equipment damage assessment and salvage, and communications recovery. The team's responsibilities include assessment of damage to facilities, equipment, and supplies; repair or relocation of the damaged facility; replacement or repair of equipment and supplies; and preparation for return of data center operations to the original data center site (if applicable). The DRP should include procedures detailing the steps to be taken to notify the team of the disaster, coordinate the necessary support at the disaster site, manage and perform assessment activities, and communicate with internal and external entities on the progress of the recovery effort. The facility restoration team leader may also need to assist in finding a temporary data center that meets predesignated criteria established in the plan.

2.1.3.1.3 The Recovery Headquarters Team

The Recovery Headquarters Team is one of three data center recovery teams, the others being the Computer Operations Recovery Team and the Disaster Site Recovery Team. The Recovery Headquarters Team is responsible for internal and external notification and communication activities, as well as the administrative support activities that will be needed throughout the disaster recovery operation.

2.1.3.1.4 Developing the Initial Disaster Alert Procedure

The *initial disaster alert procedure* addresses the decision-making process from the time data center representatives are notified until the decision is made to activate (or not activate) the DRP. This procedure establishes who notifies the IS recovery management team of a disaster, who on the team is to be notified, how to verify that the disaster requires activation of the DRP, and who has authority to activate the recovery plan. The initial disaster alert is important for companies that have determined they would suffer a serious loss if their computers were not quickly operational following a disaster and that have contracts with commercial hot-site vendors or have established their own in-house backup sites.

2.1.3.1.5 Performing an Applications Impact Analysis

The *applications impact analysis* is a process used to identify the impact on the organization of not being able to process a computer application as scheduled. It is performed to identify which applications are critical to the organization and which are less critical. The impact analysis provides information that can be useful in developing the computer backup site strategy. For example, if the results of the applications impact analysis indicate that an application cannot be delayed long beyond its scheduled processing point without causing a significant negative impact, use of a hot-site may be justified.

2.1.3.1.6 Selecting a Computer Processing Recovery Strategy

An organization can select from a number of strategies for resuming computer processing following a disaster or business interruption affecting the data center. The options include use of a commercial hot-site, company-owned backup site, reciprocal agreement, and cold-site. Companies that need immediate processing might choose a computer hot-site. Companies that do not have an immediate processing need might choose a reciprocal agreement or a cold-site.

2.1.3.1.7 Protecting and Recovering Computer Data

The protection and recovery of data is the most important element in the DCRP because without the data, the recovery operation will fail. It consists of the rotation of backups to the off-premises storage location and the reconstruction steps needed to bring the backup data to a satisfactory point for the user of the application.

2.1.3.1.8 Testing and Exercising the Plan

After the IT Disaster Recovery Plan is documented and tested to ensure that it works, the plan then moves to a maintenance and exercise phase. The DRP coordinator needs to establish a policy for plan maintenance; this usually involves reviews and updates on at least a quarterly basis.

The plan should also be flexible enough to allow recovery teams to update their section of the plan whenever a significant change has occurred. For example, changes in routine computer operations can occur frequently during the quarter, and some of these changes might affect the DRP. These changes should be reflected in the DRP as soon as possible after they occur.

In summary, The IT Disaster Recovery Plan includes the following teams: the Computer Operations Team, the Disaster Site Recovery Team, and the Recovery Headquarters Team. It includes procedures (such as the initial disaster alert procedure) and policies (such as the protection of data, the testing, exercising, and maintenance of the plan).

Now let us look at an overview of the second type of planning process of the BCP's Business Resumption Plan — the Business Unit's Business Resumption Plan.

2.1.3.2 The Business Unit's Business Resumption Plan

The Business Unit's Business Resumption Plan details how each business unit, or department, within the organization will resume operations following an interruption.

During the development of the Business Unit's Business Resumption Plan, business units' operations are analyzed to determine which must be resumed immediately, and which can be delayed. Just because a business function can be delayed does not mean it is not critical to the organization. It just means that it can be delayed from its normal schedule. That is, it cannot be omitted. It will be done, just a little later.

The Business Resumption Planner in the business unit would then determine all the data (or records) needed for this operation to function properly. Some of the data resides on mainframes. This data must be identified by the business unit planner to the IT planner to be sure it is being copied and stored off-premises (in another building). (Sometimes, the term "off-site" is used for data storage. This means that the data is stored somewhere else other than the floor on which the mainframes, or microcomputers, are located.) As we now know from the "lessons learned" in the World Trade Center collapses (9-11), those basements were not accessible for months, if at all.

An overview of the Business Units' Business Resumption Plan follows.

2.1.3.2.1   The Business Impact Analysis

The *business impact analysis* (BIA) is designed to ensure a thorough understanding of the vital business functions and systems within the organization. The impact of loss on each of these functions is identified, evaluated, and categorized according to the required time frames for recovery of the function. The recovery priorities are set on the basis of this analysis.

The purpose of the impact analysis is to identify the consequences of the interruption in terms of financial loss, additional expense, embarrassment to the organization, and the maximum time period of interruption that the organization can tolerate.

After the analysis is complete, it should be reviewed and verified by management and all participants. Management is then ready to establish recovery priorities. System and application recovery time frames are driven by the recovery priorities.

21.3.2.2   Identifying and Documenting Critical Business Functions

The BIA identified the critical business functions at the level of business units and their major supporting systems and applications. This next stage in developing the business unit operations resumption plan builds on that analysis. For each of the identified critical business units, the planning professional must now identify the critical processes performed by the business unit. An inventory of these processes is developed, and each process is broken down into its component tasks (e.g., order entry is a process; each activity performed to enter an order is a task). The individual applications that support each of these processes must also be identified. Having established an inventory of processes and related tasks, the processes can be evaluated to identify those that are most critical and should therefore receive a high priority for recovery.

Two structured methods can be used to obtain the necessary inventories of critical processes and tasks. The first method involves the use of a questionnaire to collect data; the second involves interviewing key employees. These data collection methods are independent of each other, and either can be used.

21.3.2.3 Identifying and Documenting Resource Requirements

For each process performed by the business unit, a set of resources or tools is necessary to complete the process. Resource planning identifies the resources that business units need to reestablish their operations at an alternate location.

First, the number and type of personnel needed for the recovery is determined. This information allows the planner to determine such other resource requirements as recovery facilities and equipment, because these depend, at least in part, on the number of people that require support during the recovery effort. For example, the number of employees involved in the recovery helps determine the size of the recovery facility and the number of desks, phones, computers, and supplies needed. Planning for recovery of facilities and such basic resources as voice and data communications requires determining the expected volume and use of these resources.

Other types of dependencies must also be taken into consideration. For example, the power requirements of specific items of equipment must be assessed to determine overall power requirements for the recovery facility.

Resource planning also identifies who is responsible for installing and configuring equipment. The results of this analysis must be shared with all participants in the planning process so that the parties responsible for providing the necessary resources understand what is expected of them. Depending on the availability of internal resources, the planner and service providers may have to go outside the organization for assistance.

2.1.3.2.4 Organizing the Business Unit Operations Recovery Teams

The *business unit operations recovery teams* are responsible for responding to and managing any serious interruption of business operations. Some organizations choose to create separate programs and teams for handling specific types of threat events. A disaster recovery team might handle any immediately apparent disaster (e.g., an explosion, fire, or earthquake) that interrupts business operations. A crisis management team might be organized to handle such threats as criminal activity, workplace violence, product contamination, and accidents involving hazardous materials that pose a danger to the organization but do not interrupt operations. An emergency-preparedness team might be assigned responsibility for the safety of employees, customers, or the public in a crisis or disaster.

Other organizations choose to manage all types of crises and disasters using primarily two types of teams: one that is chiefly responsible for coordinating the company-wide recovery effort and the other for managing recovery of specific business units at the alternate sites designated in the recovery plan.

The purpose of recovery management is to minimize damage to the organization and its employees. The first priority is to protect human life, whether of employees or consumers of a company's products or services, while terminating and recovering from the incident as quickly as possible. The recovery teams must act prudently to ensure that a relatively minor incident does not become a major disaster.

The recovery teams must also attempt to protect the organization's assets. These include financial and commercial assets as well as such intangible assets as the organization's goodwill and reputation.

In responding to a disaster, the organization must seek to maintain the confidence of its customers and shareholders. It must also maintain good relations with law enforcement, regulatory and other governmental agencies, and comply with all applicable laws and regulations. A key objective is to minimize the risk of legal liabilities to the organization.

The organization must set up an emergency operations center for the Crisis Management Team to use in managing the disaster. The Crisis Management Plan describes the chain of command, areas of responsibility for managing the recovery, and certain basic operational procedures. However, it is not possible to document how specific recovery decisions should be made. Such decisions will differ, depending on the type of disaster and expected length of the outage, the nature of the affected organization and its organizational structure, and the mix of experts available at the emergency operations center.

It is possible to outline a basic framework for response and recovery activities. The Crisis Management Team must know under what circumstances it is to respond to a disaster or crisis. The organization might choose to designate response or escalation levels, each level assigned according to the expected length of the interruption and the appropriate response for that level. For ease of communication and use, one set of response procedures should be used by all parties involved in managing the incident. These procedures include notification of the disaster, damage assessment, activation of the emergency operations center and of the recovery teams, and restoration of facilities.

2.1.3.2.5 Recovery Planning for Microcomputers

Many applications that previously resided on mainframe systems are now processed on microcomputers; these include an increasingly large number of mission-critical applications. The microcomputers may, in turn, be connected to other internal and external networks as well as to mainframes. Even if a system appears to serve a single business application, its applications and data might reside on multiple computers, although the connections may never be apparent to users. In addition to networked systems, stand-alone microcomputers are now sufficiently powerful to support important, mission-critical applications.

Whereas most companies have comprehensive programs in place for mainframe disaster recovery, far fewer address recovery of microcomputers.

2.1.3.2.6 Business Units Operations Recovery Plan Testing, Maintenance, and Training

The business operations resumption plan must change in response to changes in the organization. The plan must be maintained in a timely manner so that it reflects the most recent changes in operations, systems, and management structure. It must be periodically tested to ensure that it is workable.

Recovery team members must be trained so that they understand how to perform their duties during a recovery operation. They must also be tested in the documented recovery procedures to ensure they are capable of carrying out the plan in a crisis.

The primary goal of testing is to ensure that the procedures for recovering business operations are feasible in practice. This involves testing the readiness of the organization to recover business operations as well as testing recovery of specific systems and applications.

The primary cause of failure for many plans is the lack of proper maintenance. An inaccurate plan can be misleading and cause management to make incorrect decisions or delay the recovery. For example, if key vendor contact information is not valid, the delays in contacting and obtaining a response might extend the interruption. The users of the plan should provide the information and have primary responsibility to ensure that their specific part of the plan remains current. To encourage active participation in maintaining the recovery plans, ease of plan use and maintenance are key.

Training provides an opportunity for team members to address problems that would almost never occur under normal business conditions and to do so in a more relaxed atmosphere. Tests and training exercises provide the best form of training for the recovery teams. They offer an opportunity for team members to use systems in an unfamiliar environment, accomplish critical tasks with minimal resources, and develop the team attitude and processes required for successful recovery.

In summary, the Business Unit's Business Resumption Plan includes the following elements: the Business Unit Operations Recovery Teams, and policies and procedures dealing with the Business Impact Analysis, Documenting of Critical Business Functions, Documenting of Resource Requirements; Recovery Planning for Microcomputers, and the procedures for the testing, exercising and maintenance of the plan.

Now let us look at an overview of the second type of planning process of the BCP's Business Resumption Plan — the Crisis Management Plan.

2.1.3.3 The Crisis Management Plan

The Crisis Management Plan consists of responsibilities for the executives of organizations to follow when a disaster, or a nonphysical crisis, has struck the organization.

As discussed in Chapter 1, the Crisis Management Plan is a documented plan, detailing the actions the executives want to be taken when a crisis strikes the organization. It is designed to put order into confusion. After a crisis has surfaced, executives selected to serve on the Crisis Management Team will work together to achieve control of the crisis and minimize the impacts of the crisis.

A crisis generally passes through three stages. The first is referred to as the Pre-Crisis Stage. No one outside the organization is aware of the growing problem. If the problem is not managed properly and it becomes known outside the organization, the problem has moved to the Acute-Crisis Stage. After the organization contains the crisis, the Post-Crisis Stage begins. (These three stages are discussed in detail in Chapter 3.)

When a crisis has reached the Acute Stage, the Crisis Management Team will employ the following steps to contain the crisis:

1. Take charge quickly.
2. Determine the facts.
3. Tell your story.
4. Fix the problem.

(The four steps in managing a crisis are discussed in detail in Chapter 4.)

The Crisis Management Plan identifies the members of the Crisis Management (CM) Team. It also identifies the members of the Executive Management Team, key executives selected by the president or chief executive officer. Chapter 5 discusses the Executive Management Team's role with the Crisis Management Plan while Chapter 6 focuses on the Crisis Management Team's role. Chapter 7 concentrates on the Crisis Management Team Command Center, and Chapter 8 will discusses the importance of testing and exercising the Crisis Management Plan. Chapter 9 deals with an approach that can be used in developing and implementing the Crisis Management Plan.

In summary, the remaining chapters of the book concentrate on addressing: the three stages of a crisis, the four steps in managing a crisis, the role of the executive management team, the roles of the members of the crisis management team, preparing a CMT command center, testing and exercising the plan, and an approach to developing the Crisis Management Plan.

Now let us look at some of the differences between the Business Resumption and the Crisis Management Plans.

2.1.3.4   Differences between the Crisis Management Plan and the Business Resumption Plan

Crisis Management Planning is a term used to describe a methodology used by executives to respond to and manage a crisis. The objective is to gain control of the situation quickly so a company can efficiently manage the crisis and minimize its negative impacts. It is defined in the *American Heritage Dictionary* as "special measures taken to solve problems caused by a crisis." It is considered more an art than a science, because an art is defined as a nonscientific system of principles and methods employed in the performance of a set of activities, while a science is defined as a methodical activity, discipline, or study.

In a Crisis Management Plan, if a crisis strikes the company, the crisis management team will activate and manage the crisis until its conclusion. In a Business Resumption Plan, if a disaster strikes a computer center, causing injuries to employees, or damage to the equipment or to the building, the IS/IT department would need support. The Crisis Management Team will activate and provide support to IS/IT until the department's business operations are back to normal. This team's support is, in essence, crisis management support.

2.1.3.4.1   Differences

One difference between the two plans relates to *scope*. The Business Resumption Plan deals with incidents that cause physical damage to assets of the company, while the Crisis Management Plan deals with incidents that do not cause physical damage to assets of the company. This is one area of difference between the two planning concepts.

Another difference relates to the *actions taken*. When the cause is a disaster, with physical damage, the Business Resumption Plan indicates that the Crisis Management Team will provide support to the affected business units until the business units resume normal operations. However, when the cause is a crisis, with no physical damage, the Business Resumption Plan indicates that the Crisis Management Team will manage the crisis until its conclusion.

A third difference is the *use of scenarios*. The scenarios used in crisis management planning are different from the scenario used in the business resumption planning.

In Business Resumption Planning, business units build their plan based on one scenario, a worst-case disaster scenario. They do not build a plan to resume business from each type of disaster that they could possibly experience (e.g., fire, explosion, internal floods, damage from storms, etc.).

Why does the Business Resumption Plan use a "worst-case scenario?"

In the mid-1970s, companies started building their disaster recovery plans with actions to respond to different scenarios. They were developed and documented as "what-if" Contingency Plans. "What if" the computer equipment failed? "What if" the computer software failed? "What if" we lost power? Companies carried that thinking over to their Disaster Recovery Plans. They began developing a DRP for a fire, another one for a flood, and a third one for a storm.

Disaster Recovery Planners realized that most of the information used to resume business operations from one specific type of disaster was the same as, or similar to, resuming business operations from an entirely different type of disaster. Whether it was a fire, a flood, or a storm that struck their location, their plan called for them to:

■ Activate their alternate operating location.
■ Retrieve their backup files from the off-premises storage location.
■ Relocate key people to the alternate site to resume time-sensitive business operations.

The same concepts would be used, the same recovery resources would be used, despite the fact that the cause of the disaster was different.

The planners realized that much of the information in the plan was redundant. They decided that if the plan would work in "a worst-case disaster," then that is the scenario that would be used. They recognized that the "worst-case disaster," as rare as it is, provided all the planning actions they would need. If the disaster that they would need to recover from was less damaging than a "worst case," the plan could still be used. Some of the elements would need to be activated, and other elements would not.

On the other hand, with Crisis Management Planning, they build their plan to address specific types of crises. The reason for that is that the actions needed to manage one type of crisis could be quite different from the actions needed to manage a different type of crisis. For example, if the company faces a "sudden market shift" crisis, company executives would manage the crisis entirely differently than a "product safety" crisis. In an organization that could realistically be faced with each of these crises, the company should preplan the actions, and options they could take in each case, to minimize the impact to the company.

2.1.4 History of Business Continuity Planning

When discussing the Business Continuity Plan, we are talking about a number of different plans that have been rolled up under one umbrella. At one time or another, different departments within the organization have managed these plans. For example,

- Parts of the Prevention Plans have been under the jurisdiction of the Security department, while the other parts were under the jurisdiction of the Facilities/Building Engineering department.
- Emergency Response Plans have been under the jurisdiction of the Facilities/Building Engineering with input coming from the Human Resources and Legal departments.
- Business Resumption Plans have been under the jurisdiction of the department for which they were written. The first plan was the IT Plan, developed in the 1970s. The business unit Business Resumption Plans became a standard operating policy back in the mid-1980s. The Crisis Management Plan was in the process of evolving during the early years.

The Prevention and Emergency Response Plans have evolved significantly during the last 50 years. As lessons were learned from a disaster experience, policies and procedures were changed and updated. Thus today, resources are available that were never even thought of 50 years ago. These resources provide organizations with sophisticated controls (detection systems, suppression systems, etc.) to minimize actual incidents from occurring.

The same concept has taken place with the technology used in an organization. Years ago, a Contingency Plan was developed to respond to a technology problem (computer or telecommunications). As a result of lessons learned from actual incidents, this plan was changed. Eventually we reached the point in time when the Business Continuity Plan became the generally accepted term to depict the Prevention Plans, the Emergency

Response Plans, and the Business Resumption Plans coming together under one executive, as one plan, to provide the safest environment in which an organization can operate.

Business Continuity Planning actually began as early as the mid-1960s. Of course, it was not called Business Continuity at that time. The name it bore related to the scope the planning took at the time. For some understanding of the evolution of the process, let me explain how I experienced its growth.

The Crisis Management Plan started out as a support section of the IT Plan in the late 1970s. It then became part of the organization's Company-Wide Business Resumption Plan. Through the 1990s, it became imperative that it should be a stand-alone element of the Business Resumption Plan. The difficult part of developing and implementing the Crisis Management Plan was merging the roles and responsibilities of members of the team when they had to deal with a disaster, or with a crisis.

Perhaps it would be a good idea to visit the history of the Business Continuity Plan; I present the milestones and changes as I saw and experienced them.

2.1.4.1   Contingency Plans, 1965

Organizations with in-house mainframe computers installed began developing "Contingency" Plans. These plans were designed to limit an interruption to computer processing schedules. It was not uncommon in the mid to late 1960s for computers, or their peripheral equipment (tape or disk drives), to fail (crash). In addition, at that time, human error in operating computers was a common problem.

Certainly many senior people in the IT field have shared, or least heard, stories of a computer operator experiencing a crash on a disk drive. Disk packs were removable at the time. On occasion, a disk pack would be damaged when they were being removed. The damage was not discovered until the pack was placed back in a disk drive. Operators were trained to check a disk pack for damage if it caused a disk drive to crash.

Human error. On occasion, an operator would remove the disk pack after the disk drive malfunction and place the it on another drive — without checking for damage to the pack. If they experienced another disk drive crash, the operators would know there was a problem with the pack.

We old timers have all heard, or known, operators who have moved a disk pack (that was obviously damaged) from one disk drive to another, causing multiple disk drive crashes — without recognizing that the problem was with the disk pack. Eventually after having done this exercise a couple times, the operator would realize that the problem was with the disk pack, not the drives.

First- and second-generation computers needed a great deal of maintenance to prevent equipment failures. For this reason, companies that relied on computers needed to provide a "Contingency" Plan to ensure that computer processing outages would not create major problems for the company.

I worked for the IBM Service Bureau Corporation in the mid-1960s. SBC, as it was known in the industry, was providing computer processing services (as its name says, Service Bureau). In today's terminology, it was an outsourcer. Many of the companies that placed an order for a computer, and were waiting for it to arrive (which could take 12 to 18 months), would contract with a service bureau to provide the same services for which the computer was ordered. SBC was one of the most successful "outsourcers" at the time.

In addition, SBC also offered a Payroll System service that was one of the best in the country. Many small companies that could not afford to have their own in-house computer would contract with SBC, or its competitors, to provide payroll services. In a number of cases, companies that did have their own in-house computers chose to have SBC, or a competitor such as ADP, process their payroll. They felt that the in-house computer should be used for applications that contributed to the making of money. The idea behind the computer was that it allowed organizations to process profit-making applications rapidly, allowed management to have access to information rapidly, and to improve the overall operations of the organization. In the mid-1960s, the computer and its peripheral equipment cost millions of dollars. Payroll was taking away resources that could be used to add to the overall success of the organization. Basically, the payroll system did not make money for an organization.

The SBC Contingency Plan. Recognizing the importance to the customers of the applications they were processing, the Service Bureau Corporation developed a "Contingency" Plan for each of its locations throughout the country. SBC owned and operated 72 different computer sites throughout the United States. When they developed the "Contingency" Plan, they identified a sister site, or backup site as we refer to it today. Every night, at the completion of the processing schedule, backup tapes were created, packaged, loaded into a van, and driven to another SBC computer site nearby. In the Philadelphia location, we sent out backup tapes to the Washington, D.C., location. The SBC site in Washington, D.C., sent its backups to Philadelphia.

There was the question of whether the Philadelphia site's application schedule could be run on a timely basis at the Washington, D.C., site, and vice versa. To verify this capability, all Philadelphia's processing was run for two consecutive weeks at the Washington, D.C., site. The applications scheduled for Philadelphia and Washington, D.C., would be processed together for the two-week exercise. To assist the backup location with the logistics, the Philadelphia office would send a couple of computer operators to the Washington site for the duration. If they needed applications or systems programming assistance, the Washington, D.C., personnel would provide it.

Later in the year, this process would be repeated with the Washington schedule being moved to the Philadelphia location.

The "Contingency" Plan also included a list of people, and their home telephone numbers, who would be called whenever there was a problem with computer equipment, systems software, or applications software.

The "Contingency" Plan was an "informal plan" when compared to today's Business Continuity Plans. It contained sketchy documentation. It was more of an "escalation plan" with procedures on who to call. And it was limited to the Data Processing department

It was a "What-if" plan. "What if" the computer went down? "What if" the peripheral equipment was down? "What if" the disk or tape drives crashed? "What if" there was a systems software problem? "What if" there was an applications programming problem?

2.1.4.2 The Fire in Hawthorne, New York, 1972: The Incident That Changed the Scope from Contingency Plans to Disaster Recovery Plans

In September 1972, as a result of a fire that destroyed a computer center in Hawthorne, New York, computer managers faced a change to their Contingency Plan scenario. The new scenario had to include the destruction of a computer mainframe, the damage to computer tapes in the tape library, and the contamination of tapes in the data safe.

> *Incident.* A fire erupted in the basement area of the IBM Program Information Department (PID), Hawthorne, New York. The PID developed software for IBM users. A smoke detector alerted a security guard and the fire department. Flames were too extensive to be controlled with handheld extinguishers. The building had no sprinklers. A carbon dioxide fire suppression system in the basement tape vault operated as designed and protected the tape records. It took the firefighters 12 hours to extinguish the fire.

> *Damage assessment.* The fire spread through the air conditioning ducts to the computer room directly above. Plastic fluorescent light diffusers melted and dripped down onto computer equipment, causing severe surface damage. Three major computer systems

were completely destroyed. (IBM-360-65 mainframes). IBM activated its emergency plan.

Disaster recovery. Brought the system to the operational stage in five days, and brought the systems completely current in 19 days.

Records recovery. Tape backups were retrieved from Canada and Europe in order to resume business.

Damage assessment. Estimated damage was $6 million.

2.1.4.2.1 Planning Changes

The fire changed the scope of the Contingency Plan. It created a different scenario for computer managers to use in their planning. This resulted in the following changes to the "Contingency" Plan.

- *Change 1: change in scope.* The term "Contingency Plan" was changed to "Disaster Recovery Plan" (DRP). The scope was no longer a minor interruption to the computer; it now was a disaster. The DRP identified teams such as the Alternate Computer Operations Team, the Disaster Site Restoration Team, and the Recovery Headquarters Team:
  - The Alternate Computer Operations Team consisted of the members of the recovery team who would deal with getting the systems programming software, the applications programming software, and the computer backup files operating at the temporary computer center.
  - The Disaster Site Restoration Team consisted of the members of the recovery team who would deal with repairs to the computer facility, and repair or replacement of computer equipment.
  - The Recovery Headquarters Team consisted of the members of the recovery team who would function as the communications control point throughout the disaster recovery operation; and would also deal with getting assistance from staff and administrative departments (e.g., Security, Facilities, Medical, Personnel (HR), Public Relations (PR), Insurance, Legal, Finance, etc.).
- *Change 2: change in the format.* Originally, the Contingency Plan was an informal document. Now, the Disaster Recovery Plan required a formal, documented plan. The document included:
  - "What" has to done
  - "When" it has to be done,
  - "Who" will be responsible to do it
  - "Where" it will be done
  - "How" it will be done

2.1.4.3 The Fire in Philadelphia, Pennsylvania, 1978

This is an incident that changed the scope: it added the beginning of Crisis Management Plans to the Disaster Recovery Plans.

Another change occurred to the "Disaster Recovery Plan" in 1978 when an insurance company in Philadelphia, Pennsylvania, experienced a fire in the headquarters building. In addition to the business units, the building also housed the computer mainframe operation.

> *Incident.* The fire started in the room adjacent to the mainframe room. It was the computer forms storage room. After investigating the cause of the fire, the Philadelphia Fire Department determined that the cause of the fire was arson. They determined that an accelerant was used on the paper stored in the room to start the fire — and assisted it in spreading. The smoke from the fire contaminated much of the computer equipment, and also the computer tapes that were located on the same floor. An interesting side issue of the recovery was that while some of the computer disk drives could be cleaned and put back into service, others had to be replaced. The tape drives that were salvaged were of the IBM-3330 variety — removable; the tape drives that were not salvageable were of the newer IBM-3350 variety — fixed drives.

The insurance company did have a Disaster Recovery Plan for the computer department but did not have one for the executives (that would form today's Crisis Management Team) to follow. So when a local newspaper reporter began asking questions about the fire, the reporter approached the president and chief executive officer. The CEO apparently thought he was speaking "off the record." The next day, the CEO's comments were printed in the fire article on the front page of the newspaper: "the fire was on the floor where the computer was located. The computer system handles all the company's premiums, policies and claims. To the computers alone, we're talking about millions of dollars in damage."

This statement resulted in many concerned policyholders contacting the company the next couple of weeks checking on the status of their policy. The large, unexpected avalanche of calls resulted in a chaotic couple of weeks for the employees.

The fire changed the scope for the Disaster Recovery professional. It created a different scenario for computer managers to use in their planning. This resulted in the following change to the Contingency Plan. This incident stressed the need to pre-establish who the spokesperson for the organization will be.

- *Change 1:* The change was in the level of documentation. The incident with the news media stressed that in addition to being knowledgeable and articulate, the spokesperson needed to be trained on how to deal with the media. In today's Business Continuity Plan, there should be a Crisis Management Team Plan. The CMP would include a Crisis Communications Plan (Public Relations Plan). This plan ensures that the spokesperson is well-trained for dealing with the media. (See also Chapter 6.)

2.1.4.4   Fire in Minneapolis, Minnesota, 1982

This is an incident that changed the scope — from Disaster Recovery Plans to Business Resumption Plans (BRPs). In November 1982, as a result of the fire in Minneapolis, Minnesota, disaster recovery plan manager/directors were faced with another change to their Disaster Recovery Plan scenario.

> *Incident.* This fire occurred in the 16-story headquarters building of Norwest Bankcorp. The fire started on the seventh floor. It spread upward, climbing from floor to floor, until it reached the top floor. The bank's business units' operations were affected. Much of the equipment, furniture, and records were destroyed by the intensity of the fire. Fortunately, the mainframe computers were located in another building four blocks from the headquarters building.

As a result of the Norwest fire, the new scenario had to include the business units throughout the company that were not computer departments; rather, they were the revenue generators. Some of these departments had no computers in their areas but they did have critical equipment and records.

The fire, and the new scenario that Disaster Recovery managers were faced with, resulted in the following changes to the Contingency Plan.

- *Change 1:* The business units of an organization now had to build a plan to resume operations following a disaster. While the earlier Disaster Recovery Plans concentrated on the data processing department, the planning process now shifted to the business units. The methodology used in developing and documenting Data Processing Disaster Recovery Plans could be followed to develop the revenue-generating business unit business resumption strategies.

    But early on in the process, we noticed that the business units did not want to call their plans Disaster Recovery Plans. They wanted a title that carried a more positive message.

Speaking of a title change, when I was talking with a bank president and CEO during a contract, he asked me what he was going to receive when we finished the contract. I explained that he was going to receive a plan to quickly resume the bank's operations following a disaster. He thought for a second, and then said, "That's great. I thought I was just going to receive a Disaster Recovery Plan. But what you're telling me is that I'll actually receive a Business Resumption Plan for revenue-generating departments that have been damaged by a disaster. I like that. How can I help in this process?"

So to differentiate between the two areas of planning, (data processing and revenue-generating departments), Devlin Associates began calling the plan for the Data Processing Department (now known as the IT Department) the Disaster Recovery Plan, and we called the plan that dealt with the business units the Business Resumption Plan (BRP).

The Business Resumption Plan was a formal document. For each business unit, it included:

- "What" has to be done
- "When" it has to be done
- "Where" it will be done
- "Who" will be responsible for doing it
- "How" it will be done

The revenue-generating departments' Business Resumption Plan concentrated on the "resumption" of time-sensitive business functions and identifying the resources needed to resume operations. The resources included information such as:

1. Alternate work locations
2. Equipment needed to resume operation
3. The Information, records, or other forms of data needed to resume operations
4. The recovery of "delayable" business functions
5. The restoration and repair of the damaged site — or relocation to a new, permanent site

- *Change 2:* The Business Resumption Planning effort also included formal plans for the staff and administrative departments. (Security, Facilities, Insurance, Medical, Human Resources, Purchasing, Legal, etc.) For each staff and administrative department, the formal plan included:
  - "What" has to be done
  - "When" it has to be done
  - "Where" it will be done

- "Who" will be responsible for doing it
- "How" it will be done

Some examples of critical data needed by these departments included:

- Security — hazardous material
- Facilities — engineering diagrams
- Insurance — claims information
- Medical — confidential files
- Human Resources — employee files
- Purchasing (Procurement) — vendor information
- Legal — current legal activity

- *Change 3:* This fire resulted in a regulation, BC-177, that required banking operations to provide a recovery capability following any disaster.

2.1.4.5 Bombing in New York City, 1993

This is an incident that changed the scope — from Business Resumption Plans to Business Continuity Plans (BCPs).

In February 1993, as a result of the bombing of the World Trade Center garage, disaster recovery plan managers/directors were faced with a change to their Disaster Recovery Plan scenario.

Incident. A bomb exploded at approximately 12:17 p.m. in the parking areas under the buildings. It killed five people and injured more than 1000 (smoke inhalation). The bomb created a 200-by-100-foot crater.

Damage assessment. Six floors were affected. The force of the explosion collapsed the floors and the walls on the B-3 and B-4 levels. (The B-4 level is the PATH train entrance and platform.) The Vista Hotel main floor was damaged. It caused damage to both of the 110-story towers; Tower 1 was more affected (smoke). Smoke traveled up both towers through elevator shafts and stairways.

Emergency response. Mechanicals failed. Eugene Fasullo, the Port Authority's chief engineer, said the bomb had been placed where it would do maximum damage to the safety and utility systems.

The high-tension cables running to five of the eight Con Edison electrical feeders had been severed by the blast.

The remaining feeders were subsequently turned off while the fire was extinguished.

Without power, the building's ventilation system also failed.

He said no structural columns had been damaged, and that the center could probably not be brought down by a bomb of such size because it is a "tubular" structure with 25 steel columns per side, supports that bear the building's weight.

Emergency response. Evacuation plans: Charles Makish, the director of the WTC, said they had an elaborate evacuation plan. The plan involved directing a network of fire safety marshals on every floor of each tower to the safest location. The plan was practiced two or three times a year. But the evacuation plans for the WTC were rendered useless because the explosion devastated its police command and operations centers. It knocked out their electricity, telephones, closed-circuit television monitors, and public address system. A set of emergency generators that could have powered the building's emergency systems was also knocked out when lines carrying water used to cool the generators were severed. The public address system and other communications components are the linchpins of an evacuation plan. As a result, tens of thousands of office workers were left to fend for themselves amid terrifying confusion as they groped their way down as many as 100 flights of stairs in darkness and thick smoke with no organized leadership.

Prevention. At least six years before the incident, the Port Authority (of New York and New Jersey) was warned by its terrorism task force that it needed to take steps to protect the Trade Center from a car bomb. Port Authority officials acknowledged the report's existence. The report was prepared by a task force of Port Authority police and civilian engineers, and was reviewed by an outside engineering consultant who approved the recommendations, said two senior authority officials who asked not to be identified. The recommendations included:

Elimination of public parking from the center's garage to prevent terrorists from placing a bomb where severe damage could be done

Protecting the building's power supply by moving the main and backup electrical systems farther apart so one blast could not knock out everything

Moving the police station and emergency command center farther apart.

Installing battery-powered emergency lighting in the stairwells

According to sources, the only recommendations that were followed involved some security upgrades on the 67th floor, where the executive director's office is located and the board meets.

2.1.4.5.1 Planning Changes

The bombing changed the scope of Business Resumption Plans. In addition to the data processing plans and the business units' plans, now the Business Resumption professional had to merge in the Prevention and Emergency Response Plans.

- *Change 1:* Merging the Prevention and Emergency Response Plans in with the Business Resumption Plan. This change in scope required that the title of the plan be changed. In most organizations, Business Continuity Plan seemed to best describe the new role of the three plans. The definition of "continuity" — a continuous function — defined the new role of the plan. The Prevention Plan was designed to minimize the potential for the disaster to occur; the Emergency Response Plan was designed to respond quickly and efficiently when a disaster does occur; and the Business Resumption Plan was designed to resume business operations quickly and efficiently after the disaster is over.
- *Change 2:* The manager of the new Business Continuity Plan had to be chosen. This required the support of the executive management team, because the head of the Security department managed the Prevention Plan and the head of the Facility department managed the Emergency Response Plan. In addition, the heads of the Human Resources and Legal departments had input into the policies and procedures used in the Emergency Response Plan, especially in the Life Safety element. It was obvious that the manager of the Business Resumption Plans should not be the new manager of the Business Continuity Plan. Without a titular head, this would have become a political football. (It would be like the FBI and the CIA sharing information with one another as well as the other intelligence organizations in the government.) The decision on the new manager and his authority had to be made on the executive management team level.

(***Author Note:*** Many organizations are still operating the BCP with co-managers and joint responsibility.)

2.1.4.6 Bombing in Oklahoma City, Oklahoma, 1995

This is an incident that changed the scope — from Stand-alone Business Continuity Plans to the merging of public/private sector plans.

On April 19, 1995, a truck parked in front of the Murrah Federal Building exploded. The explosion caused the front of the building to collapse, killing 169 people. Nearby buildings were also damaged.

Incident. A yellow Ryder rental truck parked at a meter on Fifth Street in front of the Murrah building burst like a bubble into a spray of steel, chrome, and glass. A bomb in the truck exploded at 9:04 a.m. and destroyed the building. The entire north side of the nine-story building was blown off. It sent bullet-like glass shards over ten blocks and was felt at least 15 miles away.

Damage assessment. The bombing killed 169 people and injured more than 500. Some 25 structures in the blocks surrounding the site were rendered unfit for occupancy; 350 businesses were affected. The bomb caused 14 buildings to collapse; 30 others suffered severe structural damage. The estimated property and business loss was $650 million.

Communications. Long-distance phone calls to Oklahoma rose sharply as news of the blast spread, causing overloaded circuits and delays. Priority was given to Oklahoma City callers who were dialing out.

Emergency Response. FEMA teams (six 56-member urban search-and-rescue teams) arrived from Phoenix, Sacramento, Virginia Beach, New York City, Los Angeles County, and Montgomery County, Maryland. Each 56-member team was self-sufficient; they arrived with 15 tons of food, fuel, tools, search dogs, and equipment, enough to sustain them through 72 straight hours. Firefighters (600 firefighters), working in two-hour shifts, searched the rubble to find the living and remove the dead. Police Department: 1200 members pulled victims and survivors from the rubble and kept the gawkers away. Medical teams coordinated triage, performed first-aid and surgery, and counseled survivors and their families. The Oklahoma National Guard (177 members) worked with the police to disperse onlookers. Architects and engineers, using time-lapse cameras, examined the building's stability and installed beams to keep the structure from collapsing, especially as rain swelled the debris. The Red

Cross (more than 1400 volunteers) aided victims' families and helped feed rescue workers.

2.1.4.6.1 Planning Changes

The bombing emphasized the need for the private sector to pre-establish a working relationship with the public-sector authorities.

■ *Change 1:* Organizations needed to be prepared to work with the public sector better. As Elizabeth Dole said, when she was president of the American Red Cross, "The midst of a disaster is the poorest possible time to establish new relationships and to introduce ourselves to new organizations. … When you have taken the time to build rapport, then you can make a call at 2 a.m. when the river's rising and expect to launch a well-planned, smoothly conducted response." ("Managing the Crisis You Tried to Prevent," by Norman R. Augustine)

2.1.4.7 The Millennium Change (Y2K), 2000

This is an incident that changed the scope — strengthen the Business Resumption element of the Business Continuity Plan.

In 1998 and 1999, organizations throughout the world stepped up to the Y2K threat. As a result, a great deal of planning was done for the contingency that computers and chips would fail.

Incident. For years, all programs written for computer applications with a date field used the MM/DD/YY field. With the approach of the year 2000, there was a fear that computer applications would not function properly when faced with a 01-01-00 field. The thought was that the computer would assume that the date field was referring to the year 1900, rather than 2000. This, in turn, would cause applications, or equipment with computer chips, to fail on January 1, 2000.

Many dollars and much time was invested in fixing software to ensure it would not fail. But just in case, organizations throughout the world developed and implemented Y2K contingency plans. "What if?"

What if the computer hardware fails?
What if the peripheral equipment fails?
What if the systems programs fail?

What if the application programs fail?
What if the building's infrastructure fails?
What if the utility companies have problems?
What if the vendors and suppliers have problems?
What if the customers or business partners have problems?
What if Embedded chips fail?

2.1.4.7.1 Planning Changes

The serious threat caused business units to develop "work-around" plans, identifying how things would be accomplished if there was a disruption to business operations, that is, if compliant, or noncompliant, systems fail.

■ *Change 1:* The first change was in the depth. Business units heretofore were not very responsive to the value of business continuity planning. But due to the threat, they took the task of developing "work-around" procedures to heart. They developed excellent work around plans. How do we know they were excellent? Because, the plans were tested. And they were tested again. And when they were tested just before the turn of the calendar, they actually worked.

(***Author's Note:*** The shame of the whole thing is here we are, 6 years later, and very few of the business units kept the work-around plans current.)

■ *Change 2:* The second change was in the premise in the plan. Prior to this threat, many employees responsible for the business units' plans felt that they would never really have to use them. It would never happen to them. But because the threat was real, and because the time it was going to occur was known, these same employees (responsible for the business unit plans) assumed something would fail. In fact, the premise of their work was "planning for the failure." They developed "work-around" plans, identifying how things would be accomplished if there were a disruption to business operations, that is, if compliant, or non-compliant systems fail.
■ *Change 3:* The planning included the organizations vendors, suppliers, and business partners. Questions were raised as to what the organization would do if its vendors, suppliers, or business partners suffered a Y2K outage. To minimize this from happening, in 1997–1998 organizations began requesting a "compliance" report from their vendors, suppliers, and business partners. They wanted to make sure the dependencies were addressing the future problem.

The value of the Y2K threat was that it raised awareness of the problem. In addition to causing organizations to change their software programs, and in some cases to purchase new hardware, Y2K compliant, it also it forced executives to think through the hated contingency planning process. Executives provided large budgets to ensure that the organization's operations would not be affected by the Y2K bug.

After the calendar rolled into the year 2000, and relatively few glitches occurred, many executives across the country complained about the money spent and time wasted on Y2K preparations. The unappreciated response of management, and some employees, who felt this was a waste of time, forced me to write an article in a newsletter I was producing in 2000 and 2001. An excerpt from the newsletter follows:

> "The Y2K rollover went extremely well. Congratulations to all of you. You did a tremendous job. There were very few Y2K problems. This is a tribute to all of you, the Business Continuity Professionals, the Facility managers, the Security managers, and the business unit representatives on the Y2K team. In addition, the coordination between the private and public sector[s] was tremendous. I don't believe we ever experienced such cooperation before. You can be very proud of your accomplishment.

> "I have to admit that I was skeptical about the rollover. Having been associated with the IS area for 35 years, I expected that small glitches would occur for a week or two, resulting in business interruptions or personal inconveniences.

> "Unfortunately, because you did such a good job, you will never be given the credit you deserve. Many people are saying this was 'much ado about nothing.' These same people have no idea how easy it would have been for failures to occur. On the other hand, we all know the truth. The job was gigantic. All of the IS applications had to be reviewed to determine which had to be fixed before January 1. Then you had to test them to ensure that all 'fixes' worked. In addition, all the microchips used in various components located in either the equipment used by the business units, or the building in which the business unit was located, had to be tested to ensure they would roll over properly. It's unfortunate that most people do not understand the tremendous effort you and your peers put in, in order to make the rollover as smooth as it was. Again, congratulations for doing a great job.

"Business units have prepared detailed 'work-around' procedures to respond to potential Y2K problems. As a result of the testing of these procedures, they actually work. These same procedures can be used in a Business Resumption operation. You need to establish a program that will motivate the business units' representatives to maintain these "work-around" procedures.

"Most companies developed strong Crisis Management plans and established command center locations where the glitches would be managed. These elements, the crisis management plan and the command center, need to be retained as part of standard operating procedures (SOP). This same plan can be used in the future to manage the varying crises that your organization may face."

7-Eleven Stores: An interesting incident occurred of January 1, 2001, not on January 1, 2000. *USA Today* reported the following on January 4, 2001. The 7-Eleven Stores experienced a computer glitch on January 1, 2001. Cash registers in 7-Eleven stores this week read the new year as 1901 instead of 2001 and inconvenienced customers who wanted to make credit card purchases. A spokeswoman said the problem was fixed late Tuesday night and most stores were operating normally yesterday. Officials thought they had nipped calendar-related computer glitches a year ago when, like many big corporations, they geared up for an onslaught of Y2K bugs that never came. 7-Eleven said it spent $8.8 million preparing its in-store computer systems for the rollover from 1999 to 2000. It was working fine until *Monday.*

Blackout of 2003: Wall Street officials credited preparations for the Y2K computer bug as well as additional disaster-recovery planning following the September 11, 2001, terrorist strikes for the financial industry's ability to cope with the outage.

2.1.4.8   The Terrorist Attack on the World Trade Centers in New York City

This is an incident that forced a reassessment of the Business Continuity Plan — 2001

On September 11, 2001, terrorists flew two hijacked airliners into the World Trade Centers in New York City and one hijacked airliner into the Pentagon. After the crashes into the WTC buildings, the two buildings collapsed, resulting in the deaths of more than 2900 people. The incident caused Business Continuity Plan professionals to re-think their plans, starting with the three fundamental principles: prevention, emergency response, and business resumption.

Incident. On the morning of September 11, 2001, the World Trade Centers experienced an attack by terrorists in the form of commercial jet airliners crashing into the upper floors of the North and South Towers. The commercial planes were hijacked by a team of terrorists.

The North Tower was struck between floors 96 and 103 at approximately 8:46 a.m. by American Airlines Flight 11, which had taken off from Boston en route to Los Angeles with 92 passengers aboard. When it struck the tower, it had most of its 20,000 gallons of jet fuel remaining in its tanks.

Approximately 20 minutes later, at 9:06 a.m., a United Airlines plane, Flight 175, which was also hijacked, with 65 passengers aboard, after it took off from Boston en route to Los Angeles, struck the South Tower between floors 80 and 86.

Buildings Collapse:

At 10:00 a.m., the South Tower (2-WTC) suddenly collapsed. (Cause — 2000-degree temperatures, the steel supports gave way. It remained erect for 56 minutes, then crumbled in 10 seconds.)

At 10:29 a.m., the North Tower (1-WTC), weakened by the collapse of the South Tower, collapsed. It remained erect for 102 minutes, and then crumbled in 8 seconds. As it collapsed, debris from the building fell on # 4-WTC building below.

At 5:25 p.m., the 7-WTC building collapsed.

The other buildings that comprise the World Trade Center complex either collapsed or were seriously damaged.

There were an estimated 283 businesses located in the North and South Towers. Some of the well-known organizations with offices in the North Tower: the Port Authority of New York and New Jersey leased six floors; Cantor Fitzgerald had offices on floors 101 to 105; Empire BC/BS; Marsh USA; Brown & Wood; Bank of America; Dai-Ichi Kangyo Trust; Kemper Insurance, as well as many others. Some of the well-known organizations with offices in the South Tower included Morgan Stanley Dean Witter, the single largest tenant in the south tower, leasing 21 floors; Guy Carpenter; Fiduciary Trust Co. International; Oppenheimer Funds Inc.; AON Corporation; Fuji Bank; as well as many others.

An estimated 2900 people were killed in these attacks. This number includes people in the building, airline victims, as well as rescue workers.

In addition to the New York City attack, the Pentagon, outside Washington, D.C., also had a hijacked airliner crash into it. This attack left 184 victims dead.

A fourth hijacked airliner that was headed toward Washington, D.C., crashed near Shanksville, Pennsylvania. This attack left 44 victims dead.

These attacks required Business Continuity professionals to do a lot of rethinking of their plans. Every element of the BCP needed to be reevaluated. The scenario also needed changes to be made. The assumptions identified in all BCPs needed to be changed.

2.1.4.9 Business Continuity Plan: Reassessment

2.1.4.9.1 Prevention: The Risk Management Process

Prior to 9-11, I do not remember any questions being asked in any "Risk Analysis Questionnaires" concerning the potential threat from an attack by a fully loaded (fuel) commercial airliner.

- *Change 1:* We need to add questions heretofore unallowable. They were unallowable because the person asking the question would have been perceived as a fool.

2.1.4.9.2 Prevention: The Security Plans

What is our plan to prevent an airplane from intentionally crashing into our building? I know we never asked non-military organizations about their potential resources to prevent an airplane from crashing into a building. In fact, the fourth plane the terrorists hijacked was believed headed for the White House.

For some reason I was under the impression that the White House did have resources somewhere in it, or on it, ever since a "crazy" tried to hit the White House with a small plane. In September 1994, a Maryland truck driver, Frank Corder, crashed a small plane just a few yards from the Oval Office in September 1994. The motive was never identified. I was under the impression that stories following the incident indicated that protective measures had been enhanced that would prevent this from ever happening again.

- *Change 1:* We need to add protective measures. Organizations need to address tighter security in the future. Most organizations had security policies and procedures in place but they needed to enhance them. Obviously some things were done throughout the country because we know of no comparable terrorist incidents inside the country, to date. (***Author Note:*** There could be a new incident between the time the book is written and published.)

2.1.4.9.3 Prevention: The Facility Plans

■ *Change 1:* We need to address building construction to determine that it will remain standing, at least until we evacuate the building. The WTC's extra width and special reinforcement allowed it to withstand the immediate impact of two hijacked jetliners better than most high-rises could have, according to an international building industry task force (Council for Tall Buildings and Urban Habitat, a trade group based in Bethlehem, Pennsylvania). "These two qualities, and these two alone, allowed the towers to stand for nearly $1^1/_2$ hours after the initial impact, whereas most other buildings would have collapsed at least partially upon impact." Each of the twin towers was 209 feet across. Most U.S. skyscrapers average 120 to 140 feet across. High-rises outside the United States tend to be even narrower. The wider structure of the Manhattan buildings prevented an immediate collapse. The trade group is recommending that architects and builders implement new high-rise safety features. Among suggested steps: relocating ventilation systems and emergency power generators to where they are less vulnerable to attacks; new emergency-exit strategies, incorporating Britain's system of designating fire-resistant elevators for rescuers; and providing high-rise occupants with detailed safety and evacuation instructions (from "Engineers derive lessons from WTC demise," *USA Today*, December 12, 2001).

2.1.4.9.4 Emergency Response: Incident Response

This was a case where the employees inside the building did not have to notify the fire department that there was an incident occurring. People near the buildings saw what was happening and immediately called "911" or the fire departments to report the "accident." (Initially, it was believed to be an accident — at least until the second plane crashed into the South Tower.)

2.1.4.9.5 Emergency Response: Life Safety

The evacuation process took place quickly. From stories from some of the survivors, it appears that a number of floor wardens responded well to the incident. They quickly analyzed the situation and started ordering people out of the building using the stairwells.

■ *Change 1:* We need to look at the evacuation plan. "Despite the loss of so many lives, many safety engineers who watched the towers fall remain astonished at how many people were able to escape in the hour and 45 minutes after the initial strike. I think what we are seeing anecdotally is that the evacuation systems in those two buildings performed very well," said Jake Pauls, an evacuation consultant.

This surprise success has implications for both tactics and building codes. For one thing, it appears to prove the value of improvements in stairwell lighting, exit signs and disaster planning made by the World Trade Center as a result of the confused and sluggish evacuation after the 1993 bombing. This raises the question of whether similar reforms should be extended to all high-rise buildings.

Further, the rapid collapse of the buildings undermines evacuation procedures that assume there will never be a need to empty a high-rise quickly. Thanks to smoke detectors, sprinkler systems and aggressive fire suppression, most high-rise fires are extinguished without the need to empty more than a few floors (from "A New View of High-Rise Firefighting" — *Los Angeles Times*, September 24, 2001).

Pauls, who gained his expertise planning for bomb attacks in Canada's separatist violence, has long advocated the opposite approach — planning evacuations to get everyone out as fast as possible. Terrorists, he argues, wield more devastating weapons than fire.

2.1.4.9.6 Emergency Response: Damage Assessment

The damage assessment element for businesses must stress the importance of identifying all critical resources before an incident occurs. Once the resources are identified, the organization needs to determine where they would be able to acquire the resources quickly if a similar incident occurred.

If the resource is equipment, is it located somewhere else in the organization? In a different building? Can the vendor provide it quickly? In adequate numbers?

If the resource is data, or critical records, the business units must ensure that copies are available from an off-premise location, that is, records storage location, another building housing business units from your organization, etc.

■ *Change 1:* The damage was so complete that people were stunned. The plans prior to the 9-11 attacks assumed that the building would be damaged, but would remain standing. The assumption was that a salvage team would be able to go into the building, when it was deemed safe to enter, so they could determine what was destroyed and would have to be replaced, and what was damaged and could be repaired. Now this assumption must be changed.

An article published in the October 15, 2001, edition of *Fortune Magazine* and entitled "Telco on the frontline" is a good example of how bad the damage was. The article was about the tremendous efforts made by Verizon employees to get communications back after their building was damaged.

> For Verizon, ground zero is 140 West Street, the switching center severely damaged by the 7 World Trade Center collapse. A striking, 29-story art deco structure completed in 1926, the building evolved over the years into a telecom super center that fed the huge appetite of the downtown financial sector. Robust fiber-optic lines from all over lower Manhattan snaked through the building on their way to other parts of the city. Wireless-phone companies relied on the facility to transmit cellular calls to their own networks. Four giant switches zipped voice and data calls from Wall Street to the rest of the world. In all, the office handled more than 3.5 million high-capacity circuits in a 25-block area in the heart of the evacuation area, as well as 300,000 plain old telephone lines — about as many as in the entire city of Reno, Nevada.

> When Verizon officials were able to enter the building the following day, they were dumbstruck. "I have 29 years in the business," says Paul Lacouture, president of network services. "I've gone into our buildings after fires. I've restored our networks after floods and earthquakes. This was a combination of all those things, times a factor of three or four." Basements were flooded from broken water mains. Steel beams from 7 World Trade had pierced the sides of the building, opening six-foot holes. All the equipment was covered in ash.

2.1.4.9.7 Business Resumption Plans: IT Recovery Plans and Business Unit Plans

The organizations residing in the World Trade Center area suffered tremendous losses on September 11, 2001. The damage was extensive. The number of employees lost in the disaster was horrific. The country was at a virtual standstill for a couple of days. Companies that stored their backup data in off-premises storage locations had to come up with some alternative to move them to the alternate processing location. Why? So many organizations expected the backup data to be moved via airplane. But airplanes were not allowed to fly in the United States for a couple of days.

This was just one of the unplanned for situations that Business Continuity professionals had to deal with after 9-11.

An article published in the *USA Today* on September 28, 2001, entitled "New York firms strive to get back to work," identifies difficulties organizations faced that were not included in the earlier versions of Business Continuity Plans. An excerpt of that column follows:

> Companies also have learned that their people and their organizations can be destroyed in the blink of an eye. Some organizations lost a generation of leaders and can-do workers. The organizations have no handbook on how to cope with a tragedy of this magnitude. They are rewriting the book on crisis management. Business Resumption Planning for floods, earthquakes and fires is no longer enough.

> More than 500 businesses were destroyed in the Trade Center complex, the port authority says. More than 14,000 businesses in Lower Manhattan have been affected. They are scrambling to set up new offices, customer links, charitable funds, grief counseling and temporary housing for dislocated workers — all while staying in business. The logistics have been a nightmare.

> Companies are focusing on employees like never before, spending millions on counseling, beefed-up security, memorials, charitable funds and travel.

> Some managers expect employees haunted by images to have trouble returning to work. Workers from one unit of ITT Industries saw body parts drop from the sky as they fled their office near the Trade Center. 'People will need a little extra care,' says ITT executive Jonathan Blitt. He's counting work missed as paid leave, and he's letting people work from home.

2.1.4.9.8 Business Resumption Plans: Crisis Management Plans

Organizations realized very quickly that they had to find out the status of their employees, find alternate working locations, beef up security, provide physical and emotional support for employees that needed it, etc. Crisis Management teams were working around the clock to ensure the organization had the resources needed to resume business operations as soon as realistic.

There were a number of stories published on how well organizations with business resumption plans responded to the disaster. There were a few stories about organizations that were struggling to resume their operations because their plans did not work.

- *Change 1:* The Crisis Management Plan had to address the replacement of members of the Crisis Management and Executive Management Teams due to the deaths of key individuals.
- *Change 2:* The Crisis Management Plan had to reassess the section dealing with employee support in dealing with Post-Traumatic Stress Disorder (PTSD). An article published in *USA Today* on March 28, 2002, pointed out the immense problem New Yorkers had with PTSD:

> More than 130,000 people living in Manhattan suffered from post-traumatic stress disorder or depression after the Sept. 11 attack on the WTC, says a study out today. In the study, 13 percent of Manhattan residents reported symptoms of PTSD or depression 5 to 8 weeks after the disaster. That rate is nearly three times higher than the prevalence of these disorders in the general population, the study authors say. The study, which appears in today's *New England Journal of Medicine* is a snapshot of the number of folks struggling with psychological distress up to two months after the disaster. No one really knows how many people in New York still suffer from PTSD or depression, says John Tassey, a spokesman for the American Psychological Association. The symptoms of PTSD can occur right after the event or may take years to surface. The good news is that PTSD and depression can be treated with counseling and medication. In some cases, the symptoms of PTSD won't go away without treatment.

In summary, there have been a number of changes since Contingency Planning became the standard for protecting the computer center from lengthy outages and resuming operations quickly when an interruption did occur.

Now let us move to Chapter 3, which provides an in-depth review of the three stages of a crisis: the Pre-Crisis stage, the Acute-Crisis stage, and the Post-Crisis stage.

Chapter 3

STAGES OF A CRISIS

3.1 INTRODUCTION

This chapter discusses the three stages of a normal crises:

1. *Pre-Crisis Stage,* when the "critical situation" starts and the organization becomes aware of it
2. *Acute-Crisis Stage,* when the "critical situation" is not being controlled during the Pre-Crisis stage and it becomes visible outside the organization
3. *Post-Crisis Stage,* which occurs when the crisis is contained and the organization is trying to recoup its reputation and/or losses

(***Author Note****:* In doing research for this book, I noticed that other authors of crisis management books and articles have shown the normal crisis passing through as many as six different stages. I feel the three I have chosen to discuss will make it easier for the reader to determine which stage a crisis is in at the time they are dealing with it.)

3.1.1 The Pre-Crisis Stage

When someone in an organization discovers a "critical* situation," they usually bring it to the attention of their executives. This is known as the Pre-Crisis "warning." (It is also called a "precursor" stage by some crisis management consultants.) At this point in time, the "critical situation" is known only inside the organization and is not yet visible outside the organization.

---

* Critical — relating to, or being a turning point or specially important juncture; exercising or involving careful judgment or judicious evaluation.

When the executives are told of the "critical situation," their job is to analyze it to determine if it has the potential to become serious — that is, an acute crisis.

If the executives are comfortable with it and feel it will go away without any action on their part, they will not take any action. If, on the other hand, they see the critical situation as a serious problem, they will take action to mitigate it.

3.1.2   The Acute-Crisis Stage

A crisis moves to the acute stage, from the pre-crisis stage, when it becomes visible outside the organization. At this point in time, the executives have no choice but to address it. It is too late to take preventative actions. The actions taken are more of a "damage control."

Once the problem moves to the "acute" stage, the Crisis Management Team should be activated. The actions members of the Crisis Management Team take at this point are designed to minimize the damage. The steps include taking charge quickly, establishing the facts, telling your story, and fixing the problem. (These steps are discussed in detail in Chapter 4.)

3.1.3   The Post-Crisis Stage

A crisis moves from the acute-crisis stage to the post-crisis stage after it is contained. This is when the organization will try to recoup their losses. The executives must show the customer, the shareholder, and the community that the organization cares about the problems the crisis has caused them.

3.2   THE PRE-CRISIS STAGE

Chapter 1 defined a "crisis" as an unstable time for an organization, with a distinct possibility for an undesirable outcome. This undesirable outcome could interfere with the normal operations of the organization, it could damage the bottom line, it could jeopardize the positive public image, or it could cause close media or government scrutiny.

A normal crisis passes through three stages, the Pre-Crisis Stage, when the organization first becomes aware of the situation; the Acute-Crisis Stage — when the crisis becomes visible to others outside the organization; and the Post-Crisis Stage when the crisis is contained and the organization is trying to recoup its losses.

3.2.1   What Is the Pre-Crisis Stage?

The pre-crisis stage is the earliest stage of a crisis, the time when the organization first becomes aware of the situation. The "developing situation" is small at this time, and is not yet visible to the outside world. Although it is small, it still has the potential to move to the acute-crisis stage, where it can have a negative impact on the organization.

Management must address this "developing situation" while it is still in the pre-crisis warning stage. This is an opportune time to take action that will nullify or make the pre-crisis situation go away. At this point in time, management must ask what, if anything, can be done to alter the currently developing situation so it does not move to the acute stage.

> Let us try to relate the pre-crisis stage to our own personal lives. We have all experienced crises in our personal lives. When you have been in the middle of a crisis, have you ever said to yourself, "If I had only known…, I would not have made the decision that caused this problem." Or maybe you have said, "If only I had done…, then I would not have this problem to deal with."

> We may not have thought about the problem facing us in terms such as pre-crisis, acute-crisis, and post-crisis, but nevertheless we probably experienced the three stages. We may have missed the pre-crisis warning when it occurred. But when we were in the middle of the problem, during the acute-crisis stage, we could have thought that had we done things differently, we could have avoided the situation we were currently in.

This is exactly what happens in an organization. If a pre-crisis situation is not managed properly, and the situation moves to the acute-crisis stage, executives begin questioning how they got in the mess. They think, "If I had only known …" or "If I had done something else." Then they begin questioning why they did not know this crisis would happen. Did someone drop the ball?

This is why organizations need to have a viable Crisis Management Plan, one that enables them to recognize pre-crisis warnings when they occur. Once the executives are warned of an impending crisis, they can take the appropriate actions and nullify it, and make it go away.

> (**Author Note:** Some crisis management consultants prefer to use another term rather than pre-crisis warning, that is, "precursor" — one that precedes and indicates the approach of another; or "forerunner" — a premonitory sign or symptom, or "premonitory" — previous notice or warning. I prefer to use "Pre," "Acute," and "Post.")

3.2.2 When Someone Discovers a Potential Crisis Developing, What Should They Do?

When someone inside the organization recognizes a developing crisis situation, what is he supposed to do? Has your organization trained employees as to what they are supposed to do when they uncover a developing crisis situation? Has your organization provided employees with a means to notify executives of the impending crisis?

3.2.3 Pre-Crisis Actions Taken

Once the executives are made aware of it, it is their responsibility to manage it and prevent it from moving into the acute-crisis stage. This is considered a *time of opportunity,* to turn this from a negative situation into a positive one.

The first issue is to recognize the situation for what it is — and what it might become. They need to determine if the situation is serious, or if they believe that it will go away. Is it something that could damage the bottom line, or jeopardize the positive public image, or cause close media or government scrutiny? If they determine that it could damage the organization, they need to take appropriate action.

The danger is when executive management feels the problems are not serious, and they are wrong. In these situations, the pre-crisis situation will move to the acute-crisis stage, and the executives will have to activate the Crisis Management Team so they can effectively minimize the damage to the organization and its reputation.

The goal of a Crisis Management Plan is to prepare executives to recognize that a pre-crisis situation exists.

3.2.4 Organizations Apparently Are Very Effective in Managing Pre-Crisis Situations

Why do I say this? According to crisis management experts, pre-crisis situations occur frequently. These experts believe that small "developing situations" (problems) occur in organizations every month. Some think that the executives of some large organizations are faced with them every week.

At any rate, because we do not see organizations experiencing acute-crisis situations every month, apparently those "developing situations" that crisis management experts spoke of are managed immediately and never reach the acute-crisis stage.

3.2.5 Why Do Crises Move from the Pre-Crisis Stage to the Acute-Crisis Stage?

While there are a myriad of reasons why pre-crisis situations move to the acute-crisis stage, four stand out: (1) they underestimate them, (2) they overestimate their ability to manage them, (3) they are not aware of the developing crisis, or (4) they intentionally ignore the warning.

3.2.5.1 Underestimate

Sometimes, executives "underestimate" the damage the pre-crisis situation could do to the organization. In this case, they will let it run its course, only to find that it was serious and now they are managing an acute crisis. An example of where an acute crisis occurred because executives underestimated the damage the crisis could cause was the Intel Corporation crisis in 1994.

> *Intel Corporation.* You may recall that this crisis was based around the Pentium chip error. A math Professor at Lynchburg College (Virginia) noticed that his Pentium-based computer was making mistakes. The professor contacted Intel. Intel pleaded ignorance. A free replacement was out of the question unless people could prove to Intel they were affected by the flaw. The professor sent an e-mail to colleagues, pointing out the flaw. It ended up on the Internet. Intel says the typical user would encounter a wrong answer once every 27,000 years.

> After a story about the flaw appeared in *Electronic Engineering Times,* the Pentium chip flaw became a significant issue. Intel's image was under attack: "Intel is being painted as the Exxon of the chip industry. Eventually, Exxon cleaned up the Valdez mess, but it never cleaned up its image," according to Dan Hutchinson, president of VLSI Research, in San Jose, California.

> Seven weeks after the crisis erupted, Intel announced a new policy to avoid long-term damage to its reputation.

> First, Intel ran ads in major newspapers saying it wants to "sincerely apologize. To some users, the old policy seemed arrogant and uncaring. We were motivated by a feeling that this (replacement of the chip) was not necessary for most people. We still believe that, but want to stand behind our product," according to CEO Andrew Grove.

> Second, Intel agreed to send a new chip within 60 days,

> Third, Intel agreed to help the people install the chip themselves or pay to have someone do it for them.

(Underestimated) "Intel's stubbornness turned what could have been a minor problem, perhaps limited to a few scientists and engineers, into a costly fiasco," according to Richard Zwetchkenbaum, analyst at IDC in Framingham, Massachusetts.

Intel discovered the flaw last July, but kept quiet about it. If it had revealed it then and offered to replace chips for free, only a few users probably would have responded.

3.2.5.2 Overestimate

Sometimes, they may "overestimate" their ability to manage the crisis while it is still in the pre-crisis stage. In these cases, they find that the pre-crisis situation have overwhelmed them and moved on to the acute stage. An example of where an acute crisis occurred because executives overestimated their ability to manage it is the Exxon Valdez crisis.

> *Exxon, 1989.* In this acute-crisis, there was more than one pre-crisis warning. Maybe each warning, taken by itself, did not indicate that the incident would definitely occur. But taking all the warnings together, one could see the potential for an accident to occur.

Let us look at what Exxon executives knew, or should have known:

1. They knew there was a 1700-page Emergency Response/Oil Spill Plan in place containing detailed information of the actions to be taken if there was an oil spill.
2. They knew the captain of the Exxon Valdez (Joseph Hazelwood) had a drinking problem. He had tried treating it professionally in the past.

   (***Author Note:*** Having worked up on the North Slope with another oil organization, I was informed of the strict stipulations for working in that area. If a person was found drinking alcohol, or using drugs, they had effectively resigned their position with the company. This organization that I was consulting with took this business philosophy to the point that I, and all my consultants working on the project, had to sign a release stipulating just such an agreement. I was told it was standard operating procedure for all oil companies operating in Alaska.)

3. They knew there was the increase in floating ice from the Columbia Glacier.

4. They knew there was the previous record of poor spill response tests and exercises, which should have warned them that something was not right.

3.2.5.3 Not Aware

Then there are times when the executives have not been given a pre-crisis warning. This happens in organizations where employees fear the response to such a message will be to "kill the messenger." In some organizations, this approach, "kill the messenger," still exists.

This fear — to warn executives of an impending problem — is generated because in the past executives have not accepted constructive criticism or suggestion. An employee who warned the executives of a pending problem had made a career-ending mistake. The result of past incidents such as this usually causes all remaining employees to keep their thoughts or observations to themselves.

If executives find that they are experiencing a large number of "acute" crises, and they have not been receiving pre-crisis warnings from employees, they should look at the way the organization operates. There is a good chance that employees perceive that they would receive the same "kill the messenger" response if they were to warn the executives of what the employee sees as a potential crisis brewing.

Two examples of where the "kill the messenger" response to a pre-crisis warning may result in employees choosing to avoid telling executives of an impending crisis in the future are as follows:

> *Xerox, 2000:* When James F. Bingham, an assistant treasurer at Xerox, started warning top Xerox executives about the aggressive accounting, which he believed was being used to hide larger problems, he was fired. Bingham went public and filed a lawsuit accusing Xerox of firing him for objecting to accounting fraud. He also became a star witness in a Securities and Exchange Commission investigation of Xerox.

> A spokeswoman for Xerox described Bingham as a "disgruntled former employee" who has based many of his accusations on "hearsay and speculation."

> In May, 2001, after months of calling Bingham's claims "baseless," Xerox restated its results for the previous three years and acknowledged that it had "misapplied" accounting rules in a variety of ways, including improperly using a $100 million reserve to offset unrelated expenses — precisely one of Bingham's criticisms.

In the footnotes of an SEC filing, the company revealed for the first time that its pretax profits in 1998, 1999, and 2000 had been boosted by a total of $845 million through a series of one-time transactions and changes in accounting "estimates." That was a hefty chunk of the $2.1 billion in pretax profits reported for the three years. (Excerpt from an article in the *Wall Street Journal,* June 28, 2001, entitled "How Ex-Accountant Added Up to Trouble For Humbled Xerox.")

Coca-Cola, 2003. Matthew Whitley, a former finance director in Coca-Cola's fountain division, warned Coke's executives of accounting problems. Shortly after this, he was terminated by the organization.

In May 2003, Whitley sued Coke, saying he had been wrongfully terminated for alerting executives to what he asserted was a $2 billion accounting fraud within the Atlanta firm.

When Coca-Cola announced that "federal prosecutors are investigating allegations of accounting and marketing fraud raised by a former manager at the beverage firm," a lawyer for Mr. Whitley, Marc Garber, said his client was "very gratified that federal prosecutors will investigate Coke's misconduct." (Excerpt from an article in the *Wall Street Journal,* July 14, 2003, entitled "Coca-Cola Says U.S. Is Probing Fraud Allegations.")

(For more examples of "kill the messenger" or whistleblowers, see Appendix 03.01.02.

3.2.5.4 *Intentionally Ignore the Warning*

Finally, executives may choose to ignore it. Recently we have seen a number of crises that organizations have experienced where the executives have been involved in fraud and unethical practices. Obviously they were not going to fix the problem when they were the cause of the impending crisis.

Examples of where an acute crisis occurred allegedly because executives choose to ignore any pre-crisis warnings are the following.

3.2.5.4.1 *Cendant, 1995–1997*

Cendant Corp. announced that CUC International Inc., one of the companies that it merged with to create the franchising business, falsified records for three years, creating "fictitious revenues" and prompted a criminal investigation.

The former Stamford, Connecticut-based CUC International Inc. (which merged with HFS Inc. of Parsippany in December to form Cendant) was responsible for the "accounting errors made with an intent to deceive" and "fictitious revenues." Cendant said CUC artificially inflated its revenue by classifying restructuring charges as revenues, recording long-term revenue as short-term revenue, and delaying recognition of membership cancellations. The company also invented "fictitious revenues" for the first three quarters of 1997, Cendant said. The accounts-receivable entries for the first three quarters of 1997 were "fabricated, had no associated clients or customers and no associated sale of services," the company announced. It said the practice also occurred in 1995 and 1996.

The "widespread and systemic" accounting practices affected all the major business units at CUC, which primarily handled discount club memberships.

Cendant, which owns the brand names of Avis car rentals and Century 21 real estate brokerages, said the latest problems would decrease its 1997 earnings by $200 million to $250 million. They will also force Cendant to revise earnings for 1995 and 1996, as well as estimates for this year.

Walter Forbes, the former head of CUC and current president of Cendant, said he was "dismayed" by the problems, which led to the firing of an executive vice president and the resignation of two other CUC executives in April. Forbes said he had no knowledge of the problems while at CUC.

Embattled Chairman Walter Forbes (age 55) and eight of his allies on the board of directors resigned amid an accounting fraud scandal. Forbes, the former CEO of CUC International, submitted his resignation during a six-hour meeting with the board.

Former Chairman Walter Forbes and Vice Chairman E. Kirk Shelton bear responsibility for the massive accounting fraud, concludes a report that will be submitted to Cendant's board. The report by the audit committee said they should have known about it. They also helped foster an environment in which sloppy accounting practices could flourish. Forbes was CEO at CUC until he resigned July 28, and Shelton was president until he resigned in the spring. The report (more than 200 pages) is based on findings by accountants specializing in fraud from Arthur Andersen. This resulted in the firing of an executive vice president and the resignation of two other CUC executives in April. (From *Philadelphia Inquirer*, July 29, 1998.)

3.2.5.4.2 Enron Corporation, 2000

"Six senior lawyers from Enron Corp. and the company's outside law firm, Vinson & Elkins, were grilled by congressmen about why they didn't do more to alert the company's top managers of problems that contributed to the company's collapse.

"Members of a House Energy and Commerce Committee subcommittee took particular aim at Vinson & Elkins's investigation following an August 2001 letter in which former Enron executive Sherron Watkins told Chairman Kenneth Lay that she feared the company would 'implode' in accounting scandals.

"Congressmen criticized James V. Derrick Jr., former Enron general counsel, and Joseph C. Dilg, the Vinson & Elkins partner in charge of the Enron account, for limiting the scope of the inquiry. The firm (Vinson & Elkins) agreed not to question Arthur Andersen LLP's accounting advice, and not to undertake a full-scale analysis of every transaction involved.

"Committee members also noted that Ms. Watkins in her letter to Mr. Lay had warned that Vinson & Elkins shouldn't be retained for an investigation because the firm could have conflicts of interest.

"Mr. Derrick said that he took Ms. Watkins's letter 'extremely seriously,' but chose Vinson & Elkins for the job because the company wanted to get started on a review 'promptly.' 'To have turned to firms with no knowledge of these complex transactions would necessarily have required them … to expend a very significant amount of time getting up to speed,' he said. Mr. Dilg said he viewed the assignment as only a 'preliminary review.'

"Part of what he and a second Vinson & Elkins partner did in examining Ms. Watkins's complaints, was to make sure that Arthur Andersen had all the facts, and 'was still satisfied with their accounting advice.' The law firm, he said, 'was not in a position to ultimately second guess Arthur Andersen.'

"Mr. Dilg, who is also Vinson & Elkins's managing partner, insisted that the firm didn't have a conflict of interest because 'we were not being asked to review our own work,' and there were no allegations of 'infirmities' in the legal work." (*Wall Street Journal,* March 15, 2002.)

3.2.5.4.3   HealthSouth Corp. (Executives Admitted to Orchestrating Financial Fraud)

HealthSouth and two of its top executives were charged with securities fraud in a scheme federal officials say caused the company to overstate earnings by at least $1.4 billion since 1999. One of yesterday's charges was filed under the Sarbanes-Oxley Act, which Congress passed in the summer to crack down on corporate wrongdoing. Federal officials believed this was the first charge brought under the law.

FBI agents raided the headquarters, seizing documents that federal officials said would be used in the ongoing investigation into the company by the SEC and the U.S. Justice Department.

Smith, who was Chief Financial Officer for a year until August, pleaded guilty in federal court to criminal charges of securities fraud, and conspiracy to commit securities and wire fraud. He also pleaded guilty to criminal charges of certifying false financial records "designed to inflate the company's revenues and earnings by hundreds of millions of dollars." The false certification charge was brought under the Sarbanes-Oxley Act. ("Charges of fraud for giant in heath," *Philadelphia Inquirer,* March 20, 2003.)

HealthSouth's board of directors fired the company's chairman and CEO Monday, bringing Richard Scrushy's reign at the rehabilitation hospital chain he founded in 1984 to an inglorious end. The board had placed Scrushy on administrative leave two weeks ago, when the SEC charged him with masterminding a scheme to inflate HealthSouth's earnings by at least $1.4 billion since 1999.

Two top executives, Weston Smith and William Owens, have admitted to orchestrating the financial fraud and, on Monday, a third executive pleaded guilty to similar charges. Emery Harris 33, an assistant controller at HealthSouth, admitted in federal court that he was part of a group of executives at the company, known as the "family," which met every quarter to plug "holes" in the company's earnings statements.

Other HealthSouth executives are believed to be cooperating with Martin's probe, which extends to Scrushy and outside parties who did business with HealthSouth.

The SEC filed charges against Smith, Owens and Harris on Monday, accusing the trio of violating various securities laws for their roles in inflating HealthSouth's earnings.

The rehabilitation center company, whose stock has plummeted since the accounting scandal, was dropped from the New York Stock Exchange and trades for pennies. Last year, it traded in the $15 range but had sunk to $3.91 March 19, when the SEC suspended trading in the stock.

Scrushy's firing is certain to bolster the cause of Plaintiffs attorneys, who have accused him of inside trading. Last year, Scrushy sold $100 million in stock before jolting investors in August with an announcement that, contrary to previous guidance, the company would announce an unexpected quarterly loss. (From "Hospital chain fires CEO after scandal," *USA Today*, April 1, 2003.)

In a stunning blow to the government's crusade against business malfeasance, the jury has rendered a not guilty verdict in the first major trial under the 2002 Sarbanes–Oxley Act. (From "Former HealthSouth Corp. CEO Richard M. Scrushy Acquitted," Stephen Bainbridge; Professor-Bainbridge.com.)

Birmingham, Ala. (AP) — HealthSouth Corp. is responsible for $17 million of Richard Scrushy's legal bills stemming from his trial and acquittal on charges of directing a $2.7 billion fraud at the rehabilitation chain, an arbitrator decided. (From "Judge says HealthSouth must pay $17 million for Scrushy defense," The Associated Press–9/12/2006.)

3.2.6 Some Pre-Crisis Warnings Are Obvious, While Others Are Not So Obvious

An example of an obvious warning is when the executives have been advised that one, or more, of the buildings owned by the organization is exposed to a fire because the building does not have adequate fire protection and suppression systems.

Fires are one of the most common disasters to strike a building today. The National Fire Protection Association (NFPA) produces statistics on the number of fires that occur in the United States every year. Over the past two decades, fires reported to fire departments in the United States number close to two million every year.

> (***Author Note:*** The NFPA organization accumulates a variety of information about the fires that occur every year, that is, where they occur, why they occur, what type of fire protection was installed, etc. I have found this organization's information a most valuable resource for examining fires.)

3.2.6.1 Sprinklers

Sprinklers are considered one of the most effective resources for containing a fire and minimizing the damage the fire can cause. Yet when we look at the well-publicized fires that cause significant damage, and therefore receive the most news media coverage, we find that the buildings did not have sprinklers installed, or were only partially sprinklered.

Some examples of large fires that have damaged organizations in recent years are in buildings that are not sprinklered, or only partially sprinklered, such as:

- High-rise buildings:
  - Reliance Insurance fire in Philadelphia, Pennsylvania, in November 1978
  - Westvaco building fire in New York City, in June 1980
  - MGM Grand Hotel and Casino in Las Vegas, Nevada, in November 1980
  - Norwest Bank fire at the headquarters in Minneapolis, Minnesota, in November 1982
  - U.S. Postal Service fire at the headquarters building in Washington, D.C., in October 1984

- Alexis Nihon Plaza fire in Montreal, Canada, in April 1986
- Penn Mutual Life Insurance Co., in Philadelphia, Pennsylvania, in May 1989
- Meridian Plaza fire in Philadelphia, Pennsylvania, in February 1991
- Los Angeles County Health Department building in Los Angeles in February 1992
- Pacific Bell Telephone switching center in Los Angeles, California, in March 1994
- State of Pennsylvania — Transportation Department headquarters building in Harrisburg, in June 1994
- Delaware Trust Building in Wilmington, Delaware, in April 1997
- Cook County Administration Building in Chicago, Illinois, in October 2003.
- Low-rise buildings:
  - Olin Corporation's fire at the headquarters in Stamford, Connecticut, in July 1981
  - Chesapeake & Potomac Telephone Co. building in Silver Springs, Maryland, in July 1986
  - New York Telephone Co. switching center in New York City, in February 1987
  - Illinois Bell Telephone Co. switching center in Hinsdale, Illinois, in May 1988
  - University dormitory in Kansas in January 1989
  - Walt Whitman Shopping Mall fire in Huntington Station, New York, in May 1991
  - Logan Valley Mall in Altoona, Pennsylvania, in December 1994
  - Southside Regional Medical Center in Petersburg, Virginia, in December 1994
  - Mary Pang's Food Products Inc. in Seattle, Washington, in January 1995
  - Howard Johnson Motel in Bowling Green, Kentucky, in January 1996
  - Seton Hall University dormitory in South Orange, New Jersey, in January 2000;
  - Comfort Inn Motel in Greenville, South Carolina, in January 2004

(*Author Note:* One of the large fires that I omitted was the First Interstate Bank building fire in May 1988 in Los Angeles, California. While there were no operative sprinklers in the building, the bank was in the process of installing a total building sprinkler system. They were approximately 90 percent complete when the fire occurred. Had the sprinkler system been completely installed and operating at the time of the fire, I am sure that the damage to the building would have been much less.)

3.2.6.2 Fires during Renovations

Another Pre-Crisis warning that is missed is the potential for a fire while the building undergoes renovations. Fires often occur during this time. How many times do you read about a fire in your area where the story points out the building has been undergoing renovations, or the like?

When your organization, or any other organization located in the same building, is undergoing renovations, it should be a red flag to the managers in the facility and security departments.

Take a look at a few examples of fires during renovations:

- *One Meridian Plaza, Philadelphia, 1991.* Fire occurred during renovations. The fumes from the varnish, which was being used on the wood paneling, ignited. Oily rags left by a wood refinisher on the 22nd floor triggered spontaneous combustion. The damage to this 38-story building was so severe that it had to be torn down.
- *University of Georgia, Athens, 1995.* Fire burned through the roof of Brooks Hall, the University of Georgia's business school. Welding by roofing workers was believed to cause the fire that gutted the business school, officials said.
- *Department of Treasury (U.S. Government), Washington, D.C., 1996.* Fire damaged the roof of the five-story Treasury building. The northeast side of the building suffered "extensive damage." Other areas suffered water and smoke damage. The cause was believed to have been workers using a propane torch on roof. A newspaper report indicated that parts of the building were uninhabitable for up to a year.
- *St. Louis Children's Hospital, St. Louis, Missouri, 1997.* A four-alarm fire damaged part of the hospital. It started in an atrium where workers were using a blowtorch.
- *A Shoe Factory in San Antonio, Texas, 1998.* A four-alarm fire started when a spark from a welder's torch ignited insulation. The fire destroyed a shoe factory and a shoe store.
- *Children's Mercy Hospital, Kansas City, Missouri, 1999.* A three-alarm fire forced the evacuation of three floors in a wing of the hospital. The fire started in roofing materials on top of the five-story structure, in rolls of tarpaper that workers had heated with propane torches to soften them.
- *City of Newton, Newton, Massachusetts, 2000.* Fire consumed the top two floors of a four-story, non-sprinklered, multiple-business building, across from the Mall at Chestnut Hill. During the height of the fire, the top two floors of a portion of the building collapsed. (The building at 200 Boylston St. was built in 1955 and housed 50 tenants.) Numerous people were trapped.

15 people were rescued by firefighters on ladders. The fire caused the deaths of five people. The building was undergoing roof and window renovations.

■ *CIA Building (U.S. Government), McLean, Virginia, 2001.* A fire that forced evacuation of CIA headquarters in suburban Virginia was accidental. Workers using a torch doing repairs on the top floor of the building started it. Estimated damage was $1 million.

3.2.6.3 Workplace Violence

A sudden crisis can occur when a person attempts to injure people in one of your locations. Most of the time, organizations do not expect to be attacked in this way.

Nevertheless, they must realize the potential that this could occur. Many organizations have found themselves facing lawsuits from the families of those killed and people wounded. A few of the 2003 examples of workplace violence include:

■ *Firestone Tire & Service Center, Bensalem, Pennsylvania, 2003.* Bensalem police upgraded charges against tire and service center employee (Ken Kim) (30) to first-degree murder after the store's manager died. Kim had been charged with attempted murder and aggravated assault in the December 12 shooting of the manager. (Joseph Phillips) (39). Phillips was critically wounded after reprimanding Kim, a repair technician at the Firestone store. (From *Philadelphia Inquirer,* January 13, 2003.)

■ *Windy City Core Supply, Chicago, Illinois, 2003.* A man who was fired from an auto-parts warehouse six months ago came back with a gun and killed six employees before being shot to death by police. Salvador Tapia, 36, lost his job at Windy City Core Supply for causing trouble at work and frequently showing up late or not at all. Tapia died in a gun battle he waged with police inside and outside the building. It was the nation's deadliest workplace shooting since July 8, when Doug Williams shot 14 co-workers, killing five, at a Lockheed Martin plant in Meridian, Mississippi, before taking his own life. (From *Philadelphia Inquirer,* August 28, 2003.)

■ *Andover Industries, Andover, Ohio, 2003.* A factory worker, Ricky Shadle, 32, who was denied vacation because he filled out a form improperly, and he had just learned he had cancer, opened fire at an auto-supplies plant in Andover, Ohio, killing a woman and wounding two others before he was killed. (From *Philadelphia Inquirer,* August 20, 2003.)

■ *MBNA America Bank, Hockessin, Delaware, 2003.* Kenneth Tripp, 42, fatally shot his former boss and injured a co-worker before killing himself. He was upset about his career. Tripp left a 16-page packet consisting of a type-written journal of his conversations with co-workers at MBNA America in Wilmington, his resume, and e-mail messages. The collection of documents revealed "perceived problems with his career, his divorce, and failures in the stock market." Both shooting victims were named in the documented conversations and e-mail messages, as were four other former co-workers. (From *Philadelphia Inquirer,* August 12, 2003.)

■ *Lockheed Martin Aeronautics, Meridian, Mississippi, 2003.* A factory worker known as a racist "hothead," Doug Williams, 48, who talked of killing people, opened fire with a shotgun at a Lockheed Martin plant, killing five fellow employees before committing suicide. Nine people were injured, including one critically, in the nation's deadliest workplace shooting in 2-1/2 years. (From "Gunman 'mad at the world' kills 5, then himself in MS," *Philadelphia Inquirer,* July 9, 2003.)

■ *Modine Manufacturing Co., Jefferson City, Missouri, 2003.* A factory worker, Jonathan Russell, 25, who was close to be fired for missing work too much pulled a gun in the middle of the plant floor and killed three co-workers and later killed himself during a shootout with the police. Five employees were wounded. (From "Worker kills 3 in factory, then kills himself," *Philadelphia Inquirer,* July 3, 2003.)

■ *Case Western Reserve University, Cleveland, Ohio, 2003.* Biswanath Halder, 62, walked the halls of Case Western Reserve University's Peter B. Lewis Building and fired hundreds of rounds. He killed one person, wounded two others. Halder, who graduated from Case Western in 1999 with a master's degree in business administration, had sued a university computer lab employee who was in the building but escaped during the standoff. The lawsuit, which accused the employee of having "added and deleted things from a personal Web site" belonging to Halder, was dismissed and Halder lost an appeal about a month ago. (From *Philadelphia Inquirer,* May 13, 2003.)

3.2.6.4 Many Pre-Crisis Warnings Are Either Missed or Ignored by the EMT

Some examples include:

■ *City of Philadelphia, School District, 2001.* Jonathan Cozzolino suffered a fatal head injury when a lunch table fell on him in 2001. The boy was in a lunch line at an elementary school in northeast Philadelphia. He leaned on a 12-foot-long table that was folded in half and standing on end. The table tipped and crashed down on him.

- (Pre-Crisis) Twelve years earlier, in 1989, the U.S. Consumer Product Safety Commission had launched a nationwide warning program to alert school officials to the dangers posed by vertically stored cafeteria tables, which can weigh as much as 350 pounds. Cecilia Cummings, Communications Director for the Philadelphia School District, said that all cafeteria tables were inspected after the boy's death and that more than 1000 were deemed faulty and thus discarded.
- A Chicago manufacturer has agreed to pay $10 million to settle a negligence case, according to Thomas R. Kline. Kline said Midwest Folding Products had agreed to the settlement with the mother of Jonathan Cozzolino. Klein said he developed evidence through his suit showing that the model of table fell on Jonathan was known to be tip prone and unstable when upright, but that Midwest failed to alter the design to reduce the danger. (From *Philadelphia Inquirer,* January 28, 2004.)
- *Motiva Enterprises, Delaware City, Delaware, 2003.* The operator of a Delaware oil refinery has agreed to pay $36.4 million to settle a lawsuit by the family of a Bucks County worker killed when a tank of sulfuric acid exploded and collapsed in 2001.
    - (Pre-Crisis) A month before the accident, one inspector had recommended that it be shut down immediately and repaired. Another inspector warned in a memo: "This tank farm needs attention now!" (From "$36.4 million settles suit in refinery blast," *Philadelphia Inquirer,* September 11, 2003.)
- *New York Times, New York City, 2003.* A scandal that broke when the *New York Times* acknowledged repeated outright fakery by reporter Jayson Blair has left *Times* staffers, their press colleagues and their readers anxious, angry, and appalled.
    - (Pre-Crisis) – "This sorry tale raises uncomfortable questions about why large organizations — be they the *Times,* Enron or NASA — don't hear the whistles blown by truth tellers from within. For four years at the *Times,* Jayson Blair (27) made mistakes, turned in sloppy work, acted unreliably and exhibited all the hallmarks of a hungry journalist with more ambition than actual accomplishment. The *Times'* investigation discovered that of the 73 reports Blair filed since October as a roving national correspondent, 38 had proven unreliable. (A *Boston Globe* report yesterday confirms that Blair left a similar trail when he worked there.) I'd like to believe that anyone with a track record like that would be out the door quicker than you can spell "deadline." Yet the charming, charismatic Virginia native — who implied that he was graduated from college when he wasn't — managed to advance despite unmistakable

warnings from key editors. Warnings don't get more direct than the blunt note Metropolitan Editor Jonathan Landman wrote last year: "We have to stop Jayson from writing for the *Times*. Right now." (Excerpt from *Philadelphia Inquirer*, May 13, 2003.)

■ *NASA, Columbia Shuttle Accident, 2003.* Space-program pioneers told Columbia investigators that shuttle wings were never designed to be struck by anything and suggested that NASA should have taken the potential problem much more seriously. NASA's quick dismissal of wing damage to Columbia from a chunk of foam insulation also was criticized during the daylong public hearing by Diane Vaughan, a Boston College sociologist who spent nearly a decade studying and writing about the 1986 Challenger explosion.

NASA never fixed the underlying institutional problems that led to that tragedy, and many of them were repeated during Columbia's doomed flight three months ago, Vaughan said. Each of the disasters killed seven astronauts. "Neither one of these accidents … require Ph.D.s in physics to understand," said Robert Thompson, who headed the shuttle program during the 1970s and helped design the spacecraft.

■ (Pre-Crisis) "Erosion rates on an 0-ring, when there should be no erosion, is an obvious thing," he said, referring to the cause of the Challenger explosion. Before the failure of the Challenger, a series of memorandums to the solid rocket motor company's management from various of its engineers contained such impassioned pleas, highly unusual for technical documents, as "HELP! The seal task force is constantly, being delayed by every possible means." Another memo implored, "If we do not take immediate action to … solve the problem with the field joint … we stand in jeopardy of losing a flight along with all the launch pad facilities." (From "Shuttle wings weren't meant to take hits, pioneers report," *Philadelphia Inquirer*, April 24, 2003.)

3.2.7 Why Is Crisis Management Important?

Remember that the outcome of a crisis affects the lives and the job of innocent people — people who are totally dependent on the skills of management to see them and their families through the crisis, to enable them to continue to put bread on their tables.

—Steven Fink
Crisis Management: Planning for the Inevitable

3.2.7.1 Look for the Pre-Crisis Warning

In a well-founded crisis management plan, the executives, and their managers, must be trained to examine every out-of-the-ordinary situation for what it is — a warning. And having recognized the warning, the executives must then question what, if anything, they can do about it. (This is another form of contingency planning; it is asking "what-if" questions.)

3.2.7.2 Executive Has Missed the Warning

The problem is that when someone does recognize a warning and does sound the alarm, but no one listens, then executives must take a closer look inside their organization to find out why the warning was missed. Not only have executives missed an excellent opportunity to *change the direction* of the "developing situation," but they also have a "recognition" problem in their organization.

Executives need help from their employees. Why? The executives are often focused on the bottom line for the current year. Or they are focused on the profit for the current quarter. Many are focused on an acquisition of another organization. Others are focused on fighting the hostile takeover. Needless to say, there are a number of potential reasons why they are not focusing on pre-crisis warnings.

3.2.7.3 Could Our Product Be Harming Our Customers?

Dow Corning, Detroit, Michigan, 1992. For years, critics were contending that gel leaking from ruptured breast implants caused a variety of ailments, including cancer, painful arthritis, and debilitating auto-immune disorders. Dow maintained the breast implants were safe. In 1992, under pressure from the FDA, Dow Corning released an 800-page collection of documents showing the breast implant maker knew for more than a decade that its product was unsafe but kept the information to itself.

One of the documents released was an 11-year-old inter-office memo from a salesman (Bob Schnabel) complaining about leaking silicone breast implants. It was a graphic demonstration of a company in which salesmen and scientists expressed concerns that were brushed off by higher-ups for years. Schnabel wrote his superiors that a California plastic surgeon had complained about three pairs of "greasy" silicone gel breast implants that bled through their shell. "It has been brought to my attention that this particular lot was put on the market with prior knowledge of the bleed problem; to put a questionable lot.... on the market is inexcusable. I don't know who is responsible for this decision, but it has to rank right up there with the Pinto gas tank." (Pre-Crisis Warning 1)

In a memo dated December 15, 1977, employee Frank Lewis recounted reports by four Ohio and Michigan doctors that said 52 out of 400 implant procedures had resulted in ruptures. "As of this date, the problem is still recurring at an inordinate rate. I am sure some of these were the fault of the doctor, but that alone could not account for such a high percentage (13 percent) of ruptures." (Pre-Crisis Warning 2)

(Pre-Crisis Warning) The Dow Corning documents show that as long ago as 1971 and as recently as 1987, the company was hearing from plastic surgeons who were worried and angry about ruptured implants. (*USA Today,* September 9, 1998) — Dow will pay $3.2 billion to about 400,000 women, including thousands who say they suffered immune-related illnesses from its silicone-gel breast implants. (Executive Account) — John Ludington, chairman and Lawrence Reed, CEO were removed from their positions by the company. (*Philadelphia Inquirer,* February 2, 1992.)

3.2.8 What Is the Pre-Crisis Stage?

Management must address this pre-crisis or "developing situation" while it is still in the pre-crisis warning stage. This is the opportunity for executives to take action that will nullify, or make the pre-crisis situation go away.

At this point in time, management must ask what can be done to alter the "developing situation" so it does not move to the acute stage.

We may not have thought about the problem facing us in terms such as pre-crisis, acute-crisis, and post-crisis, but nevertheless we have probably experienced the three stages. We may have missed the pre-crisis warning when it occurred. But when we were in the middle of the crisis, we could have thought that had we done things differently, we could have avoided the situation we were currently in.

This is why organizations need to have a viable Crisis Management Plan. One of the benefits in developing and implementing a CMP is to prepare executives to recognize when a pre-crisis warning has been uncovered.

Once someone in the organization warns the executives of an impending crisis, the executives can take the appropriate actions and nullify it, or make it go away.

> (***Author Note:*** Some crisis management consultants prefer to use terms other than "pre-crisis warning," and those include "precursor" — one that precedes and indicates the approach of another; "forerunner" — a premonitory sign or symptom; or "premonitory" — previous notice or warning. I prefer to use "Pre," "Acute," and "Post.")

3.2.8.1 Apparently Organizations Are Very Effective in Managing Pre-Crisis Situations

What is meant by "apparently organizations are very effective in managing pre-crisis situations"? Most of us know of a large number of crises that have negatively affected organizations in the past couple years.

The reason I say that organizations must be very effective in managing the pre-crisis warnings is that according to crisis management experts, pre-crisis situations occur frequently. These same experts believe that small "developing situations" (problems) occur in organizations every month. Some think that organizations are faced with them every week. And yet we do not see that many organizations experiencing acute-crisis situations, or we do not see an organization facing that many acute-crisis situations every month. Apparently, those pre-crisis or "developing situations" are being managed immediately and never reach the Acute-Crisis stage.

3.2.8.2 Why Do Crises Move from the Pre-Crisis Stage to the Acute-Crisis Stage?

While there are a myriad of reasons why Pre-Crisis situations move to the Acute-Crisis stage, four reasons stand out: executives (1) might underestimate them, (2) might overestimate their ability to manage them, (3) might intentionally ignore the warning, or (4) might not be aware of the developing crisis.

3.3 THE ACUTE-CRISIS STAGE

A crisis is considered to have reached the Acute-Crisis stage when the "developing situation" becomes known outside the organization. For example, when customers begin complaining about the "situation," or creditors show they are worried, it will not be long before the news media are sure to pick up on the news. Once the media start reporting on it, it is officially in the "acute" stage.

When the situation reaches the Acute-Crisis stage, it is too late to prevent it from causing damage, either to the organization's reputation or its financial status. At this point, the executives, recognizing the organization's reputation is at stake, need to activate the Crisis Management Team (CMT). Once the organization's reputation is under attack, the damage can have serious consequences. (The Crisis Management Team (CMT) is the group of executives who have been chosen by the CEO to manage a crisis when it reaches the acute stage. They have been selected due to their expertise in certain areas of the business operations.)

Because it is too late to take preventative actions, the executives should undertake "damage control" actions designed to minimize the damage and to prevent any further damage from occurring. They should ensure that all resources needed by the members of the CMT are made available.

CMT members will take the following steps:

1. Take charge of the situation quickly.
2. Gather all the information they can about the crisis and attempt to establish the facts.
3. Tell your story to the appropriate groups that have a vested interest in the organization, namely, the media, the general public, the customers, the shareholders, the vendors, and the employees.
4. Take the necessary actions to fix the problem.

(***Author Note:*** These elements are the basis for and discussed in detail in Chapter 4.)

3.3.1   When? — After the Crisis Is Known Outside the Organization

After the crisis reaches the acute stage, and is being reported on by the news media, it is not unusual for customers to be shocked. Organizations have experienced situations where their product or services come under attack. It is common for shareholders and creditors to become concerned.

Other effects that occur after the crisis has moved to the acute stage include:

1. Managing may be weakened. Organizations have experienced a breakdown of respect for senior managers. Decisions, formerly taken for granted, are now challenged.
2. Once a crisis reaches the acute stage, infighting begins in management circles. Differences that formerly were set aside now begin to emerge.
3. Organizations experience a "brain drain," as the best managers and key employees leave the organization and seek safety elsewhere. When an organization comes under siege, people's loyalties begin

to erode; they feel embarrassed that their company's name is being dragged through the mud. Desertions are common and can be a major problem. Headhunters see the crisis as a signal to start making discreet contacts.

3.3.2 Result: Managing May Be Weakened

Another negative result after it is visible for all to see is that managing may be weakened. Oftentimes, there is a breakdown of respect for senior managers. Decisions formerly taken for granted are now challenged.

After it is visible for all to see, managing the organization may be difficult because there may be a breakdown of respect for top managers. Situations formerly taken for granted by middle managers, may be challenged and debated. Management differences that formerly were set aside, begin to emerge, and the infighting begins.

3.3.3 Disgruntled Employees Attempt to Take Revenge: Examples

Examples of disgruntled employees attempting to take revenge on the organization include:

- *Bear Truss & Components, St. Louis, Missouri, 1992.* Shortly after (12/18/1992) the Christmas party in which no bonuses were given, a 911 call reported a fire at the company. The owner of the company felt the fire was arson — caused by two disgruntled employees. Financial crisis led to no bonus. No bonus was believed to be the cause for the fire. Resulted in $1.25 million loss.
- *Broward County Courthouse, Ft. Lauderdale, Florida, 1980.* Fire that caused an estimated $150,000 damage to computer area. It was the computer room of the case filing office that was set on fire. Word processing equipment was destroyed. A disgruntled employee was arrested. She confessed to starting the fire. She entered the lobby at 7:00 a.m. and signed in with the security guard so she could go to the 6th floor. Twenty minutes later she returned to the lobby and tried to scratch her name out of the register. As she left the building, the smoke alarm sounded, indicating a fire in an upstairs office. The woman was upset about her job, and her manager. No specifics given. Obviously there was the perception by the employee that she was dealing with a crisis with her manager.
- *City of Los Angeles, California, 1995.* Willie Woods (42), disgruntled 12-year employee; thought he was about to be fired. Woods had received negative reports from supervisors and was getting job counseling. Shot and killed four supervisors for the LA Fire Department. Woods was arrested.

■ *DuPont Hotel, Puerto Rico, 1986.* The fire erupted minutes after a Teamsters Union meeting at which members voted to strike at midnight. The fire killed 97 people. Damage was estimated at between $190 and $200 million. The hotel did not reopen until 1994.

A crisis developed when negotiations reached an impasse. A couple union members wanted revenge, so they set a fire in the hotel casino on New Year's Eve day.

After confessing to the arson, a federal judge sentenced three men to prison terms of up to 99 years for the New Year's Eve fire at the Dupont Plaza Hotel that killed 97 people. A 35-year-old man, who confessed to setting the blaze, received two concurrent 99-year terms. A 40-year-old man, who pleaded guilty to a federal arson charge for inciting another union member to set the fire, was sentenced to 99 years in prison. A 29-year-old man, who also pleaded guilty to arson for bringing the man who set the fire a can of cooking fuel used to set the fire, was sentenced to 75 years in prison. A bartender at the San Juan Dupont Plaza Hotel killed himself by leaping from a building. A newspaper reported that he faced questioning about the New Year's Eve fire.

■ *Pacific Bell, Los Angeles, California, 1987.* (Tony Apodaca) disgruntled former employee. Took four employees and security guard hostage. Pumped 200 shotgun rounds into critical central office equipment, causing an estimated $10 million in damages. Surrendered. Caused 15,000 customers a phone outage for 22 hours. Motive: upset about his retirement benefits.

■ *U.S. Government Postal Service, Dearborn, Michigan, 1993.* (Larry Jasion) (45), a disgruntled mechanic, shot a fellow employee. He then shot himself to death. Motive: he was upset that a female co-worker had gotten a clerical job he wanted. The woman and his supervisor were injured when he shot up the garage.

3.3.4   Product (or Services) Come under Attack: Examples

■ *Arnott's, Australia, 1997.* An extortionist tampered with six packets of Arnott's biscuits on a shelf in a Brisbane supermarket in 1997. Australia's largest cookie-maker conducted a nationwide recall of its products after a threat was made to poison its products on supermarket shelves.

The irony according to Chris Roberts, the former managing director of Arnott's biscuits, was that the extortionist rescued the company from a potentially crippling public image crisis. By tampering with the packets of biscuits, the extortionist unintentionally swung public sympathy behind the biscuit manufacturer for the first time in more than two years. Children and pensioners responded to a massive recall that cost Arnott's $35 million by sending the company the money they (consumers) would have otherwise spent on biscuits. At that time the public had turned its back on Arnott's because the American-based Campbell Soup Company had taken control of an Australian icon. The takeover had been carried out piece by piece under the 3 percent creep-provision of the Companies Code. Months of negative publicity had thrown the credibility of the Arnott's brands out the window.

■ *Audi Motors, 1995.* When Audi owners complained that their cars accelerated spontaneously, Audi's response was to blame the drivers. Customers' faith plummeted, and Audi lost two thirds of its market share in three years. (From *Philadelphia Inquirer,* December 22, 1995.)

■ *Central Sprinkler Co., Lansdale, Pennsylvania, 1997.* Allegations against Central Sprinkler focus on the company's line of Omega sprinklers made before June 1996. The lawsuit maintains that the sprinklers have failed in at least six instances across the country in the last two years. 80 percent of the 10 million Omega heads produced during the last 15 years had been made before the 1996 design-flaw correction.

(Public Warning) Underwriters Laboratories, the independent firm that certified the Omega head as reliable, issued a public warning, "Omegas do not and will not function in a significant percentage of instances." (*USA Today,* December 28, 1997.)

3.3.5 Creditors Become Concerned and Want to Be Satisfied: Examples

Some examples of organizations whose creditors became concerned and wanted to be satisfied include: Enron Corporation; Safety-Kleen Corporation; HealthSouth Corporation; Adelphia Communications; Boston Chicken Inc.; and Dow Corning.

■ *Enron Corporation, Houston, Texas, 2001.* After reporting a big third-quarter loss, and the replacement of its CFO who ran two of the controversial partnerships, and an investigation by the SEC had just been announced, Houston-based Enron stock price has plummeted by about 75 percent. The SEC filing raises further questions about Enron's accounting procedures and disclosure policies. Enron will restate its financial results from 1997 through the third quarter of 2001, reducing previously reported income by $586 million and boosting previously reported debt to $628 million at the end of 2000, concedes three entities run by company officials should have been included in its consolidated financial statements, based on generally accepted accounting principles.

(Creditors) A 2000-page report by Neal Batson of Atlanta law firm Alston & Bird, a second in a series requested by U.S. Bankruptcy Judge Arthur Gonzalez, suggests that creditors might be entitled to as much as $2.9 billion in assets that Enron transferred or sold before its Dec. 2, 2001, bankruptcy reorganization filing. Batson says Enron might be able to seek recovery of the more than $74 million lent to Lay in 2000 and $53 million paid to Enron employees in late 2001, when the company was presumed to be insolvent.

The report also calls into question some $5 billion in loans disguised as transactions that Enron entered into with Citibank and J.P. Morgan Chase. "Both Citibank and J.P. Morgan knew that Enron accounted for its obligations under the prepay transactions as liabilities from price risk management activities rather than debt," the report said. "They also believed that Enron reported the cash as cash flow from operating activities rather than financing activities."

■ *Safety-Kleen Corp., Columbia, South Carolina, 2000.* Safety Kleen Corp., the hazardous waste-disposal company, based in Columbia, South Carolina, said in a filing with the SEC that a restatement of financial results reduced its earnings by about $534 million for the fiscal years 1997 through 1999. Safety Kleen unveiled a net loss for 2000 of $833.2 million, or $8.27 a share, including charges for asset impairment, as it undergoes a reorganization under new management.

Allegations of accounting irregularities at Safety-Kleen surfaced in March 2000 and have triggered investigations by a federal grand jury in New York and the SEC. Safety-Kleen said an audit of its financial results for the years ended August 31, 1997, 1998, and 1999 revealed a host of improper accounting practices, ranging from inappropriate establishment and use of reserves for some acquisitions made between September 1, 1996, and August 31, 1999, to recording uncollected revenue.

(Creditors) In addition, Safety-Kleen said about $174 billion in proofs of claim had been filed from creditors against it and its affiliates as of May 18. The value of Safety-Kleen's assets was $3.13 billion as of August 31, 2000. ("Safety-Kleen Says Restatement Reduced Earnings for Fiscal 1997 through 1999" *Wall Street Journal*, July 10, 2001.)

■ *HealthSouth Corp., Birmingham, Alabama, 2003.* On March 19, five more executives involved in the company's internal accounting procedures pleaded guilty to participating in the scheme to inflate HealthSouth's earnings. They all admitted their roles in the company's quarterly campaign to make its earnings look better than they actually were. HealthSouth runs 1700 rehabilitation hospitals around the world.

(Creditors) The company, whose stock has plummeted to penny status after the revelations of accounting fraud, is fighting to stave off a push for Chapter 11 bankruptcy protection from its creditors. (From "Scrushy breaks silence — through his lawyer," *USA Today*, April 4, 2003.)

■ *Adelphia Communications, Coudersport, Pennsylvania, 2002.* Adelphia's stock has plunged since March, and was delisted from the Nasdaq on Monday. The No. 6 cable operator's shares fell to 30 cents yesterday, a collapse from $20.39 a share before the off-the-books debt was disclosed in March.

(Creditors) The company has missed deadlines for filing financial reports, and is in default on agreements with creditors.

■ *Boston Chicken Inc., 2002 report.* Boston Chicken Inc., whose stock crashed to earth amid questionable accounting, filed for bankruptcy-court protection in 1998.

A lawsuit filed last year in U.S. District Court in Phoenix by Boston Chicken's bankruptcy trustee, alleging that Arthur Andersen helped Boston Chicken create "a facade of corporate solvency" by hiding its franchisees' losses. The franchisees were nominally independent, but the lawsuit alleges they were controlled by Boston Chicken to manipulate the parent's financial results.

(Creditors) The trustee's lawyer, says Boston Chicken's creditors lost more than $1 billion following the bankruptcy filing; the suit seeks triple damages under state racketeering statutes. (From "Boston Chicken Case Mirrors Enron Failure," *Wall Street Journal*, March 13, 2002.)

■ *Dow Corning, Detroit, Michigan.* In 1995, the Supreme Court let stand a $7.34 million verdict won from Dow Corning by a woman in Sebastopol, California, for injuries she suffered when her breast implants ruptured. Dow contended expert testimony from defense witnesses wasn't scientifically sound and the $6.5 million in punitive damages to punish Dow was excessive. The decision could encourage more women to sue on their own rather than join the 200,000 registered for a $4.2 billion settlement fund.

(Creditors) Dow Corning has been under bankruptcy protection since 1995, overwhelmed by creditors and implant-related legal claims. Both sides were instructed not to discuss the case. (From *USA Today*, September 9, 1998.)

3.3.6 Shareholders Are Concerned and Begin Dumping Their Stock: Examples

Some examples of organizations whose shareholders became concerned and began dumping their stock include Enron Corporation; Freddie Mac; HealthSouth Corporation; and Schering-Plough Corporation.

■ Enron Corporation, Houston, Texas, 2001.

(Acute Crisis) Enron Corp. reduced its previous reported net income over the past 4 years by $586 million, or 20 percent, mostly due to improperly accounting for its dealings with partnerships run by some company officers.

(Stockholders Dump) The company's stock price plummeted by about 75 percent in that time. (From *Wall Street Journal,* November 9, 2001.)

■ *Freddie Mac, Washington, D.C., 2003.* In January, Freddie Mac restated its earnings for 2000–02, after its new auditor recommended changes to its accounting policies to reflect higher earnings from the complex financial instruments called derivatives. The company has 3900 employees. The federal agency that oversees Freddie Mac, the Office of Federal Housing Enterprise Oversight, is investigating the company's accounting.

In June of 2003, Freddie Mac announced abruptly that it had fired its president because he did not fully cooperate with an internal review of the company's accounting, which also is being investigated by federal regulators. In a surprise shake-up, the government-sponsored company whose stock is widely traded said that it had fired the president and chief operating officer, "because of serious questions as to the timeliness and completeness of his cooperation and candor" with lawyers hired in January by the board of directors' audit committee to review the accounting problems that span three years.

(Stockholders Dump) Freddie Mac shares dropped 16 percent, or $9.61, to close at $50.26. The loss wiped out about $7 billion in shareholder value. (From *Philadelphia Inquirer,* June 10, 2003.)

■ *HealthSouth Corp., Birmingham, Alabama, 2003.* In March of 2003, HealthSouth's board of directors fired the company's chairman and CEO, bringing Richard Scrushy's reign at the rehabilitation hospital chain he founded in 1984 to an inglorious end. The board had placed Scrushy on administrative leave two weeks ago, when the SEC charged him with masterminding a scheme to inflate HealthSouth's earnings by at least $1.4 billion since 1999. Two top executives had admitted to orchestrating the financial fraud.

Then a third executive pleaded guilty to similar charges. The executive, who was an assistant controller at HealthSouth, admitted in federal court that he was part of a group of executives at HealthSouth, known as the "family," which met every quarter to plug "holes" in the company's earnings statements. Other Health-South executives are believed to be cooperating with the probe, which extends to Scrushy and outside parties who did business with HealthSouth.

(Stockholders Dump) The rehabilitation center company, whose stock has plummeted since the accounting scandal, was dropped from the New York Stock Exchange and trades for pennies. Last year, it traded in the $15 range but had sunk to $3.91 March 19, 2003 when the SEC suspended trading in the stock. Scrushy's firing is certain to bolster the cause of Plaintiffs attorneys, who have accused him of inside trading. Last year, Scrushy sold $100 million in stock before jolting investors in August with an announcement that, contrary to previous guidance, the company would announce an unexpected quarterly loss. (From "Hospital chain fires CEO after scandal," *USA Today,* April 1, 2003.)

■ *Schering-Plough Corp, Kenilworth, New Jersey, 2003.* The SEC brought and settled a case against Schering-Plough Corp. and its former chairman for alleged violations of news-disclosure rules, penalizing an individual for the first time under Regulation Fair Disclosure. Without admitting or denying any wrongdoing, the drug maker agreed to a cease-and-desist order and to pay a $1 million civil penalty, the SEC said.

In late September 2002, according to the SEC, the former CEO met privately with analysts and portfolio managers at four institutional investment firms and disclosed that analyst estimates for the company's earnings prospects were too high. They also allegedly disclosed that Schering-Plough's earnings in 2003 would significantly decline.

(Stockholders Dump) The three days following the meeting, the price of Schering-Plough's stock declined by more than 17 percent. While the Kenilworth, N.J., company's stock was plunging, the SEC said, the former CEO held another private meeting with about 25 analysts in early October 2002, during which he said that Schering-Plough's 2003 earnings would be "terrible." Only after this meeting did the company issue a press release disclosing earnings would be materially below the company's prior guidance, the SEC said. (From "SEC Settles Schering-Plough Disclosure Case," *Wall Street Journal*, September 10, 2003.)

3.3.7 Damage to a Company's Reputation Can Have Serious Consequences: Examples

Another critical problem for an organization in the middle of a crisis is that the damage to its reputation can have serious consequences.

- *American Red Cross— Liberty Fund, Washington, D.C. USA Today,* November 6, 2001:

  The American Red Cross acknowledged that some of the $550 million in donations to the Liberty Fund, a special fund established for the victims of the Sept. 11 terrorist attacks, will be used for other broad-based needs instead. But a portion of that money will go to broad-based activities such as a blood reserve program, a national outreach effort, and a telecommunications upgrade. Of the $550 million pledged so far, the Red Cross expects to spend more than $300 million over the next several months on disaster relief related to the attacks.

  - $100 million has been set aside for its Family Gift program, which provides victims' families with money to help cover immediate expenses.
  - $100 million will go to disaster relief services in New York City, Washington, Pennsylvania and other sites.
  - $50 million for a blood readiness and reserve program that would increase the group's blood inventory from two or three days to 10 days.
  - $26 million in nation-wide community outreach.
  - $29 million would be spent on relief infrastructure, including telecommunications, information systems, database management, contribution processing and other overhead costs.

  Normally donations to the Red Cross typically go into its Disaster Relief Fund, a general account designed to meet emergencies of all types. This resulted in a crisis where the future donations to the ARC were at risk.

  Disputes among board members and criticism that not enough money is going to the victims, have prompted the relief agency to wage a campaign to restore its image. High-profile former President Bernadine Healy (57) was forced from her $450,000-a-year post.

  The ARC said that all the money donated to the Liberty Fund would go to people affected by the Sept. 11 terrorist attacks, reversing a plan to set aside some of the money for other needs. The Red Cross' interim chief executive officer, Harold Decker, apologized for what he called "a failure in communications between the American Red Cross and the American public." *(Philadelphia Inquirer,* November 15, 2001.)

■ *Arthur Andersen, Chicago, Illinois, Wall Street Journal,* January 21, 2002:

The SEC has been investigating Arthur Andersen's role in Enron's complex accounting, including questionable partnerships that kept about $500 million in debt off the books and allowed Enron executives to profit from the arrangements. The SEC sent a letter to Enron on October 17, 2001, asking for information after the company reported hundreds of millions of dollars in third-quarter losses. David B. Duncan, of Andersen — called an urgent meeting on October 23 to organize an "expedited effort" to destroy documents a few days after he learned that the SEC had requested information. Two weeks later, Duncan's assistant said: "Stop the shredding." A day before that, Andersen had received a federal subpoena for the documents.

The unfolding Enron saga could have a detrimental effect on Andersen, which employs 85,000 people in 84 countries and last year had U.S. revenue totaling $9.3 billion. As with all accounting firms, Andersen's ability to attract and retain audit clients depends on having a sterling reputation. The more its reputation comes into question, the more likely it becomes that investors will view an audit opinion by Andersen with skepticism or distrust.

■ *United Way, Chairperson for Fund That Abused Funds:*

William Aramony resigned after his lavish spending and management practices spelled an end to his 22-year tenure as president. The government charged the former president of United Way of America and two fellow executives with conspiracy and mail and tax fraud yesterday, accusing them of spending more than $1 million of the charity's money on vacations, real estate and air travel.

Elaine Chao succeeded William Aramony as national president of United Way. Her major concern was the potential negative impact the scandal will have on donations to the United Way.

3.3.8 Managing the Organization Becomes Difficult

After it is visible for all to see, managing the organization may be difficult because there may be a breakdown in respect for top managers. Situations formerly taken for granted by middle managers may be challenged and debated. Management differences that formerly were set aside begin to emerge, and the infighting begins.

3.3.8.1 *Problem: Loss of Personnel*

During the Acute-Crisis stage, an organization faces the loss of key personnel. One of the critical problems for an organization in the middle of a crisis is the brain drain, as the best employees seek safety elsewhere.

■ Arthur Andersen, 2002:

Employee morale at Andersen is taking a beating as the accounting giant's reputation is tarnished. Workers are grappling with tough questions about how the companies' predicament could imperil their own careers.

"When the image of a company is tarnished, that leads to turnover," says Elaine Hollensbe, an assistant professor in management at the University of Cincinnati. "Employees may not want to be identified with a company when there's impropriety going on."

"If the code of ethics isn't followed at the top, the blocks tumble," says Nan DeMars, an ethics behaviorist and author of *You Want Me To Do What?* on workplace ethics. "People always championed Arthur Andersen. Now they're embarrassed. Their confidence is shaken."

(Company Image) "Andersen carried a reputation for integrity and competence in the fields of auditing and accounting." Now the reputation is in tatters. (From "Andersen employees' morale rattled," *USA Today,* January 21, 2002.)

■ Exxon Corporation, 1989:

Employees at Exxon Corp.'s Credit Card Center have been under a state of siege for two months as angry customers — including more than 17,000 who canceled their accounts — vehemently protest the Alaskan oil spill.

1. Workers at the credit card center here are wearing special gloves to handle protest letters purposely soaked with oil.
2. They spend hours piecing together torn-up credit cards in order to determine the account numbers that customers want canceled.
3. They apologize on behalf of their company dozens of times a day. "There are mornings when I don't want to go to work," Barbara Domino said. "I just tell myself I can't let it get to me."
4. Many of the returned credit cards are torn to shreds, covered in oil or burned. They also are accompanied by notes reading "You ought to be hung" — for the oil spilled by an Exxon Shipping Co. tanker March 24.

The crisis is taking its toll through-out the Exxon organization. Employees, confronted daily by criticisms of Exxon in the media and by friends and family members, are questioning their faith in the corporate giant. "It's been deeply painful for every employee that I've worked with, talked with and met," said Larry Stockman, a psychologist on retainer with Exxon. "They feel devastated by what's happened." A week and a half into the crisis, one of the women at the card center hung up after a call from an enraged customer and started to cry. One by one, her office mates started crying as well. Her supervisor, Joyce Jackson, stood among them, handing out tissues. Stockman said employees are "embarrassed, they're hurt, they're sad. Some are angry, but that passes because they don't know who to be angry with. It's like a death."

The company has taken steps to maintain its employees' confidence. At Exxon's downtown building, videos presenting management's side of the story are shown throughout the day. Despondent workers have come up with their own morale boosters. Employees of the shipping company said they were being shunned not only by the public but by Exxon employees from other divisions. So they printed up buttons proclaiming "I Work for Exxon Shipping and I'm Proud of It." ("Morale sinks at Exxon as hate mail pours in," (From *Philadelphia Daily News,* May 22, 1989.)

3.3.8.2 Loss of Key Employees

One of the critical problems for an organization in the middle of a crisis is the loss of key employees as they seek safety elsewhere.

■ Exxon Valdez, Prince William Sound, Alaska:

(03/24/1989, Executive Management Team) Allowing the crisis to move from a Pre-Crisis situation to an Acute-Crisis situation. They were guilty of an over-optimistic opinion of their capabilities. They also had a false sense of security conditioned by the 12-year history of an estimated 6000 tanker trips without incident. They were also guilty of "a false sense of security" because they had a Contingency Plan. The plan was 1700 pages, containing detailed information of the actions to be taken if there was an oil spill. The Contingency Plan was viable when it was put in place, because the resources it referred to were available. A documented manual does not mean it will work. The strategies have to be first tested, and then exercised regularly — to ensure the strategies work when needed. A positive lesson learned from the Exxon experience is that all oil companies have learned from the spill situation; and all companies have learned how to avoid a "public relations" disaster. (*USA Today,* June 22, 1999.)

"Many factors contributed to the action of the operators, such as deficiencies in their training, lack of clarity in their operating procedures, failure of organizations to learn the proper lessons from previous incidents, and deficiencies in the design of the control room." Sounds like the reason for this incident. Actually this was the findings of the investigation of the Three Mile Nuclear accident incident in 1979.

3.4 THE POST-CRISIS STAGE

After the crisis is under control, the Post-Crisis stage begins. It is during the Post-Crisis stage that the company must attempt to recoup their losses. This is the time for the company to show the consumer or customer that they care about the problems the crisis has caused them.

After an organization gets the acute crisis under control, the executives can concentrate on actions to take during the Post-Crisis stage. Their goals during the Post-Crisis stage should be to:

1. Recoup losses.
2. Evaluate the organization's performance during the crisis.
3. Make any changes that were identified as being needed during the crisis.

3.4.1 How Long Will This Last?

The Acute-Crisis stage eventually ends. On the other hand, the Post-Crisis stage can be lengthy and in some instances endless. Therefore, you need to plan for the Post-Crisis stage *during* the Acute-Crisis stage. How can you predict a long, drawn-out Post-Crisis phase? Depending on the nature of your crisis, if the crisis and/or the company fits certain profiles, you can make certain, well-reasoned assumptions. Such business profiles would include a public company; a highly visible, household-word company; and a celebrity-type CEO or other senior executive. Such crisis profiles would include any crisis that:

1. Involves the loss of lives, especially in large numbers (Arco)
2. Almost costs lives
3. Creates a panic (Enron)
4. Demonstrates an industry weakness or trend (Arthur Andersen)
5. Is exposed by the media (especially if it makes good copy)
6. Entails conspiracies, moral offenses, kickbacks, bribes, or swindles (Tyco)

"Why" is a luxury question during the Acute-Crisis stage. But during the Post-Crisis stage, "why" is asked again, along with "how" and "what" and "when" and "where," and so on. These questions were first asked during the Acute-Crisis stage and are repeated again in the Post-Crisis stage. If you can prepare for it, even while still in the midst of the Acute-Crisis stage, you will be more in control of the Post-Crisis stage.

3.4.1.1 Take Notes

In anticipation of the Post-Crisis stage, try to capture your activity during the Acute-Crisis stage. The organization needs to assign someone from the Crisis Management Team (CMT) to that task. This is an excellent opportunity to use a tape recorder. Tape-record all planning sessions, CMT meetings, fact-gathering reports, etc.

Write down, or dictate into a tape recorder, the thoughts, feelings, and reasons for making decisions, etc. Ask other members of the CMT to do the same.

Your organization might even consider having a photographer (or video camera operator) on hand at all times. This will allow you to freeze a particular point in time that you will be asked to relive and explain actions taken — perhaps for years.

If you have a credible and accurate record from which to quote, it will make it easier to get through the post-crisis stage and will help to speed up the post-crisis stage itself. Having records will also aid you if you find yourself in an uncomfortable position during an acute crisis — where you are advocating one course of action in the face of stiff opposition.

If you take the time to duly record appropriate comments and events during a crisis, then when you respond to "why," your response will be more credible.

Do not spend time wondering why the investigations (articles, hearings, etc.) seem to be going on and on.

> There may be some up-and-coming investigator (reporter, prosecutor, politician, etc.) out to make a name for him- or herself at your expense. If there is no apparent malice, you may have to suffer ignominiously.
>
> You can consult with your lawyers or public relations consultants to find out if you can pursue certain remedies, such as lawsuits or editorial briefings for the media, to put an end to your ordeal. But, by and large, you may just have to tough it out.

This is all the more reason for doing whatever is necessary during the Acute-Crisis stage to be prepared for the Post-Crisis stage.

Two other headaches to guard against are (1) the almost inevitable attacks on your other corporate entities or subsidiaries and (2) the invidious comparisons of subsequent crises to yours.

3.4.1.2 Guilt by Association

When a company suffers a mega-crisis at one of its locations, there is a natural tendency on the part of the news media, community leaders, and government officials to point at other locations owned by that company and put them under a similarly powerful microscope.

A good example is the Union Carbide experience after the Bhopal, India, incident. The media, and even government officials, pointed at other plants owned by that company (such as Union Carbide's plant in Institute, West Virginia) and put it under similar scrutiny.

> ■ *Charleston Daily Mail,* November 11, 1985: Officials at the plant still aren't sure what caused a toxic gas to leak from a storage tank, sending about 135 people to area hospitals. Carbide spokesman Dick Henderson said a buildup of pressure in the storage tank containing up to 500 gallons of aldicarb oxime caused a gasket to rupture, releasing a white odorous plume of gas into neighborhoods near the plant. Hospitals treated people for eye, throat and lung irritation after being exposed to the pesticide ingredient; injuries were not considered serious.

As long as this continues, you know that the Post-Crisis stage of your crisis still is underway. But the extreme comparisons — perhaps due to our insatiable appetite for superlatives — may continue long after the Acute-Crisis phase, depending of course on the crisis.

3.4.1.3 The Worst Example of a Crisis Will Not Go Away

The news media are guilty of perpetuating the crisis. How? They usually compare the incident they are writing about with the "worst" prior incident; for example, "The worst nuclear accident since Three Mile Island." Or, "The most widespread case of product tampering since the Tylenol poisonings ...." Or, "The most deaths from a chemical plant accident since Union Carbide's Bhopal disaster."

> Those are the sorts of comparisons that make corporate public relations people cringe. To their way of thinking, the media should stop dredging up ancient history. But it is the nature of the media to "dredge up ancient history" when it enhances the story. And the sad and frightening truth is that the only thing that will make the media stop comparing chemical plant accidents to Union Carbide's is to have a worse accident to take its place.

> **—Steven Fink**
> *Crisis Management: Planning for the Inevitable*

Comparisons are made by the news media and the Internet. When a significant disaster strikes, invariably the media print a list of other similar disasters. This was the worst hurricane since "Andrew." Or the worst flood in this region in 50 years. In April of 2005, Pennsylvania and New Jersey experienced a huge rainstorm. Flooding along the Delaware River and a number of other rivers and creeks in Pennsylvania and New Jersey were compared to a storm in 1955. The tragic tsunami of 2005 was compared to a number of other tsunamis going back a century.

3.4.1.4 Learn from Other Crises

Just because a crisis is not yours does not mean that you cannot find opportunity in it. During someone else's crisis, look around to see what mistakes were made and whether or not you are vulnerable to the same or similar problems. As someone once said, "The only thing better than profiting from your mistakes is profiting from someone else's."

> There is not a power plant in the country today that does not have some sort of crisis management plan in case of an "incident." But, how many of these plans were in existence prior to Three Mile Island? Few, if any.

> Today, look at how many over-the-counter consumer drugs and other ingestible products come in "tamper-proof" containers, which feature warnings not to use the product and to return it to the store where it was purchased if a safety seal is broken. You can credit the Tylenol poisonings for this.

The point should be clear: although it may not be sporting to kick your opponent while he is down, if you can be affected by the same type of crisis, find out where they were vulnerable and why, and act accordingly. If your competitor is vulnerable, are you also?

3.4.2 Evaluating the Organization's Handling of the Crisis

3.4.2.1 Evaluating the Organizations' Handling of the Crisis — Objective: Recoup Losses

One of the best ways to recoup losses is to have the executives show consumers that they (the executives) care about what the crisis did to them (the consumers). Then the executives should show the consumers what the organization is doing to prevent this from happening again. An example of executives showing that they do care about what the crisis did to the consumers is:

Johnson & Johnson/McNeil Co. Tylenol Tampering Case: A good example of recouping losses, and regaining market share, is the Johnson & Johnson (McNeil Co.) handling of the Tylenol tampering case. When J&J was made aware of the tampering incident, the executives' major concern was to ensure the safety of the public. The company recalled over 30 million capsules from store shelves and homes around the country. In that way, the organization demonstrated its concern. Consumers realized that the cost of the recall was significant.

J&J told its story using full-page ads in newspapers and television ads across the country. The actions taken by the executives restored trust in the organization, and consumers began buying Tylenol again. Within a few months, Tylenol regained much of its pre-crisis market share.

(Post-Crisis) Johnson & Johnson/McNeil redesigned the Tylenol packaging. This repackaging would alert consumers that the package was in its original state when it left the plant, or that it had been tampered with. The packaging shows a warning not to use the product and to return it to the store where it was purchased if the safety seal was broken.

"From a business perspective, the result of the Tylenol crisis was that Johnson & Johnson demonstrated both its concern for its customers and its commitment to the corporation's ethical standards. Although this was a tragic episode, the company clearly was regarded even more highly after the episode than before. The operative word is trust … and whether people will take one's word when one badly needs them to do so will depend on how much confidence has been built in the organization over the years before the crisis occurs." (Excerpt from Norm Augustine's article published in *Crisis Magazine* and entitled "Managing the Crisis You Tried to Prevent").

Coca-Cola Co. – Europe. On Thursday, June 10, 1999, 31 schoolchildren fell ill in Bornem, Belgium, after drinking Coke. At least one person was hospitalized, showing symptoms of hemolysis, an excessive destruction of red blood cells that causes anemia and vomiting. On Monday, June 14, 40 more students were hospitalized in Lochristi, Belgium. Health Minister Luc Vandenbossche said doctors across Belgium have reported cases of illness after people drank Coca-Cola products.

Vandenbossche banned all sales of Coke and other Coca-Cola brands such as Fanta, Sprite, Aquarius and Bonaqua, and Minute Maid fruit juices.

While the world's largest soft-drink maker contended that the products were safe, the scare that prompted Belgium to ban all Coke soft drinks spread to its neighbors. Luxembourg imposed a similar ban, France banned Coke in cans, and the Netherlands, Spain, Germany, and Switzerland recalled Coca-Cola products coming from Belgium.

A week after the illnesses began, (Thursday, June 17), Philippe Lenfant, general manager of Coca-Cola Belgium reported that a pesticide exposure in one bottling plant, and a substandard carbonation gas in another, led to the contamination of Coca-Cola products that sickened dozens of Belgians. Lenfant said separate errors occurred at two Coca-Cola plants, one in Dunkirk, France, just across the Belgian border, and the other in the northern Belgian city of Antwerp.

The company has been slow to address public concerns, said Paul Holmes, editor and publisher of *Reputation Management,* a publication focused on corporate and brand name management. "Nobody at Coke in the U.S. took charge of the incident immediately or recognized that it could develop into an international crisis," Holmes said. It costs more to a company's image "the longer you stay silent in the beginning," he said.

(Losses) Coca-Cola Co. said second-quarter earnings fell 21 percent, the result of depressed sales overseas and the discovery of contaminated Coke products in Europe. Coke warned that its third-quarter earnings would fall short of analyst estimates because of a product recall in Europe, higher marketing costs and sluggish sales in struggling foreign countries. And Coke also said the withdrawal of its drinks in Europe will also hurt fourth-quarter profit, though it did not give specifics.

(Post-Crisis) In order to show consumers that the organization cared about the crisis, during the third quarter, Coke boosted advertising and introduced new packaging in Belgium to help win back customers. It instituted a free-drink giveaway to show potential customers that Coke was safe. It put Coca-Cola "greeters" in supermarkets to talk with consumers.

Herron Pharmaceuticals, Australia: The company's products were recalled nationwide when two Brisbane men were treated in hospital after taking Herron headache tablets (Paracetomol) laced with strychnine. (Cause) — A former Herron employee, Garry Sakowski (32), was subsequently arrested and charged with extortion and other offences against the company, but police said his arrest was connected to previous extortion threats, in 1993. Mr. Sakowski has been granted bail to appear in court on August 7.

(Post-Crisis) Herron, meanwhile, has embarked on a campaign to regain its 20 percent share of the Paracetomol market after its products were put back on store shelves two weeks ago. New packaging, described as the most "tamper-evident" in Australia, features heat-fused ends. (From *The Age*, Australia, June 7, 2000.)

Salomon Bros.:

(Acute-Crisis) Salomon Brothers was accused of breaking the rules at the Treasury market auctions by submitting bids in the names of customers without their authorization.

Salomon admitted to breaking the rules. Paul Mozer improperly purchased $4.7 billion of the notes in direct bidding and through other dealers, giving the firm more than the 35 percent allowed by any one company.

The negative impact to Salomon was significant.

1. The British Treasury announced on September 9, 1991, it had fired the firm as the lead underwriter in an $8 billion sale of shares in British Telecommunications PLC in the United States.
   The departure of customers has ominous implications, says a senior U.S. Treasury official: "If confidence goes, no institution can survive."
2. The California State pension fund, one of the nations biggest investors, suspended purchases of government securities through Salomon.
   "Even though Salomon has made a good deal of money for us, we can't look the other way when the law is broken," Gray Davis, California state controller.

3. The California Public Employees' Retirement System, expressing "outrage and concern," said it would stop buying government securities through Salomon "for an indefinite period pending the outcome of the firm's reorganization activities and findings of continuing investigations."
Salomon did not say how much revenue it would lose with the California pension account.

(Post-Crisis Actions) Warren Buffett, Salomon Bros. chairman, said the actions of Mozer, Salomon's 36-year-old ex-government bond chief, were not the actions of a rational man.

Mr. Buffett said the actions of John Gutfreund, who waited months before reporting Mozer's abuses, were "inexcusable."

Buffett called for tighter scrutiny for the freewheeling treasuries market. He said "I have no problems with tough rules, tough cops and tough execution."

Salomon terminated John Gutfreund (the former CEO), Thomas Strauss (the former President), John Meriwether (the former vice chairman), and Donald Feuerstein (the former chief legal officer). They would receive no severance pay, future legal expenses, or compensation from the firm. That decision followed Kansas Democratic Rep. Jim Slattery's pronouncement during the hearings that "there should not be a dime spent by the firm to defend the wrongdoers.... these men should be in striped suits, sweeping up Wall St." (*From Philadelphia Inquirer,* August 21, 1991.)

3.4.2.2 *Evaluating the Organizations' Handling of the Crisis — Objective: Show Consumers You Care about What You Did to Them*

Some organizations have taken full-page advertisements in newspapers around the country. Some have sent letters to individual customers, stockholders, and employees explaining the situation.

Bayer AG:

(Acute-Crisis) Lipobay, marketed as Baycol in the U.S. was linked to a rare muscle wasting syndrome and about 100 patient deaths. Bayer pulled Lipobay after it was linked to the deaths. (From *Wall Street Journal,* January 13, 2004.)

(Post-Crisis) Bayer said it has reached more than 2000 settlements related to the 2001 withdrawal of a cholesterol lowering drug. It has paid out $782 million without admitting guilt.

Bank of America (USA Today, October 8, 2003): Bank of America on Tuesday promised to reimburse additional mutual fund shareholders and beef up efforts to tackle internal problems related to improper fund trading practices.

Following a rapidly expanding government probe, the USA's largest consumer bank said it has hired independent experts to review its mutual fund practices, policies and compliance systems.

Bank of America already had pledged to repay mutual fund shareholders of its own Nations funds family of funds who lost money because of trading violations under investigation by New York Attorney General Eliot Spitzer. Last month, Spitzer settled charges with a hedge fund, Canary Capital Partners, that it engaged in illegal trading practices with the mutual fund arms of Bank of America and Bank One, and mutual fund providers Strong Financial and Janus Capital.

(Exec-Account) One former Bank of America broker, Theodore Sihpol, has been charged with larceny and securities fraud by Spitzer. The bank fired Sihpol and two other executives who have been linked to allegations of improper trading.

(Post-Crisis) (Step-4-FTP) Bank of America says it will set up a restitution fund to repay shareholders harmed by Canary's violations. It has hired the retired chairman of General Electric Investment, Dale Frey, to lead the independent review, and the former General Counsel of U.S. Trust and State Street, Maureen Scannell Bateman, to conduct a compliance review. It also hired a company headed by former bank regulator Eugene Ludwig to review its compliance and trading systems. The bank is taking the right steps by hiring independent experts to conduct a review, says Mercer Bullard, a University of Mississippi law professor and head of Fund Democracy, an advocacy group. But he adds that it's unrealistic to expect too much. "They should investigate the independent fund directors, but I doubt that they will." Others say that calls for an internal review should be coming from Nations funds' board of directors, instead of from Bank of America. "The Nations funds board may not have been completely quiet, but they've been missing in action," says Gary Gensler, co-author *of The Great Mutual Fund Trap.* ("Bank of America to repay fund holders")

3.4.2.3 Evaluating the Organization's Handling of the Crisis — Objective: What Are You Doing to Prevent This from Happening Again

Johnson & Johnson/McNeil:

(Acute-Crisis) Extra-Strength Tylenol Capsules laced with cyanide. Killed 7 people: a 35-year-old flight attendant (Paula Prince); two brothers in their 20s and the 19-year-old wife of one of them; a 12-year-old girl (Mary Ann Kellerman); a 27-year-old mother of four who had just come home from the hospital with a 5-day-old infant, and a 31-year-old mother of two. (Step-4-FTP) McNeill and J&J management took swift and responsible action; they removed all Tylenol capsules from the shelves. (22 million bottles of Tylenol capsules at a cost of $100 million.)

(Company Image) The move preserved the reputation of the company. The company regained Tylenol's share of the market within a year. Fewer than 75 capsules were ultimately found to be poisoned.

(Post-Crisis) (Change) J&J ultimately discontinued the production and sale of capsules and introduced tamper-resistant Tylenol packages and/or caplets. (*Philadelphia Inquirer,* May 14, 1992.) (Extortion) (James Lewis) the prime suspect was convicted of trying to extort $1 million from Johnson & Johnson. He was sentenced to 10 years. (Post-Crisis) Johnson & Johnson, elevated management of the crisis to corporate level and managed to recover market share within nine months.

City of Chicago, River Leak (Chicago Resource, April 13, 1992): A company that drove pilings for a new bridge into the Chicago River bed caused the leak by cracking an aging tunnel system that runs beneath a 12-square-block area of Chicago's Loop. A hole developed in a branch of the tunnel. A large whirlpool formed. An estimated 250 million gallons of river water rushed through car-size hole flooding the tunnel and building basements in the Loop (Chicago's principal business district), at a rate of two feet per hour.

In the ensuing flood, power failures and water damage forced the immediate evacuation of 200,000 people, leaving commerce at a standstill and the city's business community reeling from losses exceeding $1 billion. According to the *Chicago Resource* newsletter, 229 buildings and 7671 business tenants were affected.

Large-scale computer failures sent more than 30 companies rushing for cover at hot sites and business recovery centers maintained by service bureaus. Nearly as many firms put their back-up service on notice. Business Units moved Personal Computer's and Local Area Network equipment to temporary locations.

(Post-Crisis) In the aftermath of the flood, the city made major repairs in the tunnel and started new inspection routines. Old buildings in the Loop got mechanical and wiring repairs. Some are talking about the need to repair bridges, roads and the rest of Chicago's infrastructure.

Days Inn/Alamo Rent-A-Car, April 21, 1993: Jorg Schell, 59, a tourist from Germany was shot and killed helping his wife, who was being mugged as she got out of a rental car in the Days Inn parking lot in Homestead, Florida. He was the sixth tourist to have been slain in Florida in the last five months. His family filed a $10 million lawsuit contending Alamo Rent-A-Car and the Days Inn motel chain contributed to his death.

(Post-Crisis) Alamo Rent-A-Car decided to remove logos and stickers that identify vehicles as rentals. Hertz and Avis took similar action earlier. Police believe people driving rental cars may be singled out by violent robbers who prey on visitors. The state has also stopped issuing special license plates to rental cars, which had made them crime targets.

Merrill Lynch (Blodget): Merrill Lynch reached a settlement with New York Attorney General Eliot L. Spitzer, who accused the company's analysts of misleading investors. Spitzer said Merrill Lynch's analysts praised the stock of companies whose investment banking business Merrill wanted to win. Investment banking brings brokerage firms hefty fees for helping to arrange new stock offerings and corporate mergers. The settlement required the company to devise a new way of compensating analysts.

(The Post Crisis) Merrill said it would pay its analysts based on the accuracy of their forecasts. The new system for paying

Merrill's 800 analysts is effective immediately. It will base analysts' pay on how accurate they are in their stock forecasts and how their recommendations benefit investors, among other factors. The firm will use surveys and input from clients to help gauge the latter. "Investment banking will not have input into analyst compensation."

Merrill also announced plans for a stock-rating system intended to be easier for investors to use. The new stock-rating system, which reduces the number of ratings to three (buy, neutral, sell) from the previous four-level ratings system (strong buy, buy, neutral, reduce/sell), will be implemented in September. It was not required under the settlement with Spitzer. (From *Philadelphia Inquirer,* June 8, 2002.)

3.4.2.4 Evaluating the Organization's Handling of the Crisis — Objective: Organizations Are Too Weakened to Continue Operations

Central Sprinkler, 1998: Santa Clara County filed a lawsuit alleging that one of the nation's leading manufacturers of automatic fire sprinklers is putting out a defective product. Santa Clara County's suit, filed on behalf of any public agency in the nation that may have faulty Central sprinklers, is believed to be the first case brought by the public sector.

> According to the lawsuit, the allegations against Central focus on the company's line of Omega sprinklers made before June 1996. The lawsuit maintains that the sprinklers have failed in at least six instances across the country in the last two years.

Approximately 80 percent of the 10 million Omega heads produced during the previous 15 years had been made before the 1996 design-flaw correction. The Omega model has since been overtaken by a less complex "quick-response" model, and represents less than 5 percent of Central's sprinkler-head sales.

(Omega's failures during fires) The first two 1995 fires — one in a hotel near Detroit, the other in a Veterans Administration Hospital in Canandaigua, New York — were cited in the government announcement. It said that four similar 1997 failures have come to light, one of which caused $3 million in damages to a marina in Gulf Breeze, Florida. No one was seriously injured in the fires.

The company said that in each incident in which an Omega head may not have operated, "other heads in the system have activated to successfully assist in controlling the spread of the fire."

Central Sprinkler's spokesperson responded within minutes of the government announcement, saying it "strongly disagrees" with the complaint. "The Omega works. It has been successfully controlling fires for 15 years. We intend to defend our product and our ongoing remediation program." The company also said the commission's conclusion "is based on a methodology that does not apply to installed sprinkler systems."

Central's CEO George G. Meyer blamed: (1) sloppy work by installers; and (2) the use of illegal leak-stopping products by maintenance workers not employed by his company.

Tal Briddell, interim CEO, said Central had learned a valuable lesson from the Omega crisis. He said the situation reminded him of a quote from Shakespeare, who "said something like, 'Learn from life's experience when it is in its infancy.' Don't let the challenge mature.... As a general philosophy, if you have a challenge, deal with it early and deal with it effectively."

(Post-Crisis) (*Philadelphia Inquirer*, June 16, 1999). Central Sprinkler Corp. was sold yesterday to its major rival, Tyco International Ltd. for $115 million. Central chief executive E. Talbot Briddell, a turnaround manager hired last July, said the cost of its Omega sprinkler product-liability crisis — more than $65 million — left the company without enough capital to compete effectively. The sale to Tyco "assures that Central will survive the Omega crisis and that the firm's 1480 employees will have jobs," Briddell said.

Hudson Foods, 1997: Suspected of shipping 40,000 pounds of beef contaminated with *E. coli* bacteria will be targeted for more inspections, a USDA official said. Hudson recalled 25 million pounds of hamburger due to bacterial contamination and faces a criminal probe into its handling of the recall.

In a statement released Friday, Hudson said, "We wish to state emphatically that Hudson Foods has moved with all dispatch as information became available and has in no way tried to hide any information from the USDA or the public. The reason for the expansion of volume in the (beef) recall was that the USDA, acting out of an abundance of caution ... with Hudson Foods to ensure the public's safety, expanded the volume to include all production of the days in question rather than portions of that production. When it comes to the public's safety we are not going to take any chances."

(August 22, 1997) "Ground Beef Pulled Back in Massive Recall"; What might be the largest meat recall in U.S. history began yesterday as the beef company linked to the latest outbreak of *E. coli*-tainted hamburgers agreed to pull off the market and destroy 25 million pounds of ground beef. Under pressure from the U.S. Department of Agriculture, Hudson Foods Co. also agreed yesterday to shut down its plant in Columbus, Nebraska, and not reopen it until the company erases all the government's doubts that its processes are safe.

Following a massive bad-beef recall, Burger King has pulled Hudson Foods' burgers off its grills — forever, a spokesman for the fast-food chain said yesterday. "No more Hudson Beef is in the Burger King system, nor will we be buying any more Hudson Foods Inc. beef," said David Nixon, a spokesman at Burger King's headquarters in Miami.

(Post-Crisis) (*Philadelphia Inquirer*, September 5, 1997). Tyson Foods, the nation's largest poultry producer, is buying Hudson Foods for $642 million just weeks after Hudson recalled a record 25 million pounds of hamburger in a contamination scare. "They have made us a very good offer, and the Hudson Foods board and I have decided that it is in the best interest of our shareholders, associates, growers and customers to accept," Hudson chairman James "Red" Hudson said yesterday.

3.4.2.5 Evaluate the Organization's Performance during the Crisis — Objective: Investigations

After the crisis is under control comes "the investigation." How did the organization handle the adverse publicity? What could have been done better? How did the organization handle investor communications? What could have been done better? How did the organization handle employee communications? What could have been done better?

For example, were there any customer problems?

▪ Did the problems result in any loss of current business?
▪ Did the problems result in any loss of future business?
▪ Did the problems result in any contractual disputes, and any lawsuits being filed?
▪ What could have been done better?

Another concern that should be addressed during the investigation is: Did the crisis result in any doors being opened to other potential crises?

When Alaska Airlines Flight 261 crashed, the investigation ended up resulting in a review of maintenance problems with *all* its airplanes. Another example of the crisis causing other doors to be opened was the SEPTA lawsuit by Shareif Hall's family over the escalator accident. During the court trial, it was uncovered that the officials at SEPTA tried to cover up their prior knowledge of the problems with the escalator.

> *Three Mile Island, 1979.* There were a lot of investigations following the TMI incident, for example, by the U.S. Congress, the Nuclear Regulatory Commission, the Commonwealth of Pennsylvania, as well as features and background pieces by national and local news media.
>
> (Post-Crisis) Post-crisis investigations are needed as long as they focus on legitimate concerns for public safety and well-being of people. Others are only used in witch-hunts, or to grab attention or headlines for the vehicle performing the investigation. The value of the investigation is that it often brings to light certain previously unknown information that may be considered damaging, or at least embarrassing, to the company involved. This information may shed new light on the cause of the crisis, reveals that the company tolerated shoddy workmanship, or inaccurate reporting to government agencies. "Human error" was really "management error" — meaning that the company simply had not been doing a good job of managing a nuclear power facility. (*Kemeny Report.*)

Depending on the nature and magnitude of your crisis, you will be placed under a series of powerful microscopes by a variety of operators, investigative reporters or government agencies (federal, state, or local), along with their inquiries/investigations, congressional hearings, political position papers, lawsuits, depositions, etc. The organization will receive a sudden level of interest a from a whole host of people. As soon as you get the first inkling of the nature of your acute crisis and can envision or even predict a protracted chronic phase, take necessary steps during to be prepared to answer the question "why" during the chronic phase.

During the crisis, stop every once in a while to assess the situation. Am I doing all I can do? Are we, as a company, doing all that we can do? Do I feel confident about my decisions, about my ability to continue to manage this crisis? Such questions are meant as additional working tools for you to use during the chronic phase of the crisis.

3.4.2.6 Evaluating the Organization's Handling of the Crisis: Investigations

Post-crisis investigations are needed as long as their focus is on legitimate concerns for public safety and well-being of people. However, they should not be used as witch-hunts or to grab headlines.

> *Broyhill Furniture Plant Explosion and Fire.* Uncovered that the facility had not been inspected for 19 years. It resulted in new regulations requiring state safety workers to conduct a follow-up inspection within five years of any manufacturing plant where a fatality has occurred.

Accounting Industry (*Wall Street Journal,* January 14, 2002):

> (Post-Crisis) Enron Corp.'s collapse — and the failure by its auditor Arthur Andersen LLC to detect questionable bookkeeping — is intensifying the spotlight on the accounting industry's peculiar self-policing system, which since its inception 25 years ago has never called for disciplinary action against any large accounting firm. The government has almost no formal role in monitoring how accounting firms conduct their audits of publicly traded companies. Instead, under the "peer review" system adopted by the industry in 1977, the firms periodically review each other. Questions about the system's effectiveness have been underscored lately by a string of auditing scandals, in which Big Five accounting firms allegedly failed to detect major financial irregularities at companies such as Waste Management Inc., Rite Aid Corp., Sunbeam Corp., Xerox Corp and Enron. Arthur Andersen LLP audited all.

The industry's rules allow firms to withhold audits from peer review while litigation is pending. Critics in Congress and in the accounting profession say the problem may be more fundamental. Former SEC Chairman Arthur Levitt, among others, has taken the industry to task for marketing highly profitable consulting services to the same companies they audit. He has argued that this creates an incentive for firms to go easy on the audits. In 2000, Andersen received $52 million in fees from Enron, of which more than half was for non-audit work, such as consulting. (From "Accounting Scandals Have Some Peering at the Industry's System of Self-Policing.")

American Red Cross — Liberty Fund (*USA Today*, November 6, 2001):

(Acute-Crisis) The American Red Cross acknowledged that some of the $550 million in donations to the Liberty Fund, a special fund established for the victims of the Sept. 11 terrorist attacks, will be used for other broad-based needs instead. But a portion of that money will go to broad-based activities such as a blood reserve program, a national outreach effort, and a telecommunications upgrade. Of the $550 million pledged so far, the Red Cross expects to spend more than $300 million over the next several months on disaster relief related to the attacks.

> $100 million has been set aside for its Family Gift program, which provides victims' families with money to help cover immediate expenses.
> $100 million will go to disaster relief services in New York City, Washington, Pennsylvania and other sites.
> $50 million for a blood readiness and reserve program that would increase the group's blood inventory from two or three days to 10 days
> $26 million in nation-wide community outreach.
> $29 million would be spent on relief infrastructure, including telecommunications, information systems, database management, contribution processing and other overhead costs.
> Normally donations to the Red Cross typically go into its Disaster Relief Fund, a general account designed to meet emergencies of all types.

(9-11) (Company Image) The abrupt resignation of its outspoken president, disputes among board members and criticism that not enough money is going to the victims, have prompted the relief agency to wage a campaign to restore its image. (Exec-Account) High-profile former President Bernadine Healy (57) was forced from her $450,000-a-year post. (10/26/2001). (From "Red Cross reverses itself on Liberty donations," *Philadelphia Inquirer,* November 15, 2001.)

The ARC attempted to fix the problem when it said that all the money donated to the Liberty Fund would go to people affected by the Sept. 11 terrorist attacks, reversing a plan to set aside some of the money for other needs. The Red Cross' interim chief executive officer, Harold Decker, apologized for what he called "a failure in communications between the American Red Cross and the American public."

(*U.S. News & World Report,* November 19, 2001) (Post-Crisis) Typically, the Red Cross has not been in a position of publicly explaining itself to Congress. But there are limits to the charity's independence. It is chartered by Congress and required to operate according to terms outlined by the federal government. The Red Cross can expect either a written reprimand from Congress or another Capitol Hill hearing to discuss possible redress. ("Red Crossroads")

And the spotlight could also engender a slump in giving and in confidence in charities. So now the Red Cross is scrambling to regain the public's good graces. "If we don't subject ourselves to public scrutiny, we will never have public trust," says David McLaughlin, chairman of the Red Cross's board of governors. ("Red Cross may triple aid to victims")

British Petroleum (BP America), (February 7, 1990). When the American Trader oil tanker spilled nearly 400,000 gallons of oil on February 9, 1980, the vessel's owner quickly set up a claims advice office to instruct people as to what types of documents they would need to support a claim and how to keep the records they would need. Claims numbered more than 400 for everything from oil from the beach tracked onto carpets, to business lost while the beach was closed.

(Post-Crisis) Then the oil company assessed its job. Webster candidly said the review showed communications deteriorated at some points. "Messages got confused between point A and point B over items like equipment requirements and the charge that not all workers were sufficiently trained. It took months to fully review the soft spots."

(Hire Consultant) The company hired crisis management consultant Robert Irving, author of the book, *When You Are the Headline,* for a case study. In June it called a conference to share its findings with other oil companies. Interest was not confined to the oil industry. Reports of the success of the operation had brought a flood of inquiries from disaster management people in every line of business, Webster said, from chemicals to consumer products. "It opened up a lot more dialogue about crisis management and its application to non-marine incidents," Webster continued. Oil companies that do not transport by water were also jolted by Valdez. ("After Valdez — Oil Companies Reassess Their Readiness")

3.4.2.7   *Evaluating the Organization's Handling of the Crisis: Change Is Needed*

After the bombing of the World Trade Center in February 1993, it was apparent that there were changes needed in the Prevention and Emergency Response policies of the New York Port Authority.

Changes were made; the building was retrofitted. Changes included:

- The parking garage can be used for tenants only.
- Identification will be needed to use the elevators.
- New Communication and Control Centers will be established in the sky lobbies (where elevators to upper floors are located).
- Stairwells and elevators were to get battery-operated emergency lights and phosphorescent signs.
- Portable backup generators would be set up outside the World Trade Center complex.

Other examples include the following:

Internal Revenue Service, Colorado Springs, Colorado. (Post-Crisis) After a fire, believed to be caused by an arsonist, caused $1 million in damage to its offices, the IRS relocated to a new office with new rules: no one is allowed in without an appointment.

U.S. Postal Service, Washington, D.C. (Post-Crisis) (Change is Needed) Security concerns after the TWA Flight 800 explosion brought a change in airmail handling. Beginning August 16, parcels that weighed a pound or more had to be presented to a post office clerk, instead of dropped in the mailbox. Aim was to decrease chances a bomb will get aboard a plane. Spokesman

Jim Van Loozen said the change was expected to affect less than 1 percent of parcels because most people go to a postal counter anyway. (From *USA Today,* August 8, 1996.)

3.4.2.7.1 Name Changes

Some organizations have changed their organization's name after a crisis or disaster. After the plane crash in Florida, ValuJet Airlines changed its name to AirTran. After the WorldCom scandal broke, WorldCom decided to change its name to MCI.

> *ValuJet Airlines.* Flight-592 crashed into the Everglades after taking off from Miami en route to Atlanta. Encountered a fire near the cockpit. Pilots tried to turn back to Miami. 110 people on board died — 105 passengers and 5 employees. ValuJet was grounded after the crash.

> ValuJet 's planes flew less than half full in January as competitive pricing and a slow travel month cut into the company's discount airline service. Load factor, or percentage of seats filled, was 41.5 percent. Load factor in January 1996 was 48.5 percent. The company has discounted fares in an effort to win back customers after the crash last May and a 3-month federal shutdown that ended in September. The airline reported $54.7 million in costs associated with the crash. (Pre-Crisis) The spotlight is turning to the FAA. There was mounting evidence of ValuJet's alleged maintenance and safety problems. In fact, the FAA released documents that seemed to confirm that its monitoring of the airline was flawed. An internal report by the FAA, completed just nine days before the Florida crash, ranked ValuJet's safety record as the second worst among 14 discount carriers.

> (Post-Crisis) ValuJet acquired another discount airline named AirTran. After the plane crash crisis moved to the Post-Crisis stage, ValuJet changed its name to AirTran. (From *USA Today,* June 18, 1996.)

Chapter 4

STEPS IN MANAGING A CRISIS

4.1 INTRODUCTION

This chapter discusses the major steps to follow after the "pre-crisis situation" has moved to the "acute" stage, where it is visible for all to see, — the employees, the shareholders, the customers, the vendors, government agencies, and the news media.

Contrary to popular belief, a crisis is not necessarily bad. It is characterized by a certain degree of risk and uncertainty. Handled properly, a crisis can position a firm in a positive light. Steven Fink defines crisis management as "the art of removing much of the risk and uncertainty to allow you to achieve more control over your own destiny."

(*Crisis Management: Planning for the Inevitable,* by Steven Fink; AMACOM Publishing, p. 15.)

As I mentioned in Chapter 1, Steven Fink pointed out, crisis management is an art, not a science. Science is knowledge acquired through study or practice, or knowledge covering general truths or the operation of general laws. It is a system or method based on scientific principles. Art is a skill, acquired by experience, study, or observation; the faculty of carrying out a plan.

If it were a science, companies would have no problem hiring a person to fill the role of crisis management officer.

After the situation moves to the Acute-Crisis Stage, the Crisis Management Team should be activated. This act establishes that the executive's have given the Crisis Management Team the authority to take actions necessary to manage the crisis in an effective and timely manner. The Crisis Management Team (CMT) consists of executives with specific expertise that will be needed to support business units and executive management during the crisis. They could include the heads of, or designated representatives of, the following departments:

- Public Relations
- Human Resources
- Facilities
- Security
- Finance
- Insurance
- Purchasing
- Transportation

The responsibilities of the members of the Crisis Management Team will be to:

1. *Take charge quickly.* The CMT needs to take charge quickly, or the crisis will end up dictating the actions that will be taken, rather than having the Crisis Management Team dictating the actions.
2. *Establish the facts.* The CMT should reconstruct the events that led to the crisis. They should determine which employees were directly involved in the incident and speak with those employees about what happened. Getting good information about what happened is difficult. Much of what is being reported is tainted by emotion. Information that is available is also subject to differing interpretations.
3. *Tell your story.* Make contact with all of the important segments of your public (i.e., the media, the general public, customers, shareholders, vendors, and employees).
4. *Fix the problem.* This is the stage in which the tough decisions must be made — and made fast. The goals are to recoup losses, to evaluate the organization's performance, and to make any changes that were identified as needed.

If the CMT follows these steps, it will be able minimize the damage, be it physical damage to the assets or a crisis causing damage to the perception of the organization. The executives (Executive Management Team) will assist the members of the CMT where needed, but their main responsibility will be to continue running the organization.

(***Author Note:*** Chapter 5 discusses in detail the members and roles of the executives during a crisis. Chapter 6 discusses in detail the members and roles of the CMT.)

Now let us look at the details of Step 1: Take charge quickly.

4.1.1 Take Charge Quickly

The first step an organization needs to address when a crisis situation moves to the acute stage is to *take charge quickly*. Taking charge quickly includes activating the Crisis Management Team, identifying the crisis manager (may be different, depending on the type of crisis), establishing a command center, and opening lines of communication.

4.1.1.1 Activate the Crisis Management Team

Immediately after recognizing that the organization is facing an acute-crisis situation, the executives need to activate the CMT and turn the managing of the crisis over to them. This act establishes that the executives have provided the CMT with the authority to take actions necessary to manage the crisis in an effective and timely manner. While the members of the CMT make decisions and take actions, the executives will continue to run the day-to-day organization activities.

The CMT consists of executives with the specific expertise needed to support the business units and executive management during the crisis. They could include the heads of, or designated representatives of, the following departments: Public Relations, Human Resources, Facilities, Security, Finance (Treasury), Insurance (Risk Management), Purchasing (Procurement), Transportation, etc.

The CMT needs to be activated quickly so they can begin to take charge of the situation. This allows them to be *pro*active in managing the crisis, not *re*active.

The members of the CMT should be notified and told where to report (i.e., Command Center). After arriving, the crisis situation should be evaluated and the CMT should determine the actions that need to be taken. They should also clarify who will manage the crisis, based on the "type of crisis."

4.1.1.2 Establish the Crisis Management Command Center

If the crisis has occurred in a location a distance from the organization's headquarters, the crisis manager should go to the spot of the crisis, set up a command post, and open lines of communication. This provides for the crisis manager to be in a position to obtain and digest all the information available on the crisis and monitor the media for the latest developments. (This does not mean that all members of the CMT would go to the spot of the crisis. Many members of the CMT would operate from the command center in, or near, the headquarters building.) (Chapter 7 discusses the command center in more detail.)

By having the crisis manager near the spot of the crisis will show the people affected that your organization is taking the problem seriously. On the other hand, if your organization's senior people do not show up at the site of the crisis, it will appear your management does not care about the problem they have created. Examples in which an organization gave the impression that the management did not care follow.

4.1.1.2.1 The Exxon Crisis in Alaska on March 24, 1989

The president of Exxon Co., USA, William Stevens, did not fly to Alaska until President Bush sent three officials to survey the damage. It took until Thursday (March 30) for Exxon chairman, Lawrence Rawl, to comment publicly. He appeared on television to apologize for the accident.

Any goodwill the company engendered by its early candor could evaporate much faster than the stubborn oil sludge as the company stumbles over cleanup operations and related communications.

According to Gerry Meyers, a Crisis Management expert, the oil giant's biggest mistake was when the Chairman-CEO Lawrence G. Rawl waited six days before discussing the spill — from New York. In Meyers' opinion, Rawl "should have been out of his chair and there (in Alaska) in flying time. You get off your ass and get on the scene, and get your picture taken there. The top guy has got to take charge, step forward and say, 'I am going to personally manage this crisis.'"

Some Crisis Management experts feel Rawl's failure to follow crisis management criteria has soured everything the company has tried since then. That includes Rawl's apologies to Alaska and the United States on TV and to Congress, and a full-page ad that cost $1.8 million to run in 166 newspapers.

They made it appear that he had little interest in the problem, which was growing in leaps and bounds.

4.1.1.2.2 The Coca-Cola problem in Belgium in 1999

After their product allegedly sickened children in Belgium starting on June 10, 1999, the Coca-Cola executives apparently decided that the best person to handle the crisis was the local person in Europe. The executives from the United States did not show up in Europe for over a week.

After having the small crisis explode into a major international crisis, with Coca-Cola's products being removed from shelves all over Belgium, Luxembourg, France, and the Netherlands, the CEO from headquarters decided to go to the Crisis Management Command Center in Belgium.

On June 19, 1999, Coca-Cola Co. Chairman, Douglas Ivester, flew to Europe to oversee the company's efforts to persuade officials and consumers that its beverages were safe and to contain a health scare that had spread across the continent.

The company has been slow to address public concerns, said Paul Holmes, editor and publisher of *Reputation Management,* a publication focused on corporate and brand-name management. "Nobody at Coke in the U.S. took charge of the incident immediately or recognized that it could develop into an international crisis," Holmes said. It costs more to a company's image "the longer you stay silent in the beginning," he said. (From "Coke chief tackles scare in Europe." *Philadelphia Inquirer,* June 19, 1999.)

4.1.1.3 Identify the Person Who Will Manage the Crisis

Why is the crisis manager selected based on the type of crisis? Remember that the CMT consists of executives with different areas of expertise. The executive with the expertise in dealing with the "type" of crisis being faced should manage the crisis. For example:

- If your organization finds that *one of their products is causing harm to the customers,* who would be the likely selection to manage the crisis?
- If your organization has *a financial problem* that is now known by your customers, or your investors or shareholders, or your vendors or suppliers, who would be the likely selection to manage the crisis?
- If your organization has created a *public image problem,* who would be the likely selection to manage the crisis?
- If your organization is faced with an *industrial relations problem,* such as an employee strike, who would be the likely selection to manage the crisis?
- When a *physical disaster caused by an act of nature (e.g., earthquake, flood, tornado, etc.) occurs* at one of your locations, and the building housing your employees is damaged, who would be the likely selection to manage the crisis?
- When a *physical disaster caused by an intentional act (e.g., terrorism, bombing, vandalism, etc.) occurs,* who would be the likely selection to manage the crisis?

You probably would not want the same person to manage each of the crises mentioned above because each crisis requires a different type of expertise. Quite frequently, the people selected to manage one of the preceding examples are:

- If your organization finds that one of their products is causing harm to the customers, the crisis manager would probably be *the head of engineering or operations.*
- If your organization has a financial problem that is now known by your customers, or your investors or shareholders, or your vendors or suppliers, the crisis manager would probably be the *chief financial officer, or if they were the problem, the chief executive officer.*

- If your organization has created a public image problem, the crisis manager would probably be *the head of public relations*.
- If your organization is faced with an industrial relations problem, such as an employee strike, the crisis manager would probably be *the head of human relations*.
- When a physical disaster caused by an act of nature (e.g., earthquake, flood, tornado, etc.) occurs at one of your locations, and the building housing your employees is damaged, the crisis manager would probably be *the business continuity officer*.
- When a physical disaster caused by an intentional act (terrorism, bombing, vandalism, etc.) occurs, the crisis manager would probably be *the head of security*.

4.1.1.4 Let People within Your Organization Know Who the Crisis Manager Is

After determining which member of the CMT will manage the crisis, let people inside your organization know who the manager is. The manager should go to the location of the crisis and set up a command post at that location, if possible. The crisis manager should ensure that lines of communication are opened with the appropriate people, that is, with:

- The media
- Customers
- Investors
- Employees
- Various government officials and agencies

The ongoing communications with specific groups, such as government officials, investors, and customers will be handled by someone other the Crisis Manager or Crisis Communications spokesperson.

4.1.1.5 Take Charge Quickly — Before the Organization Weakens

It is important that your organization acts quickly, before the organization weakens and the employee loyalty begins to fade. The longer it takes for the organization to "take charge," the more likely that it will weaken. Why?

4.1.1.5.1 Organization Weakened by Management Differences

The organization will weaken as soon as middle management begins to openly question whether or not they should follow the executives who allowed the crisis to get out of hand. They may feel that the executives are inefficient, or indecisive. As long as the crisis controls you, and not you controlling the crisis, your leaders will appear to be indecisive. Nothing is worse for an organization than having indecisive leaders.

Decisions and strategies formerly taken for granted are now going to be challenged. Decisions will be debated rather than followed. Management differences emerge and in-fighting will start. The organization's goals are no longer clear.

4.1.1.5.2 Organization Weakened When Employee Loyalty Wanes

The organization could be weakened because the employee loyalty begins to erode. If the crisis gets out of hand, employees will feel embarrassed about their organization, and that they personally are being blamed for the crisis. Once employees feel this way, it is not uncommon to see employees resign from the organization in crisis and join one that is not in crisis. And when employee loyalty begins to erode, placement personnel will start making discreet contacts with the organization's best people. This could contribute to an even greater loss of key personnel.

This loss of key personnel can be a major problem. These are the same people you are counting on to lead the organization back to normalcy. Once they are gone, you have to use alternates. Some alternates are not as strong as the key individuals that have jumped ship.

Another concern is how well were the alternates trained and tested to take over the responsibilities of the employees who have left.

4.1.1.5.3 Organization Weakened by Slow Response

The organization will be weakened when the executives fail to "take charge quickly." The response by Isuzu Motors to a negative article in *Consumer Reports* magazine would appear to be a good example of a slow response.

> *Isuzu Motors Co., 1996. Consumer Reports* magazine warned car buyers to stay away from the Isuzu Trooper sport-utility vehicle. "To consumers considering buying one of these models, our advice is don't." (R. David Pittle; *Consumer Reports'* technical director.) The magazine called a press conference on August 20, 1996, demanding a recall of 1995 and 1996 Troopers. The magazine said its tests showed that the trucks could tip over during emergency maneuvers at speeds as low as 33 mph.

> Car buyers listened: Trooper's sales plunged 83 percent in September from the prior year. Isuzu said the plunge looked especially bad because sales in the year prior were especially strong for the Trooper, according to Susan Von Der Ahe, Isuzu's spokesperson.

Isuzu held a press conference on September 12 to explain that Trooper met all federal safety standards. (From *USA Today*, October 8, 1996.)

This is an example of poor "crisis communications" planning. Isuzu should have responded shortly after the article was published, not three weeks later.

4.1.1.5.4 Weakened When Organization Refuses to Accept That It Has a Crisis

Before an organization can begin "taking charge quickly," it must first recognize that it is experiencing a crisis. No crisis can be managed effectively unless it has first been identified. Many people I have worked with have said that it would be obvious to everyone that the organization is experiencing a crisis. While that is generally true, it is not always the case. Some organizations can be in denial. Look at the following example.

Central Sprinkler Corp., Lansdale, Pennsylvania, 1999. Santa Clara County filed a lawsuit alleging that Central Sprinkler Corp., one of the nation's leading manufacturers of automatic fire sprinklers, was putting out a defective product. Santa Clara County's suit, filed on behalf of any public agency in the nation that may have faulty Central sprinklers, is believed to be the first case brought by the public sector, Acting County Counsel Ann Ravel said. According to the lawsuit, the allegations against Central focus on the company's line of Omega sprinklers made before June 1996. The lawsuit maintains that the sprinklers have failed in at least six instances across the country in the last two years.

Central Sprinkler's spokesperson responded quickly. Within minutes of the government announcement, Central's spokesperson said it "strongly disagrees" with the complaint. "The Omega works. It has been successfully controlling fires for 15 years. We intend to defend our product and our ongoing remediation program."

Central's CEO George G. Meyer blamed the failures not on the sprinkler, but on (1) sloppy work by installers, and (2) the use of illegal leak-stopping products by maintenance workers not employed by his company. (This is another strategy that is frowned upon during a crisis — blaming someone or something else — and is discussed in Chapter 7.)

Tal Briddell, interim CEO who replaced Mr. Meyer, said Central Sprinkler had learned a valuable lesson from the Omega crisis. He said the situation reminded him of a quote from Shakespeare, who said something like, "Learn from life's experience when it is in its infancy. Don't let the challenge mature.… As a general philosophy, if you have a challenge, deal with it early and deal with it effectively." (*Note:* Another way of saying that is "take charge quickly.")

Central Sprinkler was sold on June 15, 1999, to Tyco International. Central chief executive E. Talbot Briddell, a turnaround manager hired last July, said the cost of its Omega sprinkler product-liability crisis —more than $65 million — left the company without enough capital to compete effectively. The sale to Tyco "assures that Central will survive" the Omega crisis and that the firm's 1480 employees will have jobs, Briddell said.

Columbia Broadcasting System, 2004. Just look at the "Memogate" crisis that CBS experienced in September of 2004. There were reports "that insiders were worried that the credibility of the network's news division has been grievously damaged by anchor Dan Rather's persistent defense of a story, which relied on questionable documents about George W. Bush's National Guard service." (*Newsweek*, September 27, 2004.)

After determining that the records were bogus, Mr. Rather apologized — for the questionable records. But he did not apologize to the CBS viewers, nor did he apologize to President Bush. He apologized to the management of the network.

At the same time as the CBS National News program began experiencing a significant drop-off in viewers, CBS News President Andrew Heyward publicly backed Mr. Rather. Apparently CBS, and Mr. Heyward, were unaware that CBS was "in crisis." If they were aware, they would have taken charge quickly, gathered the facts, told their story, and fixed the problem.

"Effect of Taking Charge Slowly. Four CBS News execs got the ax in January after an independent panel issued a scathing report charging they were sloppy with the facts in their "myopic zeal" to get a scoop, running a story about President Bush's National Guard Service based on dubious documents. The bulky 224-page report accuses the sacked newsies and CBS anchor

Dan Rather of rushing a story on to the air even though they had "failed miserably" to make sure it was true. Making matters worse, investigators say, they continued to defend the September 8 piece for nearly two weeks despite strong indications that it hinged on bogus documents. "The fact is that basic journalistic steps were not carried out in a manner consistent with accurate and fair reporting," says the report, "leading to countless misstatements and omissions." The only vaguely positive finding was that Rather did not have a "political bias" as conservatives had charged. "We deeply regret the disservice this flawed 60 Minutes Wednesday report did to the American public," said CBS President Lee Moonves." (From "Bad News," *U.S. News and World Report,* January 24, 2005.)

On the other hand, compare the CBS "Memogate" crisis situation to the one CNN faced with their "Operation Tailwind" story in 1998. CNN-Time claimed in a telecast on June 7, 1998, that the military used sarin gas in Laos during a mission to find and kill Americans who defected during the Vietnam War. According to the story, "Tailwind" was approved by the Nixon White House as well as the CIA, quoting as its main source retired Admiral Thomas Moorer, a Vietnam-era chief of naval operations and chairman of the Joint Chiefs of Staff."

CNN "Takes Charge Quickly," 1998. When the story created a firestorm, CNN hired First Amendment lawyer Floyd Abrams to investigate the report. Abrams concluded that the story was broadcast and published based on information that could not be proven and where evidence indicated that the reporters overlooked contradictory evidence.

Based on the findings of Abrams, CNN took charge quickly when it:

> Retracted the report alleging U.S. military use of nerve gas during Operation Tailwind
> Also disowned the work of Jack Smith and April Oliver, the two producers
> Terminated Smith and Oliver (CNN said the firing was necessary on a story alleging war crimes and cover-up at the highest levels of government)

Now let us look at the second step to address when a crisis situation moves to the acute stage: "establish the facts."

4.1.2 Establish the Facts

The second step an organization needs to address when a crisis situation moves to the acute stage is to "establish the facts." Establishing the facts includes reconstructing the information to obtain the facts, recognizing the problems that will be encountered.

4.1.2.1 Facts Not Completely Known

Many times, the facts are not known at the time the crisis moves to the acute stage. There are many versions of the story; some are rumors, and others are exaggerations.

> The problem in this stage is that usually you don't know what you don't know. There may be too little information, or there may be far too much, with no way to sift out what is important.
>
> **—Norman Augustine**
> "Managing the Crisis You Tried to Prevent,"
> *Risk Management Magazine*, 1996.

4.1.2.2 Information Tainted

Getting good information about what is happening is difficult. Much of what is being reported is tainted by emotion. Some of the other information that is available is subject to differing interpretations.

Your organization may have to investigate the information that is available to determine the facts. In the early stages of the investigation, it is important for the organization to find out which employees were involved with the crisis. The officials responsible to establish the facts should speak with those employees who were directly involved in the situation.

Getting good, accurate, unbiased information about what happened, or is happening, is difficult sometimes. In many cases, the information being provided by an employee is being influenced by emotions. When a number of employees are providing information, it is normal to have stories that differ. This is because the information is subject to differing perceptions and interpretations.

For example, I have read a number of stories following an explosion and fire where one employee has been quoted as saying, "I heard the explosion and then saw a fireball." Another eyewitness account was, "I saw the fire and then heard an explosion." Which was eyewitness was right? It is difficult to tell because there are emotional responses that could affect their perception. You would have to know the emotional state of the eyewitness at the time they were talking.

Absorb all the information available on the crisis: the information provided by eyewitnesses, and the latest developments being reported by the news media.

4.1.2.3 Gather Information: Use Crisis Communications Team Members

Obviously, the "crisis manager" cannot be out gathering facts and also be responding to all other aspects of the crisis at the same time. The Crisis Communications Team needs to assign people to specific areas being affected by the crisis. The assigned people should report back to the Crisis Communications Team from the scene, or from any departments the impact of the crisis reaches. This will provide the organization's crisis manager with up-to-date information.

> (***Author Note***: Chapter 7 discusses the Crisis Communications Team in more detail.)

4.1.2.4 Prepare Your Story

After identifying the "facts," the crisis manager, along with the Crisis Communications spokesperson, should prepare the organization's story. No matter how terrible the event is, you can still influence the perception of your company when telling your story. Let there be no misunderstanding in preparing your story; be honest, factual, and concerned. Also, be willing to accept whatever blame rightfully attaches to the company (see PECO example).

4.1.2.5 Get and Give Facts as Early as Possible

The important thing for the organization to remember is they have to *get and give facts as early as possible*. When your organization is the victim of a disaster, or of a crisis, you are in the spotlight. The news media will ensure that everyone is looking at your organization and, in turn, your executives. So it is incumbent upon you to get your story out quickly.

4.1.2.6 Difficulty in Getting an Accurate Story out Quickly

A good example of the difficulty in establishing the facts immediately is the story given after the terrorist attack on the USS Cole destroyer that killed 17 sailors and injured 39 in Yemen in October 2000.

> The initial reports on the bombing given by the Navy said that "the destroyer had tied up at a fuel station in the port of Aden

nearly two hours before the bombing." Admiral Vern Clark, chief of naval operations, told reporters that the Cole crew's "ability to deal with this kind of attack" had been "limited" by the mooring operation that he said was under way.

A week later, the Navy revised its account of the terrorist attack. The Navy explained that the original story had been based on unconfirmed reports from the stricken ship. Now it said it had obtained additional information from the Cole's records that changed at least three points of fact in the official timeline:

1. The explosion occurred at 11:18 a.m. local time, or about an hour earlier than originally reported.
2. Refueling began at 10:30 a.m. and was going on at the time of the attack. Earlier, the Navy said refueling had not yet begun.
3. The Cole was completely tied up at the fueling dock in Aden harbor at 9:30 a.m., nearly two hours before the attack. The Navy had said the mooring operation was completed just minutes before.

A Navy representative explained the changes by stating that "As is often the case, these initial relayed reports contained some errors and in some cases were misunderstood." This points out that as part of your Crisis Communications strategy, you should endeavor to have basic information prepared ahead of time as part of your pre-planning efforts. Using these statements, along with some of the early information you have gleaned, you are prepared to provide an initial news media briefing shortly after the crisis breaks. Then you must continue to gather information, sort out the rumors and exaggerations, establish only the facts, and provide additional briefing for the media with new or changed information.

I remember reading the details of the Tylenol incident. In one of the early media briefings, the crisis communications spokesperson assured the media that the type of cyanide found in the capsules that were tampered with was not found anywhere inside the McNeil Labs buildings. A couple days later he found out that there was a container of cyanide located in one of the maintenance rooms of a building.

Continue to gather information and provide additional update briefings. The spokesperson immediately called a media briefing in which he revealed that there was a container found in a maintenance room, but it had not been opened. The fact that he was forthcoming with the media eliminated the concern on the part of the reporters, and the cyanide in the building never became an issue.

4.1.2.7 Inaccurate Information

Another reason you have to be prepared to get your story out quickly is due to *inaccurate information*. On occasion, a story is written based on incorrect information. If you do not respond to it quickly, the perception of readers and listeners of the news media is that the story is true. Take a look at the following example.

> *Plain Dealer of Cleveland newspaper, 1998.* The *Plain Dealer of Cleveland* newspaper published a story in January 1998 that the FAA had found serious safety-related violations at the AirTran Airline Company. Violations included falsified documents and faulty repairs. The documents, based on a three-week inspection that ended November 7, showed that the airline had more serious violations than the 1996 report that recommended that ValuJet be grounded. (From *USA Today,* January 12, 1998.)
>
> AirTran officials responded quickly by first saying that they "understand that the outcome (of the probe) was excellent." Then they began gathering the facts related to the special inspection. Then on January 14, 1998, *USA Today* published a story that indicated that federal aviation officials said that a special inspection found no systemic safety problems at AirTran despite a published report indicating widespread trouble at the discount airline. FAA managers said action already would have been taken against the airline if serious problems had been found.

Another example is given in which an environmental group felt that a news media source was reporting "inaccurate information" in 2000.

> *ABC Television, 20/20 Show.* When John Stossel presented a report in July 2000 on ABC's *20/20* television show questioning the safety of organic produce, the Environmental Working Group was quite upset. The report, first aired in February and repeated in July, seemed to debunk the common belief that organic foods may be safer than regular foods because no pesticides are used. Stossel said on the air that tests conducted on produce for ABC News "surprisingly found no pesticide residue on the conventional samples or the organic."
>
> The environmental group knew this could not be right. They went about gathering the facts. They said that chicken had been tested for pesticides at ABC's request, and that traces were found on the regular poultry but not on the organic poultry.

That finding, favorable to the organic-food proponents, was not mentioned on the show. They contended that pesticide tests on produce were never conducted for the show.

After an investigation, ABC confirmed that the tests were not done. ABC said Stossel had relied on inaccurate information provided to him by a staff member. "We are reviewing the circumstances surrounding the error." A producer mistakenly believed that a test done on chicken had also been done on produce.

ABC News has acknowledged that a 20/20 report by John Stossel questioning the safety of organic produce was wrong and that the reporter would apologize on the air for his mistake on the next show. (From *USA Today,* August 9, 2000.)

Now let us look at the third step to address when a crisis situation moves to the acute stage: "tell your story."

4.1.3 Tell Your Story

Step 3 in managing the crisis in its acute stage is to "tell your story." Telling your story includes selecting your spokesperson, making contact with the media, and also making contact with your customers, shareholders (if you have shareholders), and employees.

4.1.3.1 *Spokesperson: Who Should Be the Spokesperson?*

Organizations must make this decision before a crisis strikes. This decision should become part of the Crisis Communications Plan "policy."

> (***Author Note:*** Chapter 7 discusses the "Crisis Communications Plan" in detail.)

Should the spokesperson be the CEO? Or should the spokesperson be the head of Community or Public Relations?

In many cases today, the spokesperson is the CEO. This usually works for consumers because they feel that the organization cares about the crisis and what it did to the community.

It also works well with the news media because they feel they will receive less "spin" from the CEO than they might from a crisis communications or public relations person. (Most crisis communications specialists or public relations people know how to answer the questions and how to deal with the news media in general.)

On the other hand, some CEOs are not the best spokespeople. While they are very strong at running an organization, marketing their products or services, dealing with shareholders and government agencies, they may not be able to show the proper concern for the incident to the media.

> After the Exxon Valdez oil spill, Exxon did not have Lawrence Rawl as the spokesperson. Instead, Exxon selected Dave Parish as the official spokesperson. In addition, Frank Iarossi, president of Exxon Shipping Co., was also a spokesperson. Within 48 hours after the Exxon Valdez struck an undersea reef off the Alaskan coast, Iarossi, acting as a spokesperson, said that Exxon took financial responsibility for the oil spill. He also told reporters that an uncertified officer was piloting the tanker at the time of the collision.

> In hindsight, not having Rawl as the spokesperson may have been a bad decision, but that is hindsight. One of Rawl's strengths may not have public relations. If that is the case, then Exxon did not make the wrong decision by having another person as spokesperson.

> Such a plan anticipates who is in charge the minute events demand a response. Delegating authority to a designated spokesperson and giving that individual authority to contact media, issue an initial statement, provide background information, et c. is essential to minimize the damage. (From "In Business, One's Reputation is the Bottom Line," by Alan Caruba, *Disaster Recovery Journal*, September 1994.)

4.1.3.2 Make Contact with the Media

Making contact with the media is a requirement. You need to gather the facts regarding the crisis. (Step 2 in Managing), and tell your story (Step 3 in Managing).

Recognize that in the age of instant news, there is no such thing as a "private" crisis. No matter how terrible the event is, there is still your story. Provide the company's interpretation of the event. Be sure to give background information and any pertinent prior events.

In your initial briefing, tell the media what you can. Be honest, factual, concerned, and willing to accept whatever blame rightfully attaches to the organization. The organization that is willing to take the blame — willing to accept whatever blame rightfully attaches to the company — will be able to put the crisis behind quickly. More importantly, this stance will win the critics over as well.

An example of accepting whatever blame rightfully attaches to the organization is the PECO Energy Co. headquartered in Philadelphia, Pennsylvania.

On December 19, 1995, a gas leak caused an explosion that killed two people and seriously injured a third. PECO received a report of a gas odor at 12:31 a.m., but its emergency technician did not arrive on the scene until 1 hour and 45 minutes later. By that time, the gas that was leaking caused one home to explode and the adjoining twin to burst into flames. (PECO's unofficial policy is to respond within one hour to reports of leaks).

PECO threw away what is often the standard corporate playbook when it shouldered the blame for the explosion. (The standard corporate play book is to avoid any responsibility for the incident.) "PECO Energy takes full responsibility" for failing to respond to reports of a leak in time to avert the tragedy, CEO Corbin A. McNeill, Jr., said in a prepared statement. He called PECO's delay in dispatching a technician "unacceptable and regrettable."

McNeill acknowledged that his words could make the company more vulnerable to lawsuits and damage judgments. But he said it was the right thing to do, both morally and pragmatically, "regardless of any potential increases in liability." It was morally right because "we recognize that we had not responded properly, and there was such a tragic outcome that we ought to come forward and admit that." But it was a good business decision as well. "The community wants to deal with a company that has integrity and accountability, and this is the way to achieve that."

But PECO has won plaudits for admitting forthrightly that it failed to respond promptly to reports of a leak.

PECO's acceptance of blame was called "refreshing candor" that "doesn't happen very often" by Edmund B. Spaeth, Jr., a dean of the Philadelphia Bar, who is of counsel at Pepper, Hamilton I & Scheetz and teaches professional responsibility at the University of Pennsylvania Law School. Usually, companies say they are afraid to admit responsibility for fear it will expose them to liability, Spaeth said.

Honesty can be good a good business decision, according to Steven B. Fink, president of Lexicon Communications Corp., a Los Angeles public relations and crisis management firm. Even companies that try to cover up their liability are frequently sued, so it is not clear how much money is saved in stonewalling. Meanwhile, the waffling can destroy customer loyalty, employee morale, and investor confidence — creating problems that are much more serious.

More companies are seeing "how breathtakingly powerful honesty is," according to Brian Tierney, President of Tierney & Partners, a Philadelphia public relations and crisis management firm. Still, "a lot of companies just don't have the nerve to do it."

4.1.3.3 Dealing with the Media

During the initial meeting, assure the media that you will stay in touch. It is a good idea to schedule news media briefings every day. Tell them what you have found out since the last briefing, and encourage them to contact you if they have useful information to pass on. This will give you a "heads-up" on any rumors that may have started. Your organization wants to correct any rumors before they become fact.

> "First state clearly that you do not know all the facts. Then promptly state the facts you do know. One's objective should be to get it right, get it quick, get it out, and get it over. You see, your problem won't improve with age."

> **—Warren Buffet**

When dealing with the media, be prepared to answer the following questions:

- What did you know?
- When did you know it?

Remember that a "no comment" can imply guilt and that it is often best to take your lumps in one big news story, rather than in dribs and drabs.

4.1.3.3.1 Do Not Provide Misinformation

In an era of instant news, with a sophisticated public demanding answers, one cannot ignore the press or present misinformation, instead of the facts. All the misinformation does for the company is provide an environment where anger results when the true dimension of the situation is revealed.

> *Three Mile Island crisis, 1979.* As pointed out in Steven Fink's book *Crisis Management: Planning for the Inevitable*, the Three Mile Island crisis has become a legendary example of how "not to manage" a crisis. As Fink points out, the term "crisis management" was literally born as the nuclear reactor was dying.

> (***Author Note:*** The executives for three Mile Island provided so much misinformation that no one knew what to believe and what was "spin.")

> Fink goes on to point out that five years after the Three Mile Island event, the first-ever graduate school program in crisis management was started by Carnegie Mellon University in Pittsburgh.

What is frequently forgotten is that news is now. Instant electronic media communications of news requires an on-the-spot response. It cannot be postponed until the following day "when we have reviewed all the facts" because the facts are that something went terribly wrong or that a charge has been leveled of misconduct.

4.1.3.4 Make Contact with the Employees

Communicate with employees before their loyalties begin to erode. The employees feel embarrassed that their organization has caused the problem. Some employees feel they are personally being blamed for the crisis.

4.1.3.4.1 Employees Personally Blamed

Employees at Exxon Corp.'s Credit Card Center in Houston were under a state of siege for two months as angry customers — including more than 17,000 who canceled their accounts — vehemently protested the Alaskan oil spill. They had to apologize on behalf of their company dozens of times a day.

> Workers at the credit card center had to resort to wearing special gloves to handle protest letters purposely soaked with oil. They spent hours piecing together torn-up credit cards to determine the account numbers that customer's wanted canceled. One employee said, "There are mornings when I don't want to go to work. I just tell myself I can't let it get to me." Many of the returned credit cards were torn to shreds, covered in oil, or burned. They also were accompanied by notes reading, "You ought to be hung" for the oil spilled by an Exxon Shipping Co. tanker March 24.
>
> The crisis took its toll through out the Exxon organization. Employees, confronted daily by criticisms of Exxon in the media and by friends and family members, were questioning their faith in the corporate giant. "It's been deeply painful for every employee that I've worked with, talked with and met," said Larry Stockman, a psychologist on retainer with Exxon. "They feel devastated by what's happened." A week and a half into the crisis, one of the women at the card center hung up after a call from an enraged customer and started to cry. One by one, her office mates started crying as well. Stockman said employees are "embarrassed, they're hurt, they're sad. Some are angry, but that passes because they don't know who to be angry with. It's like a death." (Excerpted from an article entitled "Morale Sinks at Exxon as Hate Mail Pours in," *Philadelphia Daily News,* May 22, 1989.)

As a result of their embarrassment or stress, many employees will resign from the organization. They will look to find another organization that does not have a crisis. The unexpected loss of key employees will weaken any organization, and in some organizations the loss of key individuals creates another crisis.

4.1.3.4.2 Resign from Organization during Crisis

Employee morale at Arthur Andersen is taking a beating as the accounting giant's reputation is tarnished. Workers are grappling with tough questions about how the company's predicament could imperil their own careers.

> "When the image of a company is tarnished, that leads to turn-over," says Elaine Hollensbe, an assistant professor in management at the University of Cincinnati. "Employees may not want to be identified with a company when there's impropriety going on."
>
> "If the code of ethics isn't followed at the top, the blocks tumble," says Nan DeMars, an ethics behaviorist and author of *You Want Me To Do What?* on workplace ethics. "People always championed Arthur Andersen. Now they're embarrassed. Their confidence is shaken. Andersen carried a reputation for integrity and competence in the fields of auditing and accounting." Now the reputation is in tatters. ("Andersen employees' morale rattled," from *USA Today,* January 21, 2002.)

The crisis management team should inform the employees about the situation and how they are managing it. Employees feel embarrassed that their organization and they personally are being blamed for the crisis (see Exxon example). This can result in some of the better employees "jumping ship." The last thing the organization needs at a time like this is to have employees consider leaving the company in the middle of a crisis. After all, these are the people who are going to play an instrumental role in the recovery.

4.1.3.5 Make Contact with the Customers

Customers will become worried. Your organization needs to contact them and assure them that you have the situation under control.

4.1.3.5.1 Coca-Cola — Europe, 1999

Douglas Ivester's initial public response to the crisis did not come until June 22, 1999, when he issued a statement saying

Coke would do whatever it took to ensure the quality of its products. He then flew to Brussels for a quick visit, but he made no public appearance while there. His lack of public visibility throughout the week made it seem Coke was not being totally open about what was happening, especially on a matter of high importance to Europeans.

While Coke did a good job describing what went wrong two weeks ago, before them now is the harder task of rebuilding the trust of its consumers. "The public fundamentally does not trust big companies, and they tend to believe negative health information," says Eric Dezenhall of Nichols-Dezenhall, a Washington, D.C., firm that advises companies on how to deal with emergencies.

"The company has to address two questions from its customers: 'Am I going to be OK?' and 'What are you doing about it?' (From "CEO Washes Down Crow with a Tall Glass of Coke," *USA Today,* June 22, 1999.)

4.1.3.5.2 Arnotts Ltd., Australia, 1997

An extortionist tampered with six packets of Arnott's biscuits on a shelf in a Brisbane supermarket in 1997. Australia's largest cookie-maker conducted a nationwide recall of its products after a threat was made to poison its products on supermarket shelves.

Mr. Chris Roberts, the former managing director of Arnott's biscuits, who was thrust into the public glare of daily television interviews, said the plan required that they protect the interest of all stakeholders — the consumers, the company and its shareholders — and work through the incident as quickly as possible.

Tell Your Story — "We did everything in front of television cameras, the withdrawal of products from the shelf, the trucks dumping the products at the tip and later the restocking of supermarkets. We ran information ads in different states because in each state the circumstances were different." He said it was a campaign designed to show that Arnott's had been completely open and it worked. "We came out of that fiasco smelling like a rose."

In a lesson well learned, "Arnott's followed a script written in 1982 after the still-unsolved murders of seven people in Chicago

who had swallowed cyanide substituted for the analgesic Tylenol."
(From the *Age Newspaper,* Australia, June 8, 2000.)

4.1.3.6 Make Contact with the Shareholders or Investors

Investors will begin selling stock shortly after learning of the crisis. This
selling of stock will continue until the investors feel that the organization
is in control. Some examples of where worried investors began selling
the organization's stock include the following.

4.1.3.6.1 Cendant Corporation, 1998

Cendant revealed that that CUC Int'l was responsible for
"accounting errors made with an intent to deceive" and "fictitious
revenues." CUC International Inc., (Stamford, CT) merged with
HFS Inc. of Parsippany in December to form Cendant. CUC
International was in the business of discount travel, dining and
shopping clubs, while HFS was a franchiser, Ramada, Avis, Days
Inn, Coldwell Banker and Century 21.

Cendant said CUC artificially inflated its revenue by classifying
re-structuring charges as revenues, recording long-term revenue
as short-term revenue, and delaying recognition of membership
cancellations. The company also invented "fictitious revenues"
for the first three quarters of 1997.

Worried investors began selling stock — Panicked investors
dumped Cendant's shares and by mid-summer Cendant had lost
nearly $23 billion in market value.

Cendant cleaned up its books. It lowered previously reported
earnings for 1997, 1996 and for 1995. The announcements did
win back support on Wall Street and begin the recouping of
about $20 billion in market value the company had lost.

Cendant, slammed by accounting irregularities in 1997, is the
new comeback kid. The franchiser of motels — Ramada Inn,
Days Inn, and Howard Johnson — and owner of Avis and
Budget rental cars has cleaned its balance sheet, paid off debt,
improved governance, and now generates $2 a share in free
cash flow, notes Robert Lyon, president of Institutional Capital
which owns 2.5 percent of Cendant in its $10 billon portfolio.
(From "Cendant Comes Back," *Business Week,* May 12, 2003.)

4.1.3.6.2 Freddie Mac, 2003

Mortgage-market giant Freddie Mac announced abruptly yesterday (June 9, 2003) that it had fired its president because he did not fully cooperate with an internal review of the company's accounting, which also is being investigated by federal regulators. In a surprise shake-up, the government-sponsored company whose stock is widely traded said that it had fired the president and chief operating officer, David Glenn, and that the chairman and chief executive officer, Leland Brendsel, had resigned. Vaughn Clarke, the McLean, Va., company's executive vice president and chief financial officer, also resigned.

Freddie Mac is the nation's second-largest buyer of mortgages. The company does not believe fraud or criminal misconduct was involved, said Gregory Parseghian, the new president and CEO, told shareholders, financial analysts and reporters in a conference call yesterday.

Worried investors began selling stock — Freddie Mae shares dropped 16 percent, or $9.61, to close at $50.26 each on the New York Stock Exchange. The loss wiped out about $7 billion in shareholder value. (*Philadelphia Inquirer*, June 10, 2003.)

4.1.3.6.3 HealthSouth Corporation, 2003

HealthSouth's board of directors fired the company's chairman and CEO, bringing Richard Scrushy's reign at the rehabilitation hospital chain he founded in 1984 to an inglorious end. The board had placed Scrushy on administrative leave two weeks ago, when the SEC charged him with masterminding a scheme to inflate HealthSouth's earnings by at least $1.4 billion since 1999.

Worried investors began selling stock — The rehabilitation center company, whose stock has plummeted since the accounting scandal, was dropped from the New York Stock Exchange and trades for pennies. Last year, it traded in the $15 range but had sunk to $3.91 March 19, when the SEC suspended trading in the stock. (*USA Today*, April 1, 2003.)

4.1.3.6.4 Rite Aid Corp. of Camp Hill, Pennsylvania, 1999

On October 18, 1999, Rite Aid Corp. of Camp Hill announced that it had inflated its profits by about $500 million the last three years and that its chairman and chief executive officer, Martin L. Grass, had resigned.

Worried investors began selling stock — Rite Aid, which began as a single drugstore in Scranton, is the nation's third-largest discount drugstore chain, and the largest in the Philadelphia region. Rite Aid's outstanding common stock was valued at $11 a share, sharply off the $51.125 a share at which Rite Aid stock was trading in January of 1999. (*Philadelphia Inquirer*, October 19, 1999.)

4.1.3.6.5 Tyco International, 2003

Worried investors began selling stock — Shares of Tyco International Ltd. tumbled after the company fired the president of its fire and security systems division and lowered its profit outlook because of accounting problems in that department. (*USA Today*, March 4, 2003.)

Now let us look at the fourth step to address when a crisis situation moves to the acute stage: Fix the Problem.

4.1.4 Fix the Problem

The fourth step an organization needs to address when a crisis situation moves to the acute stage is to "fix the problem." Fixing the problem includes trying to recoup the losses and making any changes that were identified as being needed.

Following the crisis, an organization must concentrate on survival. It can do this by trying to recoup the losses sustained as a result of the crisis. A good example is Johnson & Johnson/McNeil Labs. While there was no way it was going to recover the losses of the recalled capsules, it wanted to regain the market share that Tylenol had prior to the tampering incident. As a result of the executives knowing what their corporate culture was, and their commitment to the safety of their consumers, they were able to exhibit such a concern for the customers that the customers felt they did not have to buy a competitor's product.

After a crisis is visible for all to see, culpability is not the issue — how the company managed the crisis is the issue. Throughout the crisis, the Tylenol manufacturer showed everyone that it was trying to "fix the problem."

"You have to be able to identify the problem and be able to say you're fixing it. If you're not fixing it, you don't have much to say." This quote from Mary I. Woodall, group director of the special-situations unit of Hill & Knowlton public relations firm, when commenting on Exxon's

Oil Spill in Alaska in 1989, shows the difference in perspective with the management of the two early crises that everyone uses to build their Crisis Management Plan.)

4.1.4.1   Recoup Losses

One of the best ways to recoup losses is to have the executives show consumers that they care about what the crisis did to them, and furthermore to show the consumers what the organization is doing to prevent this from happening again. An example of executives showing that they care about what the crisis did to the consumers is to show consumers you care about what happened to them.

4.1.4.1.1   Show Consumers You Care About What Happened to Them

To show consumers that they care about what happened to them, some organizations have taken full-page advertisements in newspapers around the country. A couple organizations that used ads in newspapers include:

> *Veryfine Products Inc., Littleton, Massachusetts, 1989.* Veryfine is an apple-juice manufacturer. They learned that *60 Minutes* would probe the safety of Alar (Daminozide), a growth regulator used on apples. Veryfine quickly moved to spread word that it had stopped processing Alar-treated apples in 1986.

> (Ads in newspapers) To drive the message home, the company placed advertisements in newspapers in its 20 largest markets. The executive vice president believes that Veryfine responded well to the crisis. But he also thinks that the company's crisis management skills could be sharpened. "We need to have more formal data and more formal plans available and ready to act on." (From "Keeping a Crisis from Careening toward Catastrophe," by Barbara Carton.)

> *Sears Roebuck & Co., Auto Repairs, 1992.* Between January and April of 1992, state investigators paid 12 visits to 6 Sears shops. A wire had been disconnected causing the alternator light to keep lighting. It could have been fixed for $5 to $10. The shops did not fix the wire, instead they wrote estimates for unnecessary repairs that averaged $400. Consumer officials in California began action to revoke state auto-repair certificates at all 72 California Sears auto-shops after an 18-month probe showed the facilities allegedly overcharged undercover investigators an average $233. Sears agreed to pay $200,000 to settle accusations

arising from a consumer fraud investigation of its auto repair centers in NJ. Sears shops wrote estimates for unnecessary repairs that averaged $400. Sears will also: (1) stop paying commissions to car repair employees, (2) eliminate goals for selling specific products and hire outsiders to pose as consumers to check on workers.

(Ads in newspapers) Sears began an advertising blitz aimed at repairing damage done to its auto-repair business charges of overcharging and fraud. Ogilivy & Mather Inc. designed the ads in which Edward Brennan, Sears Chairman, acknowledges that "mistakes have occurred". He explains the steps Sears has taken to guard against such things happening in the future. "When our integrity is on the line, we must do more than just react — we must overreact," Brennan said. (From *Philadelphia Inquirer,* September 12, 1992.)

Intel Corporation, Pentium Chip Error, November 7, 1994. After receiving a call from a math professor at Lynchburg College (Virginia) that he noticed his Pentium-based computer was making mistakes, Intel pleaded ignorance. Intel says typical user would encounter wrong answer once every 27,000 years. After some complex calculations, IBM announced the chances of getting an error from the Pentium chip were much higher than Intel claimed — once every 24 days, not once every 27,000 years.

Intel stock falls 2 percent on 11-25-1994 in Wall Street's first reaction to publicity about the flaw.

"Intel is being painted as the Exxon of the chip industry. Eventually Exxon cleaned up the Valdez mess, but it never cleaned up its image," according to Dan Hutchinson, president of VLSI Research, in San Jose, California.

(Ads in newspapers) On 12/02/1994, seven weeks after the crisis erupted, Intel began running ads in major newspapers saying it wants to "sincerely apologize." "To some users, the old policy seemed arrogant and uncaring. We were motivated by a feeling that this (replacement of the chip) was not necessary for most people." After Grove announced the new policy, Intel's stock rose 3-7/16 to $61-1/4 a share. Analysts and investors saw this move (apologize on Internet and in newspapers) as the stopping of the crisis.

In cases following disasters, organizations have used newspapers to thank the local authorities and vendors and employees for their assistance during the crisis. The Olin Corporation took full-page ads out in a number of the newspapers in Connecticut and New York following the fire that damaged its Stamford headquarters in 1981. This type of response was used by the following organizations — Northwest Bank following the fire in their headquarters building in Minneapolis in 1982, First Interstate Bank following the fire in their headquarters building in Los Angeles in 1988, and Penn Mutual Insurance Company following the fire in their headquarters building in Philadelphia in 1989. (These are just a few examples of organizations that have taken the opportunity to use ads in newspapers to help the image during their efforts to recoup their losses.)

Some organizations have even sent letters to individual customers explaining the situation. An example of an organization whose CEO took the story directly to the customers was:

> *US Airways, 1994.* After USAir light 427 crashed approaching the Pittsburgh airport, killing all 132 on board, USAir chairman (Seth Schofield) mailed letters to one million of the airline's most-frequent fliers assuring them that USAir is safe. Schofield reiterated that he would ground USAir's fleet if he had any qualms about the company's safety. "Safety never has been, not ever will be compromised at USAir," he said. (*USA Today,* October 4, 1994.)

4.1.4.2 Make Any Changes That Were Identified as Being Needed

One example that can validate the need for change to "fix the problem" is the Johnson & Johnson Tylenol incident.

> In 1982, the division of Johnson & Johnson's that manufactured Tylenol (McNeil Labs) was faced with a tampering incident that resulted in the deaths of eight people. An unknown individual placed cyanide in Tylenol capsules. While the company truly was an innocent victim, it needed to ensure the public's safety and to restore trust in the company. J&J/McNeil pulled 30 million capsules from store shelves and home medicine cabinets around the nation. They gave all consumers full credit for any capsules they returned. There was a cost associated, but the cost of protecting a reputation that would have been tarnished would have been much costlier.
>
> (Fix of the problem) They redesigned the packaging to protect against future tampering. The result of their crisis management

efforts was that within three months Tylenol regained 95 percent of its pre-crisis market share.

Many organizations whose products have been determined a safety hazard have recalled their products to "fix the problem" and to ensure that no additional people were injured or sickened. There are too many to list.

4.1.4.2.1 Some Organizations Have Made Changes to the Management of the Organization

City of Chicago, 1992, Change in Management. After the City of Chicago experienced the flood in the tunnels under the Chicago River in April 1992, the Mayor of Chicago terminated a number of people for failing to fix the leak when they first found out about it.

The American Red Cross, 2001. After the terrorist attacks on 9-11, the Red Cross took the unusual step of creating a special account for donations that was designated specifically for terrorism relief efforts. They termed this special account The Liberty Fund. After an estimated $550 million was donated to the fund, the American Red Cross acknowledged that it planned to use some of the $550 million in donations to the Liberty Fund for other broad-based needs instead, such as a blood reserve program, a national outreach effort, and a telecommunications upgrade. Of the $550 million pledged so far, Red Cross spokesman Mitch Hibbs said, the Red Cross expects to spend more than $300 million on disaster relief related to the attacks. (From "Red Cross diverting some disaster funds," *San Diego Union-Tribune*, October 30, 2001.)

The American Red Cross came under heavy criticism from members of Congress on Tuesday for not funneling all of the $564 million it raised after the Sept. 11 terrorist attacks directly to victims.

Bernadine Healy, the controversial Red Cross president, bore the brunt of the congressional ire as members of a House subcommittee looked into how charities are distributing more than $1.1 billion in donations collected since the attacks.

(Change in Management) Healy announced October 26 that she would resign at the end of the year. (From "Red Cross assailed on victim funds," *USA Today*, November 7, 2001.)

Adelphia Communications, 2002. Adelphia Communications disclosed that over the past few years, it funneled millions — often without the board's knowledge — to private businesses controlled by founder John Rigas and his family.

(Change in Management) John Rigas and sons Timothy, Michael and James resigned from their jobs at Adelphia and left the board. (From "SEC filing reveals Rigas' use of Adelphia's assets," *USA Today,* May 28, 2002.)

The Boeing Company, 2003. (Change in Management) Boeing is taking disciplinary action against 6 current employees, including demoting the head of its Delta IV military rocket program, after determining they were embroiled in corporate espionage that netted the company proprietary Lockheed Martin Corp. documents in the late 1990s. Boeing hopes the move will help persuade the Air Force that the company has cleaned up its ethical lapses and should be reinstated as a Pentagon rocket supplier. (From "Boeing Employees Are Disciplined In Espionage Case," *Wall Street Journal,* December 12, 2003.)

4.1.4.2.2 Some Organizations Have Made Changes to Their Policies and Procedures

World Trade Center, New York City, 1993. After the bombing of the World Trade Center in February 1993, it was apparent that there were changes needed in the Prevention and Emergency Response policies of the New York Port Authority. The building was retrofitted. Some changes made included:

> The parking garage can be used for tenants only.
> Identification will be needed to use the elevators.
> New Communication and Control Centers will be established in the sky lobbies (where elevators to upper floors are located).
> Stairwells and elevators were to get battery operated emergency lights, phosphorescent signs.
> Portable backup generators would be set up outside the World Trade Center complex.

Alamo Rent-a-Car, 1993. Police believe people driving rental cars may be singled out by violent robbers who prey on visitors. An Alamo logo was on the front of the car rented to Berlin schoolteacher Barbara Meller Jensen, who was beaten to death after getting lost on her way out of Miami international Airport.

(Change) Alamo Rent a Car, stung by the slayings of 2 German customers vacationing in FL, is removing logos and stickers that identify vehicles as rental. Hertz and Avis took similar action earlier. (From *USA Today,* May 6, 1993.)

Now let us move on to Chapter 5, "The Executive Management Team."

Chapter 5

THE EXECUTIVE MANAGEMENT TEAM

5.1   INTRODUCTION

Chapter 5 focuses on the role of the Executive Management Team (EMT) during the three stages of a crisis; that is, during the Pre-Crisis stage, the Acute-Crisis stage, and the Post-Crisis stage.

During the Pre-Crisis stage, the EMT plays the major role. The EMT's responsibility includes recognizing that the organization is faced with a developing situation that could be disruptive to the organization and preventing it from moving into the Acute stage.

During the Acute stage, the role the EMT plays is a more minor role as it relates to managing the crisis situation. The major role now continues to be to manage the day-to-day operations of the organization. The EMT will turn the managing of the acute crisis over to the Crisis Management Team (CMT). The members of the CMT have unique areas of expertise that are needed when the crisis is most volatile. When the crisis is turned over to the CMT, the authority to take action to manage the crisis effectively is also turned over to them. (The CMT is discussed in detail in Chapter 6.)

During the Post-Crisis stage, the role of the EMT changes again — back to a major role. During this stage, the members of the EMT will have to work to recoup the losses caused by the acute crisis, evaluate the response of the organization during the crisis, and make the changes it feels are necessary to allow the organization to move forward.

5.1.1   The Executive Management Plan

The Executive Management Plan (EMP) contains information that can be used by the members of the EMT during the Pre-Crisis and Post-Crisis stages. During the Pre-Crisis stage, they will be responsible for analyzing information and making a decision as to whether it will go away on its own, or it will need help. During the Post-Crisis stage, they will be responsible to recoup the losses, to investigate the organization's performance during the crisis, and to make the changes deemed necessary to minimize the potential of a similar crisis to occur.

During the Acute-Crisis stage, the EMT will turn the managing of the acute crisis over to the Crisis Management Team.

5.1.2 Who Are the Members of the Executive Management Team?

The members of the EMT include the Chief Executive Officer (CEO), Chief Financial Officer, (CFO), Chief Operations Officer (COO), Chief Legal Counsel, Public Relations Officer, Human Resources Officer, Chief Information Officer, Chief Regulatory Officer, Risk Management Officer, and the Chief Privacy Officer. The core member of the EMT is the Chief Executive Officer.

The CEO will usually select the CFO and COO as members of the EMT.

5.1.3 Is There a Predefined List of Executives Who Comprise the EMT?

Would that it were. No, there is no pre-identified group of executives that comprise the EMT. This is an individual decision made by the CEO. If we look at the executives chosen by the CEO in 10 different organizations, we would find that they are different between organizations. We would probably find that most of the executives identified above would be found on some of the Executive Management Teams of the 10 organizations, but there would be differences. In some cases, the differences could be dramatic.

Why is that? The members are hand-picked by each CEO, based on the business strengths of the individuals. But in addition to that selection criteria, the CEO will choose as members of this select group, executives who have demonstrated their trust to the CEO, and their loyalty to the organization. When they meet behind closed doors during a crisis, the policy for the members of EMT is *nothing discussed in the room leaves the room*. This way the CEO knows that all members of the EMT will feel comfortable contributing to the discussions. (***Author Note:*** I do not think any CEO wants to have another Paul O'Neill on the EMT, someone who will write a book critical of the executives or the organization.)

The CEO usually selects the Chief Financial Officer (CFO), and if the organization has one, the Chief Operations Officer (COO).

The remaining members of the EMT should include one or more of the following executives:

■ Chief Legal Counsel
■ Public Relations Executive

- Human Resources Executive
- Chief Information Officer

(**Author Note:** I have been in one-on-one meetings with CEOs where they have told me in no uncertain terms that "X" will not be on the Executive Management Team. When I ask why, they have responded that they do not feel comfortable discussing problems with these executives anymore. They no longer trusted them in confidential meetings.)

Perhaps this story, entitled "Shaking Up Coke Abroad" and published in *Business Week* (April 4, 2005), describes the importance of the loyalty needed by CEOs.

Not long after Neville Isdell came out of retirement last May to become CEO of Coca-Cola, he set off on a whirlwind world tour of Coke's far-flung operations. On March 23, the outcome of Isdell's trip became evident with a restructuring that does everything from beefing up Coke's marketing to splitting the key European and Asian regions into smaller groups.

As part of the shuffle, Asia chief Mary Minnick gets a job overseeing both marketing and new product development in Asia. Isdell recruited French bottling exec Dominique Reiniche to oversee European operations. And he brought back Coke alum Muhtar-Kent to oversee one of the restructured Asia divisions.

Now that Isdell is surrounded by a band of loyalists, perhaps he can avoid the internecine warfare that undermined his two predecessors, Doug Ivester and Doug Daft. 'He's building a team that's going to be loyal to the leader,' says a former executive.

Others members the CEO could select for the EMT include, but are not limited to:

- Chief Regulatory Officer
- Risk Management Officer (see Appendix 5A)
- Chief Privacy Officer (see Appendix 5B)

All in all, the majority of people identified in the first paragraph paragraph comprise Crisis Management Teams around the country. Some of these people will be deleted in some organizations and some additions will be made in others.

5.1.4 Do Organizations Not Already Have an Executive Management Team?

The answer is no — and yes. To be more specific, maybe. Many organizations have an Executive Management Committee. This committee consists of executives who could be called together if the CEO feels a need for their advice or opinions. However, this committee is not a formal team; it is more of an ad hoc committee.

The Executive Management Team, as identified and defined in the Crisis Management Plan (CMP), is a formal team, established to (1) manage the Pre and Post stages of a crisis and (2) meet the requirements of the Board of Directors.

Its members and their responsibilities have been preplanned and documented during the development of the CMP. The CMP has been validated as a viable plan, first during the development and then during the training and exercising efforts made throughout the year. The members of the team have documented responsibilities, and the plan contains checklists with resource information for them to use in managing a crisis. During the training exercises, the members have the opportunity to recognize that they need to make changes to their responsibilities or their checklists.

The EMT will meet when a potential problem is first noticed (i.e., the Pre-Crisis stage). They will meet during the Acute-Crisis stage with the members of the Crisis Management Team (CMT) to discuss the daily activities used in managing the crisis. They will then meet after the crisis is over (Post-Crisis stage) to perform a post mortem.

The CEO and the members of the Executive Management Team's main responsibility during a crisis is to move the organization forward. They will continue to manage the organization's day-to-day operations, and attempt to lessen the potential for financial losses, negative publicity, regulatory investigations, lawsuits, etc.

5.1.5 What Do They Do When They Are Made Aware of a "Developing Situation"?

When they are made aware that a "developing situation" that threatens the normal operations of the organization, they will be responsible for managing it to ensure that it either goes away on its own, or goes away with the assistance of the EMT. As mentioned in Chapter 3, this "developing situation" is identified as being in the Pre-Crisis stage.

Once the "developing situation" moves from the Pre-Crisis stage to the Acute-Crisis stage, the EMT will activate the Crisis Management Team (CMT). The CMT will be responsible for managing the acute crisis until it is controlled. At that point, the situation will move to the Post-Crisis stage, and will be managed by the EMT. During this time, the EMT will do what it can to recoup any losses and make any changes t feels are needed to ensure that this situation does not occur again.

5.1.5.1   What Does the Executive Management Team Do?

Members of the EMT normally assist in managing the day-to-day operations of the organization.

When a "developing situation" is threatening the normal operations of the organization, EMT members come together at the behest of the CEO. This "developing situation" is also known as the Pre-Crisis warning stage. During this point in time, it is their responsibility to manage any and all of the pre-crisis situations that threaten the organization.

If they are unsuccessful in preventing the situation from moving to the acute stage (i.e., if the situation becomes known outside the organization and the media is reporting on it), they will turn over management of the acute stage to the members of the Crisis Management Team (CMT).

During the Acute-Crisis stage, the members of the EMT will do what they are supposed to do, which is to continue to manage the day-to-day operations of the organization. As to the status of the acute crisis, they will continue to stay in touch and monitor the status of the Acute-Crisis stage through communications with the CMT.

When the crisis moves from the Acute-Crisis stage to the Post-Crisis stage, the EMT will resume managing the crisis and its impacts on the organization. The Post-Crisis stage is very important to an organization because this is the time to resume moving the organization forward again and leaving behind the effects of the crisis.

5.2   EMT ROLE DURING THE PRE-CRISIS STAGE

When the EMT is made aware of a "developing situation" that could threaten the organization, they play the major role in managing the developing situation. The Pre-Crisis situation becomes their priority. They will be responsible for analyzing all the available information and make a determination: will it go away on its own, or will it need help?

As discussed in Chapter 3, the management of an organization must address a "developing situation" while it is still in the pre-crisis warning stage. This is an opportune time to take action that will nullify, or make the pre-crisis situation go away. At this point in time, management must ask what, if anything, can be done to alter the currently developing situation so that it does not move to the acute stage.

Once the executives are made aware of it, it is their responsibility to manage it and prevent it from moving into the Acute-Crisis stage. This is considered a "time of opportunity," to turn this from a negative situation into a positive one.

The first issue is to recognize the situation for what it is — and what it might become. They need to determine if the situation is serious, or if they believe that it will go away. Is it something that could damage the bottom line, or jeopardize the positive public image, or cause close media or government scrutiny? If they determine that it might damage the organization, they need to take appropriate action.

5.2.1 Remove the Threat

The goal is to manage the problem in a way that will lessen any "negative" publicity, or do any harm to the company. Most problems are defused before they become an acute crisis. Few people outside the company ever hear about them. Apparently, the EMTs of organizations have been very effective in managing pre-crisis situations and removing the threat.

The reason that organizations must be very effective in managing the pre-crisis warnings is that, according to crisis management experts, pre-crisis situations occur frequently. These same experts believe that small "developing situations" (pre-crisis warnings) occur in organizations every month. Some experts think that organizations are faced with them every week — and yet we do not see that many organizations experiencing "acute-crisis" situations. Apparently those pre-crisis or "developing situations" are being managed immediately and never reach the Acute-Crisis stage.

5.2.1.1 Avoid the "Opens the Door" Crisis

If the members of the EMT successfully manage the "developing situation," it not only minimizes the effects already experienced, but also avoids opening doors that lead to another, thus far unknown, secondary crisis.

One of the frustrating things that results from a crisis is the secondary effect — the first crisis "opens the doors" to other situations that crop up during the investigation of the first crisis. To make matters worse, the second crisis can be just as serious as the first. A couple of examples that will demonstrate this point include Alaska Airlines following the crash of flight 261; Coca-Cola's many investigations that were made by European countries regarding the possibility that Coke had violated competition rules; *New York Times* terminations of executive editor Howell Raines and managing editor Gerald Boyd after the scandal of Jason Blair; and Three Mile Island post-crisis investigation findings that inadequate, improper, and criminal procedures had been used for certain leak-rate tests at TMI-2, and that these events had occurred prior to the accident. The point here is that if the first crisis had never happened, then the second crisis would never have occurred.

Alaska Airlines, 2000. In January of 2000, Alaska Airlines Flight 261 crashed in the ocean off the coast of California. All 88 people aboard were killed. In February, divers seeking clues to the crash recovered a damaged jackscrew that moves the aircraft's horizontal stabilizer. The jackscrew seems to be the cause of accident.

> *(Opens the Door 1)* In the wake of the January crash, the FAA is launching a thorough inspection of Alaska Airlines. Its personnel are being investigated for allegedly falsifying maintenance records. (From *USA Today,* March 27, 2000.)
>
> *(Opens the Door 2)* In March of 2003, the U.S. Attorney's office in San Francisco reopened a criminal probe into the crash of Alaska Air Flight 261. The action follows a December report by the NTSB that blamed shoddy maintenance for a lack of grease, excessive wear and eventual failure of Flight 261's jackscrew, a component in the jet's tail that helps move the stabilizer and sets the angle of flight. (From *USA Today,* March 13, 2003.)

Coca-Cola – Europe, 1999. Just weeks after millions of cases of Coca-Cola products were recalled in Europe after dozens of people became sick after drinking Coke products, the Coca-Cola Co. said European Commission officials have seized internal company records in four European nations, acting on a tip that the beverage giant had violated competition rules. A company spokesman said authorities raided its offices in Britain, Germany, Austria and Denmark and also seized records from three Coca-Cola bottlers. (From "Coca-Cola records are seized in Europe," *Philadelphia Inquirer,* July 22, 1999.)

> *(Opens the Door 1)* "We suspect that Coca-Cola has … offered three types of incentives, all of which are unlawful for dominant companies m any market," European antitrust chief Karol Van Miter said in a statement. Under EU rules, a dominant company is restricted in its use of incentives to get retailers to raise sales, carry more of its products or drop a rival. (From *USA Today,* July 23, 1999.)
>
> *(Opens the Door 2)* Instigated by a complaint from rival PepsiCo Inc., Italy's antitrust authorities have been investigating Coca-Cola Co. for unfair business practices for more than a year, Italian officials said. A report sent to Coca-Cola accuses the company of dominating the market through

questionable trade practices, damaging its competitors' ability to business. Italy is the latest country to announce it is reviewing antitrust allegations against Coca-Cola. In July, European Union officials raided Coca-Cola's offices in Austria, Denmark, Germany and Britain as part of an inquiry into the company s marketing practices. Alessandro Magnoni, spokesman for Coca-Cola Italia in Milan, and the company is aware of the inquiry. (From "Italy Joins the List of Countries Investigating Coca-Cola," *Philadelphia Inquirer,* September 14, 1999.)

New York Times, 2003. Jayson Blair, 27, a *Times* reporter for nearly four years, was fired after the *San Antonio Express-News* complained to the *Times* that much of a Blair story about the mother of a missing soldier — a story ostensibly reported and written from Texas — was substantially identical to one published by the *Express-News.* The *Times* later discovered that for months, and perhaps longer, Blair had been stealing material from other papers or simply making up people quoted in his stories. Although a number of his stories carried date-lines indicating they had been filed from West Virginia, Ohio, or other places outside New York, it appeared he had rarely left his apartment in Brooklyn. The *Times* bared all of Blair's deceptions it could uncover in a four-page self-expose Sunday. In it, blame appeared to rest solely with the reporter. (From "Media cornerstone violated in scandal," *Philadelphia Inquirer,* May 16, 2003.)

> *(Opens the Door 1)* The Gray Lady's two top newsmen collapsed under the pressure of the Jayson Blair scandal yesterday — resigning from their positions at the head of the nation's "paper of record." The departure of *New York Times* executive editor Howell Raines and managing editor Gerald Boyd was announced in a newsroom meeting yesterday (From "Paper of Wreckage" — "Top editor & No. 2 quit amid story-fake scandal," *New York Post,* June 6, 2003.)
>
> *(Opens the Door 2)* The shock waves from the scandal have rippled through the media world. Reporting and editing procedures are being examined and tightened at other outlets. The scandal threatened to cast a shadow on all news media, says Arlene Morgan, assistant dean at the Columbia University Graduate School of Journalism. "The *Times* is considered the most credible source of news in the world. When something like this happens there,

it really confirms to people who do not trust the press that we're only in this business to sell papers and to sensationalize stories," says Morgan, a former *Philadelphia Inquirer* editor. (From *New York Post,* June 6, 2003.)

Three Mile Island, 1979. One of the nuclear power units shut off automatically and alarm sirens sounded to alert the men working that shift at 4:00 a.m. on March 28, 1979. A series of events escalated the accident into the worst crisis to date experienced by the nation's nuclear power industry, equipment failures, inappropriate procedures, and human errors and ignorance. The danger on Three Mile Island from "this incredible sequence of avoidable events" (Steven Fink) was from the possibility of a "melt-down." This could occur if the nuclear core were to drop into the water coolant at the bottom of the chamber, in turn causing a steam explosion. The possible explosion could break the four foot thick concrete walls of the container and release deadly radioactive gas into the atmosphere. It could have been a nuclear holocaust.

> *(Opens the Door 1)* During one of the post-TMI investigations, it was revealed that there was cheating on some of the exams required to become licensed to be an operator at the plant. The cheating that was first revealed happened after the TMI incident and involved TMI-1, the reactor that was not damaged in the accident. When the qualification tests were re-administered under much closer supervision, one third of the licensed operators failed the test.
>
> *(Opens the Door 2)* But most damaging of all, subsequent digging indicated — and a guilty plea from Met Ed ultimately confirmed — that inadequate, improper, and criminal procedures had been used for certain leak-rate tests at TMI-2, and that these events had occurred prior to the accident.

By managing a pre-crisis effectively, the members of the EMT can also avoid those secondary crises that result from a crisis that moves to the "Acute" stage.

5.2.2 Look for the Pre-Crisis Warning

One of the benefits of developing and implementing a Crisis Management Plan is to prepare executives to recognize when a pre-crisis warning has been uncovered.

"In a well-founded crisis management plan, the executives, and their managers, must be trained to examine every out-of-the-ordinary situation for what it is — a warning. And having recognized the warning, the executives must then question what, if anything, they can do about it."

—Steven Fink
Crisis Management: Planning for the Inevitable

The EMT must address this pre-crisis or "developing situation" while it is still in the pre-crisis warning stage. This is the opportunity for executives to take action that will nullify, or make the pre-crisis situation go away. It should ask, what can be done to alter the "developing situation" so it does not move to the acute stage?

Once someone in the organization warns the executives of an impending crisis, the executives can take the appropriate actions and nullify it, or make it go away.

5.2.2.1 Warnings Missed

As discussed in Chapter 3, there are times where the executives have not been given a pre-crisis warning. This happens in organizations where employees fear the response to such a message will be "kill the messenger." In some organizations, this approach, "kill the messenger," still exists.

This fear — to warn executives of an impending problem — is generated because in the past executives have not accepted constructive criticism or suggestion. An employee who warned the executives of a pending problem has made a career-ending mistake. The result of past incidents such as this usually causes all remaining employees to keep their thoughts or observations to themselves.

If executives find that they are experiencing a large number of "acute" crises, and they have not been receiving pre-crisis warnings from employees, they should look at the way the organization operates. There is a good chance that employees perceive that they would receive the same "kill the messenger" response if they were to warn the executives of what they see as a potential crisis brewing.

Two examples of where the "kill the messenger" response to a pre-crisis warning might result in employees choosing to avoid telling executives of an impending crisis in the future are the (1) James F. Bingham of Xerox in 2000 and (2) Matthew Whitley of Coca-Cola in 2003. In addition to Bingham and Whitely, there have been others cases of whistle-blowers alleging problems internally in an organization which result in negative publicity and investigations by regulatory authorities. For example:

Hercules, 1998. Hercules agreed to settle a nine-year battle brought by Katherine A. Colunga, a former employee and whistle-blower, who alleged that there were deficiencies in Hercules' quality assurance program for rocket motors sold to the U.S. Government. Subject to court approval, Hercules will pay $36 million to settle the Colunga case plus $19 million to cover attorneys' fees, expenses and other costs incurred by plaintiff Colunga. Hercules said it settled to avoid the cost of protracted litigation. (Excerpt from *Philadelphia Inquirer,* May 16, 1998.)

Onvoy, Inc., 2003. To his supporters in some of the nation's biggest phone companies, James C. Krutchen (36) is a whistle-blower angered by what may be a massive criminal fraud perpetrated by MCI and another company he once worked for, Onvoy Inc. Two companies, Onvoy Inc. and MCI, are accused by competitors Verizon Communications Inc., AT&T Corp., and SBC Communications Inc. of illegally disguising calls to avoid paying access fees to local companies for the use of their lines, potentially defrauding them of hundreds of millions of dollars.

Federal prosecutors in New York, relying largely on a sworn statement from Mr. Krutchen, have launched an investigation. Dan Stark, a top internal lawyer for AT&T, declined to talk about the informant's integrity but stressed the company had been able to verify his claims. Executives at Verizon said the company did a background check on Mr. Krutchen and found he had no criminal past, and stressed other witnesses had corroborated his allegations. "We remain convinced that the information he provided is accurate," Verizon spokesman Peter Thonis says. (Excerpt from "Views Diverge on Credibility of MCI Informer," *The Wall Street Journal,* August 8, 2003.)

Plummer Precision Optics Co., 2000. A precision-optics company. (Falsifying Data) — Makes artillery sights for the Army's M-1 tank and other weapons systems. Pleaded guilty to faking inspection reports and shipping millions of dollars worth of defective parts to the military. Plummer agreed to pay a fine of more than $875,000 and will pay an additional $2.3 million to the government to settle a separate civil lawsuit. Two former executives, Walter Lagger and Max Haskins, are expected to plead guilty in the next few days.

> The allegations stemmed from a whistle-blower lawsuit that the company's former marketing director filed in March 1997. John L. Plummer and his company were accused along with several Plummer officials and others of engaging in "a systematic and continuous scheme" to defraud the government over the course of 10 years. Plummer has since died and his company changed its name to Blue Jaunte Company Inc Lawsuit said plant inspectors who complained that products did not meet government specifications were threatened to keep them quiet. (Excerpt from *Philadelphia Daily News,* December 20, 2000.)

The early warning system, if set up properly, can ensure that executives are warned of an impending crisis at the earliest stages. Just make sure that the organization has a procedure for employees to follow to report these early warnings. And make sure that managers are not punishing employees for coming forward.

The biggest threat to an organization is to have an employee find out there is a potential situation developing, but caused by their manager. Who do they go to? Does your organization provide a procedure for employees to report "developing situations" to an executive above their immediate manager?

5.2.3 Seek the Support of Outside Consultants

The question that often comes up is: Why do organizations need outside consultants when they already have internal capabilities? One reason is that the internal capabilities may not have any experience with this type of "developing situation." Gaining this experience on-the-job during a pre-crisis or developing situation could end up costing the organization a lot in both dollars and reputation.

Large organizations generally have a Public Relations staff in-house yet they seem to use outside consultants frequently. Why? Their answer is because they want someone who has experience with this type of crisis. In addition, they sometimes feel that the outside consultant provides objectivity.

5.2.3.1 *Selecting an Outside Consulting Firm*

Hire a crisis specialist the way you would hire a surgeon: ask for a recommendation from someone who has used the outside consultant in the past. You should be able to get a list of some of their clients so you can check them out. Keep in mind that, for security and reputation reasons, "crisis specialists generally refuse to discuss their clients in detail, noting that the best managed disasters are the ones no one ever hears about." (Gerry Meyers)

5.2.3.2 Outside Consulting Firms and Specialists

Does your company use a crisis management specialist, or has it used one in the recent past? Do you have a list of crisis management specialists included in your Business Resumption Plan?

There have been articles in industry magazines that identify some of the larger consulting groups and even identify some of their clients. One article, entitled "Who Can You Call?" listed:

- *Fleishman-Hillard* counseled MGM Grand Hotels Inc. in the early 1980s when a slew of lawsuits arose after a fatal 1980 fire at its Las Vegas hotel.
- *Ketchum Public Affairs* advised Wendy's International Inc. earlier this year after a fatal shooting at one of its restaurants in Queens.
- *Shandwick International's* newly acquired unit, Rowan & Blewitt, helped advise Exxon after the Exxon Valdez oil spill in 1989, and BIC following a slew of safety allegations concerning its disposable lighters in the 1980s.
- *Porter Novelli* advised produce growers in the wake of a 1989 scare about Alar, a chemical pesticide, on apples, and Audi during its "unintended acceleration" controversy in the mid-1980s.
- *BSMG Worldwide* advised tobacco giant Philip Morris Cos. since the start of national tobacco-settlement talks in 1997.

Others mentioned in various articles include Vorbaus & Co., a New York firm; Landor Associates, a unit of Young & Rubicam; Barr, Hill & Knowlton; and Giuliani Partners.

> (***Author Note:*** There are many more organizations available to assist organizations in the throes of a crisis, but due to space limitations, I have not identified them.)

What is the relationship between you, the client, and an outside crisis consultant? Can they resign from their contract? Can they reveal confidential information?

The best answer to those two questions can be answered by excerpts from an article published in the *Wall Street Journal* on September 8, 2000, entitled "The Perils and Potential Rewards of Crisis Managing for Firestone."

> "What happens when a crisis management consulting firm walks away from a client in frustration. This happened to Bridgestone/Firestone during the tire crisis.
>
> "Although neither side will publicly discuss why Omnicom Group Inc.'s Fleishman-Hillard quit the Bridgestone/Firestone

account, those familiar with the situation say the giant public-relations firm grew disturbed with Firestone's refusal to communicate the breadth and seriousness of its problems. Fleishman, according to people familiar with the situation, was unaware that a tire problem loomed that would put Firestone, a unit of Japan's Bridgestone Corp., in crisis mode only two weeks after the agency was hired. Firestone's announcement that it was recalling 6.5 million tires effectively put the company under siege. As the crisis unfolded, Fleishman executives concluded they were receiving incomplete and questionable information from Firestone executives in the U.S. This made it difficult to give good advice or to effectively represent the company, say individuals familiar with the situation."

In any case, Firestone didn't follow most of Fleishman's advice, relying instead on the cautious counsel of its lawyer's, individuals familiar with the matter say. The agency, for example, is said to have urged Firestone to move forward with a proactive plan of action to restore consumer confidence. This included issuing an immediate apology for the faulty tires and quickly recalling and replacing those tires."

The article shows us that the outside consultant has the right to walk away from the contract. The consultant does need a justifiable reason to do this so that its reputation will not suffer.

Most observers say that Fleishman made the right call in resigning and doubt the decision will affect its crisis-management business — or scare away future clients. "They had to resign the business. It would do more damage to their reputation than anything else out there," says Allen Adamson, a managing partner at the brand consulting firm Landor Associates, a unit of Young & Rubicam. (From "The Perils and Potential Rewards of Crisis Managing for Firestone," *Wall Street Journal,* September 8, 2000.)

As to "Can they reveal confidential information?" the answer is clear. No! Unless the company in crisis was foolish enough to discuss confidential information before it signs a non-disclosure agreement, it would not be legal. Furthermore, it would not be prudent for a professional consulting organization to discuss any information with other people or organizations.

The crisis-management consulting profession, or industry, is one of the hot areas of corporate consulting. According to the article in the *Wall Street Journal* (September 8, 2000), "Some date the industry back to the 1960s, when companies encountered civil-rights and environmental challenges to products like the pesticide DDT."

> "Back then, Burson-Marsteller, for one, conducted seminars with plant managers on how to deal with protests or explosions for its manufacturing client Owens Corning," says Harold Burson, the founder and chairman of Burson-Marsteller. The firm counseled Dow Corning on how to deal with groups protesting its manufacture of deadly chemicals during the Vietnam War. And it advised Johnson & Johnson during the poisoned Tylenol episode, a major early success for crisis management. ("The Perils and Potential Rewards of Crisis Managing for Firestone." *Wall Street Journal,* September 8, 2000.)

More than 60 firms nationwide now counsel corporations involved in product recalls, labor disputes, and environmental disasters, among other issues. In 1999, public-relations revenue grew about 30 percent from the prior year to nearly $3 billion, according to the Council of Public Relations Firms, a trade group. Crisis management accounted for slightly less than 4 percent of the total, or roughly $100 million.

In the past five years, the biggest advertising and marketing corporations, including Omnicom and Interpublic, have bought leading public-relations agencies that boast crisis management units. Omnicom bought Fleishman-Hillard, now the largest public-relations firm in the United States, in 1997. And a year later, Interpublic acquired Shandwick International, which owns the crisis management firm Rowan & Blewitt.

5.3   EMT ROLE DURING THE ACUTE-CRISIS STAGE

Once the crisis becomes known outside the organization, the EMT will activate the Crisis Management Team (CMT) (see Chapter 6). Managing the crisis during the acute stage will be the responsibility of the members of the CMT.

When CMT members are made aware of a "developing situation" that could threaten the organization, they play the major role in managing the developing situation. The Pre-Crisis situation becomes their priority. They will be responsible for analyzing all available information and make a determination as to whether it will go away on its own or need help.

As previously discussed, the management of an organization must address a "developing situation" while it is still in the pre-crisis warning stage. This is an opportune time to take action that will nullify, or make the pre-crisis situation go away. At this point in time, management must ask what, if anything, can be done to alter the currently developing situation so it does not move to the acute stage.

Once the executives are made aware of it, it is their responsibility to manage it and prevent it from moving into the acute-crisis stage. This is considered a "time of opportunity," to turn this from a negative situation into a positive one.

The first issue is to recognize the situation for what it is — and what it might become. They need to determine if the situation is serious, or if they believe that it will go away. Is it something that could damage the bottom line, or jeopardize the positive public image, or cause close media or government scrutiny? If they determine that it could damage the organization, they need to take appropriate action.

5.3.1 How Does the EMT Allow a Pre-Crisis Situation to Move to an Acute Crisis?

This question was discussed in Chapter 3 but it is appropriate to ask and answer again in this chapter.

Sometimes, executives *underestimate* the damage the pre-crisis situation could do to the organization. In this case they will let it run its course, only to find that it was serious and now they are managing an acute crisis. An example of where an acute crisis occurred because executives underestimated the damage the crisis could cause is the Intel Pentium Chip incident in 1994. Initially, Intel pleaded ignorance.

> Intel's actions turned what could have been a minor problem, perhaps limited to a few scientists and engineers, into a costly fiasco according to Richard Zwetchkenbaum, analyst at IDC in Framingham, MA. Intel discovered the flaw last July, but kept quiet about it. If it had revealed it then and offered to replace chips for free, only a few users probably would have responded.
>
> *—USA Today*
> *December 24, 1994*

Sometimes, executives *overestimate* their ability to manage the crisis while it is still in the pre-crisis stage. In these cases, they find that the pre-crisis situation has overwhelmed them and moved on to the acute stage. An example of where an acute crisis occurred because executives overestimated their ability to manage it is the Exxon Valdez crisis.

Then there are times where the executives have not been given a pre-crisis warning. This happens in organizations where employees fear the response to such a message will be to "kill the messenger." In some organizations, this approach, still exists. This fear — to warn executives of an impending problem —— is generated because in the past executives have not accepted constructive criticism or suggestion. An employee who warned the executives of a pending problem has made a career-ending mistake. The result of past incidents such as this usually causes all remaining employees to keep their thoughts or observations to themselves. Examples of "kill the messenger" were given earlier in Section 5.2.2.1.

Finally, they may choose to ignore it. Recently we have seen a number of crises that organizations have experienced in which the executives themselves have been involved in fraud and unethical practices. Obviously they are not going to fix the problem when they are the cause of the crisis. Two examples: Cendant (1997) and Enron Corporation (2000).

The notion that one person, sitting atop a corporate hierarchy, can regularly and successfully guide the daily actions of tens of thousands of individual employees is a pleasant confection created, some would suggest by, academics and certain business leaders. Only the truly brave or the truly foolish would make this claim. However, the one aspect of business in which a chief executive's influence is measurable is crisis management. Indeed, the very future of an enterprise often depends on how expertly he or she handles the challenge. Crises tend to be highly formative experiences — watershed experiences, sometimes even life-threatening experiences — for a business. Nowhere else is the leadership of a chief executive more apparent or more critical to the long-term prospects of an enterprise. So by all means avoid involving your business in a crisis. But once you are in one, accept it, manage it, and try to keep your vision focused on the long term. The bottom line of my own experience with crises can be summarized in just seven words: Tell the truth and tell it fast. (Norman R. Augustine – "Managing the Crisis You Tried to Prevent")

5.3.2 Activate and Empower the Crisis Management Team to Take Action

Once a Pre-Crisis situation moves to the Acute-Crisis stage, the members of the EMT should activate the CMT and turn over the managing of the acute crisis to them.

When the crisis reaches the "acute" stage, members of the EMT should concentrate on running the organization's day-to-day operations. They should continue to manage the organization and maintain a continuity of operations. Their goal should be to lessen the potential for financial losses, and to minimize negative publicity and lawsuits, etc.

The EMT should authorize the members of the CMT to take whatever action is needed to fix the problem. The CMT should take charge quickly, determine the facts, tell your story and fix the problem. (See Chapter 4.)

Remember that the selection of members was based on the ability of the executives selected to the CMT to manage the crisis management issues.

Selecting CMT members was done during a non-crisis, non-stressful time (during a calm time), and was based on their ability to manage a crisis when one would strike.

Now the CEO needs to show confidence in the members of the CMT by providing them with the power to make decisions.

They should determine which member of the CMT will be the "crisis manager." This will be determined based on the type of crisis and the expertise of the CMT members.

5.3.2.1 Support the Crisis Management Team

After authorizing the activation of the CMT, the EMT should maintain a communications link with the CMT command center. As part of that role, the EMT should establish a schedule for a meeting to review the activities of the crisis management operation. In many Post-Crisis reviews that have been discussed, you often find mention of the time of the day when the executives (EMT) met with the members of the CMT — each day at, for example, 6:00 p.m. or 7:00 p.m.

When the EMT meets with the CMT, the CMT will want answers to questions such as:

■ What is happening?
■ How did this happen?

Sometimes, the answers to these questions do not come as a surprise. They had been warned that this might happen but they chose not to take any action, or any successful action.

In some situations they find out that the crisis struck with such speed that there was no early warning system. (Following the successful managing of and conclusion to the crisis, a new early warning system is put in place.)

CMT members may need to have access to the executives on the EMT on short notice, and at any time during the day or night.

5.3.2.2 Review the Executive Management Team's Crisis or Disaster Agenda

The EMT should assemble at the Executive Management Team's Executive Operations Center (EOC).

There they will meet the members of the Crisis Management Team at a prescribed time to review the status of the crisis. The questions the EMT will want answers to include:

■ What happened?
■ Why did it happen?
■ When did we know about it?
■ How could we have prevented it?
■ Where in the building did this happen?
■ Who is located on that floor(s)?

The executive management committee's priority is to run the normal day-to-day operations of the organization, even during an acute crisis. But they will still want to review the day-to-day status of the acute crisis. They will expect the members of the CMT to report on all the "positives" as well as "negatives" that have occurred since their last meeting together. They will be able to maintain a communications link about the activities through the EOC.

5.3.2.2.1 Develop the EMT Agenda

When they get together, they will review the status of the crisis using the EMT's agenda. This "agenda" consists of a list of questions the team will ask the members of the CMT after a crisis occurs.

A list of questions will be developed for physical disasters to the organization's assets (e.g., fire, flood, explosion, etc.). Another list of questions will be developed for non-physical crises (e.g., product problems, company image problems, financial problems, etc.).

The Business Continuity Plan professional will be responsible for developing and documenting the list of questions.

Step 1: Develop and document a list of questions to be used if a disaster has struck a building housing key business units of the organization.

Step 2: Arrange for a meeting with the CEO in which you will describe the disaster scenario. After explaining the scenario, the BCP professional should ask the questions in the "proposed agenda." Ask the CEO if the questions should be changed, added to, or subtracted from. Then ask the CEO if this type of disaster ever did occur, whom would the CEO want on the Executive Management Team. When the CEO finishes with the agenda, prepare a "draft document" of the EMT agenda.

Step 3: Send the "draft" to the CEO for their final input, changes or approval. Also send a list of executives the CEO wants to be on the EMT for a final change or approval.

Step 4: Arrange for a meeting with the members of the EMT. (They have been assigned by the CEO.) At that meeting, explain the purpose of the CMP. Explain that they have been selected by the CEO to be on the EMT. During this meeting, the BCP professional should make a presentation using a scenario.

Sample Scenario: Let us use a fire as the sudden crisis that has struck your organization. Shortly after the executives on the EMT have arrived at the EOC, they will want to have answers to questions about the fire.

(**Author Note:** The EOC is the name for the command center that will used by the members of the EMT throughout the crisis. It is not the same as the CMT Command Center (CMTCC), where the members of the Crisis Management Team will function throughout the crisis. That is a different location.)

Your list of questions for the EMT agenda should include:

- Were there any injuries to personnel?
- What was the cause of the fire?
- Have security precautions been implemented?
- What is the damage to the organization's assets?
- Is there a potential for adverse publicity?
- Do we have any contractual concerns?
- Does our insurance policy cover our losses?
- What is the status of the affected business functions?
- Where are the business functions located? Is this a temporary situation?
- How did the employees get to the temporary sites? Transportation support? Monies?
- How is the network operating? Do we have communications with the key organization and people?

(*Author Note:* See Appendix 5C, EMT Agenda Worksheet.)

Then ask the members to review the EMT "agenda." Members of the EMT should provide input on how they would like the agenda changed. In some cases they will want to add areas to the agenda; in other cases they may want to delete areas from the agenda.

Following the meeting, document the EMT agenda with any changes suggested by members of the EMT. After completing the documentation, the BCP professional should send each member a copy of the agenda. The BCP professional should request that they review it to ensure that the BCP professional did not misunderstand their comments or opinions. After all of the members of the EMT have responded, prepare a final document. Distribute it to each member of the EMC. Send a copy of the final version to the CEO.

(*Author Note:* For specific information regarding the EMT agenda, see Chapter 8.)

5.3.3   Act as Spokesperson, if Necessary

While the organization will have a formal team (the crisis communications team) prepared to work with the media to get out your side of the story, it sometimes is a good thing to have the CEO serve as the spokesperson.

A few examples of where the CEO acted as spokesperson, or made direct remarks that were later reported in the news media, include:

Arco Chemical Co. – Houston, 1991. Arco Chemical experienced an explosion at its flagship plant in Channelview, Texas. The plant is the nation's largest producer of an additive that ARCO, Shell, Exxon, and several other companies have blended with their gasolines to reduce toxic emissions. The blast, which occurred about 11:30 p.m. (Thurs.), shot flames into the sky and rocked houses miles away. The fiery explosion at the petrochemical plant killed 17 workers and injured five others. The concussion damaged private houses for miles around the plant.

When I was an EVP for Sungard Planning Services, Arco Chemical was a client of ours. I was actively involved in the project to help them develop their company-wide Business Recovery Program. My specific role was to meet with the senior executives and explain the program, and their roles in it. When I had the opportunity to meet with the CEO (early one morning, very early), I found him (Hal Sorgenti) to be very interested in the crisis management plan. We discussed which executives he would expect would be the source of information following a disaster. We went on to discuss an overview of the roles of these executives who would comprise the "crisis management team." When we discussed the person that would deal with the news media, he identified the executive that headed up the Public Relations department.

But then he went on to say, "Ed, if the disaster results in injuries to my employees, or negatively impacts the community nearby, I will be the spokesperson for the organization." I of course felt this was great, because that is whom the media would prefer as the spokesperson. He went on to say that he considered it his role in an instance like this (injuries or community impact). I then asked him, "Who will run the day-to-day operations of the organization?" He responded, "Our CFO." I thanked him for his time and left. I sent a copy of the documented Crisis Management Plan to Mr. Sorgenti for his approval, or changes. It was accepted as written.

Six weeks later, the explosion occurred. As mentioned above, the explosion killed 17 workers and injured a number of others. In addition, the concussion damaged private houses for miles around the plant.

As I understand the situation at that point in time, Sorgenti had just arrived in Europe, along with Lod Cook (the Chairperson of Arco Corporation) and the Chief Financial Officer, for a business meeting. After being told about the explosion, Sorgenti and Cook immediately flew back to the United States, to Houston, to deal with the situation. But before he left Europe, Sorgenti told the CFO that he was in charge of the day-to-day operations until Sorgenti was sure that this crisis was "under control."

One of the first things Sorgenti and Cook did was address the news media. "We are deeply grieved and saddened by this tragic event and offer our heartfelt, deepest sympathy," said Sorgenti.

Sorgenti handled the situation so well that the news media stories, which were predominant the first couple days after the explosion, dried up by Sunday and Monday. The news media had difficulty finding anyone from the community who was unhappy with this corporate giant, and the threat it provided.

This was a result of the crisis management team following through on its plan to reduce the negative impact of a crisis. There is no question that the incident was a tragedy, but the Arco organization took full responsibility for it, and the CMT worked with the community of neighbors to resolve the damage.

Ortho Pharmaceutical, Division of Johnson & Johnson, Raritan, New Jersey, 1992. Ortho employees shredded thousands of documents about the marketing campaign for Retin-A, a day after learning of the federal investigation. The company reported the shredding to prosecutors in 1992 and fired three senior Ortho employees.

CEO-Spokesperson: "The document destruction was absolutely wrong, and should never have occurred," said Ralph S. Larsen, Chairman and CEO of J&J.

Southwest Airlines, 2000. A Southwest Airlines Boeing 737 jetliner skidded off the end of a runway at Burbank Airport and crashed through a barrier, then hit two cars on a street before coming to rest a few feet from a gas station located across the street from the airport. The flight from Las Vegas to Burbank carried 137 passengers and a crew of five. Six people were injured; the most seriously injured was the pilot, who suffered cuts to his scalp. The injured people were transported to a nearby hospital. The plane was towed back through the broken fence onto airport property the next morning. (From *USA Today,* March 20, 2000.)

CEO-Spokesperson: About three hours after the accident, Southwest's CEO Herb Kelleher held a press conference.

(***Author Note:*** For more examples of CEOs acting as the spokesperson during a crisis, see Appendix 5D, CEO Acts as Spokesperson.)

5.4 EMT ROLE DURING THE POST-CRISIS STAGE

Once the crisis is considered "contained," or "under control," it moves to the Post-Crisis stage.

The CMT will now provide support where needed, but the management moves back to the EMT. Just because the crisis is considered "under control," it is not over. In fact, this is the time when the organization needs to take significant action.

The EMT will begin planning to recoup the losses, investigate the organization's performance during the crisis, and make the changes that will minimize the potential of a similar crisis from occurring.

5.4.1 Recoup Some of the Losses

As pointed out in Chapter 3, one of the best ways to recoup losses is to have the executives show consumers that they care about what the crisis did to them and furthermore to show the consumers what the organization is doing to prevent this from happening again. Some examples used in Chapter 3 included:

> *Johnson & Johnson/McNeil Co. Tylenol Tampering Case.* A good example of recouping losses, and regaining market share, is the Johnson & Johnson (McNeil Co.) handling of the Tylenol tampering case. Johnson & Johnson/McNeil redesigned the Tylenol packaging. This repackaging would alert consumers that the package was in its original state when it left the plant, or that it had been tampered with. The packaging shows a warning not to use the product and to return it to the store where it was purchased if the safety seal is broken.

> *Coca-Cola Co. – Europe, 1999.* After the crisis in Europe over the children getting sick, Coke, in order to show consumers that the organization cared about the crisis, took three important steps: they (1) introduced new packaging in Belgium to help win back customers, (2) instituted a free-drink giveaway to show potential customers that Coke was safe, and (3) put Coca-Cola "greeters" in supermarkets to talk with consumers.

5.4.1.1 *Apologize*

One of the strategies that helps soothe the public during as well as after a crisis is for the organization to apologize. It should apologize for what it did to its customers, its shareholders, its vendor and suppliers, and its employees.

An example of an organization that was interested in soothing an acute-crisis situation was the *Cincinnati Enquirer*.

The Cincinnati Enquirer – Chiquita, Cincinnati, Ohio, 1998. *The Cincinnati Enquirer*, apologized to Chiquita in a front-page story. The apology was made after a series of stories about Chiquita that questioned the company's business practices. In the apology, the newspaper explained the story was based on stolen voice mail and drew "untrue conclusions."

Executive Fired: The newspaper said it has fired reporter Mike Gallagher and agreed to pay more than $10 million to Cincinnati-based Chiquita, which is the world's biggest distributor of bananas. (From *Newsweek,* July 13, 1998.)

In an attempt to fix the problem, *The Cincinnati Enquirer:*

Agreed to pay more than $10 million to Chiquita
Ran an apology — front page, three days running — renouncing the story, expunging its afterlife on the Web
Fired the lead reporter on the project, Mike Gallagher, for being "involved" in the theft of voice mail at Chiquita's headquarters

The Enquirer wrote that "the representations, accusations and conclusions are untrue and created a false and misleading impression ... but never told readers what, exactly, was untrue."

5.4.1.1.1 Apology Made by CEO

United Airlines, 2000. When it comes to apologizing to the customers, many public relations experts feel the CEO should apologize. For example, back in the summer of 2000, United Airlines experienced a lot of flight cancellations.

Executive Apology: In September of 2000, United began running advertisements addressing this situation. "In the ad, United's CEO, Jim Goodwin, stepped up to the camera and apologized for United's summer of disruptions. In shirtsleeves, straight face and solemn tone, the chief of the world's biggest airline tried to reach out to thousands of angry United customers." (From *Newsweek,* September 2000.)

"We felt like we had to communicate with passengers, and we wanted to reach of lot of people," explained Julie Thomson, spokeswoman for Fallon Worldwide, United's advertising agency. "This ad will never win any awards, it just seemed like the right thing to do." (From "CEOs Now Love to Say Sorry," *USA Today,* September 8, 2000.)

According to Steven Fink, considered one of the top crisis management experts, "The ad was 'sincere,' it took the right approach by not deflecting blame."

5.4.1.2 How Effective Are These Apologies?

Communication professor Bill Benoit of the University of Missouri, author of *Accounts, Excuses and Apologies,* says apologies by CEOs can either be "very effective or fall flat on their face."

"At the university, we've done research on this: people want to hear apologies when companies make mistakes," he says. "Next, they want you to fix the problem, to clean up the mess or make sure it never happens again. An apology without some kind of solution doesn't fly with the public," he says.

An apology is not a decision made lightly. There is usually a lot of discussion about the value, or risk of an apology, when the EMT meets. Dennis Cesa, senior vice president at Cohn & Wolfe Public Relations, commented on this situation.

"Very often in a crisis, a high-level group of people are pulled together as a crisis committee. Usually there's great debate as to the benefits and detriments of an apology, and the CEO listens to arguments on all sides. Lawyers representing the company often discourage it for fear of lawsuits from consumers. Fear of business repercussions can inspire a circle-the-wagons reaction rather than remorse." And then there's human nature: most people, especially leaders accustomed to power and success, hate to apologize. (From "CEO's Now Love to Say Sorry," *USA Today,* September 8, 2000.)

Keith Hearit, communications professor at Western Michigan University (who is writing his own book on corporate apologies), thinks CEOs apologies are increasing. Hearit used Toshiba's technology sale to the USSR as an example. The executives at Toshiba not only apologized, they resigned. But rather than fall on their swords, CEOs in American organizations just apologize, they do not usually resign. In fact, Hearit adds, "In America, the CEO apologizes and then fires some poor soul who was at the switch."

> "Done right, expressions of regret can deflect criticism, create drama and touch on the public's beliefs about the value of confession and contrition." (From "CEOs Now Love to Say Sorry," *USA Today,* September 8, 2000.)

5.4.2   Make Changes Necessary to Fix the Organization

What could our organization have done to manage the crisis better? Based on the information gleaned from the investigations that followed the crisis (post-mortem), the organization usually needs to make changes to prevent the problems from occurring again.

After the problem is contained, the EMT will make the necessary changes to minimize the potential for a similar crisis to occur. For example, the following are some examples of organizations that made changes where the executives were fired, resigned, or reassigned.

5.4.2.1   *Changes to Their Management: Executives Fired*

The following crises resulted in executives being terminated from their organization.

> *Fleming Companies, Lewisville, Texas, 2003.* Fleming, the largest U.S. grocery distributor, has ousted chairman and CEO Mark Hansen, a week after it said the SEC formalized an accounting investigation. Fleming said that the SEC formalized an inquiry into how the company accounted for payments to vendors. Some of Fleming's suppliers have alleged that Fleming deducted fees from customer bills to bolster profit. Wholesalers can receive fees when they place goods with retailers or in advance, sometimes for promising sales of a given level. The practice becomes a problem when companies book money before actually receiving it, analysts said. Hansen, who took over in 1998, was overseeing a reorganization that included a contract to exclusively supply Kmart Corp., its biggest customer. (From *Philadelphia Inquirer,* March 5, 2003.)

> *Computer Associates International Inc., Islandia, New York, 2004.* Computer Associates, which has been under the cloud

of a long-running accounting investigation, fired nine people in the software company's legal and finance departments, after the audit committee acknowledged that Computer Associates "prematurely recognized revenue" in fiscal 2000. (From *Philadelphia Inquirer,* April 20, 2004.)

CBS — Columbia Broadcasting System, New York City, 2005. Four CBS News execs got the ax last week after an independent panel issued a scathing report charging they were very sloppy with the facts in their "myopic zeal" to get a scoop, running a story about President's Bush's National Guard Service based on dubious documents. The bulky 224-page report accuses the sacked newsies and CBS anchor Dan Rather of rushing a story on to the air even though they had "failed miserably" to make sure it was true. Making matters worse, investigators say, they continued to defend the September 8 piece for nearly two weeks despite strong indications that it hinged on bogus documents. "The fact is that basic journalistic steps were not carried out in a manner consistent with accurate and fair reporting," says the report, "leading to countless misstatements and omissions." The only vaguely positive finding was that Rather did not have a "political bias" as conservatives had charged. (From *U.S. News & World Report,* January 24, 2005.)

(*Author Note:* For more examples of executives being terminated as a result of an ongoing crisis, see Appendix 5E, "Changes Made: Executives Fired.")

5.4.2.2 Changes to Their Management: Resignations

The following crises resulted in executives resigning their positions with their organizations.

Dynegy Inc., Houston, Texas, 2002. The chief executive of Dynegy resigned Tuesday (05-28), the latest casualty of the turmoil that spread through the energy trading industry since the Enron scandal broke last fall. Chuck Watson, who spent 17 years at Dynegy and was one of its co-founders, leaves amid an SEC investigation of the company's trading practices and a nearly 90 percent drop in Dynegy's stock during the past year. He is the second head of a U.S. energy trader to quit within a week. (From *Colorado Springs Gazette,* May 29, 2002.)

Rent-Way Inc., Pittsburgh, Pennsylvania, 2003. Rent-Way said that it had agreed to pay $25 million to shareholders who accused the national rental chain of manipulating its books and inflating earnings. Two years ago, shareholders filed a federal lawsuit against Rent-Way, an Erie-based furniture, appliance, and computer-rental chain, and its accounting firm, Pricewater-houseCoopers, alleging that officers used faulty accounting practices to drive up the stock price. The company revealed in October 2000 that improper entries had been made into its accounting ledger to the tune of $75 million.

Matthew Marini, Controller & Chief Accounting Officer, was fired, and Jeffrey Conway, the company's former president & COO, was asked to resign. (From *Philadelphia Inquirer,* March 21, 2003.)

Delphi, Detroit, Michigan, 2005. Alan Dawes, CFO of Delphi, the biggest U.S. auto parts supplier, resigned Friday (03-04) amid a company probe that uncovered accounting errors dating back to 1999, when the auto parts supplier was spun off from General Motors. (From *USA Today,* March 7, 2005.)

(***Author Note:*** For more examples of executives who were forced to resign as a result of an ongoing crisis, see Appendix 5F, "Changes Made — Executives Resigned.")

5.4.2.3 Changes to Their Management: Reassigned

The following crises resulted in executives being reassigned.

World Trade Center, October 3, 2001. After the 9-11 attack on the World Trade Center, executives at the Boston Logan Airport made personnel changes.

Some employees were demoted or reassigned by Massachusetts Gov. Jane Swift, who says the move is necessary to restore public confidence in the facility where hijackers boarded the two planes that slammed into the World Trade Center towers Sept. 11.

> While Joseph Lawless, the chief of security at Boston's Logan Airport, repeatedly stressed there was no evidence that showed any of the ten Boston hijackers breached airport security to gain access to the two aircraft on Sept. 11, he was reassigned.

Aides to the governor say that repeated disclosures about security lapses at Logan since the hijackings has made Lawless' position untenable.

Massport has acknowledged that 130 security badges that give wide access to airport grounds are missing.

Lawless was demoted and reassigned from his post as head of all security operations for Massport, to a post where he will just oversee security at the harbor operations.

Federal Aviation Authority, October 3, 2001. The FAA acknowledged it had reassigned Mary Carol Turano, the director of its security field office at Logan.

(***Author Note:*** For more examples of executives being reassigned as a result of an on-going crisis, see Appendix 5G, "Changes Made: Executives Reassigned.")

5.3.3.4 *Changes Made to Procedures and Controls*

The following crisis resulted in changes being made to minimize the potential for a similar crisis to occur.

Lawrence Livermore National Laboratory, Livermore, California, 2003. A set of keys that unlocks gates and offices at a nuclear-weapons lab disappeared last month, but officials have since changed the most important locks and said that national security was not compromised. The incident at Lawrence Livermore National Laboratory is the latest embarrassment to the University of California, which manages the lab for the Energy Department. It also manages Los Alamos National Laboratory in New Mexico. Livermore guards discovered April 17 that the keys were missing. They have yet to be located, lab spokeswoman Susan Houghton said yesterday. Houghton said there had been no indications of any attempts to access the lab with the missing keys, one of about 200 such sets. For security reasons, she could not say how many locks the missing keys would unlock, but about 100 of the most important ones have been changed, she said.

Lab officials have begun three internal investigations to determine whether the keys were stolen or simply misplaced. The guard who last had the keys says he returned them to a locker when his shift ended April 16.

The House Energy and Commerce Committee will ask the Energy Department's inspector general to investigate, committee spokesman Ken Johnson said. Anyone with the keys would still have to get through other security safeguards, such as electronic key-card locks and computer-controlled access systems. Nevertheless, "this is an incident I take very seriously," lab director Michael Anastasio said in a statement. "We are reviewing this aggressively and making the necessary improvements to our key handling and storage procedures." *Congressional Quarterly* first reported the key loss Monday. (From "Locks are changed at nuclear lab after keys vanish," *Philadelphia Inquirer,* May 12, 2003.)

Merrill Lynch (Blodget), New York City, 2002. Merrill agreed to pay $100 million and change how it monitors its stock analysts, to settle the New York State Attorney General's inquiry into allegations that the nation's largest brokerage firm misled individual investors about the stock of its investment-banking clients. In Merrill's case, damaging e-mails provided explosive evidence that Merrill analysts harbored private doubts about stocks that were being pushed to small investors with positive ratings through the firm's brokerage network. In one e-mail, a Merrill analyst referred to an Internet stock the firm was touting as a "piece of s---." Mr. Blodget, in another e-mail to a colleague, wrote: "Can we reset this stupid price target and rip this piece of junk off whatever list it's on. If you have to downgrade it, downgrade it."

Apology: Merrill issued a statement of contrition, which was less than the admission of wrongdoing Mr. Spitzer had sought. "We sincerely regret that there were instances in which certain of our Internet sector research analysts expressed views that at certain points may have appeared inconsistent with Merrill Lynch's published recommendations," the firm said in its statement. "We view this situation as a very serious matter." The firm also said that some of the e-mails "violate internal policies" of the firm.

Change 1: Under the other terms of the Merrill deal, Merrill vowed to take a series of steps to separate its investment-banking and research departments. Analysts, for instance, no longer will be evaluated and paid based on their role in helping the firm win investment-banking business, but only for work they do in helping investors. Mr. Spitzer gave up, his demand that investment-banking business be spun off entirely. (From "Merrill Lynch to Pay Big Fine, Make Changes to Settle Inquiry," *Wall Street Journal,* May 22, 2002.)

Change 2: Merrill said it will pay its analysts based on the accuracy of their forecasts. The new system for paying Merrill's 800 analysts is effective immediately. It will base analysts' pay on how accurate they are in their stock forecasts and how their recommendations benefit investors, among other factors. The firm will use surveys and input from clients to help gauge the latter. "Investment banking will not have input into analyst compensation."

Change 3 — Rating System: Merrill also announced plans for a stock-rating system intended to be easier for investors to use. The new stock-rating system, which reduces the number of ratings to three (buy, neutral, sell) from the previous four-level ratings system (strong buy, buy, neutral, reduce/sell), will be implemented in September. It was not required under the settlement with Spitzer. The changes come less than a month after Merrill Lynch reached a settlement with New York Attorney General Eliot L. Spitzer, who accused the company's analysts of misleading investors. Spitzer said Merrill Lynch's analysts praised the stock of companies whose investment banking business Merrill wanted to win. Investment banking brings brokerage firms hefty fees for helping to arrange new stock offerings and corporate mergers. The settlement required the company to devise a new way of compensating analysts. (From "Merrill set to base pay on accuracy," *Philadelphia Inquirer,* June 8, 2002.)

(***Author Note:*** For more examples of executives being reassigned as a result of an ongoing crisis, see Appendix 5H, "Changes Made: Procedures and Controls.")

Now, let's move on to Chapter 6, "The Crisis Management Team." This chapter discusses in detail the members of the CMT and their projected duties in successfully managing a crisis.

Appendix 5A

RISK MANAGEMENT OFFICER

"Executive Offices Make Space for Managers of Risk," *USA Today,*
May 2000

—Del Jones

The star executive of the 1980s was the chief financial officer. In the 1990s, the chief information officer rose. And now?

The new hot executive might be the chief risk officer, which students of Intel chairman Andy Grove's book, *Only the Paranoid Survive,* may recognize as the chief paranoid officer. These are times when hackers can shut down Yahoo.com and Time Warner can flip the switch on ABC. Paranoia is moving into the corner office as CRO's make jeopardy a science.

"There are over 100 CRO's globally, all in the past four or five years," said James Lam, founder of erisk.com. "You're likely to see that number grow to over 1000 in the next two years." What does a CRO do?

That might be best answered by a look at Microsoft. The software giant likely had early and scattered warnings long ago that it was at risk of an antitrust action.

Risk carries two elements: the probability that something bad might happen and the consequences if it does.

Even if the odds of antitrust action were judged to be slight at Microsoft, a CRO might have estimated the price to be paid. Microsoft may have monitored lobbying efforts by competitors more effectively. It could have toned down a culture that squashes opposition, or even warned employees to lighten up on e-mail language later used against it in court.

CRO's are finding work in utilities, where deregulation has led to summer price swings that can go from $30 per kilowatt-hour to $7000 per kilowatt-hour. The industry lost $500 million last year, but Gary Lavey, general manager of global risk for Cincinnati-based Cinergy brags that risk management helped his firm sidestep the loss.

Companies must "approach risk offensively, not just defensively," said Jack Rose, a global partner at KPGM. Risk must be managed within departments, said Suzanne Labarge, chief risk officer at Royal Bank of Canada. Information technology staffs must have contingency plans; legal staffs must try to sidestep potential lawsuits. In short, the CRO's job is to look across all departments to anticipate risk, and choose the ones worth taking. "Somebody had a wonderful phrase," Labarge said. "Risk management is the speed bump on the way to a bonus."

Appendix 5B

CHIEF PRIVACY OFFICER

"The Newest High-Level Position: Chief Privacy Officer"

—Philadelphia Inquirer
July 12, 2000

WASHINGTON – Move over CEO, CIO and COO. Your titles are passe compared to the newest position in high demand from corporate head-hunters: chief privacy officer.

With consumers increasingly concerned about their privacy, and new technology able to track Internet users click by click, companies are rapidly hiring privacy officers, and giving them broad powers to set policies that protect consumers from invasion and companies from public-relations nightmares.

In many cases, the privacy officers report directly to the chairman or chief executive officer. And their hiring has become a litmus test for a company's dedication to customer privacy.

Corporate icons such as American Express Co., Citigroup Inc. and Prudential Insurance Co. have hired privacy officers. American Telephone & Telegraph added one last month.

"Privacy went from being a minor issue in most companies to something that could threaten their basic revenue model, or make their costly merger turn to dust," said David Westin, a privacy expert who helped a congressional committee write the Privacy Act of 1974.

Westin said companies failed to fully address the issue for two decades. That changed thanks to a recent spate of lawsuits by consumers, the government alleging a loss of privacy, and high-profile publicity surrounding how easy it is to track people with technology.

To deal with the growth, Westin has even created a training course for new private officers.

Lance Hoffman, a computer science professor at George Washington University, said privacy officers are being hired from universities, and promoted from government affairs and policy positions within companies.

They are being asked to educate their company, the public and legislators about privacy, said Hoffman, head of the university's Cyberspace Policy Institute, which studies security, E-commerce and intellectual- property issues.

"It attracts people who have a knowledge of history and law," Hoffman said. "They know something about technology, and they can't get techno-dazzled by explanations that don't hold water. They appreciate what technology can do for good and for evil."

In 1994, Shelley Harms became the executive director for public policy and privacy for Bell Atlantic Corp., which recently became Verizon Communications after merging with GTE Corp.

Harms, a public-policy lawyer, helped develop the company's privacy principles. She said her job was primarily teaching, although she sometimes has to take a more active role.

For instance, she became involved in the company's reverse-directory search product, making sure that unlisted numbers could not be searched and customers would feel comfortable.

"There's a lot of education that has to be done," Harms said. "Sometimes people get very zealous about their product, and they want to gather information and use it without telling the customer. But that's not what we do."

Michael Lamb, who was named AT&T's privacy officer last month, said: "Some companies name a CPO because they have a problem, and some do because they don't have a problem and want to keep doing the right thing."

Appendix 5C

EMT AGENDA WORKSHEET: (FOR A FIRE)

These are standard questions the EMT will ask the members of the CMT.

What happened?

_____

_____

Why did it happened?

_____

_____

When did we know about it?

_____

_____

How could we have prevented it?

_____

_____

Where in the building did this happen?

_____

_____

Who is located on that floor(s)?

_____

_____

In addition, they will probably want answers to questions such as:

Were there any injuries to personnel?

_____

_____

What was the cause of the fire?

_____

_____

Have security precautions been implemented?

_____

_____

What is the damage to the organization's assets?

_____

_____

Is there a potential for adverse publicity?

_____

_____

Do we have any contractual concerns?

_____

_____

What is the status of our insurance policies? Will they cover our losses?

_____

_____

What is the status of business functions?

_____

_____

Where are the business functions located? Is this a temporary situation?

_____

_____

How did the employees get to the temporary sites? Transportation support? Monies?

_____

_____

How is the network operating? Do we have communications with the key organization and people?

_____

_____

Appendix 5D

CEO ACTS AS SPOKESPERSON

- *Ashland Oil, Floreffe, Pennsylvania, 1988.* A 3.8 million gallon storage tank collapsed at Ashland's Floreffe's terminal (south of Pittsburgh), a tidal wave of diesel fuel surged over the containment dikes, into the parking lot and escaped into a storm sewer. An estimated 750,000 gallons of the diesel fuel flowed into the Monongahela River, affecting the drinking water for 300,000 people.
  - (CEO-Spokesperson) The CEO (John Hall), acting as spokesperson, agreed to pay Pennsylvania a record $4.6 million fine for costs and civil penalties.
- *Burroughs-Wellcome, Triangle Park, North Carolina, 1991.* When Sudafed capsules were laced with cyanide causing the death of two customers, the organization issued a nationwide recall. Nearly 1 million packages were recalled. The FBI reported that tests found cyanide in one of three altered capsules recovered after the tamperings were announced.
  - (CEO-Spokesperson) Philip R. Tracy, president & CEO, spoke with the news media. He explained "We are moving rapidly to alert the public and retrieve all Sudafed 12-hour capsules from the retail stores. Our sympathies go to the families of the individuals involved, and they have our assurance that the company will investigate these incidents quickly and thoroughly."
  - During the investigation into the person who caused the tampering, Tracy again met with the news media where he offered a $100,000 reward for information.
- *Central Sprinkler Corp., Lansdale, Pennsylvania, 1998.* U.S. Consumer Product Safety Commission said that Omega fire-suppression sprinklers posed a substantial hazard, and that all 10 million should be recalled. "All of the approximately 10 million Omegas, manufactured from 1982 through the present, could fail to function, and members of the public may suffer bodily injury and/or death as a result."

Citing tests showing unacceptable failure rates, the U.S. CPSC sued the manufacturer last month to force it to recall the Omegas.

Central responded within minutes of the government announcement, saying it "strongly disagrees" with the complaint. "The Omega works. It has been successfully controlling fires for 15 years. We intend to defend our product and our ongoing remediation program." The company also said the commission's conclusion "is based on a methodology that does not apply to installed sprinkler systems."

- ■ (CEO-Spokesperson) In April, Central's CEO (George G. Meyer) spoke to the media. He blamed sloppy work by installers and the improper maintenance — over which his organization had no control. (One of the strategies used in most crisis communications plans is — Don't blame someone else.) (See Chapter 7; (*Philadelphia Inquirer,* March 5, 1998.)

■ *Diversified Records Services, Inc., West Pittston, Pennsylvania, 1997.* A Diversified Records Services' building was damaged by flames on May 5, 1997. The fire burned for nearly a week. The estimated damage is $6 million. It was the first fire Diversified Records has had at any of its 14 locations.

- ■ (CEO-Spokesperson) "At a May 9 press conference, president Clifford Metberger detailed response efforts, explaining that the company had remained in close contact with clients and was seeking additional space in the West Pittston area to meet storage needs." ("Another Records Center Fights Fire," *Contingency Planning & Management,* June 1997.)

■ *Firestone Tire Co., 1999.* Federal investigators are examining deaths that they think could be linked to faulty Firestone tires. Complaints suggesting that the tread of the Firestone models peel off. ("In probe of Firestone tires, 46 deaths are investigated," *Philadelphia Inquirer,* August 8, 2000.)

- ■ (CEO-Spokesperson) John Lampe, the successor to Masatoshi Ono as CEO, said, "We know that many people, not just in the United States but around the world, are now questioning our integrity and the safety of our tires. And we know that we can't blame anyone else for people losing trust in Firestone products — not our customers, not our business partners, not the media or Congress. The responsibility is ours," Lampe said.

■ *Food Lion – ABC Prime Time Live, 1992.* A story on an ABC's *Prime Time Live* in 1992 charged Food Lion, a grocery chain, with doctoring and selling spoiled meat. The story focused on lax sanitation and pressures to sell rotten food. According to *Prime Time Live,* workers at Food Lion said they were told to rewrap spoiled meat, to change "sell by" dates in order to increase shelf life, to camouflage rotting meat and fish by dipping old meat in bleach, and to disguise tainted chicken with barbecue sauce.

- ■ (CEO-Spokesperson) Hours after the program aired, President and CEO Tom E. Smith, issued a statement peppered with, "These lies have got to stop." The next day Smith also spoke out in new commercials.

■ *Ortho Pharmaceutical, Division of Johnson & Johnson, Raritan, New Jersey, 1992.* Ortho employees shredded thousands of documents about the marketing campaign for Retin-A, a day after learning of the federal investigation. The company reported the shredding to prosecutors in 1992 and fired three senior Ortho employees.

- ■ (CEO-Spokesperson) "The document destruction was absolutely wrong, and should never have occurred," said Ralph S. Larsen, Chairman and CEO of J&J.

■ *PECO, Norristown, Pennsylvania, 1995.* A gas leak caused an explosion that killed 2 people and injured a third.

- ■ (CEO-Spokesperson) Instead of following the standard corporate playbook, PECO shouldered the blame. The CEO (Corbin A. McNeill Jr.) said "PECO Energy takes full responsibility" for failing to respond to reports of a leak in time to avert the tragedy. He called PECO's delay in dispatching a technician "unacceptable and regrettable." McNeill acknowledged that his words could make the company more vulnerable to lawsuits and damage judgments. But he said it was the right thing to do, both morally and pragmatically, "regardless of any potential increases in liability." It was morally right because "we recognize that we had not responded properly, and there was such a tragic outcome that we ought to come forward and admit that."

■ *United Airlines, Chicago, Illinois, 2000.* United Airlines explained that "illegal job actions" by mechanics was the cause for a recent rise in flight cancellations at the world's largest airline as contract talks with the workers' union intensify. The airline said it canceled 99 flights Tuesday, more than twice as many as expected and about 4 percent of its 2270 daily flights. The number of aircraft taken out of service for repairs has risen in the past several weeks. The union denied that its members were engaged in any concerted job action. The airline still is on a reduced schedule due to delays and cancellations earlier this year that United blamed in part on pilot contract talks.

- ■ (CEO-Spokesperson) When United Airlines CEO Jim Goodwin stepped up to the camera in a TV spot last month, he apologized for United's summer of disruptions. In shirtsleeves, straight face and solemn tone, the chief of the world's biggest airline tried to reach out to thousands of angry United customers. United's decision to go on the air with the apology followed weeks of dizzying cancellation numbers and traveler horror stories. United pilots and mechanics were refusing to work overtime in protest of labor issues. "We felt like we had to communicate with passengers, and we wanted to reach of lot of people," explains Julie Thomson, spokeswoman for Fallon Worldwide, United's advertising agency.

Appendix 5E

CHANGES MADE: EXECUTIVES FIRED

The Executive Management Team (EMT) will begin make changes that will minimize the potential of a similar crisis from occurring. One of the changes could be the change in management.

Some of the crises that have resulted in the firing of executives of an organization include:

- *Arthur Andersen, Chicago, Illinois (Enron), 2002.* (Exec-Fired) On Jan. 15, five days after it announced the destruction, Andersen fired the lead auditor, David Duncan, and disciplined several members of its Houston office, which handled the Enron account. Backfired when congressional investigators released e-mails between Andersen's Chicago and Houston offices, showing that Nancy Temple had sent an e-mail about the firm's document-retention and destruction policy on Oct. 12. ("Andersen employees' morale rattled," *USA Today,* January 21, 2002.)
- *The Cincinnati Enquirer – Chiquita, Cincinnati, Ohio, 1998.* The Cincinnati Enquirer, apologizing to Chiquita in a front-page story, said a series that questioned the company's business practices was based on stolen voice mail and drew "untrue conclusions."
  - (Exec-Fired) The *Cincinnati Enquirer* newspaper said it has fired reporter Mike Gallagher and agreed to pay more than $10 million to Cincinnati-based Chiquita, after a series published by the newspaper questioned the company's business practices was based on stolen voice mail and drew "untrue conclusions." (*Newsweek,* July 13, 1998.)
- *Enron Corporation, Houston, Texas, 2001.* (Exec-Fired) Enron said that it discharged Ben Glisan, the company treasurer, and Kristina

Mordaunt, the general counsel of Enron's North America unit, in connection with investments they made in one of the officer-run limited partnerships. (*Wall Street Journal,* November 9, 2001.)

■ *Exxon "Valdez," Prince William Sound, Alaska, 1989.* (Exec-Fired) Capt. Joseph Hazelwood was fired because alcohol test results showed he had an illegally high blood-alcohol level 10 hours after the incident. Exxon USA's President, William Stevens, said, "We are all extremely disappointed and outraged that an officer in such a critical position would jeopardize his ship, his crew and the environment through such actions." (*USA Today,* June 22, 1989.)

■ *HBOC – McKesson, San Francisco, California, 2000.* Albert J. Bergonzi and Jay P. Gilbertson were indicted for securities fraud, conspiracy, mail fraud and wire fraud (former executives of McKesson). Investigators found accounting discrepancies that caused the company's stock to shed nearly half its market value when McKesson publicly announced accounting irregularities in April 1999. The indicted pair were co-presidents of HBOC & Co., an Alpharetta, Ga., maker of health-care software. The indictment accuses the two men of inflating quarterly sales to the SEC, backdating contracts, falsely reporting operating and expense outlays, providing false records to independent auditors, and conspiring to conceal their deceit. Millions of shareholders lost $9 billion in stock at the pharmaceutical and health-care-software supplier. The New York Common Retirement Fund, with $110 billion in assets, said it lost $250 million in the alleged ruse.

  ■ (Exec-Fired) McKesson ousted its top management two months after publicly announcing accounting irregularities. (*Philadelphia Inquirer,* September 29, 2000.)

■ *HealthSouth Corp., Birmingham, Alabama, 2003.* HealthSouth's board of directors fired the company's chairman and CEO, bringing Richard Scrushy's reign at the rehabilitation hospital chain he founded in 1984 to an inglorious end, when the SEC charged him with masterminding a scheme to inflate HealthSouth's earnings by at least $1.4 billion since 1999. Scrushy's firing is certain to bolster the cause of Plaintiffs attorneys, who have accused him of inside trading. Last year, Scrushy sold $100 million in stock before jolting investors in August with an announcement that, contrary to previous guidance, the company would announce an unexpected quarterly loss. ("Hospital chain fires CEO after scandal," *USA Today,* April 1, 2003.)

■ *Kidder, Peabody & Co. (General Electric), 1994.* (Exec-Fired) Kidder fired Joseph Jett, its head government-bond trader, for trades that Kidder says were intended to inflate profits and yield Jett a bigger bonus. Jett made $9 million in 1993. Six other staffers were suspended.

General Electric CEO Jack Welsh was furious about the Kidder Peabody bond-trading scandal. "What we had here was an integrity violation. It's an embarrassment," said Welsh. (*USA Today,* April 19, 1994.)

GE announced a sweeping management shuffle at its troubled Kidder, Peabody & Co. brokerage after firing Jett, installing GE's top financial officer, Dennis D. Dammerman, as Kidder's chief executive. Last month GE fired Kidder chairman Michael Carpenter, replacing him with two top GE executives. (*Philadelphia Inquirer,* June 23, 1994.)

■ *McKesson (Arthur Andersen), Chicago, Illinois, 2002.* Shareholders of McKesson HBOC filed lawsuits against Arthur Andersen claiming that Andersen's audits of HBOC in the late 1990s were negligent and failed to uncover the alleged accounting fraud.

 ■ (Exec-Resigned) Former CEO Mark Pulido resigned and

 ■ (Exec-Fired) Several other McKesson HBOC executives were fired. (McKesson HBOC case) – ("Andersen offers $50 million to settle suit," *USA Today,* April 18, 2002.)

■ *Mellon Bank, Pittsburgh, Pennsylvania, 2001.* At least 40,000 federal tax returns and payments involving $810 million were either lost or destroyed at a Pittsburgh processing facility. The tax returns and payments were sent by taxpayers in New England and parts of New York this year to a Pittsburgh lockbox run by Mellon Bank under a contract with the federal government.

 ■ (Exec-Fired) Mellon said in an e-mail that "several" bank employees were fired after an internal probe found returns were "hidden, and in some cases, destroyed." Loss of the contract resulted in layoffs of 106 other employees. (*Philadelphia Inquirer,* August 30, 2001.)

■ *Merrill Lynch (Enron), New York, New York, 2003.* The SEC accused four former senior Merrill Lynch executives yesterday of helping Enron inflate profit and mislead investors with two financing deals.

The SEC named former Merrill vice chairman Thomas W. Davis; Schuyler Tilney, an investment-banking managing director who directly oversaw corporate finance matters related to Enron; Robert Furst, a managing director in the investment-banking division; and Daniel Bayly, the global head of the division who later became the firm's chairman of investment banking.

 ■ (Exec-Fired) Davis and Tilney were fired by Merrill Lynch in September, Furst resigned in 2001, and Bayly retired last fall. (*Philadelphia Inquirer,* March 18, 2003.)

■ *Merrill Lynch (Martha Stewart) – New York, New York, 2002.* (Exec-Fired) — Late yesterday, Merrill Lynch fired Peter Bacanovic. It also fired Mr. Bacanovic's assistant, Douglas Faneuil, because he is accused of, and pleaded guilty to, a misdemeanor in connection with the case. (*Wall Street Journal,* October 3, 2002.)

- *NBC –Dateline, New York, New York – GM Truck, 1993.* (Exec-Fired) On March 21, 1993, NBC fired three top staff members on its *Dateline NBC* program over the staging of the fiery crash involving a General Motors truck. Jeff Diamond, executive producer of Dateline NBC, David Rummel, the program's senior producer, and Robert Read, who produced the segment. The decision was made after NBC president Robert Wright reviewed a report from outside attorneys hired by NBC to look into the GM fiasco. (*USA Today,* March 22, 1993.)
- *Prudential Insurance Co., Newark, New Jersey, 1994.* During a 1994 investigation of Prudential for possible misconduct in selling life insurance, Prudential said that files had been destroyed in its Cambridge, MA, office.
  - (Exec-Fired) Prudential fired the office's managing director, (David Fastenberg, Sr. VP), for "failing to abide by and enforce company directives to preserve documents." (*Philadelphia Inquirer,* June 27, 1996.)
- *Rent-Way Inc., Pittsburgh, Pennsylvania, 2000.* In October 2000, shareholders filed a federal lawsuit against Rent-Way, an Erie-based furniture, appliance, and computer-rental chain, and its accounting firm, PricewaterhouseCoopers, alleging that officers used faulty accounting practices to drive up the stock price. The company revealed in October 2000 that improper entries had been made into its accounting ledger to the tune of $75 million.
  - (Exec-Fired) Matthew Marini, Controller & Chief Accounting Officer, was fired, and Jeffrey Conway, the company's former president & COO, was asked to resign. ("Rent-Way settles for $25 million," *Philadelphia Inquirer,* March 21, 2003.)
- *Southwest Airlines, Burbank, California, 2000.* (Exec-Fired) Airline has fired the pilot and copilot of a 737 jetliner that skidded off a runway and onto a street during a botched landing at Burbank, Calif., Airport. The 737-300, arriving from Las Vegas, barreled off the runway onto a city street in March 5, 2000, striking a car, just missing a gas station. (*USA Today,* August 4, 2000.)
- *State of Texas, Fort Worth, 1995.* (Exec-Fired) (Tax Official) Don Sharp admitted transferring $4.2 million to his own account. He said he wasn't trying to steal it, but was testing the security of Tarrant County wire transfers. He was fired. (*USA Today,* January 23, 1995.)
- *Tyco International, Portsmouth, New Hampshire, 2003.* (Exec-Fired) In March, the troubled conglomerate said it had fired Jerry Boggess as head of the fire and security systems division, which includes the ADT home-security business. Boggess had been president of the fire and security systems division since 1995. ADT has been involved in

the bookkeeping problems revealed by Tyco. Part of the SEC's investigation of Tyco's accounting includes the speed at which the company depreciates capital expenses related to acquiring customers at ADT. ("Heads are rolling at Tyco, and its stock is hammered," *USA Today,* March 14, 2003.)

■ *U.S. Government – CIA, Washington, D.C., 2000.* (Exec-Fired) The CIA has fired one intelligence officer and reprimanded 6 managers, including a senior official, for errors that led to the bombing of the Chinese Embassy in Belgrade last year. The Chinese government has rejected U.S. explanations and demanded the U.S. conduct "a thorough investigation" and "severely punish the perpetrators." ("CIA holds 7 liable for bomb hit," *Philadelphia Inquirer,* April 9, 2000.)

■ *UnumProvident, Portland, Maine, 2003.* (Exec-Fired) UnumProvident fired Harold Chandler as chairman, chief executive and president as part of an effort to restore confidence in the disability insurer, which recently restated three years of earnings to resolve concerns of the SEC. Unum faces hundreds of lawsuits from policyholders who allege their benefits were unfairly denied and has had several recent multi-million-dollar jury verdicts against it. ("UnumProvident fires CEO Chandler," *USA Today,* April 1, 2003.)

Appendix 5F

CHANGES MADE: EXECUTIVES RESIGNED

The Executive Management Team (EMT) will begin make changes that will minimize the potential of a similar crisis from occurring. One of the changes could be a change in management.

Some of the crises that have resulted in the resignation of executives of an organization include:

- *Argenbright Security, 2001.* Under fire from the government, the nation's largest airport security company announced on Friday a management shake-up and policies to improve security.
  - (Exec-Retired) The company also announced that its founder, Frank Argenbright Jr., will retire from its board of directors. (*USA Today,* November 19, 2001.)
- *Cendant, Newark, New Jersey, 1998.* Cendant Corp. announced that the former Stamford, CT.-based CUC International Inc., (which merged with HFS Inc. of Parsippany in December to form Cendant), was responsible for the "accounting errors made with an intent to deceive" and "fictitious revenues." Cendant said CUC artificially inflated its revenue by classifying re-structuring charges as revenues, recording long-term revenue as short-term revenue, and delaying recognition of membership cancellations.
  - (Exec-Resigned) This led to the firing of an executive vice president and the resignation of two other CUC executives in April. Embattled Chairman Walter Forbes (55) and 8 of his allies on the board of directors resigned amid an accounting fraud scandal. (*USA Today,* July 23, 1998.)

■ *Coca-Cola Co., Atlanta, Georgia, 1999.* (Exec-Retired) The surprise announcement that M. Douglas Ivester (52) will retire as chairman and CEO of Coca-Cola stunned the beverage and business worlds. Ivester took over the top job at Coke after the death of Roberto Goizueta in October 1997. He has presided over a difficult period for the company, marked by lagging earnings reports and a pullback in the price of its shares, and the Belgian product recall. In June, nearly 200 school children in Belgium complained of feeling sick after drinking Coke products. The company appeared to react slowly, and Ivester didn't visit Belgium until the incident had exploded into a full-fledged health scare necessitating a product recall. (*USA Today,* December 7, 1999.)

■ *Coca-Cola Co., Atlanta, Georgia, 2003.* (Exec-Retired) The head of Coca-Cola Co.'s fountain division stepped down from his post in the wake of a scandal over a rigged marketing test for Burger King. The executive, Tom Moore, will remain with Coke in a transitional role, "to ensure a smooth transition," a Coke spokesman said. Moore has headed the food service division since December 1999. In June, the organization first disclosed its employees had tampered with results of a marketing test done three years ago at Burger King restaurants in the Richmond area to test the potential of a Frozen Coke promotion. Coke has since publicly apologized to Burger King, and agreed to pay as much as $21 million to Burger King and its franchisees to patch up relations with the company, which is its second largest fountain drink customer after McDonald's Corp. ("Executive at Coke Gives Up His Post in Scandal's Wake," *Wall Street Journal,* August 26, 2003.)

■ *Coca-Cola Co. – Fin. Arrange, Frozen, 2003.* (Exec-Resigned) On April 11, Gen. Counsel Deval Patrick resigned. Patrick had been feeling the heat for his handling of a whistleblower lawsuit (Matthew Whitely) that led to government probes of the company's accounting. ("More Seepage at Coke," *Business Week,* April 26, 2004.)

■ *Commonwealth Edison, Chicago, Illinois, 1999.* (Exec-Resigned) Five Commonwealth Edison executives have been asked to resign because of last summer's high-profile power outages, bringing to seven the number of company officials who have lost their jobs following an embarrassing series of blackouts. A reorganization was ordered after a severe heat wave left more than 100,000 customers without power for up to three days in July and a blackout hit part of a 30-square-block area in downtown Chicago for up to 11 hours in August. (*Philadelphia Inquirer,* November 27, 1999.)

■ *First National Bank of Bar Harbor, Bangor, Maine, 1996.* (Exec-Resigned) Orders the resignations of Peter Reilly, President of First

National Bank of Bar Harbor, and 3 bank workers. Bank must pay $1 million for selling home mortgage loans with falsified supporting documents. (*USA Today,* September 17, 1996.)

■ *Freddie Mac, Washington, D.C., 2003.* (Exec-Resigned) In a surprise shake-up, the government-sponsored company whose stock is widely traded said that it had fired the president and chief operating officer, David Glenn, and that the chairman and chief executive officer, Leland Brendsel, had resigned. Vaughn Clarke, the McLean, Va., company's executive vice president and chief financial officer, also resigned. Freddie Mac is the nation's second-largest buyer of mortgages. It said it had dismissed Glenn "because of serious questions as to the timeliness and completeness of his cooperation and candor" with lawyers hired in January by the board of directors' audit committee to review the accounting problems that span three years. The company does not believe fraud or criminal misconduct was involved, Gregory Parseghian, the new president and CEO, told shareholders, financial analysts and reporters in a conference call yesterday. (*Philadelphia Inquirer,* June 10, 2003.)

■ (Exec-Resigned) Two top executives who resigned from mortgage firm Freddie Mac amid accounting turmoil and federal investigations will be fired for alleged improper conduct, federal regulators said yesterday. By reclassifying former chairman and CEO Leland Brendsel and ex-chief financial officer Vaughn Clark as terminated, the Office of Federal Housing Enterprise Oversight could reduce the millions of dollars in compensation granted to them. ("Freddie Mac fires president over audit," *Philadelphia Inquirer,* June 10, 2003.)

Global Crossing Ltd., Bermuda, 2002. (Exec-Resigned) Gary Winnick, founder and chairman of the bankrupt telecommunications company, said that he would resign from the board of directors. Winnick said he was stepping down after helping develop a reorganization plan for the company and making good on his pledge to reimburse $25 million to employees who owned company stock in their retirement plans. Winnick deposited $25 million into an escrow account two weeks ago, although it is unclear how the money will be distributed to employees who had part of their 401(k) plans invested in company stock. Global Crossing sought bankruptcy protection in January 2002. Investors lost billions of dollars. (*Philadelphia Inquirer,* December 31, 2002.)

■ *Janus Capital Group Inc., Denver, Colorado, 2003.* (Exec-Resigned) Richard Garland, a Janus executive who investigators say gave e-mail approval to rapid trading of Janus mutual-fund shares, stepped down as head of the fund firm's international business. Mr. Garland's e-mails were featured prominently in the complaint files against hedge fund Canary Capital Partners LLP by NY Attorney General Eliot Spitzer on Sept. 3. The complaint alleged that Canary and managing principal Edward Stern had executed rapid trades in and out of several firms' mutual funds, including some at Janus. While not illegal, rapid trades known as market timing can raise the expenses and whittle the returns for a fund's other, long-term shareholders. (*Wall Street Journal*, November 18, 2003.)

■ *JCO Co., Sumitomo Metal Mining Co., Japan, 1999.* (Exec-Resigned) Moriki Aoyagi, the president of Sumitomo Metal Mining Co., said he would resign to take responsibility for what happened. He felt "socially and morally" responsible for the Sept. 30 accident, which killed one and left over 400 others exposed to radiation. (*Philadelphia Inquirer*, October 16, 1999.)

■ *Keefe, Bruyette Woods, New York City, 1999.* (Exec-Resigned) ex-CEO James McDermott, who was charged with passing on insider-trading tips to his porn-star lover, stepped down from the top job at KBW, which advises banks on merger and acquisition opportunities. But there are persistent questions on Wall Street about how KBW will regain its good name and reputation. (John Duffy) and (Joseph Berry) inherited the executive suite after McDermott stepped down in disgrace. They are working frantically to keep the company's name from sinking further. (*New York Post*, December 23, 1999.)

■ *Kidder, Peabody & Co. (General Electric), New York, New York, 1994.* (Exec-Resigned) The supervisor of Joseph Jett, Edward Cerullo, a 15-year veteran of the Wall Street firm, quit Kidder. Cerullo's resignation came about a week before a General Electric inquiry into the allegedly phony trading was to have been completed. (*USA Today*, April 19, 1994.)

■ *Micron Technology, California, 2002.* A Micron Technology executive agreed to plead guilty of obstructing an investigation into alleged price fixing of computer memory chips, the Justice Department. Regional sales manager Alfred Censullo was accused of altering and concealing documents, sought by a California grand jury that contained competitor-pricing information.

　■ (Exec-Resigned) Micron accepted Censullo's resignation and says it has been co-operating with the probe, which began in 2002. ("Micron exec to plead guilty of obstruction," *USA Today*, December 18, 2003.)

■ *Moody's Investor Services Inc., New York, New York, 1996.* Moody's pleaded guilty to one count of obstructing justice by destroying documents in 1996 during an antitrust investigation. Moody's said the incident occurred in 1996 during a Justice Dept investigation into how Moody's determined fees on bond deals and whether it improperly pressured bond issuers to hire the agency to rate their bonds. During the course of the inquiry, the company said an employee erred by destroying some internal documents subpoenaed by the Justice Dept. Moody's said it voluntarily reported the incident and turned over photocopies of the destroyed documents. The Justice Dept said it closed the larger investigation in April 1999. Moody's said the employee who destroyed the documents is no longer with the company.

- (Exec-Resigned) The company also said it accepted the resignations of three executives in its Global Ratings and Research Division: Sr. VP Donald E. Noe; Sr. VP and Chief Credit Officer Kenneth J.H. Pinkes; and Managing Director, Public Finance M. Douglas Watson Jr. Moody's said none of the men were engaged in the destruction of documents or the obstruction of justice. (*Wall Street Journal*, April 11, 2001.)

■ *NBC Dateline – GM-Truck, New York, New York, 1993.* NBC News president Michael Gartner, whose career sustained devastating damage after one of his shows blew up a General Motors pickup truck, announced yesterday he was resigning. After GM threatened to sue NBC, Gartner's mistake was to call the broadcast "fair and accurate." Staffers said that Gartner's ill-considered reaction to GM's challenge was the final straw. After GM sued, NBC admitted that it had misrepresented key details in the crash staged for the cameras.

Gartner (54), a distinguished newspaper editor before he took over NBC News almost five years ago, acknowledged that the now-infamous *Dateline NBC* story contributed to the timing of his departure. In that scandal, the network faked crash-test results on a GM pickup truck and was forced into an apology Feb. 9 to settle a defamation lawsuit.

- [*USA Today,* March 22, 1993] (Exec-Fired) NBC yesterday fired three top staff members on its *Dateline NBC* program over the staging of the fiery crash involving a General Motors truck. Jeff Diamond, executive producer of *Dateline NBC,* David Rummel, the program's senior producer, and Robert Read, who produced the segment. The decision was made after NBC president Robert Wright reviewed a report from outside attorneys hired by NBC to look into the GM fiasco. (*USA Today,* March 3, 1993.)

■ *PECO, Peach Bottom, 1988.* Control room personnel were discovered sleeping on the job at the Peach Bottom nuclear generating station in Delta, York County. The NRC ordered the plant shut down on

March 31, 1987. It stayed shut down for 2-1/2 years. During that time, PE had to buy replacement power elsewhere. An industry watchdog group criticized the firm for lax management. "A corporate culture had been allowed to develop from the top down that downplayed, rejected or ignored problems." "A lack of accountability in the corporate organization is pervasive and this situation has existed for several years." "The grossly unprofessional behavior by a wide range of personnel and condoned by superintendents, reflects a major breakdown in the management of a nuclear facility."

- ■ (Exec-Retired) The result was that John H. Austin, president and chief operating officer of Philadelphia Electric, announced that he would take unscheduled retirement as of March 1st of 1988. (*Philadelphia Daily News*, February 2, 1988.)

■ *Pilgrim's Pride Corp., Pittsburgh, Pennsylvania, 2002.* Listeria was found at Pilgrim's plant in Montgomery County, PA. (Step-4-FTP) On Oct. 12, Pilgrim's Pride recalled 27 million pounds of its poultry products from its Wampler Foods Inc. turkey-processing plant in Franconia Township. (CMT-Legal) The listeria is blamed for 7 deaths and 50 illnesses.

- ■ (Exec-Retired) After being buffeted by the largest meat recall in U.S. history, Pilgrim's said that CEO David Van Hoose would retire in March. (*Philadelphia Inquirer*, November 13, 2002.)

■ *Prudential Securities, New York, New York, 2003.* A dozen employees of Prudential Securities in Boston and New York were asked to resign in connection with the ongoing government investigation of mutual fund trading practices. An office manager and five stockbrokers based in Boston, an office manager in Long Island and five brokers in the New York area were forced out this week as a result of an internal house-cleaning by Wachovia Securities. Wachovia recently merged its securities arm with Prudential. Last month, Prudential acknowledged that Massachusetts's securities regulators were investigating improper mutual fund trades at its Boston office. In particular, regulators are looking at mutual fund timing — a practice in which investors make short-term trades to try to take advantage of price movements. Though the practice is not illegal, most mutual fund companies, including Wachovia, have policies prohibiting market timing. (*USA Today*, October 2, 2003.)

■ *Reliant Resources Inc., 2002.* (Exec-Resigned) Two Reliant executives who oversaw divisions responsible for bogus energy trades now under scrutiny have resigned, and the company placed a 30-year veteran in charge of the company's wholesale group activities. The departures were "fallout" from a continuing review of questionable transactions that artificially inflated Reliant's volumes and boosted its revenue by 10 percent. The trades took place over the last three years. Joe Bob Perkins was executive vice president and group president of wholesale businesses. Shahid Malik was president of trading in the company's wholesale group. (*Philadelphia Inquirer,* May 17, 2002.)

■ *Rite Aid Corp., Camp Hill, Pennsylvania, 1995.* (Exec-Resigned) Cracking under pressure from banks and regulators announced that it had inflated its profits by about $500 million the last three years and that its chairman and CEO, Martin L. Grass, had resigned. In announcing Grass's departure from the company that his father started in 1963, Rite Aid said it had reached a desperately needed one-year extension on $1.3 billion in bank credit that was set to expire on Oct. 29. Grass, 45, took control of the company from his father, Alex Grass, in 1995. Rite Aid said it would restate its earnings by $500 million for the fiscal years 1997, 1998 and 1999. Rite Aid Corp. shares rose 19 percent yesterday, a day after the Camp Hill drugstore chain said its chief executive quit. (*Philadelphia Inquirer,* October 19, 1999.)

■ *Royal Dutch/Shell, England, 2004.* Royal Dutch/Shell's upper management repeatedly ignored warnings starting as early as February 2002 that the company's oil and gas reserves were far overstated. The report was the company's fullest public statement about the origin of an accounting scandal that has triggered high-level resignations and government investigations since Royal Dutch/Shell first said in January that its reserves were much smaller than its investors knew. The company also said Monday: (1) It is downgrading an additional 200 million barrels of reserves to less certain categories. Counting two previous downgrades since Jan. 1, Shell has now moved 22% of its oil and gas reserves out of the "proven" category.

(2) Shell CFO Judith Boynton was replaced by another Shell executive, Tim Morrison. The report indicates that because of Shell's weak internal controls, Boynton was unaware of the problems when she signed off on Shell's financial statements. According to a summary of the investigative report that Shell released, Walter van de Vijver, the former CEO of Shell's exploration and production unit, began complaining about Shell's reserve estimates after he took over the division in June 2001.

■ (Exec-Resigned) He replaced Philip Watts, who became Shell's chairman. Both men resigned last month. The report portrays van de Vijver as an executive torn between his knowledge of Shell's oil reserve issues and his role in helping Shell mask the problem. (*USA Today,* April 20, 2004.)

- *Safety-Kleen Corp., Columbia, South Carolina, 2000.* The hazardous-waste-disposal company announced the resignations of 3 top officials who were suspended in March following an internal investigation into alleged accounting irregularities.
  - (Exec-Resigned) Kenneth W. Winger stepped down as CEO. Michael Bragagnolo resigned from his COO post. Paul Humphreys resigned as CFO. (*Wall Street Journal,* May 15, 2000.)
- *Salomon Bros., New York, New York, 1991.* Salomon has admitted breaking the rules at Treasury market auctions by submitting bids in the names of customers without their authorization. (*USA Today,* September 6, 1991.)
  - (Exec-Resigned) Executives forced to resign – John Gutfreund, former CEO; Thomas Strauss, former President; John Meriwether, former vice chairman; and Donald Feuerstein, former chief legal officer. (*Philadelphia Inquirer,* December 4, 1992.)
  - Former chairman John Gutfreund, will pay a $100,000 fine and never again run a Wall Street firm to settle civil charges stemming from the '91 government bond scandal. (*Philadelphia Inquirer,* January 7, 1993.)
  - Salomon agreed to pay $4 million to settle claims by 39 states and the District of Columbia over its role in the 1991 scandal. Half the money will go into an investor protection fund that state officials can use to battle fraud and abuse. The rest will be doled out evenly among the 40 jurisdictions. (*USA Today,* June 11, 1993.)
  - Salomon says it has agreed to pay $54.5 million plus $12.5 million in lawyers' fees to settle class-action lawsuits filed by its shareholders and bondholders after its '91 scandal. (*Philadelphia Inquirer,* August 20, 1991.)
- *Symbol Technologies, Holtsville, New York, 2003.* (Exec-Resigned) Symbol Technologies Inc., a maker of bar-code scanners, said its CEO and acting chairman stepped down amid a continuing investigation of its accounting. The Holtsville, NY, company also said it would restate financial results for 1998 through 2001 and the first nine months of 2002. President and chief operating officer William Nuti, 40, has been named Richard Bravman's successor as CEO. The company said it named its new lead independent director Salvatore Iannuzzi as non-executive chairman. Iannuzzi, 50, and two other directors were named to the board two weeks ago. Bravman, 48, voluntarily relinquished his roles "in an effort to facilitate a favorable conclusion" to the government investigation into Symbol's accounting, the company said. In spring 2001, Bravman was part of a transaction that involved the improper recognition of about $860,000

in revenue, the company said. (Symbol Technologies CEO steps down amid probe," *Philadelphia Inquirer,* December 31, 2003.)

■ *United Way, Washington, D.C., 1994.* (Exec-Resigned) William Aramony resigned after his lavish spending and management practices spelled an end to his 22-year tenure as president. The government charged the former president of United Way of America and 2 fellow executives with conspiracy and mail and tax fraud yesterday, accusing them of spending more than $1 million of the charity's money on vacations, real estate and air travel. The 71-count federal indictment named Aramony, president of United Way from 1970 to 1992; Stephen J. Paulachak, 49, a United Way executive between 1971 and 1988 and also president of an indicted spin-off company; and Thomas J. Merlo, 63, chief financial officer of the charity from 1990 until 1992. (*Philadelphia Inquirer,* September 14, 1994.)

(*Author Note:* This is in no way all the cases in which executives have resigned as part of the effort to "fix the problem" created by a crisis.)

Appendix 5G

CHANGES MADE: EXECUTIVES REASSIGNED

- *Firestone, 2000.* (Tire Failures) Firestone agreed that manufacturing problems at Firestone's Decatur, Illinois, plant were partly to blame for the tire failures. The problem tires exhibited lower adhesion than similar tires produced at other plants.
  - (Exec-Reassigned) Masatoshi Ono (63), CEO and chairman of the U.S. operations and EVP of Bridgestone Corp., will no longer manage its operations. Rumors of Ono's demotion, firing or resignation have circulated since August when the company recalled 6.5 million ATX, ATX II and Wilderness tires that have been linked to more than 150 fatal crashes worldwide. (*Philadelphia Inquirer,* October 3, 2000.)
- *Rent-Way Inc., Erie, Pennsylvania, 2000.* A rental company's reported earnings for fiscal 2000 were inflated by fictitious accounting ledger entries. Rent-Way Inc., Erie, has suspended its controller pending the results of an investigation into the accounting irregularities, which the company said inflated fiscal 2000 earnings by $25 million to $35 million.
  - (Exec-Reassigned) Rent-Way announced Monday that controller Matthew Marini has been put on leave while the audit committee of the company's board of directors conducts its investigation. The company has retained PricewaterhouseCoopers LP to help with the probe. (*Philadelphia Inquirer,* November 2, 2000.)
- *U.S. Navy, USS Greenville, Hawaii, 2001.* U.S. nuclear-powered submarine accidentally sank the Japanese trawler Ehime Maru in 1800 feet of water off Hawaii, killing 9 Japanese crew members. The fishing trawler was a 174-foot training vessel for Japanese high school students. The usual procedure, according to submariners,

251

is to both listen for surface ships with passive sonar and to scan the area visually with a periscope before surfacing.

■ (Exec-Reassigned) Capt. Scott Waddle has been relieved of duty pending investigations by both the Navy and the National Transportation Safety Board. The video and sound recording devices in the control room of the submarine were not operating during the accident, which occurred as the Greeneville practiced an emergency main ballast blow, a rapid ascent to the surface of the ocean. Sixteen civilian visitors were aboard the ship, and Navy officials acknowledged yesterday that their presence might have distracted the captain and crew. (*Philadelphia Inquirer*, February 15, 2001.)

■ Xerox, 2002.

■ (Exec-Reassigned) Treasurer Gregory Tayler was reassigned to a post in Canada in the wake of disclosures that he is being investigated for possible civil violations by the SEC. The move is the latest management shakeup undertaken by Xerox, which is struggling to convince skeptical investigators that the company has cleaned up its accounting mess. ("Xerox Treasurer Is Reassigned," *Wall Street Journal,* September 30, 2002.)

Appendix 5H

CHANGES MADE: PROCEDURES AND CONTROLS

- *BASF, Cincinnati, Ohio, 1990.* The BASF plant, a 4-story building, formerly known as the "Inmont," experienced an explosion and fire. When firefighters arrived, building walls had been blown down and heavy fire was showing from the center of the complex. Firefighters rescued a number of employees. Two employees were killed. The sprinkler systems had been blown apart by the explosion, and were doing little else than acting as a draw on the water supply. Given the widespread impact of the explosion, which was in a residential area, the 911 system was almost immediately inundated with hundreds of phone calls. This jam up of telephone calls made it virtually impossible for the fire or police department to respond to individual calls in the immediate vicinity.
  - (Change) The most important lesson learned was that communications and coordination with other agencies needed to be changed. Preplanning discussions had been held with most of the responding agencies. However the magnitude of this situation pointed out the need for improvements between all responders. (*Firehouse,* October 1990.)
- *ConAgra Foods Inc., Omaha, Nebraska, 2001.* ConAgra said that it would restate three years of financial results. The problems occurred within one of ConAgra's subsidiaries, United Agri Products Cos., which sells seed, fertilizer and chemicals to farmers. ConAgra said revisions would reduce pretax earnings for fiscal 1998, 1999 and 2000 by a total of about $123 million.

- (Investigation) ConAgra, maker of Butterball turkeys, Hunt's ketchup and Wesson oil, said it began investigating its subsidiary last year, and the SEC subsequently launched an informal inquiry of its own.
- (Change) Bruce Rohde, ConAgra's chairman and CEO, said that accounting controls would be strengthened; that personnel at the subsidiary would be changed; and that the major financial problems at the subsidiary already had been identified and addressed. Mr. Rohde said the irregularities "circumvented generally accepted accounting practices and violated ConAgra Foods' corporate policy." (*Wall Street Journal,* May 29, 2001.)
- *Ford Motor Co. – Explorer, Detroit, Michigan, 2000.* The recall of the Explorer's cost Ford about $500 million in the third quarter.
  - (Change) Ford says it will offer tire pressure monitors and other safety improvements on all its Ford-branded SUVs by 2005. The changes come as the company is dealing with the aftermath of defective Firestone tires on Ford trucks that have been linked to about 140 deaths. (*USA Today,* January 9, 2001.)
- Johnson & Johnson – McNeil, Ft. Washington, Pennsylvania – Tylenol.
  - (Change) McNeil Labs will be advising parents for the first time that too much Tylenol can harm children. Relatively small overdoses of acetaminophen have been blamed for liver damage and even deaths in children. Containers with new labeling are scheduled to reach stores shortly. McNeil will also take out magazine ads to inform parents about correct dosages.

    Deborah Regosin-Hodges, whose 14-month old daughter, Sophie, underwent a partial liver transplant in 1994, applauded the labeling change. Sophie was accidentally overdosed because her parents and physician were unaware that grape-flavored infant Tylenol is 3-1/2 times stronger than children's Tylenol, according to the lawsuit they filed against McNeil. Consumers weren't told that giving a child as little as twice the proper dose over a period of time could destroy their livers.
- *United Way, 1991.* After the William Aramony scandal broke in 1991, there was a question of how it would affect the charity's contributions needed by the United Way to operate. The scandal dealt with his lavish spending of the charity's money. Some of the allegations made about Mr. Aramony include: he received a salary of $463,000 annually, enjoyed chauffeured automobiles and traveled first class. He lent some affiliates nearly $3 million (IRS is investigating), approved several for-profit spin offs that have engaged in questionable activities.

- (Destruction of Records) Then in January of 1992, *The Washington Post* published reports that William Aramony had approved the disposal of five (5) filing drawers of financial documents. Officers of the United Way International have asked their accountants, Arthur Andersen & Co., to review the records and make sure that all that is needed be there. One purpose was to reassure edgy donors and local groups.
- (Exec-Sentenced) The former president of United Way, William Aramony was sentenced to seven years in prison for fraudulently diverting $1.2 million of the charity's money to pay for a romance with a teen-age girl friend and other benefits for himself. (*New York Times,* June 23, 1995.)
- (Changes) The agency's reforms have won high marks from outside observers. (1) The president' s salary and benefit package have been cut by more than half. Aramony was receiving $463,000; Chao gets $195,000 salary plus health insurance. (2) All travel expenses must be approved in advance, and nobody can sign his or her checks. (3) All employees must fly coach. (4) Per diem meal allowances, based on federal reimbursement rates, have been instituted. (5) Spouse travel at agency expense has been virtually eliminated. (*Philadelphia Inquirer,* October 4, 1993.)

Chapter 6

THE CRISIS MANAGEMENT TEAM

6.1 INTRODUCTION

This chapter deals with the roles of the Crisis Management Team (CMT) during a disaster, or crisis. It concentrates on the roles during the Acute-Crisis stage and discusses the following:

- The members of the Crisis Management Team (CMT)
- What the CMT does
- How the CMT provides support if their offices are affected
- "Exercising" – the value
- Role in documenting
- Examples of service level agreements
- Elements included in each CMT member's service level agreement

Once a Pre-Crisis situation moves to the Acute-Crisis stage, the members of the Executive Management Team (EMT) will activate the Crisis Management Plan (CMP) and **turn over the managing of the acute crisis to members of the Crisis Management Team (CMT).**

At this point in time, the executives on the EMT should concentrate on running the organization's day-to-day operations. They should maintain the continuity of operations. **(The EMT plays the major role during the Pre-Crisis and Post-Crisis stages.)**

The CMT's role is to respond quickly and efficiently in providing their expertise and support.

As John Paluszak, President of Ketchum Public Affairs, noted following the BP America crisis (the oil spill off the California coast), "In each crisis, there is a window of challenge that lasts for a few hours or a day. During that window, a company must show they are taking the crisis seriously and addressing it or neutralizing it."

Paluszak was comparing BP America's oil spill response to Exxon's Alaska oil spill response. In his opinion, BP America did a much better job than Exxon did.

After activating the CMP, the CMT should:

- Take charge quickly.
- Determine the facts.
- Tell your story.
- Fix the problem.

   (***Author Note:*** See Chapter 4.)

6.1.1   Crisis Management Planning Is Not a New Concept

Organizations have had a form of a "crisis management plan" and a "crisis management team" for a number of years. Earlier plans may have had a different name, but they did identify key executives to respond to a crisis when one occurred.

A perfect example is the "Corporate Communications Plan," used to respond to the news media when an organization is in the throes of a crisis. This plan, the "Corporate Communications Plan" is not the Crisis Management Plan. It is a major element within the CMP but the CMP also includes the roles of other key executives.

Still, some organizations use the term "Crisis Management Plan" to describe their security plans, or their emergency response plans. Others apply it loosely to an ad hoc committee that was set up for an important purpose earlier.

The security plans, the emergency response plans, or the "Corporate Communications Plans" are a part of the overall Crisis Management Team (see Chapter 2).

6.2   WHO ARE THE MEMBERS OF THE CRISIS MANAGEMENT TEAM?

The core members of the Crisis Management Team (CMT) will include the heads of, or assigned representatives for, the following departments:

- Facilities, Buildings, Property department
- Security department
- Public Relations or Media Relations department
- Human Resources or Personnel department
- Legal department
- Insurance or Risk Management department
- Treasury or Finance department

Other members who, because of their expertise, could participate on the CMT include the:

- Procurement or Purchasing department
- Transportation or Travel department
- Information Technology or Communications department

The CMT comprise a wide range of disciplines within the organization in order to effectively manage any type of crisis the organization might face.

6.2.1 Who Selected the Members of the Crisis Management Team?

When the EMT members agreed on the type of questions they want answered following a disaster or crisis (their "EMT agenda"), they also identified the executive, or department, that would provide the answer to those questions.

Chapter 5 used a fire as the disaster scenario that had struck the organization. The list of questions in the EMT agenda that should be answered should include:

- Were there any injuries to personnel?
- What was the cause of the fire?
- Have security precautions been implemented?
- What is the damage to the organization's assets?
- Is there a potential for adverse publicity?
- Do we have any contractual concerns?
- Does our insurance policies cover our losses?
- What is the status of the affected business functions?
- Where are the business functions located? Is this a temporary situation?
- How did the employees get to the temporary sites? Transportation support? Monies?
- How is the network operating? Do we have communications with the key organization and people?

As the members of the EMT reviewed the questions, adding or deleting as appropriate, they were asked "who" in the organization would be the best person to provide the answer to each question. When the executives identified by the best person, they also selected the members of the organization's CMT.

6.2.2 Do All Organizations Have Crisis Management Teams?

Organizations in industries that regularly experience disasters or crises usually have an "existing" CMT. When I say industries that experience disasters/crises regularly, I am referring to organizations in industries such as the chemical, oil, pharmaceutical, food, and airline industries.

The chemical and oil industries experience explosions and fires, and the pharmaceutical and food companies experience product safety, product failure, and product tampering crises. The airline industry has experienced plane accidents. According to some crisis management experts, many organizations in these industries have a permanent CMT in place at all times.

Because they seem to experience crises on a regular basis, organizations in these industries have the advantage of knowing how they performed, or how a competitor performed, in a prior crisis situation. This information provides the basis for establishing an agenda of items they want to ensure are going to be considered should they be faced with a similar crisis.

When something unexpected occurs, organizations have adjusted their CMP to accommodate these lessons:

For example, in the pharmaceutical or food industries:. When Johnson & Johnson's division, McNeil Laboratories, was faced with the "Tylenol tampering" issue back in 1982, they handled the crisis so well they became the model organization to use in developing a strategy to follow for managing a crisis.

> "Tylenol capsules containing cyanide resulted in the deaths of 8 people in the Chicago area. The manufacturer McNeil, (Division of J&J) recalled all the capsules in the United States. The quality of the product was not in question, but people were dying. J&J management took swift action. They removed all Tylenol capsules from the marketplace, at a cost of more than $150 million. This action is believed by many to have preserved the reputation of J&J, as it regained Tylenol's share of the market within a year."

> **—Steven Fink**
> *Crisis Management: Planning for the Inevitable*

Johnson & Johnson and its McNeil unit recalled, examined, and destroyed 31 million bottles of Tylenol capsules at a cost of $100 million. Fewer than 75 poisoned capsules were ultimately found.

Johnson & Johnson led an industry effort to make packaging "tamper resistant." Consumers can now tell at a glance with most products if seals have been broken or packages breached. "Almost everything that you can buy today has tamper-evident packaging, and it stems from that event. The Tylenol incident changed the whole way the pharmaceutical industry and the food industry business operate." (George Sadler, research professor of food packaging at the Illinois Institute of Technology's National Center for Food.)

Then when Burroughs Wellcome faced the Sudafed tampering issue back in 1991, it managed the crisis in a similar fashion as J&J/McNeil. The manufacturer of Sudafed 12-hour cold capsules issued a nationwide recall after two people who had taken the medication died of cyanide poisoning and a third became seriously ill. The deaths triggered the nationwide recall, a public awareness campaign against product tampering, and an FBI investigation.

Philip R. Tracy, president and chief executive officer of the company said, "We are moving rapidly to alert the public and retrieve all Sudafed 12-hour capsules from the retail stores. Our sympathies go to the families of the individuals involved, and they have our assurance that the company will investigate these incidents quickly and thoroughly." Tracy also offered a $100,000 reward for information leading to the conviction of the person involved in the tampering case.

Then again, when Arnott's Ltd., in Australia, faced a tampering incident in 1997, Arnott's followed a script written in 1982 by J&J in the Tylenol incident. An extortionist tampered with six packets of Arnott's biscuits on a shelf in a Brisbane supermarket in 1997. Arnott's, Australia's largest cookie-maker, conducted a nationwide recall of its products after a threat was made to poison its products on supermarket shelves.

Chris Roberts, the managing director of Arnott's biscuits at the time, said the plan required that they protect the interest of all stakeholders — the consumers, the company, and its shareholders — and work through the incident as quickly as possible. "We did everything in front of television cameras, the withdrawal of products from the shelf, the trucks dumping the products at the tip and later the restocking of supermarkets. We ran information ads in different states because in each state the circumstances were different." He said it was a campaign designed to show that Arnott's had been completely open and it worked.

Another example of learning from a competitor/peer's experience could be in the oil industry. In 1990, the British Petroleum Co. was able to respond to the oil spill off the California coast much better than Exxon's response to the oil spill in Alaska.

When Exxon Oil Co. was faced with the "Exxon Valdez" oil spill back in 1989, the organization handled the crisis as if it would go away in due time. The Exxon Valdez oil tanker went aground on Bligh Reef in Prince William Sound on Friday, March 24, 1989. The tanker released approximately 11.3 million gallons of crude oil. There were an estimated 60 million gallons aboard at the time of the incident.

Within 48 hours after the Exxon Valdez struck the reef, Frank Iarossi, president of Exxon Shipping Co., took financial responsibility for the oil spill and told reporters that the tanker was piloted by an uncertified officer.

Initially, Exxon responded to questions by the news media. For example, Exxon did reveal that:

- The tanker went out of normal shipping lanes (with permission from the Coast Guard).
- The captain of the ship was not piloting the tanker; and may have been under the influence of alcohol.
- A non-certified third mate was piloting.
- Exxon selected one person to be the official spokesperson — Dave Parish. In addition, Frank Iarossi, President of Exxon Shipping Co., was also a spokesperson.
- Exxon was chastised for not having Exxon USA's President, William Stevens, or the chairman (Lawrence G. Rawl) at the scene and making public statements. Rawl waited six days before discussing the spill. Rawl's failure to follow crisis management experts' suggested response plans soured everything the company has tried since then.

Then, when the British Petroleum (BP America) oil tanker, American Trader, spilled nearly 400,000 gallons of oil near Long Beach, California, in 1990, the company's aggressive effort to quickly clean up the mess won accolades from oil analysts and the public relations industry.

- Within hours of the disaster, BP public relations officials, carrying hand-held cellular telephones, were dispatched to points along the coast wherever reporters might congregate. They were supported by private public relations specialists. These specialists were flown in on the night of the disaster.
- The corporate communication's command center was located next to the cleanup command center in BP's Long Beach office.
- Two BP executives, located in the Coast Guard headquarters in Long Beach, were more than willing to give a national television interview when asked by a producer for NBC's "Today Show."

- When a television station wanted underwater footage of the hull of the ship, BP was ready to provide it. "That's part of the story," said BP crisis manager Chuck Webster. British Petroleum "put its crisis management approach on the line," reported Webster, whose position had been elevated to management after Valdez. The perception is created early on as to whether you can handle it or you do not shoot straight.
- At the height of the cleanup, there were 2050 contract workers on the beach, plus the company's 100-person command structure.

6.3 WHAT DOES THE CRISIS MANAGEMENT TEAM DO?

As Steven Fink said in his book, entitled *Crisis Management: Planning for the Inevitable*, "Crisis Management …is the art of removing much of the risk and uncertainty to allow you to achieve more control over your own destiny."

No crisis can be successfully and effectively managed unless it has first been identified and isolated.

Members of the CMT should be prepared to identify and isolate the crisis, and the effects on the organization, as best they can. Then the CMT should analyze the crisis they are faced with. They should be wise enough to understand and evaluate the situation and come up with solutions to help the organization cope with the problems.

As previously mentioned in this chapter, the CMT does the following:

- Take charge quickly.
- Determine the facts.
- Tell your story.
- Fix the problem.

Richard Wnek stated very clearly in his article entitled "Helping Employees Recover" (*Contingency Planning & Management Magazine,* July/August 2000), "The CMT is a functional team that must work together. The members of the team must communicate effectively with one another. The Crisis Management Plan they use should include the guidelines needed to respond to the crisis. The guidelines should be clear and not vague. They should also be concise."

> (***Author Note:*** For this reason, you may see an organization's documented guidelines using short statements, without a lot of explanation as to the why and how.)

CMTs must not be groups of individuals working at cross-purposes. In a crisis, there is no room for executives who have problems with operational needs, internal politics, and egos.

The CMT members must be capable of acting on the crisis, rather than a team that is designed to study the problem. Your CMP should have a team identified (CMT) with the responsibility and the authority to take actions on problems.

> (***Author Note:*** As part of the CMP policy set up by the top executives of your organization, there must be a stipulation that the members have the authority to act.)

Once a Pre-Crisis situation moves to the Acute-Crisis stage, the members of the EMT should activate the CMT and turn over the managing of the Acute Crisis to them.

They should authorize the members of the CMT to take whatever action is needed to fix the problem. Remember that the selection of members was based on the ability of the executives selected to the CMT to manage the crisis management issues. The selections were made during a non-crisis, non-stressful time (during a calm time), based on their expertise and ability to manage a crisis when one would strike.

Now the EMT needs to show confidence in the members of the CMT by authorizing them with the power to make decisions.

6.3.1 Situation: New Crisis — New Circumstances

Obviously the Crisis Management Plan (CMP) is a plan that will respond to a crisis similar to one that it has experienced before. After learning things from the prior crisis, the members of the CMT have that experience to fall back on when they are faced with it again.

But when the CMT is faced with a new crisis, or some new circumstance that has not occurred before, the members of the team must be flexible, and able to think quickly and adapt to new situations. This should enable them to deal with the crisis in a way that will counteract any of the unplanned for situations mentioned above.

6.3.2 Selecting the "Crisis" Manager

During a crisis, the CMT will be faced with all types of issues. The CMT member's response will differ depending on the type of crisis. Therefore, they should determine which member of the CMT should manage this particular crisis. This will be determined based on the type of crisis and the expertise of the individual CMT members.

For example, if the company's product is accused of being responsible for people getting sick — or worse yet, dying — the response will concentrate on people safety first, and then on the investigation of whether the product is at fault and why.

If an airline organization experiences a plane accident, the response will concentrate on the survivors' condition, the families of fatalities first, and then on the investigation of why the plane crashed.

When a crisis strikes, the members of the CMT should determine who the "crisis manager" will be. Because the CMT comprises a number of executives with different areas of expertise, the crisis manager will be selected based on the type of crisis the organization is experiencing. For example,

- You would not want a "product problem" (safety, failure, tampering) crisis managed by the Insurance department representative.
- At the same time, you would not want a "financial crisis" managed by the Insurance department representative.

6.3.3 Key Concern: CMT Duties during a Crisis

Some top executives feel that members of the CMT should continue to perform their normal duties, as well as attempt to manage and control the crisis. Once the crisis is visible, the members of the CMT should not be expected to perform any other duties except for managing of the acute-crisis situation. It should be the team's only priority.

6.4 HOW WILL CMT MEMBERS PERFORM THEIR CRISIS MANAGEMENT ACTIVITIES IDENTIFIED IN THE SERVICE LEVEL AGREEMENT (SLA) IF THEIR OFFICES ARE AFFECTED?

Another consideration during the planning phase is how will the CMT will provide the support identified in the Service Level Agreement (SLA) if their location, offices, or equipment and records have been affected by that crisis or disaster.

- What if their offices are not available?
- What if their computers, or other key equipment, are not available?
- What if their records or key documents are not available?

How will they carry out their responsibilities? The answer is that each member (department) of the CMT has developed its own Business Resumption Plan (BRP). This plan should have been documented, tested, and exercised. The BRP will be used to resume the department's business operations and to provide the support identified in the SLA.

It consists of policies and procedures for employees of the departments that form the CMT to follow *after* a disaster (or crisis) is contained. The BRP for each department that forms the CMT consists of planning elements to resume all critical activities performed by that department. Examples of members' plans appear in Appendices 6A through 6H.

6.4.1 If On-Site Resources Are Damaged

Part of the BRP for the CMT affected deals with when the on-site resources are damaged, or are not accessible. In those cases, the employees in the department will retrieve their backups from the off-premises storage areas.

6.4.1.1 Retrieve Data and Records from the Off-Premises Storage Location(s)

- Some material can be retrieved from the IT mainframe computers, or the open systems.
- Critical department back up (hard copy) resources would be retrieved from the off-premises storage areas. Many organizations use professional off-premises storage companies, while others store critical documents in other company-owned/leased buildings.
- The procedure used to retrieve these resources should be found in the department's BRP.

6.4.1.2 Reconstruct Data and Records

- The procedure used to reconstruct computer backups to a current state should also be found in the department's BRP.
- The procedure used to reconstruct or rebuild critical hard copy resources should also be found in the department's BRP.

6.4.1.3 Salvaging On-Site Data and Records

- In the event that hard copy records have been damaged and there are no copies stored in the off-premises storage location, the department's BRP should identify professional organizations that are in the business of salvaging documents that have been damaged by heat, smoke, or water.

Example—Meridian Plaza, Philadelphia, Pennsylvania, February 23, 1991. Salvage records: Floors 22 through 29 were badly damaged by the heat and flames. Floors 30 through 38 were so badly polluted with smoke and hazardous material that access to those upper floors was tightly restricted. Those permitted above the 29th floor were required to wear respirators and protective suits with hoods, boots, and gloves.

One Meridian tenants who needed to retrieve important documents from the fire zone were unable to get access to original records because of the health risks.

Instead, the requested documents were located by workers in protective gear, who copied the originals using electronic scanners and shipped the information to computers outside the building.

(*Author Note:* One tenant was reported to have said that they spent $3 million with a company trained in retrieving records from hazardous sites.)

6.5 VALUE OF EXERCISING THE CRISIS MANAGEMENT TEAM

The scenarios selected for exercises that are most effective are the ones that are based on the recent experiences of other organizations. These experiences provide the CMT with examples of what did and did not work. This is why they should select new situations when they are exercising their Crisis Management Plan.

There are a couple valuable reasons for exercising the CMT:

- Exercises will help a team learn how to deal with a crisis.
- It will enable them to evaluate the actions documented in the plan, and determine if other actions or options could be added.
- It gives the members an opportunity to work together. Many of the members know each other but have not ever worked together on a project. During a time of stress is the wrong time to find out that we have members that cannot work together. (*Author Note:* In fact, I have witnessed some exercises where it appeared that some CMT members were working against one another.)
- Exercises can identify any weak members and allow the EMT to replace them before an actual crisis occurs. Keeping an ineffective member on the CMT could result in delaying a successful crisis recovery effort.

6.5.1 How Often Do Companies Exercise Their CMTs?

Over the years, I have found that CMT members are very busy with their day-to-day operations. The only time they feel they have for a exercise is between late November and late December. The remainder of the time they are "too busy" to participate in an exercise.

On the other hand, organizations that have well-prepared CMTs schedule exercises more frequently (e.g., quarterly). This allows them to work together four times a year.

6.5.2 Value of Exercising: CMT Members Not Available

Another reason why multiple exercises each year are valuable is that they show the organization that the core members of the CMT may not be available at various times throughout the year. A crisis can strike at any time of the year, and certain core members of the CMT may not be available.

I know of one instance where the corporate communications executive was on vacation when her company was struck by a fire in the corporate headquarters building. By the time she could arrange to return to the site of the fire, a corporate communications command center had been set up, the news media had had a couple interviews with the corporate communication alternate, and everything was being handled well. This was attributable to the assignment of, and training of, the alternate — before the crisis struck.

6.5.3 Training the Crisis Management Team

CMT members must be trained. The right people, properly trained, will be in a good position to manage a crisis when it hits.

Because there are no formal training centers to teach these skills (public relations firms excepted), most organizations manage the training and exercises internally. My suggestion is for organizations to contract with a consulting company that has experience in training crisis management teams and running successful exercises.

6.5.4 Are Your Organization's Executives Prepared?

As part of the training program, members of the CMT should become familiar with other crises that organizations have experienced. Researching the facts and strategies of others who have dealt with crises will give team members important background information to draw on. They should analyze what went right and what went wrong; where strategies worked and where they failed. Who on your CMT is researching this?

Do not confine your research to competitors in the same industry. It could include any disasters/crises where the organization has been required to manage a crisis, such as:

- A product issue (e.g., where a product does not work as promised [credibility], is injuring people [safety], has been tampered with; a market-shift [sudden change, or over a long period of time]
- A negative public perception of your organization (e.g., your organization has a problem, and it appears it does not care about the problem)
- A financial problem (e.g., cash problem, fraud, or fuzzy accounting)

- An industrial relations problem (e.g., worker strike problem, employee lawsuits)
- An adverse international event (e.g., disaster at their location has jeopardized your product or service)
- Workplace violence (e.g., employees have been violently attacked while working on your organization's property)
- Executive succession problem (e.g., senior executives have died or been killed)

Again, who on your CMT is researching this? If the answer is no one, your team may struggle when it is forced to face one of these crises for the first time. And remember: organizations that have struggled with an unplanned crisis often suffer significant consequences. What is the old saying, "All for the sake of a nail."

When the multiple exercise schedule shows that members of the CMT are not always available immediately, it strengthens the need to have an alternate identified and trained for each core member.

6.5.5   Crisis Team Training

Crisis teams must be trained — raw talent will not suffice. Simulations will help a team learn how to recognize a crisis, what actions are appropriate, how to develop options, assess time, consider dimensions, and judge control. Because there are no formal training centers to teach these skills (public relations firms excepted), it will be necessary to design your own program or have a nearby university or consulting firm do it for you. If nothing else, the team should become intimately familiar with the crises other companies have gone through; just digging into the facts and strategies of others who have dealt with similar circumstances will give the team important background information to draw on.

(*Author Note:* For more information on the value of training and exercises, see Chapter 10.)

6.6   ROLE IN DOCUMENTING THE CMT SERVICE LEVEL AGREEMENT

Members of the CMT should document their roles for providing their expertise when a disaster has occurred, or a crisis has moved to the "acute" stage.

Their roles have been identified by the EMT when they put the EMT agenda together (see Chapter 5). As discussed in Chapter 5, after the activation of the Crisis Management Team, there would be a meeting between the members of the EMT and the CMT. The EMT would expect that the following questions will be answered:

- What happened?
- Why did it happen?
- When did we know about it?
- How could we have prevented it?

When reviewing these questions, and the more detailed questions located in Appendices 6A through 6H, with the CEO and members of the EMT, the Business Continuity professional responsible for the Crisis Management Plan should ask "who" in the organization they expect will have the expertise to answer the question.

By asking the members of the EMT during the development of the EMT plan, they also identify the key members of the Crisis Management Team.

Using this information, the BCP professional can schedule a meeting with members selected to be on the CMT. At this meeting, the BCP professional should present the EMT agenda questions to the attendees. Then the BCP professional should identify the executive (or department) selected by the EMT as being the most qualified to answer each question.

Following this meeting, each executive (or department) selected by the EMT to be on the CMT can begin to document their strategy. This strategy simply identifies the support, or actions, the member will take following a disaster or crisis. It is a checklist of items they will address following the activation of the CMT. (*Author Note:* I have referred to this checklist as *the service level agreement* (SLA).)

After each CMT member completes his or her SLA, there should be a joint meeting of all members of the CMT to review the SLAs. The purpose is to determine if all the key support items have been identified and documented.

The Business Continuity professional should ask the members of the CMT if they may want to:

- Add areas to the SLA
- Delete areas from the SLA

Following the meeting, the BCP professional should document any changes suggested by the members of the CMT.

After completing the documentation, the BCP professional should send each CMT member a copy of their SLA. The BCP professional should request that they review it to ensure that the BCP professional did not misunderstand their comments or opinions.

After all members of the CMT have responded, it is time to prepare the final SLAs. Distribute them to the members of the CMT. Send a copy of the final version to the CEO.

(**Author Note:** For specific information regarding the EMT agenda, see Chapter 8.)

Examples of SLAs include:

- Facilities, Buildings, Properties (see Appendix 6A)
- Security (see Appendix 6B)
- Public Relations, Media Relations (see Appendix 6C)
- Human Resources, Personnel (see Appendix 6D)
- Legal (see Appendix 6E)
- Insurance, Risk Management (see Appendix 6F)
- Treasury, Finance (see Appendix 6H)

Now, let's move on to Chapter 7, "The Crisis Communications Team." This chapter deals with one element of the Crisis Management Team — communicating with the media, customers, employees, etc. Its chief goal is to protect the reputation of the organization during a crisis.

Appendix 6A

FACILITIES DEPARTMENT: SLA ELEMENTS

Upon notification that a disaster has struck a building housing the business units of your organization, the Facilities/Buildings/Properties department representative(s) will report to the Crisis Management Team Command Center (CMTCC). (See Chapter 9.)

> (***Author Note:*** To simplify the terminology, I will use the term "Facilities department" for this service level agreement.)

As a member of the Crisis Management Team, the Facilities department representatives' role will be to use their expertise to manage the building damage caused by the disaster and repairs needed following the disaster. The representative(s) will act as the coordination point for all building matters pertaining to the organization's recovery from the disaster.

After the members of the Crisis Management Team have reported to the CMTCC and obtained all known pertinent information regarding the disaster, the Facilities representative(s) will:

- When it is safe to enter the building, assemble a team to assess the damage from the disaster.
- Assist in investigating the cause. Work with local, state, and federal authorities and the Security department.
- After assessment of damage has been made, manage all building repair activities.
- If the business units in the damaged building will need to work elsewhere, obtain "alternate operating locations."
- On occasion, the Facilities department, or the organization's "Facilities Policies," may be perceived as the cause of an organization's crisis.

In such cases, it may be better if the department representative is not involved in managing the crisis because they become too defensive.

SCENARIO: DISASTER

When a disaster has damaged one of the buildings housing one, or more, of your organization's business units, the Facilities department will obtain information pertinent to the building damage and needed repairs. Examples of information pertinent to the Facilities department include:

- Using a "fire" as the type of disaster:
  - Where did the fire start?
  - How did the fire start? Has there been any cause determined? Accidental or intentional?
  - How many floors did the fire affect?
  - Were any floors affected by water damage? Smoke damage? Hazmat problems?
  - Which business units were located on the damaged floors?
- Using a "storm" as the type of disaster (e.g., rainstorm, snowstorm, tornado, hurricane, etc.):
  - What type of damage was sustained?
  - Was the damage to the roof, walls, windows, etc.?
  - How many floors were affected by the storm?
  - Which business units were located on the damaged floors?
  - Are there any regulatory or legal issues that will result from the interruption of business operations as a result of the storm?
- Using a "sick building crisis" as the type of crisis. If a number of people become sick when they are inside the building, determine the cause. Some of the common symptoms of "sick building" syndrome include:
  - Respiratory problems
  - Congestion
  - Chemically induced asthma
  - Loss of breath
  - Sore throats
  - Coughing
  - Sneezing
  - Itchy or irritated eyes
  - Headaches
  - Rashes
  - Dizziness
  - Nausea
  - Fatigue

If the cause is identified as "sick building syndrome," arrange for the building to be fixed.

When it is safe to enter the building, assemble a team to assess the damage from the disaster.

Following a disaster, assemble the members of the damage assessment team. The damage assessment team members should include personnel from the facilities department and the security department. Other members of the assessment team would include vendors that have the expertise to assess the damage to the building (e.g., building engineers, etc.).

After it is determined to be safe to access the disaster site location, send the damage assessment team into the site to determine the extent of damage to the building and contents.

The business units located in the building should also enter their location(s) to assist in determining the damage. The business unit representatives can also retrieve critical assets that are considered salvageable (e.g., small equipment, records, documentation, etc.).

- Which area(s) of the building was damaged?
- Is there structural damage?
- Will it require the building to be closed until it can be shored up?

Assess the damage: building has structural damage.

Examples of assessing structural damage include:

- *Fire in Olin Corporation's Headquarters, Connecticut, 1981.* The damage assessment team was delayed for a time due to weakened structural supports and the danger of collapse. Workers had to shore up beams that were damaged by the heat. First floor suffered smoke and water damage; third floor suffered smoke damage.
- *Fire in a Meridian Plaza regional site, Philadelphia, Pennsylvania, 1991.* Around 11:00 a.m. Sunday morning, Fire Commissioner Roger Ulshafer ordered all his men out of the building. He was fearful it might collapse because of the structural damage. He already had lost three men fighting that fire.
- *Clifton, New Jersey, 1993.* During the Blizzard of 1993, a 100-foot section of the roof collapsed in the building housing one of the Electronic Data Systems computer centers. This computer center, located in Clifton, New Jersey, processed work for approximately 5200 ATMs, 6 percent of the total ATMs nationwide, at that time. Due to the condition of the building, local authorities condemned the facility preventing EDS management's access to the site for four days.

- *Murrah Federal Building Bombing, 1995.* The bombing of the Murrah Federal building caused the collapse of the front of the building. The explosive concussion also caused severe structural damage to nearby buildings.
  - Athenian building: front of building collapsed; receptionist on the ground floor was killed.
  - *The Journal Record:* a 3600-circulation daily newspaper next to the federal building was destroyed in the blast, the roof was blown off, there was heavy structural damage, and parts of federal building were blown into its facade.
  - Kerr-McGee Oil Co.: huge gaps scarred the 20-story tower.
  - Southwestern Bell building: interior walls collapse on the 8th and 9th floors.
  - Water Resources Board building: walls on the southeast side of building were destroyed; all windows were broken.
  - Will the building be condemned? (At least until it is shored up.)

Assess damage: building red-tagged or condemned.

Examples of buildings that have been red-tagged or condemned include:

- *Loma Prieta Earthquake, San Francisco/Oakland, California, 1989.* "After the quake, structural engineers were stunned to discover that it had badly damaged buildings they assumed would have resisted a temblor: steel-frame skyscrapers. Fractures were discovered on the connection of the columns to the beams." (Bill Holmes, a structural engineer at the engineering firm of Rutherford and Chekene in San Francisco.)
- *Spring Rain Storm — Mazda Motors, Compton, California, 1983.* An estimated 10,000 gallons of water crashed down on Mazda's computer. In addition, five tons of air-conditioning equipment located on the spot of the roof that collapsed, fell into the computer center. The data center was brought to a standstill. It normally supplied all Mazda's central computing services in 31 states. The center was idle for a week. Alternate operating procedures were invoked; end users reverted to manual methods.
- *Winter Snow Storm — Collapsed roof on building housing Electronic Data Systems computer location, 1993.* A 100-foot section of the roof collapsed under the weight of the snow, buckling the walls of the 35,000-square-foot data center. (Blizzard of 1993.) No injuries. EDS evacuated the 30 on-duty employees from the facility. Delayed Access: local authorities condemned the facility, thus preventing EDS access to the site for four days.

Assess damage: building contaminated with hazardous material.

- *New World Tower, Miami, Florida, 1985.* On May 29, 1985, a fire in an electric transformer at Miami's New World Tower caused health officials to close the tower because of PCB contamination. For three days, Manufacturers Hanover employees had to come up with alternative ways of carrying on business operations. As a result of the hazardous material contamination, critical on-site records, needed for these business operations, were retrieved by people in protective suits ("moon suits").
- *Houston, Texas, 1991.* In June 1991, a fire that started on the 8th floor of a Houston, Texas, 14-story building that was undergoing renovations forced out all tenants of the building for a couple of days. River Oaks Bank employees were denied access to the building for a couple days because the building contained asbestos.
- *Los Angeles, 1992.* Fire raced through the 7th and 8th floors of the 12-story non-sprinklered building housing the Los Angeles County Health Department. The building houses the staff for the county's hospital system and the county health records. The fire did cause asbestos contamination; it spread throughout the building by way of water used to fight the fire. Sections of the building may be closed for up to a year. According to the *LA Times,* the fire destroyed millions of computerized records.
- *Costco Retail Warehouse, Washington, 1995.* A fire turned into a hazardous materials emergency when flames raced through the automotive supplies section of the warehouse. The blaze, apparently caused by a spark from a forklift, caused an estimated $2 million damage.
- *Reichold Chemical Plant, Illinois, 1995.* Fire in a chemical plant injured 43 people. Most of the injured had inhaled hazardous fumes. Neighborhood residents were told to stay indoors.
- *Delaware Trust Building, Wilmington, Delaware, 1997.* A fire damaged the 14th and 15th floors of a 22-story office building. The blaze started in a law firm's file room on the 14th floor. Hundreds of thousands of gallons of water, contaminated by asbestos insulation, cascaded from the 14th floor to the basement. The building closed due to hazardous asbestos. The only people allowed back in were the cleanup crews and the building managers, all of which wore protective clothing. The building was closed to the public for four weeks.

Assist in investigating the cause. Work with the authorities (local, state, and federal) and the Security department.

After obtaining access to the damaged site, work with the Security department to determine if the cause of the disaster was accidental or intentional.

- A disaster would be considered an *accident* if it was caused by act of nature (e.g., earthquake, tornado, flood or hurricane). A fire could also be considered an accident when it was not started intentionally.

- Generally, floods are accidents; but if the flood was caused by a leak from inside the building, it could also be intentional. If a toilet overflowed, or a sprinkler system activated, it must be investigated to determine if someone intentionally caused the leak.

- A disaster would be considered *intentional* if a fire was arson, or if an explosion was a bomb. Examples of investigations to determine cause include:

  - *30 Rockefeller Center, New York City, 1996.* The cause of the October 10, 1996, fire in Rockefeller Center was determined to be accidental. Cabling in the electrical room on the 5th floor where service entered the building and was then distributed to other locations within the structure ignited. Four other electrical rooms then also caught fire, generating large quantities of smoke. In the room where the initial fire occurred, the cabling was in open cable supports. Over the years, as additional cabling was added, it was packed into these cable supports in such a way that there was no longer any clearance between the cables, or between the cables and the structural I-beam under which they passed.

  - *Hotel Conference Center in New Jersey, 1993.* The fire started when an overloaded electrical dimmer switch ignited paper-backed wall insulation. The 1000-Watt electrical wall dimmer switch was drawing 1947 Watts when it failed.
    The fire spread because voids in construction, and sprinklers were blocked by renovations. This allowed the fire to spread through concealed spaces before it was detected by an employee. HVAC ducts and structural framing that had been added during renovations blocked the sprinklers, thus limiting their effectiveness.

If the cause of the disaster is suspicious (e.g., fire, vandalism, sabotage), work with the Security department and local authorities regarding access to the building.

- Restrict access to only those people authorized by authorities or security.

- Provide access to people who are performing building damage estimates.

- After damage has been assessed, limit building access to just employees or contractors who have a need to be there. For example, allow employees access to retrieve critical equipment, data and records.

- After employees and contractors are permitted access, have security personnel check all cases, boxes, and bags when personnel are entering and leaving the building.

Examples of suspicious fires include:

- *South Orange, New Jersey, 2000.* The fire at Seton Hall University on January 19, 2000, that killed three students was believed to be arson. On June 13, 2003, prosecutors announced charges against two students in the Seton Hall University dorm fire that killed those students. The two students were arrested on charges of felony murder, arson, aggravated assault, and conspiring in a cover-up. The men were residents of Boland Hall, the dormitory where the fire broke out in the early morning hours. Essex County Acting Prosecutor Donald Campolo said the students used matches or a lighter to ignite a paper poster that had been torn down and placed on a couch made of highly flammable foam material.
- *South Brunswick, New Jersey, 1997.* A suspicious fire destroyed a warehouse full of corporate documents. The fire, in a building just off the New Jersey Turnpike at Exit 8, came two days after a smaller blaze damaged another warehouse several hundred feet away. That building had also been the scene of a fire on March 7. Firefighters were still battling the second blaze, in the smaller building, when the third broke out down the street. Both buildings are owned by Iron Mountain Inc., a company that stores government and corporate records at 117 sites around the country. The two warehouses contain nearly 1.25 million cartons of records belonging to 200 companies.

  A township fire marshal said that the first two fires had been deliberately set. An Iron Mountain spokeswoman confirmed the latest fire was arson when Iron Mountain offered a $10,000 reward for information about the source of the fires.
- *New York City, 1994.* A smoky fire in the basement of Saks Fifth Avenue forced the evacuation of the Manhattan department store. The fire, in trash bins, sent smoke into the sales floors. The blaze was declared suspicious because a fire was found in a second trash bin.

After assessment of damage has been made, manage all building repair activities.

- Contract for and manage the activities of vendors that will be repairing the damage caused by the disaster.
  - Activities of all building and utility vendors (e.g., contractors, engineers, electric, water, gas), including:

- Smoke cleanup
- Water cleanup
- HVAC cleaning and sanitizing
- Structural contents cleaning
- Electronic and mechanical equipment restoration
- Controlled demolition
- Debris removal
- Dehumidification and environmental stabilization
- Document restoration
- Magnetic media recovery

Floods

If the building has suffered a flood, buildings must be decontaminated before electricians can repair wiring and other repairs can be made.

- *Albany, Georgia, 1994.* Twenty-eight of the 31 buildings of the Albany State College in Albany, Georgia, were damaged by floods in July 1994. All damaged buildings had to be decontaminated before electricians could repair wiring and repairs to the buildings could be made. When the college resumed classes, the 3600 students attended classes in trailers.
- *Arlington County Courthouse, Arlington, Virginia, 1990.* Contents, EDP equipment, and HVAC systems were contaminated. Decontamination of contents and structure was followed by abatement of asbestos-containing fireproofing. Wet carpet was removed prior to treatment with a fungicide. The areas were then vented by high-efficiency particulate air (HEPA) filtration units fitted with carbon absorption beds. This process facilitated rapid structural drying to prevent mold or fungi regeneration. Fire extinguishing efforts and broken water lines contributed to damage in the basement and first three floors.

Following a disaster that has knocked out safety systems, employees will not be permitted to operate inside the building until work crews restore the safety systems (i.e., fire alarms, sprinkler and security systems).

If the business units in the damaged building will need to work elsewhere, obtain "alternate operating locations" (backup sites).

Obtain an estimate of the time needed to complete the repairs. Based on the length of time needed for repairs, the organization may need to find temporary operating locations. Determine where the affected business operations can resume those operations.

- In the event another company-owned location will be used temporarily, make all necessary arrangements to provide access to, and use of, the facilities.
- Ensure that 24-hour access is available until the location is no longer needed for the recovery operation. Many company locations are closed after normal working hours, and are not accessible without approval of the Facilities and Security department officials.
- In the event a commercial vendor will be used to resume business operations (i.e., computer hot site or a business unit workspace vendor), work with the affected business unit(s) to assist them in their move to the alternate site.

If the building houses a computer center and will be repaired, but the repairs will require an extended period of time, acquire a Temporary Computer Center location.

- Review the minimum facilities requirements.
- Locate potential sites.
- Review the sites with the IT disaster site recovery team manager to obtain guidance on which site will be used.
- Acquire and prepare the site for use.

In the event the damaged building houses a computer but will not be used again, obtain a new computer center location.

- Review the current equipment and facilities requirements with the IT DRP management team.
- Locate potential sites.
- Review the sites to ensure they meet your organization's requirements.
- Review the safety and security of the potential sites.
- Present the findings to IT management.
- When a final selection is made, acquire the site and prepare it for use.

Examples of organizations using an alternate site include:

- *Cash America International, Ft. Worth, Texas, 2000.* One of the hardest-hit buildings of the tornado was the nine-story corporate offices of Cash America International, one of the country's largest pawnshop chains. It was possible to see right through the building because windows on both sides were blown out. While a rival company offered Cash America the use of its offices, the CEO said the Facilities people found space at other company offices for essential employees. The CEO said they will find temporary quarters for the rest of his 150 headquarters staff in a few days.

▪ *Empire BC/BS, New York City, September 11, 2001.* In 2001, Empire Blue Cross/Blue Shield was headquartered on ten floors in the World Trade Center. When the terrorist attack destroyed the building, Empire initially set up emergency headquarters at a service office in Melville, New York. Two weeks later, it shifted 500 of its 1900 Trade Center staffers to facilities in Melville, Albany, and Middletown, New York. An additional 200 are working from home. More than 1200 have not returned to work because there is not enough space. It plans to call back the 1200 idled workers once it finds 390,000 square feet of space in Manhattan and Brooklyn, CEO Michael Stocker says.

▪ *U.S. Postal Service, Washington, D.C., 2002.* More than a year after anthrax killed two workers in the main mail-handling center of the nation's capital, crews began fumigating the building yesterday with toxic gas. The 17.5 million cubic foot Brentwood facility has been closed since October 2001, after anthrax-laced letters to two senators were determined to have been processed there and the two postal workers died. If all goes well, officials said, 1600 employees could return next spring to a cleaner, safer workplace. The site has operated under tight security since shortly after the building closed October 21, 2001.

▪ *West Pharmaceutical Services Inc. of Lionville, 2003.* West said that the deadly explosion and fire at its Kinston, North Carolina, manufacturing plant on January 29, 2003, would have "financial implications" for the first half of this year. The plant made syringe plungers, intravenous devices, and rubber compounds that are distributed to West's other manufacturing locations. The damaged factory is not operable. West said it expected to incur additional production costs associated with moving equipment and workers from Kinston to St. Petersburg, Florida, and Carney, Nebraska, as well as shifting "tooling and production" from Kinston to the United Kingdom and Singapore. "We believe that the timely execution of our recovery plan will minimize the interruptions in supply and loss of business," said Donald E. Morel, West's chief executive officer, in a written statement.

On occasion, the Facilities department, or the organizations "Facilities Policies," may be perceived as the cause of an organization's crisis.

In cases where the department, or its policies, may have caused the crisis, it may be better if department representatives are not involved in managing the crisis because they might become too defensive. They should recuse themselves during this specific crisis.

An example of a crisis in which the Facilities department might be perceived as being the cause, or being too defensive, is a fire in a non-sprinklered building or a fire in a building undergoing renovations.

First of all, having critical business units housed in a non-sprinklered building is a risk. (I assume this has been brought to the attention of top management personnel of the organization and that they have accepted the risk.) Examples of a fire in a non-sprinklered building include:

- *Greenville, South Carolina, 2004.* Fire broke out in a five-story Comfort Inn on January 25, while guests were asleep. Six guests were killed and at least a dozen people were injured. Wade Hampton Fire Chief Gary Downey said, "If there had been sprinkler systems in the hallways, probably the fatalities and injuries would not have been near what they were.,"

- *Chicago, Illinois, 2003.* A fire in the Cook County Building in Chicago resulted in the deaths of six employees who could not evacuate the building. The building was not equipped with a sprinkler system and was not required to because of its age, according to a spokesman for the city's office of emergency communications. The structure was built in the early 1960s and purchased by the county in 1996. At the time, County Board President argued the purchase would save the county money by allowing it to consolidate several offices in one location and eliminate the need to lease office space. Its purchase would eliminate the need for various county agencies, from the Public Guardian's office to the Public Defender, to continue to operate out of leased spaces at a current annual cost of about $3.5 million. While renovations were made to the building after the purchase, a sprinkler system was not installed.

- *Harrisburg, Pennsylvania, 1994.* The Pennsylvania Transportation Dept. Headquarters building is a 12-story, non-sprinklered building. Penn DOT occupies the 6th through 10th floors. The building was severely damaged by a fire on June 16, 1994. Five weeks after the fire, the headquarters of Pennsylvania Department of Transportation was closed to state workers after the discovery of cancer-causing PCBs in ceiling tiles. The building was eventually imploded in 1999.

- *Los Angeles, 1994.* Pacific Bell's 17-story building, housing the West Coast's busiest switching offices, suffered a fire on the 13th floor. An electrical malfunction, severed the main power source to the switching station. With power gone, PacBell could not transfer traffic to another switching office as it did during the Northridge earthquake. The building did not have a sprinkler system. According to an article in the *San Francisco Examiner* on March 16 of 1994, "the U.S. telecommunications industry has historically been reluctant to use standard, water-based sprinkler systems for a number of reasons. They fear wetting electrically energized equipment, for example. They also fear the electrolytic corrosion water inflicts on circuit boards and other items. However, these fears may not apply to the new water mist systems being developed as alternatives to sprinkler systems and possible replacements for halon systems. The NFPA is establishing an installation standard to permit this technology to be introduced into the mainstream of fire protection systems. The committee responsible for the proposed standard includes representatives from at least five countries and from user-environments ranging from the hotel and electrical power generation industries to the marine, telecommunications, and aerospace industries."

■ During renovations, the building is very exposed. Some security precautions are lax. Some buildings undergoing renovations have turned off their sprinkler systems to prevent them from accidentally activating. It is the Facilities department's responsibility to ensure that all fire protection rules are being followed during renovations. Examples of a fire in a building undergoing renovations (Facilities department involved) include:

■ *Meridian Plaza, 1991.* Eight floors of the 38-story building were gutted from a fire caused by fumes from the varnish that was being used during renovations. The varnish was being used on wood paneling in one of the offices on the 22nd floor. The can lid was not closed properly. This allowed fumes to escape and the fumes combusted.

■ *McLean, Virginia, 2001.* The fire that forced evacuation of CIA headquarters in suburban Virginia was accidental. It was started by workers using a torch during renovations on the building.

■ *County of Prince George's, Maryland, 2004.* A wind-blown fire gutted the nearby 300-year-old courthouse in Prince George's County, Maryland, but was beat back before reaching a modern wing where records are kept and trial are held. The courthouse has been undergoing a $27 million renovation, and hose taps and sprinklers had been disconnected by workers. The fire erupted on the roof.

■ *Williamsburg Lodge, Williamsburg, Virginia, 2005.* A construction fire caused an undetermined amount of damage yesterday at the Williamsburg Lodge. The fire broke out shortly before 11 a.m. in a portion of the famous hotel undergoing renovation. The fire apparently started as a worker used a torch to cut stainless steel ductwork near the hotel's kitchen, said Sophia Hart, a spokeswoman for the Colonial Williamsburg Foundation. Grease in the ductwork may have ignited, she said

Appendix 6B

SECURITY DEPARTMENT: SLA ELEMENTS

Upon notification that a disaster has struck a building housing some of your organization's business units, the Security department representative, or representatives, will report to the Crisis Management Team Command Center. (See Chapter 9.)

As a member of the Crisis Management Team (CMT), the Security department representative's role will be to use their expertise to manage any security situations that will arise as a result of the disaster. The representative(s) will act as the coordination point for all security matters pertaining to the organization's recovery from the disaster.

After the members of the Crisis Management Team have reported to the CMT Command Center and obtained all known pertinent information regarding the disaster, the Security department representative(s) will:

- Work with the local authorities regarding securing the damaged building.
- Work with the local, state, and federal authorities in investigating the cause.
- After the damaged site has been deemed safe to enter by local authorities, control access into the damaged site.
- During a workplace violence incident, or when any act of violence has taken place (e.g., riot), arrange for security guards to restrict access and protect the assets.
- On occasion, the Security department, or the organization's "Security Policies," may be perceived as the cause of an organization's crisis. In those cases, it may be better if the department representative is not involved in managing the crisis because they become too defensive.

SCENARIO: DISASTER

When a disaster has damaged one of the buildings housing one, or more, of your organization's business units, the Security department will obtain information pertinent to the Legal department.

Examples of information pertinent to the Security department include:

- Using a "fire" as the type of disaster:
  - Where did the fire start?
  - What is located in that area of the building?
  - How did the fire start? Has there been any cause determined? Accidental or intentional?
  - Will access to the building need to be restricted due to security reasons?
  - Will access to the building need to be restricted due to safety reasons?
- Using a "storm" as the type of disaster (e.g., a rainstorm, snowstorm, tornado, hurricane, etc.):
  - What type of damage was sustained?
  - Was the damage to the roof, walls, windows, etc.?
  - How many floors were affected by the storm?
  - Which business units were located on the damaged floors?
  - Will access to the building need to be restricted due to safety reasons?
- Using a "workplace violence" incident as the type of crisis:
  - Were any employees injured or killed?
  - Were any customers injured or killed?
  - Were there any security lapses that allowed the incident? During the incident?
  - Was the perpetrator apprehended?
  - Will lawsuits be filed against the organization claiming that "Security was inadequate"?

Work with the local authorities regarding securing the damaged building. Secure the site immediately.

Although it has been determined to be safe to access the disaster site location, access may be delayed because a crime investigation is taking place. Whether a fire or a storm caused the disaster, local authorities will control access to the building for safety and security reasons. When they have completed their work, they will turn the building over to the owner of the building.

The owner should ensure that the building remains in a secure situation because the assets located in the building are exposed. An organization can lose some of its equipment, information, etc., to looters. Organizations should provide 24-hour security during this time.

The Facilities department (along with the Security department) should be the interface with the local authorities (i.e., fire department, police, etc.) and the owner.

If the cause is believed to be arson, or a bombing, the Security department representative should work with local, state, and federal authorities to determine when it is safe to return to the building. Once it is determined to be a crime scene, an investigation will take place.

Examples of when an investigation has taken place include:

- *Boston, 1986.* On December 9, 1986, a fire in the basement of the One Post Office Square building in Boston, Massachusetts, caused a delay in retrieving critical files and records for the Craig & McCauley law firm. The firm had its offices on the 22nd floor. Offices were not usable for a while, so the law firm made arrangements to share space with another law firm in a nearby building. All Craig & McCauley needed was its records. According to an article in *the Boston Herald*, employees had to wait until the investigation was completed before officials allowed them to re-enter the building where they could then retrieve the backups from the on-site safe.
- *Philadelphia, 1989.* Following a major fire in the Penn Mutual Life Insurance Building in Philadelphia, Pennsylvania, on May 30, 1989, the Rubin, Quinn, Moss, & Heaney law firm's 75 employees were delayed in retrieving critical records and files. Security guards did not allow anyone from the firm back into the building until the on-site investigation of cause was complete. The fire was declared a crime scene after the cause was determined to be arson. The employees of all the organizations located in the building had to wait to gain access to their firms' files and other vital records for a couple days.
- *New York City, 1993:* Following the bombing of the World Trade Center in New York on February 26, 1993, the building owner delayed access back into the building until first, the safety could be assessed and second, the investigation was completed. When access was permitted, security guards were used to control access into the building.

  Employees who worked in the WTC had to wait in lines to be led to their offices to retrieve vital records and papers. Only 30 minutes was provided to each company (on Sunday) to retrieve any critical equipment or records. Following this opportunity to access their offices or computer centers, they had to return to the end of the line and wait for their next turn.

Access can be delayed due to regulations.

- *King of Prussia, Pennsylvania, 1984.* On January 1, 1984, a fire started on the first floor of a two-story building in King of Prussia, Pennsylvania, owned by the Worlco Company, a holding company for several businesses in the building. Worlco owned an insurance company, a data systems company, and North American Medical Centers, which operated several nursing homes. Employees for Worlco were delayed in gaining access to the building to assess the damage because "After a major fire in Pennsylvania, the law requires that the state fire marshal must inspect the premises before salvage operations can begin." This was finally accomplished by the morning of January 4th.

Access can also be delayed by the owner of the building.

Since the building owner could be sued by employees of a tenant injured when they enter the building after a disaster, they will not allow people back into the building until it has been established that it is safe to enter. Keep in mind that the owner will be concerned about:

- Safety — anyone entering the building after the disaster could be injured. The owner, and the owner's insurance company, will probably delay your return to the building until they are sure the building is safe.
- If the building is insured by commercial insurance companies, the insurance companies expect you to comply with their requirements to protect insured items against any further loss or damage.

The building should be tightly secured following a disaster due to the potential for looting or theft. The organization will be exposed to having salvageable assets walking out the door unless there is a strict security policy in effect.

Examples include:

- Penn Mutual Life Insurance Company Building, Philadelphia, 1989:
  - Following the fire, one of the roles of the Security department was to order guards to prevent anyone from entering the building until the on-site investigation of cause was complete. The fire was declared a crime scene after the cause was determined to be arson. People who worked in the building had to wait to gain access to the firm's files and other vital records for a couple days.
  - When employees of tenants that had offices in the building started to reuse the building, the security procedure was: use driver's

license, enter it into a computer to account for all people in the building. They also used a metal detector to check personnel going in and out of the building.

- The Security Department hired off-duty policemen to provide extra security bodies.
- After access is permitted, the Security personnel should check all cases, bags, boxes, etc., of people entering or leaving the building.
- Salt Lake City, Utah, 1999:
  - Following a rare tornado that knocked out power to 20,000 customers in downtown Salt Lake City, police sealed off several downtown areas where looting of damaged cars was reported.
- Panama Beach, Florida, 1995:
  - Following Hurricane "Opal," a number of looters were arrested in Panama Beach.
- Los Angeles, California, 1992:
  - During the Los Angeles riots in April 1992, employees of the FedCo Discount store in West Los Angeles reported that looters broke into the store and took an estimated $9 million worth of merchandise and then attempted to burn down the building.

Work with local, state, and federal authorities in investigating the cause. Coordinate and play an active role in any investigations (e.g., into arson, bombing) conducted by local or company authorities.

If the cause of the disaster is suspicious, work with the local authorities in investigating the cause.

- Intentional would include a disaster caused by sabotage, vandalism, arson or a bombing/terrorism.
- Play an active role in any investigation (e.g., into arson, bombing) conducted by local or company authorities.

Someone in the Security department will have had to be trained on how to investigate a fire to determine if it was arson. As explained by an arson investigator from the Philadelphia police/fire department, no untrained person is allowed into the crime scene until all evidence has been obtained. If your organization allowed an untrained person into a crime scene, there would be little likelihood that a jury could convict an accused perpetrator once the defense lawyer has suggested that your security person planted the evidence.

The arson investigator pointed out that if an untrained person was in the crime scene, they could accidentally destroy evidence; that is, walk out of the area with evidence on the bottom of their shoe.

Following a bombing or arson of a building, federal authorities will work with local authorities to attempt to determine the perpetrator(s). The area of the building being investigated could remain sealed for some time after the bombing, or arson. Delayed access by structural engineers, who would necessarily be first-in to ascertain the building's safety, can prevent them from assessing the damage.

> When Diversified Records Services, Inc. of West Pittston, Pennsylvania, experienced a fire in 1997, the security director as well as an on-site security consultant were at the site within an hour playing an active role with local police and fire crews. After an investigation of the cause, a Diversified spokesperson reported that insurance investigators have ruled out arson and "have determined that the fire was caused by an electrical malfunction."

If the cause of the disaster is suspicious (e.g., fire, vandalism, sabotage), control access into the building.

- Restrict access to only those people authorized by authorities or security.
  - Use an authorization procedure and checklist. (You can find more information on this procedure and checklist, in the book entitled *Business Resumption Planning* [Auerbach Publications].)
- Provide access to people assigned to perform building damage estimates.
- After damage has been assessed, limit building access to just employees or contractors who have a need to be there.
- At some point in time, allow employees access to retrieve critical equipment, data, and records.
- After employees or contractors are permitted access, have security personnel check all cases, boxes, and bags when personnel are entering or exiting the building.

Provide security guards in all high-profile recovery sites, as required, throughout the recovery operation.

After the damaged site is deemed safe to enter by local authorities, control access into and out of the damaged site.

Security — the building contents are now exposed to anyone interested in looting. To protect against looting of any contents, the owner can restrict access into the building.

Examples of looting following a disaster include:

- *Salt Lake City, Utah, 1999:* Following a rare tornado that knocked out power to 20,000 customers in downtown Salt Lake City, police sealed off several downtown areas where looting of damaged cars was reported.

■ *Panama Beach, Florida, 1995:* Following Hurricane "Opal," a number of looters were arrested.

■ *Los Angeles, California, 1992:* During the Los Angeles riots in April 1992, employees of FedCo Discount store in West Los Angeles reported that looters broke into the store and took an estimated $9 million worth of merchandise and then attempted to burn down the building.

The owner of the building may establish a strong security presence.

The owner may want to establish a security policy and procedure for people authorized by the tenant to enter. The owner may have security personnel check all cases, boxes, or bags of personnel leaving the building.

> *Penn Mutual Life Insurance Company building – Philadelphia, 1989:* Following the fire, one of the roles of the Security department was to order guards to prevent anyone from entering the building until the on-site investigation of cause was complete. The fire was declared a crime scene after the cause was determined to be arson. People who worked in the building had to wait to gain access to the firm's files and other vital records for a couple days.

> When employees of tenants that had offices in the building started to reuse the building, the security procedure was — use drivers license, enter it into a computer to account for all people in the building. They also used a metal detector to check personnel going in and out of the building.

> The Security department hired off-duty policemen to provide extra security bodies.

What to do after people are authorized to re-enter the building.

After people are authorized to re-enter the building, the Facilities department should document a complete list of employees authorized to enter the building and provide a copy of this list to the Security department.

The owner can also use a copy of this list to verify that those people interested in entering are actually the authorized employees of their tenant. (It is incumbent upon the owner, or the owner's representative, to check the credentials of the people purporting to be employees [e.g., employee identification card].)

The Security department guards should then identify all personnel attempting to enter the site and verify that they are authorized to enter using the list of authorized personnel.

If business units want to send employees into the building, they should submit a list of authorized employees to both the Facilities and Security representatives.

If employees are entering the building to retrieve critical equipment, data, and records, the Security guards should monitor their movement throughout the building. This is done for safety and security reasons.

> *New York, 1993:* Following the terrorist bombing of the World Trade Center in 1993, access to the building was denied for a period of time. When access was provided, it was on a limited-time basis. Only 30 minutes were provided to each company on the Sunday after the bombing, to retrieve any critical equipment or records. It is important to know where the key equipment or records are located. After the 30 minutes were up, the organization's representatives had to return to the end of the line, where they waited until all other organizations retrieved their critical assets.

When employees are exiting the building, they should pass through a security checkpoint established by the Security department. Employees, and contractors, should have all cases, boxes, and bags checked by Security personnel when leaving the building.

STRENGTHEN SECURITY POLICIES AND PRACTICES

If the cause of the disaster is believed to be *intentional,* the Security department should strengthen its Policies and Procedures. Add security to protect against a second occurrence. There will be a need to provide protection at:

- ■ Recovery headquarters
- ■ Alternate operating location(s)
- ■ Off-premises records storage location(s)

Instruct all security personnel to verify that individuals entering those sites are authorized. Check the appropriate authorized access list and the company identification of the individual. (For more information on this process, refer to the book entitled *Business Resumption Planning* [Auerbach Publications].)

Provide security guards, as required, throughout the recovery operation. For example, guards may be required during the transportation of data, reports, and materials between recovery operation locations.

The Security department's guards should *escort* people in areas of a building in which confidential records or equipment are located. This is especially true when a fire strikes a government building containing classified records or equipment. Examples include:

- The fire that forced the evacuation of CIA headquarters in suburban Virginia in 2001 was determined to be accidental. Workers using a torch doing repairs on the top floor of the building started it. During the fire, CIA uniformed security officers escorted the local firefighters through the building.
- Pacific Bell experienced a fire in 1994. The firefighters entered the lobby, where security personnel met them and advised them that the fire was on the 13th floor. They then escorted the firefighters to the fire scene.

Policies and procedures should be changed.

After incidents, Security policies and procedures should be changed. For example:

> *Harrisburg, Pennsylvania, 1993:* On February 7, 1993, an intruder crashed through the front gates at the Three Mile Island nuclear plant and was able to roam through the turbine building for four hours before being caught by the police. The government mandated that security controls would be added to beef up security at the plant. (Guardrails, reinforced gates, alarms, and video cameras will be installed at an estimated cost of $1 million.)

> Then the NRC ruled in August 1993 that all nuclear power plants in the United States must install barriers to guard against truck bombs similar to the one that exploded under the World Trade Center. The NRC had refused for years to require anti-terrorist barriers at nuclear plants, but commissioners reconsidered because of the WTC bombing and the Three Mile incident.

> *World Trade Center, New York City, 1993:* Following the bombing on February 26, 1993, new security precautions and policies were put in place to prevent a recurrence of the bombing, including:

The parking garage can be used for tenants only.

Identification will be needed to use the elevators.

New Communication and Control Centers will be established in the sky lobbies (where elevators to upper floors are located).

Stairwells and elevators will get battery-operated emergency lights, phosphorescent signs.

Portable backup generators are to be set up outside the World Trade Center complex.

During a workplace violence incident, or when any act of violence has taken place (e.g., riot), arrange for security guards to restrict access and protect assets.

During and following a workplace violence incident, Security department personnel should assist employees in obtaining safe shelter. They should also do whatever they can to assist the person attacked until emergency responders can come to their aid.

They should attempt to capture or secure the person responsible, but only if they are adequately trained for such action. Many people assigned to the Security department are not qualified to carry, or shoot, a pistol. If the Security personnel have not been trained, and have not been given adequate resources to capture or restrain the person responsible for the violence, it is best left to the authorities.

Examples include:

- *Taylor, Michigan, 2005:* A man who had just been fired from his job at the International Paper Co. plant in Taylor, Michigan, returned to his workplace with a handgun in February 2005 and shot two colleagues, killing one of them. The suspect is a 31-year-old Detroit man.
- *Detroit, Michigan, 2004:* A factory worker at Peerless Metals in Detroit killed a fellow employee with a sword in October 2004. Witnesses told police the 30-year-old man had complained he was being bullied by another worker at Peerless. The suspect had been working on the sword for several days, apparently at work, and when he finished, he struck the 40-year-old victim in the neck, nearly decapitating him. When police arrived at the factory, the suspect was having a beer.
- *2001:* In September 2001, a man fatally shot a federal officer at a security checkpoint in the lobby of the Patrick V. McNamara Federal Building when he was told he could not take a gun into the building housing the FBI. The gunman then was shot and wounded. The man entered the lobby of the Federal Building and

put the bag on a counter beside the metal detector. After his request to take the gun inside was refused, he reached into the bag and fired. The building has offices for agencies including the IRS, Veterans Affairs, the National Labor Relations Board, and Housing and Urban Development.

- *Bolton, Georgia, 2001:* In July 2001, a 22-year-old man, an ex-employee of the Home Depot store in Bolton, Georgia, fatally shot two people and wounded another at the store, and then killed himself after police arrived.
- *Romulus, Michigan, 2001:* In March 2001, an employee of the Metro Machine Works company, an engine parts manufacturer in Romulus, Michigan, shot and killed his superior after an argument. He then killed himself.
- *East Greenville, Pennsylvania, 2001:* In March 2001, a 23-year-old employee of Knoll Inc. in East Greenville, Pennsylvania, shot and killed a floor manager. He then killed himself. The shooting apparently followed several disciplinary meetings over the past several days.

During an industrial relations crisis (e.g., strike) or if protests threaten your organization's facilities, arrange for security guards to restrict access and protect the assets.

- Following the terrorist attacks on the World Trade Center attacks in 2001, Goldman Sachs posted dogs in its lobby to sniff incoming packages.

On occasion, the Security department, or the organization's "Security Policies," might be perceived as the cause of an organization's crisis.

In cases where the department, or its policies, may have caused the crisis, it might be better if the department representative is not involved in managing the crisis because he or she might become too defensive. They should recuse themselves during this specific crisis.

An example of a crisis in which the Security department may be perceived as being the cause, or being too defensive, involves the Security department scheduling an exercise that is too threatening to employees:

TCI Cablevision, Tulsa, Oklahoma, 1993: During an after-hours meeting on security, two strangers burst into the cable company's lobby, cursing and aiming guns at terrified employees and demanding money. Some of the 25 workers were shaken and physically ill as the robbers fled with the cash.

Managers then revealed the break-in was fake; the robbers were actors. The purpose, according to a memo three days later, was "to prepare the possible victims to be alert and to take action to help make them a less desirable target should a real robbery occur."

Five women at the simulated robbery quit their jobs and sued, saying the faked event amounted to a vicious assault and outrageous conduct. In depositions among the six volumes of documents in the case: one woman said she could not sleep and her hair fell out. Another said she cried a lot and was depressed, and a third said she began vomiting the day she returned to work. Each seeks in excess of $10,000 in damages from the Englewood, Colorado-based Tele-Communications Inc., its Tulsa subsidiary, and Elite Protective and Security Services Inc., contracted to run the seminar.

Memorial Hospital, Virginia, 1996: Five masked men burst into the emergency room waving guns and demanding drugs. Real, unloaded guns were pointed at the nurses during the five-minute drill, *which was arranged by the hospital's security staff.*

Police are looking into the mock assault at the hospital that left several emergency room nurses and patients badly shaken. A lawyer who represents three of the nurses said, "I don't think you can point a gun at someone's head and get away with it." (From *USA Today,* March 22, 1996.)

Security was inadequate.

The next examples involve "Security Policies" that were perceived to be the cause of the crisis. The Security department policies were inadequate and failed to prevent a crime.

Bloomingdale's Department Store, Stamford, Connecticut, 1995: Bloomingdale's must pay $1.5 million to the estate of a woman who was stabbed to death in its dim and lightly patrolled parking garage, the state Supreme Court ruled. *Bloomingdale's was warned years earlier that better security was needed.*

Denny's Restaurant, Indianapolis, Indiana, 1995: Amy and Steve Johnson, held in a 1994 Denny's hostage standoff, filed suit against Denny's. Reason: *they claimed Denny's security failed to protect them.* Their son, Justin, 6, was shot by the accused gunmen, Ron and Tom Mathisen.

Exxon Mobil, Waterford, Connecticut, 2000: The mother of a convenience store clerk who was shot to death last summer in Waterford, is suing Exxon Mobil Corp., claiming the oil giant put her son at risk. Billy Pityer, 32, of Westerly, Rhode Island, was working the night shift in a Mobil Mart on June 7 when two robbers burst into the store, pulled their guns, and shot him to death.

In her ten-page complaint filed in U.S. District Court, Pityer's mother alleges that:

1. Exxon Mobil negligently caused her son's death by failing, among other things, to have a bulletproof shield in place to protect the cashier on duty in the convenience store. In fact, the company removed a shield that had been at the store, according to the complaint.
2. Exxon Mobil was also negligent to require the Waterford store to stay open 24 hours a day, even though it was located in an area that made it susceptible to nighttime robberies and had a history of criminal conduct, the complaint states. It has been robbed before, according to Waterford police.

   Exxon Mobil also failed to use an external cash draw or some other system that would have enabled people to pay for gas late at night without going into the store, while the cashier stayed safely behind locked doors, the complaint states.

State of Florida, Department of Transportation, Clearwater, Florida, 1996: Jury awarded $450,000 to a woman who sued the state Department of Transportation *for lax security.* She was raped in the bathroom of an I-75 welcome station.

Antioch College, Yellow Springs, Ohio, 1994: A student, who has filed a $3.1 million suit, says she was raped by a man hired by the school. *The students demand better security measures and screening.*

SUNY – State University of New York, Albany, New York, 1994: A psychology major held 350 people hostage in a lecture hall for nearly two hours before he was jumped and disarmed by five students. Motive: the student had a dispute with the school over his student status. Jason McEnaney, 19, who helped tackle the gunman, was shot in the abdomen and leg and hospitalized in serious condition. On April 20, 1995, McEnaney filed a $20 million suit against the state and school officials. *McEnaney's lawyer said they should have known to keep the suspected gunman away from campus because of his history of irrational and violent behavior at school.*

Wal-Mart Store and the Mall, Memphis, Tennessee, 1996: A woman was kidnapped from the mall's parking lot in 1990. The family filed a $20 million lawsuit, *claiming that security was inadequate.*

Winn Dixie, Eustis, Florida, 1993: (Dorothy Lewis) – (Abduction) – Reason: poor lighting and the padlocking of one of two front doors at the grocery store contributed to the attack. Dorothy Lewis has reached an out-of-court settlement with the owners of a Eustis Winn-Dixie store from which she and her daughters were abducted two years ago. Lewis and her daughters were taken at gunpoint from the parking lot of the store January 30, 1993. Lewis was raped, shot, and left for dead in a remote area northeast of Eustis. She lived, but her daughters were shot to death.

Lewis argued in her suit that *poor lighting and the padlocking of one of two front doors at the grocery store contributed to the attack. The store had a responsibility to provide her with a safe entrance and exit.* Lewis's civil suit prompted a suit between Winn-Dixie and the landlord, with each claiming that if anyone should be held responsible, it was the other. Winn-Dixie and the Tanens also tried to shift blame to Hall Properties Management Company Inc. hired to take care of the shopping center. Alfonza Smalls and Richard Henyard Jr. were both convicted of first-degree murder.

In many of the cases mentioned above, the courts ruled that the "Security Policies" were the cause of the crisis.
Did security fail?
The next examples are where "Security Failed" to prevent a crime.

Essex County Courthouse, Newark, New Jersey, 1993: A shooting at the Essex County Courthouse on June 4, 1993, came three months *after metal detectors were installed* to keep weapons out of the building. A detective waiting to testify in a drug trial was "assassinated" outside a courtroom by the cousin of the two defendants. John Sczyrek, an undercover detective with the Newark Police Department, was shot in the head in the hallway outside the courtroom and died at the scene. Assistant Prosecutor Carolyn Murray said Sczyrek was a key witness against Charles Oliver and Darryl Hill, having made an undercover drug buy from the pair.

The suspect, Eddie Lee Oliver Philson, 25, of Newark, was arrested a few blocks away and a gun was recovered from bushes outside the courthouse.

The judge in charge of the courthouse — New Jersey's busiest county courthouse with many of its most serious criminal cases — immediately ordered that security be further increased. State and county officials could not recall a killing in a New Jersey courthouse before.

U.S. Government, Department of State, Washington, D.C., 1993: Geneva Jones, a secretary in the State Department with top-secret clearance, and Dominique Ntube, the "executive director and editor in chief" *of The Continent*, were charged in federal court with stealing thousands of classified documents from State Department and CIA files. The documents taken related to U.S. military operations in Somalia and Iraq. Investigators believe some of the documents were transmitted to Liberian insurgent Charles Taylor. Ntube is supporting Taylor's attempt to seize power in Monrovia, the capital of Liberia. Taylor has been carrying out a civil war since 1989. On September 14, 1994, Jones was sentenced to 37 months in prison.

Appendix 6C

PUBLIC RELATIONS/MEDIA RELATIONS: SLA ELEMENTS

Upon notification that a disaster has struck a building housing business units of your organization, the Legal department representative, or representatives, will report to the Crisis Management Team Command Center (CMT CC). (See Chapter 9.)

As a member of the Crisis Management Team (CMT), the Public Relations department representatives' role will be to use their expertise to manage the media and public relations impacts of the disaster or crisis. The representative(s) will act as the coordination point to reassure the public that the organization's representatives are in control of the situation and the crisis will be handled in an organized and timely manner.

After members of the CMT have reported to the CMT Command Center and obtained all known pertinent information regarding the disaster, the Legal representative(s) will:

- If telephone communications are disrupted by a disaster, (i.e., earthquake, hurricane, tornado, etc.) and you need to notify employees who are not at work, contact employees.
  - Assist the business units in notifying employees of the situation.
- Set up a news media meeting area in or near the Crisis Communications Command Center. Conduct and manage all press conferences.
  - TV, radio, newspapers.
  - Establish who the company spokesperson will be.
- Activate the Crisis Communications Plan strategy.
  - Ensure all employees understand that they are to make no statements to the news media.
  - Have the employees refer the news media personnel to the company spokesperson. The statement is intended to minimize adverse publicity.

- Provide employees with information on the status of the recovery progress.
    - Consider using e-mail for daily status reports, and the company's newspaper or magazine for more in-depth reports.

- Provide information about the crisis to:
    - Media — avoid negative publicity.
    - Shareholders — maintain value of company stock.
    - Customers — avoid loss of current or future business.

(***Author Note:*** This element of the Crisis Management Plan is so voluminous that it needed to be its own chapter. For more information on this department Crisis Management Team role, see Chapter 7.)

Appendix 6D

HUMAN RESOURCES/PERSONNEL DEPARTMENT: SLA ELEMENTS

Upon notification that a disaster has struck a building housing business units of your organization, the Human Resources department representative, or representatives, will report to the Crisis Management Team Command Center (CMT CC). (See Chapter 9.)

As a member of the Crisis Management Team (CMT), the Human Resources department representative's role will be to use his or her expertise to manage employee problems and situations caused by the disaster. The representative(s) will act as the coordination point for all employee and personnel matters pertaining to the organization's recovery from the disaster.

After the members of the CMT have reported to the CMT Command Center and obtained all known pertinent information regarding the disaster, the Human Resources representative(s) will:

- Determine if employees have been injured.
- If there is a need for additional personnel to assist during the "resumption" stage, obtain temporary personnel to meet the organization's operational needs.
- Following a disaster, establish a payroll policy for employees in which some employees are working and many are not.
- Monitor employees for signs of stress — Post Traumatic Stress Disorder (PTSD).

- Work with the Legal department in activating the "Executive Succession Plan" when necessary if executives are victims of the disaster.
- On occasion, the Human Resources department, or the organization's "Human Resources Policies," may be perceived as the cause of an organization's crisis. In those cases, it may be better if the department representative is not involved in managing the crisis because he or she might become too defensive.

SCENARIO: DISASTER

When a disaster has damaged one of the buildings housing one, or more, of your organization's business units, the Human Resources department will obtain information pertinent to the building damage and needed repairs.

Examples of information pertinent to the Human Resources department include:

- Using a "fire" as the type of disaster:
  - Were any employees injured by the fire?
  - Issues to be handled by the Human Resources department representative include:
    - Safety
    - Injuries
    - Notifications to "Emergency Contacts"
    - Need for additional personnel
    - Compensation for exceptional effort
- Using a "storm" as the type of disaster (e.g., a rainstorm, snowstorm, tornado, hurricane, etc.):
  - Were any employees injured by the storm?
  - Issues to be handled by the Human Resources department representative include:
    - Safety
    - Injuries
    - Notifications to "Emergency Contacts"
    - Need for additional personnel
    - Compensation for exceptional effort
- Using a "financial problem" as the type of crisis:
  - Will this crisis result in the termination or layoffs of employees?
  - Will there be a need for additional personnel to be hired temporarily?
  - Will it create any undue stress on employees?

Determine if employees have been injured.

- Determine "which" employees have been injured
- From local authorities
- From other employees
- From hospitals
    - If employees have been injured by the disaster, a representative from the Human Resources or Medical department will contact local hospitals to determine which employees have been admitted. Provide this information to management at the CMT Command Center.

Notify the families. When employees are injured, your organization needs to consider who will contact the person (family member) identified by the employee in the event of an emergency. This information is part of the Human Resources database. They are usually identified as the "Emergency Contact."

- A process must be in place for notification of family members in the event of serious injury to or the death of an employee. If possible, a person trained in bereavement issues should assist management in that process.
- Who will notify the families?
    - Local authorities: the *easiest* way to notify the person identified by the employee would be to let the local officials do the notification (i.e., Police).
    - Representative of your organization: the *best* way to notify the person identified by the employee as the "Emergency Contact" would be to have someone from your organization do the notifying because this person can show the proper concern about the employee and their situation. They can answer questions relating to medical coverage, work continuation, wage continuation., job security, medical insurance, insurance claims, etc.
- What information will the "notifier" need in order to notify the family?
    - The "Emergency Contact's" name
    - Relationship to employee
    - Address
    - Telephone number
- Who can provide this information?
    - The Human Resources representative, using the HR database.

- How will the "notifier" notify the "Emergency Contact"?
  - Go to the residence of the person to be notified?
    - Resource needed: the address
  - Call on the telephone?
    - Resource needed: the phone number

  (***Author Note:*** When American Air suffered a plane crash in Chicago in 1980, an insurance company I was assisting had four executives on the plane. They sent a senior member of the HR/Personnel department and a senior member of the Legal department to the homes of the executives to personally tell the "Emergency Contact" of the situation and to assist in any way they could.)

- Are there any special considerations your company can make to assist the family?
  - In some earlier disasters, organizations have arranged for baby-sitters to watch children while the spouse visits the employee in the hospital.
  - Another organization told me that it provided transportation for a number of days because the spouse did not drive.
- Does the "notifier" (from your organization) have any other assigned responsibilities to perform during the early stages of the Business Resumption operation?
  - If yes, what responsibility has priority? The notification or the other responsibility?
- If the personnel files are inaccessible or destroyed by the disaster, how will the notifier know who the "Emergency Contact" is?
  - Who has been designated the "Emergency Contact"?
  - What if the "Emergency Contact" are the parents of an unmarried child? Where do they live? What is their telephone number?

Advise the Business Continuity Plan (BCP) professional and Executive Management Team (EMT) of the status of "Emergency Contact" (family member) notifications. Coordinate information with the Crisis Communications/Public Relations department representative regarding news media announcements of injured personnel.

If there is a need for additional personnel to assist during the "business resumption" stage, obtain temporary personnel to meet the organization's operational needs.

In the event that a disaster has injured employees, or key employee designated business resumption responsibilities are not available, and the organization will need to have different employees perform their duties, the Human Resources personnel will obtain replacements. These replacements will only be needed on a temporary basis.

If staff is unavailable:

A key lesson Rodney Hargroder of Premier Bank in Baton Rouge, Louisiana, learned after Hurricane Andrew was that current staff may not be available to carry out their responsibilities following a disaster. Mr. Hargroder said, "We had a basic assumption in our disaster recovery plan that staff would be available for recovery, but we had some no-shows. At one point, we had one person staffing our data center." (From "Hurricane Andrew," *Disaster Recovery Journal,* 1993.)

The HR department personnel could use one, or all, of the following resources to obtain the temporary personnel:

■ Employees in other areas of the company with similar skills as the injured employees. (This information should be available in the HR database.)
■ The organization's pensioners or retirees with similar skills as the injured employees. (This information should be available in the HR database.)
■ If neither of the resources mentioned above is available, then use temporary employment agencies.
■ A less appealing and less likely option is to ask an organization that presently employs one of your organization's ex-employee if they can lend the ex-employee to your organization temporarily to assist during your business resumption operation.

Lend a former employee, Arby's and Haverty Furniture: In an unusual resolution to a personnel crisis, Arby's corporate office "borrowed" the person who had set up its Florida data center from another company. Vic Anderson, currently with Haverty Furniture in Atlanta, wrote the disaster recovery plan for Arby's Florida data center, but it had not been tested. When the hurricane knocked out windows, power, and air conditioning at the Arby's data center, Arby's asked Haverty to "loan out" Anderson to supervise their hot site recovery in Atlanta.

Following a disaster, establish a "payroll policy" for employees in which some employees are working, and many are not.

Some employees will be needed immediately after a disaster strikes. They play a vital role in the damage assessment or the business resumption efforts. At any rate, they will be working immediately, usually in difficult conditions, to support the organization's business resumption operations.

Other employees will not be needed immediately. They have either been sent home by the organization or the organization has asked them to "not report" to work. It could be that their work areas need repair before they can resume their duties. They will not be working until they are called back, which may be days, or weeks.

Establish a "payroll policy" for those employees who have been sent home by the organization, those who cannot report to work, or those who are asked to "not report" to work. Do they receive pay, or not? For example,

> *Bankers Trust.* When fire damaged three floors in the Bankers Trust Headquarters building in New York City in 1993, about half the employees were able to work in the undamaged areas, 25 percent of the employees were relocated to other offices, and 25% were told to stay home. Human Resources must establish a policy on whether the 25 percent who were told to stay home should be paid for staying home.

> *River Rouge power plant.* A fire in 1999 at the Ford Motor Company's River Rouge power plant resulted in Ford asking most of the 10,000 employees to stay home for a day while a damage assessment and repairs were taking place.

> (***Author Note***: I do not recommend that an organization not pay employees who have been directed by the organization to stay home. In fact, I have often recommended to my clients when I was consulting, that they buy a Payroll Continuation insurance policy. This strategy was explained to me in 1983 when H.C. Prange Stores, of Sheboygan, Wisconsin, explained that is what they added to their insurance portfolio after they recovered from their building disaster.

> A water main burst in the basement of the Prange headquarters building. It flooded the basement of the block-long headquarters building. The next day the center pillar in the basement began sinking into the flood-damaged soil. The building was evacuated, and then condemned by local authorities for safety reasons, until it could be shored up. The computer mainframe, which does the processing for all 42 department stores, was in the building.

> After the building was shored up, the organization removed the mainframe and relocated it to a building in Green Bay, Wisconsin, which was a former computer center.

The building in Sheboygan was declared unsafe and eventually had to be demolished.

Employees who working in that building were either transferred to another Prange store, or paid until a new store could be made operational.

The VP of Insurance told me that they did not have this payroll insurance policy in place before the flood/building collapse. But after paying a number of employees who could not be transferred for months, management decided it was appropriate to have the payroll continuation policy in place before the next incident occurred. (It would provide up to three months of pay to each employee.

To the best of my knowledge, Prange never had a "next" incident. I guess their forethought is something like the old wives' tale, "Carry an umbrella to ensure that it doesn't rain.")

Let me cite a few organizations that I am aware of that did establish a policy "to pay employees who did not work during the damage assessment or repairs."

Cigna's Metro Center building in Hartford, Connecticut: The building was flooded in 1987 when water pipes in the air-conditioning system burst. About 40,000 gallons of water poured from the break. The 1000 employees of the insurer's Group Pension Division have been asked to stay out of the building the following day. (Policy) The employees will be paid in full during their unexpected holiday.

Malden Mills, Massachusetts: A fire destroyed the Malden Mills nine-building mill complex in 1995. It left 1400 workers jobless just days before Christmas. Aaron Feuerstein, CEO, announced to the 3000 employees affected that he would continue to pay them their salary for 30 days and continue health benefits for 90 days. When the 30-day period ended, he pledged to keep paying out-of-work employees for another month. Feuerstein's uncommon deeds made him a national symbol of the model corporate citizen.

York International Corp., Pennsylvania: After an explosion at York International Corp. in 1998, officials said it would take two or three days (clean-up and investigation) before it can determine how many employees can return to work. (Policy)

They also said employees would be guaranteed their base wages until they return to work.

Formosa Plastics, Illiopolis, Illinois, 2004: A series of explosions rocked a Formosa Plastics plant in 2004. The plastics plant will be rebuilt, and the 136 employees will continue to be paid.

The examples above involve organizations that paid employees for a couple days. Are there any examples of organizations that paid their people for months? The answer is yes.

MGM Mirage Inc. (Beau Rivage), New Orleans, Louisiana, 2005: The MGM Mirage Inc., which owns Beau Rivage, paid its 3100 employees and provided insurance for three months after Hurricane Katrina gutted the lower floors of the beachfront casino and hotel.

Harrah's Entertainment Inc., 2005: Harrah's paid its 8000 employees who worked in casinos in Biloxi, Gulfport, and New Orleans full pay and benefits until November 26. (From *Philadelphia Inquirer*, December 8, 2005.)

Consider implementing an extraordinary compensation program to reward employees who extend special efforts.

John Alden Life Insurance Company, 1992: Following "Hurricane Andrew," the life insurance company ran its processing from a computer "hotsite" facility for 15 days. It had in place a recovery plan that provided for the forwarding of data and people to a recovery site (Comdisco) prior to the storm impact.

The recovery ran smoothly for its entire 15 days. Many individuals involved in the recovery operation spent time away from their homes and families during a time of extreme psychological uncertainty. They were given special considerations by the insurance organization to thank them for their loyalty.

(**Author Note:** I do recommend that an organization consider some type of "thank you" for those employees who did come in to assist immediately after the disaster. This "thank you" can take many forms. Obviously a small bonus, or extra paycheck, or compensatory time off goes a long way to making the employees feel that their efforts were appreciated.

Following the Chicago River Flood in 1992, one company sent limousines to pick up each member of the IT recovery team at the airport following the recovery efforts. In each limousine were a large box of candy and a dozen roses. Obviously the roses were for the female recovery team members, or the wives or girlfriends of the male recovery team members. The following weekend, the organization thanked them at a dinner in one of the finest restaurants in Chicago.

It did not cost the organization a lot of money to say thank you, and it was a great morale booster — not only for the recovery team members, but also for all the employees. The organization showed that it cares for employees who show their loyalty by performing during a great deal of stress.)

Speaking of loyalty, a book *entitled Loyalty Rules! How Today's Leaders Build Lasting Relationships* states that Corporate America does not grasp the relevance of employee loyalty to success. And its actions have alienated employees, who in turn alienate customers — and that hurts profits and growth. Frederick Reichheld, author of that book, finds that the typical company is lucky if 50 percent of its employees believe it deserves their loyalty, according to a study of 2000 employees that Reichheld did for Bain & Co. this year. As a result, Reichheld says, U.S. corporations lose half their customers in five years, half their employees in four years, and half their investors in less than one year. By fostering loyalty, companies can boost productivity, customer retention and referrals, and attract talented staff. "It's more important in a down market," he says. (From "When Loyalty Erodes, So Do Profits," *Business Week*, August 13, 2001.)

Imagine what the study would have shown if the organization had experienced a disaster and told employees to stay home — and did not pay them. That certainly does not generate a feeling of loyalty. On the other hand, what would the study have shown if the organization had experienced a disaster and told the employees to stay home, and that they would be paid (maybe for three months)? Furthermore, what if the organization had rewarded the employees who did work (immediately after the disaster) with some sort of extra pay or time off?

"To pay or not to pay?" In a *New York Times* article published on September 20, 2001, that question was discussed as it related to organizations that were affected by the 9-11 terrorist attacks. Many companies with offices in the World Trade Center, especially financial-services concerns, had not yet decided whether to pay victims' families the hefty bonuses that can make up a large part of employee pay. That is partly because companies often do not pay bonuses to employees who are not on their payrolls at the time that they issue bonus checks — although company policies vary in cases of death.

> *Cantor Fitzgerald LP*, which lost more than 600 of the 1000 employees who worked at the World Trade Center, posted a page on its Web site to explain benefits to victims' families. The bond-trading firm said it "expect[s] to pay all year-end bonuses that would have otherwise been paid to individual employees as soon as we possibly can." Cantor Chairman Howard Lutnick, who lost a brother in the bombings, gave a series of highly emotional interviews in the days after Cantor Fitzgerald"s offices in the Trade Center's Tower One were destroyed. He pledged to "take care of" the families of lost employees, whom he called "a new class of partners," and contributed $1 million to a fund to be distributed among victims' families.

> At *Sandler O'Neill & Partners*, an investment-banking boutique, about 10 managers, including both internal and outside consultants, are working full-time to figure out benefits for families of employees lost in the World Trade Center attack. It aims to have answers in the next 72 hours "but I hope sooner than that," says Fred D. Price, the firm's chief operating officer. The attack left 67 of the firm's 177 employees missing or dead.

> The process of determining benefits requires recreating all its personnel files, which were destroyed along with details like beneficiary information, Price says. ("From "Companies Confront the Issue of Benefits Covering Staffers Killed in the Attacks," *New York Times*, September 20, 2001.)

Monitor employees for signs of stress — Post Traumatic Stress Disorder (PTSD) — and provide employee-counseling resources.

> "Posttraumatic Stress Disorder, or PTSD, is a psychiatric disorder that can occur following the experience or witnessing of life-threatening events such as military combat, natural disasters, terrorist incidents, serious accidents, or violent personal assaults like rape. People who suffer from PTSD often relive the experience through nightmares and flashbacks, have difficulty sleeping, and feel detached or estranged, and these symptoms can be severe enough and last long enough to significantly impair the person's daily life.

PTSD is marked by clear biological changes as well as psychological symptoms. PTSD is complicated by the fact that it frequently occurs in conjunction with related disorders such as depression, substance abuse, problems of memory and cognition, and other problems of physical and mental health. The disorder is also associated with impairment of the person's ability to function in social or family life, including occupational instability, marital problems and divorces, family discord, and difficulties in parenting."

—"A National Center for PTSD Fact Sheet"

"Unaddressed, traumatic stress can devastate human health and human life, and its effects can cripple the productive and financial life of even the strongest corporation."

—Bruce Blythe, CEO
Crisis Management International
"Terrorism from Within Threatens Corporate America"

"Traumatic stress is a sudden, devastating 'blow' or series of blows to the human psyche that hits with such force that it exceeds all the normal coping abilities. It breaks through our defenses and overwhelms our abilities to respond or function effectively. Traumatic stress will impact and affect everyone involved in an emotion-packed crisis or disaster."

—Bruce Blythe, CEO
Crisis Management International
"Terrorism from Within Threatens Corporate America"

The Human Resources department representative should ensure that employees are being monitored for symptoms. Symptoms of PTSD in employees include:

- May feel "hypersensitive" or have a sense of increased arousal
- Difficulties with sleep
- Increased irritability and temper
- Difficulty with concentration
- Numbing, or loss of interest in their typical activities
- More withdrawn
- Do not take pleasure in things they used to do
- May feel detached from or apart from others
- May experience an "exaggerated startle response," over-responding, or "jumping" when there is unexpected noise, the phone, or doorbell

If the organization recognizes that employees are showing these symptoms, it should provide employees with, or obtain, psychological support for these personnel. If the organization has an in-house medical department, work with them to provide this counseling. Organizations should pre-plan for PTSD counseling. If they do not have internal resources, the organization's HR department should arrange for external professional support.

> "Management needs rehearsed guidelines and procedures. Normal management procedures may prove very inappropriate in a crisis situation, worsening the stress impact on victims. But rapid, right responses by key management can greatly lessen the damage both to individuals and the organization."
>
> **—Bruce Blythe, CEO**
> *Crisis Management International*
> *"Terrorism from Within Threatens Corporate America"*

Humans have unique, individual responses to disaster situations. Some people have emotional reactions to traumatic events that show up within the first 24 hours. These are called *acute* reactions. As time goes on, these feelings may change, or new feelings may evolve. These are called *delayed* reactions.

Some of these effects are (from *The Human Factor*):

- Disorganization and sluggishness in thinking
- Inability to make decisions
- Poor judgment
- Decreased concentration
- Decreased efficiency
- Increased errors
- Exaggerated startle response
- Breakdowns in communication
- Conflict between employees in the same business unit; between different business units
- Conflict between managers over authority

Following the terrorist attacks on the World Trade Center in 2001, "One large survey of Americans and their mental health found that of those who said they had been exposed to trauma, about 25 percent developed the hallmarks of post-traumatic stress disorder. Perhaps the only thing experts can say with any certainty is that people most directly exposed to death, injury and loss are at highest risk. Those who do develop post-traumatic symptoms will relive ... '9-11'... events in nightmares, flashbacks and images their minds cannot suppress. Any reminder — a television replay or the sound of a siren — may send their bodies on a physiological roller coaster. They may start at loud noises, sleep badly, strike out in irrational anger or try to avoid places or people that trigger memories."

—"Stress from Attacks Will Chase Some into the Depths of Their Minds, and Stay,"
New York Times, *September 18, 2001*

Steps that were taken after 9-11 to help organizations with employees suffering from PTSD symptoms were mentioned in an article published by *Philadelphia Inquirer* on October 10, 2001, entitled "For some, return is beyond capability." "Affected companies are generally letting employees take a leave or work from home. Most are offering one-on-one telephone counseling for those who cannot come in." "People who live outside the city are afraid to come back." "People in tall buildings are fearful to go up, and people who live near ground zero are afraid to go home. Managers are all asking: 'What do we do? How do we work with these people?' Most large companies forced to evacuate the World Trade Center are experiencing hesitation by at least some workers, particularly those who were emotionally fragile before the attacks."

When an organization suffers a disaster that probably will cause the employees a high level of traumatic stress, it may expect the following effects:

- Increased absenteeism
- Poor morale
- Lowered productivity
- Increased problems with drugs and alcohol
- Higher medical and mental health claims

It is important for an organization to be prepared for a traumatic event, and know what to do to care for its employees. Employees can make or break an organization during a disaster or crisis.

How well the company responds here will have crucial implications for its ability to function in the long term. Those companies that provide for the well-being of their employees often find that they are able to achieve a higher level of functioning than before the disaster.

Post-Traumatic Stress Statistics

Suicide

Earthquakes, floods, and hurricanes cause suicide rates to climb among grieving and stressed survivors, researchers report in today's *New England Journal of Medicine*. A Centers for Disease Control and Prevention research team found a 13.8 percent increase in suicides during the four years after a natural disaster. (From "Post Traumatic Stress Disorder," *USA Today*, February 5, 1998.)

Increased Drug and Alcohol Use

Twenty-three states and six cities, including New York and Washington, have seen an increased demand for drug and alcohol treatment since the September 11 attacks on the WTC, says a survey from the National Center on Addiction and Substance Abuse (CASA) at Columbia University. (From "9/11 attacks reverberate in the mind," *USA Today*, April 2, 2002.)

Depression

More than 130,000 people living in Manhattan suffered from post-traumatic stress disorder or depression after the September 11 attack on the WTC, says a study out today. In the study, 13 percent of Manhattan residents reported symptoms of PTSD or depression five to eight weeks after the disaster. That rate is nearly three times higher than the prevalence of these disorders in the general population, the study authors say. The study, which appears in today's *New England Journal of Medicine* is a snapshot of the number of folks struggling with psychological distress up to two months after the disaster. No one really knows how many people in New York still suffer from PTSD or depression, says John Tassey, a spokesman for the American Psychological Association. The symptoms of PTSD can occur right after the event or may take years to surface. The good news is that PTSD and depression can be treated with counseling and medication. In some cases, the symptoms of PTSD won't go away without treatment. (From *USA Today*, March 28, 2002.)

How is PTSD treated?

PTSD is treated by a variety of forms of psychotherapy and drug therapy. There is no definitive treatment, and no cure, but some treatments appear to be quite promising, especially cognitive-behavioral therapy, group therapy, and exposure therapy. Exposure therapy involves having the patient repeatedly relive the frightening experience under controlled conditions to help him or her work through the trauma. Studies have also shown that medications help ease associated symptoms of depression and anxiety and help with sleep. The most widely used drug treatments for PTSD are the selective serotonin reuptake inhibitors, such as Prozac and Zoloft. At present, cognitive-behavioral therapy appears to be somewhat more effective than drug therapy. However, it would be premature to conclude that drug therapy is less effective overall since drug trials for PTSD are at a very early stage. Drug therapy appears to be highly effective for some individuals and is helpful for many more. In addition, the recent findings on the biological changes associated with PTSD have spurred new research into drugs that target these biological changes, which may lead to much increased efficacy. (From "A National Center for PTSD Fact Sheet.")

Work with the Legal department in activating of the "Executive Succession Plan" when necessary if executives are victims of the disaster.

One of the critical crises that can strike an organization is the sudden death of one of its executives. This sudden loss can result in the organization's ability to keep moving forward with the various programs it was planning or implementing. The failure to respond to the sudden loss of a leader can damage a company's performance. It can also have a negative effect on its reputation or image.

Work with the Legal department to ensure there is an "Executive Succession Program" in place. Then when the organization experiences the sudden loss of an executive, work with the Legal department in applying the terms and conditions of the "Executive Succession" Plan. This is especially true in financial institutions in which is required by law to have a person designated to act as CEO of the financial within 24 hours of an incident that prevents the former CEO of performing their duties.

Many organizations are including an "executive succession program" as a standard operating procedure.

There was an interesting article published in *USA Today* on April 19, 2004, entitled "Succession plan can be critical." The article was published shortly after the death of McDonald's 60-year-old chairman and CEO, Jim Cantalupo, who died of an apparent heart attack early on the morning of April 19, 2004. McDonald's has received plaudits for its succession plan. As pointed out in the article that "McDonald's moved quickly to reassure Wall Street and its employees — by immediately naming a new management team. The reaction indicated that the board had an approved succession plan in place, says Paul Hodgson, senior research associate at The Corporate Library."

The article went on to say:

"Investor activists and institutional shareholders are demanding that boards of directors take a firm hand in planning for succession, even at companies where strong chairmen or CEOs have ruled for decades. Boards should discuss succession planning at every meeting and develop strategies to both develop internal talent and keep an eye open for outside stars, says Patrick McGurn, senior counsel to proxy adviser Institutional Shareholder Services. Referring to Cantalupo, he says, "You could not come up with a more compelling example of why you need a succession plan in place, if not a process. This is the No. 1 issue for institutional shareholders. If a board fails on this issue, then nothing else really matters.""

In another article on Executive Succession Plans published in *USA Today* on April 20, 2004, Patrick McGurn, senior counsel to proxy adviser Institutional Shareholder Services, stresses "Boards of Directors should discuss succession planning at every meeting and develop strategies to both develop internal talent and keep an eye open for outside stars."

For information on some of the crises that have resulted in the need for organizations to use an executive succession program, refer to the Legal department's Crisis Management Team section. That section addresses examples such as AGCO Corp. of Georgia; Ameripec, Inc. of Taiwan; Arrow Electronics of Greenwich, Connecticut; Bruno's Inc. of Rome, Georgia; Swire Coca-Cola of Salt Lake City, Utah; Excalibur Communications Corp. of Lebanon, New Hampshire; Fred Alger Management of New York City; Keefe Bruyette & Woods; New York City; Nashua Industrial Machine of New Hampshire; and Trump Casinos of Atlantic City, New Jersey.

On occasion, the Human Resources department, or the organization's "Human Resources Policies," may be perceived as the cause of an organization's crisis.

In cases where the department, or its policies, may have caused the crisis, it may be better if the department representatives are not involved in managing the crisis because they become too defensive. They should recuse themselves during this specific crisis.

An example of a crisis in which the Human Resources department might be perceived as being the cause, or being too defensive is terminating an employee during the time he or she is experiencing a personal crisis:

■ Example 1: General Dynamics, Santee, California, 1993:
Dean Farness of Santee, California; when he returned to work from bereavement leave after six-year-old son Brent died in a car accident, General Dynamics fired him. Firing was on March 15,

the day Brent would have turned 7. Farness said, "They just called me in and said, 'It's hard for us to do this, but we've got to do it.'"

General Dynamics spokeswoman Julie Andrews says: "People at the very highest levels are dismayed at the way this has happened." She said the plant is laying off 40 percent of its 4200 workers.

Farness worked ten years with General Dynamics. Said the Rev. Mark Wiley, family pastor: "Holding off a bit would not have made a significant dent in their profit-loss margin, but it would have been compassionate."

(*Author Note:* This is especially striking because it was at General Dynamics a year earlier that former employee Robert Earl Mack shot and killed a supervisor, after he was fired while on forced leave he believed was temporary.)

■ Example 2: Structural Dynamics Research, Cincinnati, Ohio, April 27, 1995:

Bill Means took his daughter Marisa to his office on "Take Our Daughters to Work Day." Marisa was two hours into the special day at her dad's organization when Ed Neenan, the company vice president, told Means that he was being fired.

Neenan said he did not know Mean's daughter was in the office, and conceded the "timing was truly regrettable."

Bill Means believed Neenan did not know Marisa was with him. Means position was: "I think that's part of his job, to know there are daughters in the building on 'Take Our Daughters to Work Day'."

■ Example 3: Coastal Oil Co., "Firing of Margaret Graziano," November 12, 1995:

A car had hit Margaret Graziano's son Adam on October 29 in Queens, New York. She was a credit analyst who had worked for Coastal Oil for six years. She took unpaid leave to stay close to her comatose ten-year-old son in the intensive care unit at New York Hospital – Cornell Medical Center in Manhattan.

On November 12, 1995, she was keeping a vigil at the hospital bedside of her son when her boss showed up — not for support or comfort. Instead he told her she had been laid off because the company was restructuring and had to cut 18 jobs.

Coastal knows it was "horrible timing for everybody concerned," spokesperson Steve Eames said. He said Graziano's boss went to the hospital "to try and help her work through her options" about taking care of the medical bills.

Option 1: continue on unpaid leave with her insurance intact — or
Option 2: be laid off immediately, so she could collect severance pay and apply for unemployment compensation.

Eames said Graziano knew before her son's accident that the company was restructuring and that jobs were being eliminated. He conceded that she had no way of knowing that hers was one of them.

Margaret Graziano's position was: "They should have waited for a better moment, when they knew my son was out of danger, or they could have contacted me somewhere else other than here."

The crisis caused was an "image crisis." After this was reported in the newspapers, there was a question in the minds of employees about the loyalty to the employees, and the compassion of the organization during a time of stress.

Now compare Coastal's approach with that of Safety Kleen:

Mark Hamlin, a sales representative for Safety Kleen Corp. in Fairless Hills, Pennsylvania, has spent nearly all his time with his daughter, Megan, 16, since the June 20 accident, with his employer's blessing. Megan was one of two girls critically injured when a red Toyota 4Runner ran over their heads as they sunbathed at the Anastasia State Recreation Area beach in St. Augustine, Florida. Megan Hamlin remains comatose at Brooks Rehabilitation Center in Jacksonville, where she was transferred after a two-month hospitalization.

When incidents like the three above are publicized in the news media, it can affect employee morale. The media will portray the terminations as cruel and heartless. Just as important, it can have an effect on recruiting. Some of the best recruits may shy away from organizations that appear to have little interest in the feelings of their employees.

Referring to the negative effect on employee morale, in 2002 the employees at Arthur Andersen were grappling with tough questions about how the company's predicament with Enron could affect their careers. "When the image of a company is tarnished, that leads to turnover. Employees may not want to be identified with a company when there's impropriety going on. Andersen carried a reputation for integrity and competence in the fields of auditing and accounting. Now the reputation is in tatters." This was the opinion of Elaine Hollensbe, an assistant professor in management at the University of Cincinnati. (From "Andersen employees' morale rattled," *USA Today,* January 21, 2002.)

Appendix 6E

LEGAL DEPARTMENT: SLA ELEMENTS

Upon notification that a disaster has struck a building housing business units of your organization, the Legal department representative, or representatives, will report to the Crisis Management Team Command Center (CMTCC). (See Chapter 9.)

As a member of the Crisis Management Team (CMT), the Legal department representatives' role will be to use their expertise to manage the legal impacts of the disaster. The representatives will act as the coordination point for all legal and regulatory matters pertaining to the organization's recovery from the disaster or crisis.

After the members of the CMT have reported to the CMTCC and obtained all known pertinent information regarding the disaster, the Legal representatives will:

- Provide any and all contract advice.
- If executives have been injured, or killed, by the disaster, work with the Human Resources CMT representative to handle the transition according to the conditions of the "Executive Succession Plan" (Corporate Bylaws).
- If the organization is going to be sued as a result of the crisis (or disaster), collect and coordinate all information regarding the crisis (or disaster) needed to minimize the effects of any lawsuits.
- On occasion, the Legal department, or the organization's "Legal Policies," may be perceived as the cause of an organization's crisis. In those cases, it may be better if the Legal department representative is not involved in managing the crisis because he or she may become too defensive.

SCENARIO: DISASTER

When a disaster has damaged one of the buildings housing one or more of your organization's business units, the Legal department will obtain information pertinent to the Legal department.

Examples of information pertinent to the Legal department include:

- Using a "fire" as the type of disaster:
  - Were any employees, contractors, or visitors injured by the fire?
  - Issues to be handled by the Legal department representative include:
    - Safety and insurance claims
    - Possible litigation resulting from injury or death
    - Compensation for trauma
  - Are there any regulatory or legal issues that will result from the interruption of business operations as a result of the fire?
- Using a "storm" as the type of disaster (e.g., a rainstorm, snowstorm, tornado, hurricane, etc.):
  - Were any employees, contractors, or visitors injured by the storm?
  - Issues to be handled by Legal department representative include:
    - Safety and insurance claims
    - Possible litigation resulting from injury or death
    - Compensation for trauma
  - Are there any regulatory or legal issues that will result from the interruption of business operations as a result of the storm?
- Using a "product problem" as the type of crisis:
  - If this was a product failure, safety, or tampering issue, were any customers injured?
  - Issues to be handled by Legal department representative include:
    - Safety and insurance claims
    - Possible litigation resulting from injury or death
    - Compensation for trauma
  - Are there any regulatory or legal issues that will result from the interruption of business operations as a result of the storm?
- Using a "workplace violence" incident as the type of crisis:
  - If this was a workplace violence incident, were any employees, contractors, or visitors injured?
  - Issues to be handled by Legal department representative include:
    - Safety and insurance claims
    - Possible litigation resulting from injury or death
    - Compensation for trauma
  - Are there any regulatory or legal issues that will result from the interruption of business operations as a result of the incident?

Provide any and all contract advice.

Are there any legal or regulatory requirements that might affect contractual computer processing schedules or priorities? Are there any property or real estate contracts that will be affected? Are there any equipment contracts that will be affected? Are there any computer software contracts that will be affected? These are the areas in which the Legal department may be asked to provide advice.

One of the common effects of a disaster, or crisis, is the interruption to business operations. This interruption can result in the failure to meet contract provisions with customers. The question of legal liability will have to be ironed out between the legal officials of the customer and your Legal department. Some of your contracts have specific penalties included in the contract if you deliver your product (or services) late. That is:

■ Customer delays and penalties for late delivery.

Organizations that provide computer-processing services probably are at risk if those services are not provided on time. Usually the contract indicates that the customer must have its input into the computer services organization by a certain day and time. If they meet the deadline, the contracts call for the computer processing services organization to provide the processing results no later than "a specific time."

If a disaster, or crisis, prevents the computer from meeting this schedule, the Legal department will have its hands full negotiating with the customers.

> *Shared Medical Systems (SMS),* a medical software organization in Pennsylvania, provides software that can be used on the hospital's mainframe. SMS also stores and processes information for a number of hospitals on its own mainframe.

> Back in 1989, SMS experienced a software problem. A "fault" in aging software prevented machines from accepting September 19, 1989, as a valid date and refused to work. The incident, apparently caused by a mistake in programming, demonstrates how institutions are accepting the risk that major disruptions might occur by handing out work to outsourcers. When the problems began to appear at numerous hospitals, SMS technicians advised clients to shut down parts of their computer systems. By day's end, services had been disrupted at about 100 of the 700 client hospitals. Officials said data was not permanently lost and that patient treatment was not threatened.

> As a result, about 100 hospitals around the country were forced to switch from computers to pen and paper for major bookkeeping functions. This is an example of where the Legal

department will work closely with the organization's customers to reduce the effects of such a crisis.

MCI WorldCom Inc.'s data transmission network partially disabled thousands of automated teller machines and restricted market trading of corn, soybeans, and other futures back in 1999. The problem began during a system upgrade and has disrupted high-speed data service for nearly 30 percent of MCI's global data network customers. MCI was upgrading network software, from Lucent Technologies Inc., a former AT&T Corp. subsidiary, when the system began experiencing problems in large cities such as Philadelphia, New York, Boston, Chicago, and Los Angeles. MCI technicians blamed a software problem in the Lucent switches and were working to fix the glitch. MCI said service was gradually being restored to customers, but did not have an estimate on when operations would return to normal. (From *Philadelphia Inquirer,* August 11, 1999.)

MCI WorldCom Inc. said it will lose revenue because of a ten-day breakdown of its high-speed data network. Lucent has acknowledged full responsibility for the outage. (From *Philadelphia Inquirer,* August 17, 1999.)

Review new contracts acquired as a result of the crisis (or disaster) before they are approved to ensure that the best interests of the organization are being met. As an example,

Temporary space acquisition: When the building housing the business units will be unusable for a lengthy period of time, work with the Facilities department, and the business units that are being moved to a temporary work space, in order to resume business operations on a timely basis. Review the contract being proposed by the real estate company as to the term and ability to extend, the facility modification restrictions, and the potential liabilities.

Assist the recovery teams in the preparation of any required notifications (verbal or written) to vendors concerning the activation of the recovery plan.

One obvious notification that may need to be made in writing is if leased equipment is going to be moved to a different building. If the organization that leases the equipment covers the insurance on the equipment, the new location might affect insurance premiums. Similarly, if your organization covers the insurance on the equipment, your insurance carrier must be notified. The Insurance department can make this notification. The verification that it needs to be done can be the support provided by the Legal department. This is particularly important if the equipment is costly, or if the equipment requires certain types of environment (e.g., computers, clean rooms).

If "hard-copy" versions of contracts are damaged or destroyed by the disaster, provide copies of the "original" contracts.

If the Legal department's offices are affected by the same disaster, Legal has developed, documented, tested, and exercised a business resumption plan to be used in just such an event. This plan identifies how Legal will resume business operations at an alternate location (with the assistance of the Facilities department), and the critical records "backups" that are stored in an off-premises storage location (somewhere outside the building housing the Legal department).

Information Protection and Vulnerability

Legal departments may be particularly vulnerable during disasters because of their reliance on hard copy such as pleadings, depositions, and client files. Paper is a risky medium because it can be consumed by fire, damaged by falling water (broken pipes, leaky roof, etc.), or lost in the rubble following an earthquake or tornado. (From *The American Lawyer,* October 1990.)

> (***Author Note***: BCP professionals should check with their Legal departments to determine "who" has the responsibility to protect the "original" contracts. For a number of my clients, the Legal departments said their responsibility was to review the contracts to ensure they protected the organization. If they felt it was important, they made copies, especially of changes to the boilerplate provided by the vendor or customer. Then they returned the original contract into the hands of the department that initiated the contract (e.g., Facilities, Security, etc.).)

Examine any changes to the business processes made by departments during the disaster recovery activities in order to mitigate any corporate liability.

- If "hard-copy" versions of contracts are damaged or destroyed by the disaster, provide copies of the "original" contracts from the off-premises storage location.
- Assist the recovery teams in the preparation of any required notifications (verbal or written) to customers, vendors, or regulatory agencies concerning the activation of the recovery plan.

If executives have been injured, or killed, by the disaster, work with the Human Resources department to handle the transition according to the "Executive Succession Plan" (Corporate Bylaws).

A CEO is lost in a disaster. How does an organization respond when a CEO, or senior officer, dies? The answer is: most organizations have succession plans in place. The "Executive Succession Plan" is part of the Bylaws of financial organizations. It is a requirement. In the event of the sudden loss of a senior executive, the financial institutions must notify, within 24 hours of the incident, the appropriate regulatory agency of the executive who will succeed.

This process is in place not only for a disaster situation; it can be the result of a sudden illness, heart attack, stroke, etc. The regulatory agencies want to make sure the organization has a continuity of operations during this type of crisis, rather than an internal war between executives fighting each other for the job.

When *McDonald's Co.* CEO (Jim Cantalupo) died of an apparent heart attack in April 2004, McDonald's was praised for its succession plan after naming Charlie Bell to replace Cantalupo. The death of McDonald's 60-year-old chairman and CEO, Jim Cantalupo, points up one of the most critical issues facing corporations: *succession planning.* Investor activists and institutional shareholders are demanding that boards of directors take a firm hand in planning for succession, even at companies where strong chairmen or CEOs have ruled for decades. And there are few industries where that is a bigger issue than among major media companies. (From "Succession plan can be critical," *USA Today,* April 20, 2004.)

Every organization should have a succession plan that does at least three things:

1. It must identify possible successors.
2. It should assess the successor's skills.
3. Notify everyone in the organization, and family, of the succession plan to avoid problems later.

Accidents

Agco Corp., 2002. Five Americans were killed when a private jet crashed on takeoff at Birmingham International Airport in England in 2002. The plane was registered with AGCO Corp., the Georgia-based agricultural equipment company. AGCO said its CEO and a senior vice president were killed in a crash.

Fred Alger Management, 2001. David Alger of Fred Alger Management was killed on September 11, 2001. So were 37 of his 55 employees who worked in the WTC's North Tower. Within 24 hours, Fred Alger announced that he would return from retirement and lead the firm to recovery.

Keefe Bruyette & Woods, 2001. The securities firm suffered over 60 casualties in the September 11, 2001, terrorist attack on the WTC, including Joseph Berry, the co-CEO, and David Berry, the director of research. The firm also lost five of its nine board members.

Ameripec, 2000. The Singapore Airlines plane crash on October 31, 2000, killed the company president, the vice president for finance, and a vice president of Ameripec, an organization in Buena Park, California.

Swire Coca-Cola company, 1996. An airplane crash killed the top management of the Swire Coca-Cola company of Salt Lake City, Utah, in 1996, killing the CEO, the CFO, and the vice president of marketing.

Nashua Industrial Machine of New Hampshire, 1994. The 1994 crash of USAir 427 killed 132 people, including the president and a department supervisor of this company.

Trump's Casinos, 1989. Three top-level executives of Trump's casino empire were killed in a helicopter crash in 1989. The helicopter was en route to Atlantic City. The executives were the CEO of Trump casino operations in Atlantic City; the president of the Taj Mahal casino project, and a senior vice president of the Trump Plaza casino-hotel.

Bruno's Inc., 1991. A corporate jet taking executives on a 1991 Christmas good-will tour of Bruno's Inc, a grocery store chain from Rome, Georgia, crashed into Lavendar Mountain, killing the seven passengers and two crew members on board. Killed were Bruno's chairman, the vice chairman, and three company vice presidents. Bruno's Inc., which operates more than 240 stores in Alabama, Georgia, Florida, Tennessee, Mississippi, and South Carolina. (***Author Note:*** Hearsay: When I was giving this case example during my presentation at an MIS Symposium in November 1998, an attendee told the class that Bruno's went out of business within two years of the crash.)

Arrow Electronics Inc., 1980. A fire at the Stouffer Inn of Westchester, New York, in 1980 killed the Arrow Electronics Inc. Chairman and President, and the Executive Vice President. The electronics firm sales were expected to be $300 million the year of the fire, making it the second largest electronics distributor in the world. A company spokesperson said, "We're afraid that our entire top management was wiped out."

Natural Deaths

Prominent Executives who have died in recent years include:

1994	Bailey Thomas	Chairman & CEO	McCormick & Co.
1994	Frank Wells	President COO	Walt Disney C.
1995	James Batten	Chairman	Knight-Ridder
1996	James Near	Chairman	Wendy's
1996	Jerry Junkins	President/Chairman	Texas Instruments
1996	E. Lawrence Miller	President & CEO	Bradley Real Estate
1996	Bob Magness	CEO	TCI
1997	Roberto Goizueta	Chairman & CEO	Coca-Cola
1998	Scott Mason	President & CEO	Investment Technology
1998	Gerald Pencer	President & CEO	Cott Corporation
1999	Gordon Teter	Chairman & CEO	Wendy's
1999	Andrew Huffman	CEO	Audible
1999	Bruce Abrams	Chairman & CEO	Prism Financial
2000	Arthur Goldberg	President & CEO	Park Place Entertainment
2000	Mark Hughes	Founder	Herbalife International
2001	Don Maurer	President & CEO	McKinney & Silver
2001	Norioki Morinaga	Sr. Executive VP	NTT DoCoMo
2001	Michael Chowdry	Chairmen & CEO	Atlas Air
2002	David Barry	CEO	Triangle Pharmaceuticals
2002	Dave Thomas	Founder	Wendy's
2003	John A. Mulheren	CEO	Bear Wagner Specialists
2003	Joe Magliochetti	Chairman & CEO	Dana
2004	Pierre Bonelli	Chairman & CEO	Bull
2004	Mike O'Callaghan	Chairman	Las Vegas Sun
2004	Mary-Ellis Bunim	Founder	Bunim-Murray Productions

Source: Information excerpted from *USA Today*, April, 20, 2004.

If the organization is going to be sued as a result of the crisis (or disaster), coordinate all information regarding the crisis (or disaster) needed to minimize the effects of any lawsuits.

> *Example 1: Drexel Heritage Furnishings (Event on December 31, 1986; settled in December 1991).* Drexel Heritage Furnishings (North Carolina) was sued over a fire that killed 97 people and injured 140 in 1986 at the Dupont Plaza Hotel in Puerto Rico.

The lawsuit alleged that a disgruntled hotel employee who set the fire used cooking fuel to ignite several packaged Drexel Heritage dressers that had been delivered to the hotel the day before and were being stored in an unsprinklered ballroom on the hotel's ground floor. The plaintiffs alleged that the furnishings were unreasonably dangerous because of their alleged ease of ignition and undue flammability.

Drexel maintained that its wood dressers were made of non-hazardous materials commonly used by all furniture manufacturers. Drexel defended the lawsuit for almost three years. In the course of the suit, the law firm representing Drexel established an office in San Juan and developed its own computer system to track the millions of documents and the more than 2000 depositions in the case.

Following a 15-month trial in the federal district court in San Juan, the jury reached its verdict after one week of deliberations, finding Drexel had no liability for any damages sustained by the plaintiffs.

The Legal department may have to defend the organization against a lawsuit such as:

Example 2: A "city" is sued. Joseph Brookins was shot and seriously injured by a fired worker for the City of Ft. Lauderdale, Florida, who went on a rampage. The fired worker shot and killed five former co-workers, and seriously wounded Brookins.

If the City of Ft. Lauderdale, Florida, were sued, the difficulty for the City's lawyer would be that Brookins had repeatedly warned that the worker was dangerous. Brookins told his sister, "If I don't come out of this, you sue the city because I've been telling them for a 1-1/2 years that this man was going to do this."

The sister told this story to WSVN-TV in Miami. In reality, the City had received "pre-crisis warnings" about the worker, and failed to respond. (See Pre-Crisis Warning — Chapter 3.)

Example 3: A "pawnshop" is sued. A Nevada pawnshop was sued because the seller of a handgun "should have known the gun was inappropriate for legitimate uses." The semiautomatic pistol was used in the killings of eight people in a San Francisco law firm. Camco Inc. operated Superpawn, a Las Vegas pawn-shop, where Gian Luigi Ferri bought one of the guns he used in the July 1993 killings.

Despite the fact that the sale was legal, Camco Inc. agreed to pay the victims' families $150,000. The settlement marks the "first time that a gun seller has paid damages to a victim for the sale of a particular kind of gun."

Example 4: An "automobile manufacturer" is sued. In 1994, a jury in Indiana ordered Chrysler to pay millions of dollars to the parents of a six-year-old boy who died of a fractured skull after being thrown from the family minivan in an accident because the rear latch was defective.

The jury said Chrysler was negligent in making the latch on the rear liftgate. The family's position was that "Chrysler knew about the defect and covered up the defect while at the same time advertising its minivans to Americans as safe."

Chrysler's position was that the van ran a red light, and the force of the collision threw the boy, who was not wearing a seat belt, out the side window, not through the liftgate opening.

But statistics worked against Chrysler. At least 37 passengers were killed in accidents in which they were ejected when the rear liftgates opened on Chrysler, Dodge, or Plymouth minivans sold from 1984 through 1995, according to NHTS records. The same statistics showed that at least 134 back-seat passengers have been ejected.

Example 5: A "health provider" is sued. The family of Ronald Henderson claimed that Kaiser's insurer's cost-cutting measures contributed to their father's fatal heart attack. Henderson's heart disease was allegedly left untreated due to the HMO's plan to cut hospital admissions in North Texas. Kaiser Permanente agreed to settle the wrongful death suit and pay $5.3 million.

The settlement came after it revealed that high-ranking Kaiser officials devised the 1995 cost-cutting plan during an alcohol-laced brainstorming session onboard a plane.

Richard Jewell, accused of being the bomber in the Centennial Park bombing:

- *Sued a television station.* In 1996, Richard Jewell sued NBC News because the network went too far in its characterization of him as a suspect in the Centennial Olympic Park bombing. NBC News agreed to pay ex-Olympic security guard Richard Jewell an unspecified amount in a settlement.
- *Sued a radio station.* In 1996, Richard Jewell sued his favorite rock 'n' roll station (WKLS) for plastering a "menacing" portrait of his face on about 100 billboards in Metro Atlanta. Radio station officials say the likeness is not menacing and that the billboards are coming down.
- *Sued a major newspaper.* Richard Jewell sued the *New York Post* newspaper, alleging libel. Jewell cited one story he said falsely portrayed him "as an individual with an aberrant and/or violent personality, and a bizarre employment history… who was guilty or likely guilty of criminal involvement" in the bombing. Jewell charged the *Post* libeled him in three articles, a column by longtime *Post* columnist Andrea Peyser.
- Former Olympic bombing suspect Richard Jewell has settled his lawsuit against his former employer, Piedmont College, for an undisclosed sum of money. Jewell had alleged that college officials slandered him in statements to the newspaper about his job performance as a security guard and his personality.

Legal Defense — "Legal Policies"

Sometimes the department's "Legal Policies" have taken the position that the organization is not at fault if just a few employees do something wrong. Unfortunately, according to the law, they are wrong. Federal appeals courts have repeatedly upheld prosecutors' rights to hold firms accountable for the actions of a few. A few examples include:

> *Example 1: Aydin Corp., 1994.* Aydin has agreed to plead guilty to charges of falsifying test data. The Horsham military contractor said it would take a $9 million charge against 1993 fourth-quarter earnings to settle the suit filed by the Justice Department and the Army.

> Two employees at Aydin's West Coast division pleaded guilty in March to the charges, which were filed in California.

> *Example 2: Arthur Andersen – Enron Crisis, 2002.* In an article in the *Wall Street Journal* on March 14, 2002, attorneys for Andersen said the government's case is fatally flawed because only a handful of employees were engaged in shredding documents related to Enron Corp.

Example 3: Boeing – Lockheed Martin, 2003. Lockheed Martin filed a lawsuit against Boeing alleging a conspiracy at the company to obtain and use its documents to win a 1998 competition to build the government's next-generation rocket.

In an article in the *Wall Street Journal* on December 12, 2003, top Boeing officials have long maintained the wrongdoing was limited to three rogue employees no longer with the company.

On occasion, the Legal department, or the organization's "Legal Policies," may be perceived as the cause of an organization's crisis.

In cases where the department, or its policies, may have caused the crisis, it may be better if the department representatives are not involved in managing the crisis because they can become too defensive. They should recuse themselves during this specific crisis.

Examples of a crisis in which the Legal department may be perceived as being the cause, or being too defensive, are:

Example 1: Southeast Pennsylvania Transportation Authority (SEPTA), Philadelphia, Pennsylvania. On November 27, 1996, Deneen Hall watched helplessly as her four-year-old son's foot was severely injured when an escalator at the Cecil B. Moore station of the Broad Street subway malfunctioned. Shareif's lawyer, Thomas Kline, said that on the day of the accident (11/27/1996), the escalator step dropped at the very top of the machine and Shareif's shoe went underneath. The escalator mangled Shareif's foot. It was amputated after the accident and he now walks with a prosthesis. The family of the four-year-old boy sued the SEPTA organization.

Prior to the trial, SEPTA turned over 44 pages of information about the accident to Shareif Hall's attorney. According to SEPTA's internal reports, it is unclear what caused the accident.

Following the trial, the verdict gave Shareif $50 million for the loss of his right foot. His mother was awarded $1 million, plus $65 for the sneakers he wore that day.

What makes the verdict so unusual is that Common Pleas Court Judge Frederica A. Massiah-Jackson on Monday allowed Kline to add a new civil rights claim to the original lawsuit that raised the amount of money the jury could award Shareif. The judge allowed the claim after SEPTA failed to turn over key documents that showed agency officials knew the escalator needed maintenance and could pose a hazard but did not carry out the repairs.

As mentioned above, SEPTA originally turned over just 44 pages of information about the accident to Shareif Hall's attorneys. Then on December 17, 1999, at the direction of Judge Frederica Massiah-Jackson, eight (8) SEPTA employees came to court carrying newly released documents in envelopes, file folders, large briefcases, and one brown Macy's store shopping bag.

The judge's response: "Oh, my gosh, a paper bag full of documents. I can't believe this." The judge later called the documents, in 18 files, which now cover a table in her courtroom, "just overwhelming. It's just incredible, the amount of documents here," Massiah-Jackson said.

SEPTA had a variety of excuses to explain why the documents were not provided:

> Some employees said they did not know the documents existed.
> Others have said they did not know they needed to be released.
> Several testified on Dec. 17th that finding the documents, when ordered by Massiah-Jackson, took only enough effort to call a co-worker or open a file drawer.

To make matters worse for SEPTA, Kline revealed that during the three years before the trial came to court, SEPTA filed a lawsuit against Deneen Hall (the mother), claiming she was the "sole, direct" cause of the accident. SEPTA blamed Hall because SEPTA said that the boy's shoelaces were untied. SEPTA's lawyer even produced as proof white shoelaces found after the accident.

Apparently this evidence was tampered with (by somebody), because it turns out that Shareif was wearing black shoelaces. *(From* "SEPTA's lame escalator defense; A moving violation," *Philadelphia Daily News,* December 14, 1999.)

Some observers of the case called into question SEPTA's legal strategy, wondering why it counter-sued the boy's family seeking financial redress. "That's why the jury turned so harshly," said Bruce Bodner, vice president of Transport Workers Union Local 234, which represents more than 5000 SEPTA workers. "I mean they sued the mother — who in SEPTA was responsible for that?" ("Septa Hit with $51 Million Verdict")

In a similar case, the Legal department may be perceived as being the cause is:

> *Example 2: Metropolitan Transportation Authority, Panorama City; Florida.* A Metropolitan Transportation Authority (MTA) bus struck a woman, her daughter and son as they were crossing a Panorama City, Florida, street. The woman's young daughter was killed and her son was seriously injured. The attorneys from the MTA's Legal department filed a lawsuit against Angelica Maravilla for allegedly letting her daughter run into the street. Mrs. Maravilla's attorney said, "I think the tragedy of the accident was compounded by the way the MTA treated her. Instead of coming to render aid, they came to start the process of spin control. The approach of considering the victim an enemy is not consistent with the public trust MTA has to treat accident victims with compassion."
>
> The MTA's attorney's response was: "I think it would be a mistake to perceive a thorough defense as an attack on Mrs. Maravilla," said Phil Miller, principal counsel representing the MTA. "At no point did the MTA intend to attack Mrs. Maravilla, but it at all times intended to vigorously defend itself where a defense was appropriate."
>
> (*Author Note:* Sounds like the attorneys from the Legal departments of SEPTA and the MTA went to the same school.)
>
> In 1998, the MTA's Board of Directors finally agreed to pay Angelica Maravilla $7 million to settle the lawsuit.

In a third example, the Legal department may be perceived as being the cause:

> *Example 3: Food Lion sued ABC television in 1997.* An ABC television report given on "PrimeTime Live" — narrated by Diane Sawyer — accused Food Lion of selling rat-gnawed cheese, expired meat, and old ham and fish washed in bleach to kill the smell. ABC sent two (2) reporters into Food Lion undercover as Food Lion employees for an expose on the supermarket chain. The two ABC reporters obtained jobs as food handlers and worked with tiny cameras hidden in their wigs and microphones inside their clothes. Small video decks were strapped to their bodies and activated by a switch in their

pockets. The hidden-camera report showed alleged unsanitary conditions at Food Lion supermarkets, including rat-gnawed cheese and spoiled chicken washed in bleach.

Food Lion denied the allegations of unsanitary practices. They also filed a lawsuit — not for libel, but for fraud and trespassing, alleging the reporters lied to get their jobs and spent company time snooping instead of performing the Food Lion duties for which they were being paid.

A jury found that ABC had committed fraud through the actions of attorney Jonathan Barzilay. It was Barzilay who gave the "PrimeTime Live" reporting team the legal advice to go ahead with the undercover operations. The jury ordered ABC to pay Food Lion more than $5.5 million for sending reporters undercover. Food Lion had asked for $52.5 million to $1.9 billion in punitive damages.

ABC challenged the jury's $5.5 million punitive damage award for the 1992 "Prime Time Live" expose that accused the supermarket chain of selling rat-gnawed cheese and rotten meat. The position of the Legal department's attorneys was "Making false representations in order to get into a position to see, report or photograph what has been concealed has been an integral part of investigative journalism for centuries," according to Nat Lewin, ABC attorney.

(*Author Note:* Apparently the Legal department believes that "the end justifies the means.")

Appendix 6F

INSURANCE DEPARTMENT: SLA ELEMENTS

Upon notification that a disaster has struck a building housing business units of your organization, the Insurance department representative, or representatives, will report to the Crisis Management Team Command Center (CMTCC). (See Chapter 9.)

As a member of the Crisis Management Team (CMT), the Insurance department representatives' role will be to use their expertise to manage the insurance issues caused by the disaster. The representative(s) will act as the coordination point for all insurance matters pertaining to the organization's recovery from the disaster.

After the members of the Crisis Management Team (CMT) have reported to the CMT Command Center and obtained all known pertinent information regarding the disaster, the Insurance representative(s) will:

1. Notify the insurance carriers.
2. Provide guidance on what action may be taken to salvage items without affecting insurance coverage.
3. Obtain any additional or special insurance coverages needed temporarily.
4. On occasion, the Insurance department, or the organization's "Insurance Policies," may be perceived as the cause of an organization's crisis. In those cases, it may be better if department representatives are not involved in managing the crisis because they become too defensive.

Scenario: Disaster

When a disaster has damaged one of the buildings housing one or more of your organization's business units, the Insurance department will obtain information pertinent to the building damage and needed repairs.

Examples of information pertinent to the Insurance department include:

- Using a "fire" as the type of disaster:
    - Were any employees injured by the fire?
        - Safety
        - Injuries
        - Insurance claims
    - How many floors did the fire affect?
    - Were any floors affected by water damage? Smoke damage? Hazmat problems?
    - Which business units were located on the damaged floors?
    - Will employees be moved to other locations?
    - Was the equipment damaged? Destroyed?
    - Were the records damaged? Destroyed?
    - Will business units be moved to other locations?
    - Will equipment be moved to other locations?
- Using a "storm" as the type of disaster (e.g., a rainstorm, snowstorm, tornado, hurricane, etc.):
    - Were any employees injured by the storm?
        - Safety
        - Injuries
    - What type of damage was sustained?
    - Was the damage to the roof, walls, windows, etc.?
    - How many floors were affected by the storm?
    - Which business units were located on the damaged floors?
    - Was the equipment damaged? Destroyed?
    - Were the records damaged? Destroyed?
    - Will business units be moved to other locations?
    - Will equipment be moved to other locations?
- Using a "product problem" as the type of crisis:
    - Were any employees injured by the product problem?
    - Will any employee lawsuits be filed as a result of this crisis?
        - Safety
        - Injuries
    - Were any customers injured by the product problem?
        - Safety
        - Injuries
    - Will any customer lawsuits be filed as a result of this crisis?

1. Notify the insurance carriers.

Following a disaster, the Insurance department representative will have the responsibility to notify the appropriate insurance carriers.

Where is the insurance vendor/policy information located?

- List of carriers
- Agent
- Phone number
- Policy specifics
- Limits

The list of carriers could include carriers offering All Risk Property coverage, Business Interruption coverage, Extra Expense coverage, etc.

In addition, specific industries have special insurance coverages, such as the banking industry. Banks usually buy Bankers Blanket Bond coverage and Legal Liability & Loss of Customers Property coverage.

Location of the insurance policies.

The actual insurance policies are usually stored in the organization's locations, with a copy stored by the insurance vendor.

What does the policy cover?

It is usually a good idea to review the contents of the policies annually. This will ensure that the organization has the proper coverage when a claim must be made.

As part of the policy review, the Insurance/Risk Management Business Resumption Plan documentation should be reviewed. In the Insurance BRP, each policy should be summarized and should be documented for use if the Risk Management/Insurance department is damaged by the same disaster.

This documentation would provide a summary of the location and limits coverage, the agreement synopsis, spells out what is covered, exclusions (what is not covered), how payment will be made for claims, the date the policy expires, the organization's responsibilities in the event of a claim, the alerts the Insurance representative is responsible for, and the salvage procedure to follow.

The insurance claims process must work in tandem with Accounting/Finance. When an incident occurs, the Treasury/Finance department representative should establish a special general ledger account number to use whenever any recovery expenses occur. Expenses could include materials, loss of rent, overtime, travel, and mileage, and emergency services. (Appendix 6G contains a list of items that are frequently covered by Extra Expense coverage.)

The Insurance representative will be able to use the expenses that have been captured and establish with the insurance company's adjuster whether or not they are coverable. Interfacing with the insurance company's adjuster is a major Crisis Management Team responsibility.

If more than one facility is damaged by the disaster, expenses for each facility affected must be tracked separately for insurance claims purposes.

Insurance carrier support in handling claims.

Following a major regional disaster, insurance carriers are usually proactive. Just as in the Northridge Earthquake in 1994, where many of the insurance carriers flew in claims adjusters immediately, they have responded the same in all the recent regional, or wide-area disasters.

In some cases, the insurance carriers fly in structural engineers to assess the damage and begin the claims process. To further assist policyholders, widespread television advertising can be used to notify the public of emergency phone numbers.

2. **Provide guidance on what action may be taken to salvage items without affecting insurance coverage.**

   ■ Are there are restrictions placed on your organization by the insurance carrier as it relates to the protection of contents of the building after a disaster strikes?
   ■ What should you do with non-damaged contents?
     ■ Can you move the non-damaged contents into a protected area?
     ■ Or, must you wait until an adjuster arrives to view the damage before you will be allowed to move the contents?
   ■ What should you do with damaged, but salvageable contents?
     ■ Can you move the damaged, but salvageable contents into a protected area?
     ■ Or, must you wait until an adjuster arrives to view the damage before you will be allowed to move the contents?
   ■ What should you do with non-salvageable contents?
     ■ Can you move the non-salvageable contents out of the damaged facility?
     ■ Or, must you wait until an adjuster arrives to view the damage before you will be allowed to move the contents?

Business Interruption Coverage

Many organizations buy business interruption coverage. It can significantly reduce an organization's losses following a disaster. For example:

- *Arco, Houston, 990.* The company's year-end results included $120 million received from business interruption insurance as a result of the explosion.
- *West Pharmaceutical Services, Kinston, North Carolina, 2003.* West Pharmaceutical Services Inc., of Lionville, Pennsylvania, said that the deadly explosion and fire at its Kinston, North Carolina, manufacturing plant on January 29, 2003, would have "financial implications" for the first half of this year. It was "confident" that most "property and business-interruption losses are fully insured."

On the other hand, the coverage may not be included:

Chicago River Flood, 1992. The University of Illinois estimated that $500 million in lost services was incurred by businesses in the affected 18-block area. Many companies discovered their insurance policies did not cover flood damages or power outages. Uninsured losses could go as high as $1 billion and will have to be absorbed directly by the companies affected.On a number of occasions, we read that employees want to re-enter the building quickly after a disaster because they want to retrieve personal items.

Employees' personal items.

Are there any company policies regarding the organization's liability for employees personal items that are destroyed by a disaster?

- In general, most organizations that I have consulted with have informed me that there is no insurance coverage for employees' personal items located in work locations.
- These same organizations made it perfectly clear to me that the employees have been informed of this policy. The placing of personal items inside the building is at the employee's risk.

3. Obtain any additional or special insurance coverage's needed temporarily.

If there are any special coverages or riders that will be needed following the disaster, who in your organization will be responsible to notify the insurance company?

- For temporary operating location or storage location:
    - Notify the insurance company if operations that have been moved to a different location.

- For equipment in transit:
  - Notify the insurance company if operations that have been moved to a different location.
- For temporary use of personal automobiles:
  - Notify the insurance company if employees are using their personnel cars for company business.
- Prepare insurance riders as dictated by the situation; that is:
  - Valuable papers and magnetic media (when being shipped from the normal site to various recovery sites).
  - Equipment shipment insurance coverage (when transportation company's insurance base are rated on pounds rather than value of item, e.g., mainframe computer).
  - Employee travel insurance (employees traveling for the organization to assist during the recovery operation may require additional coverage).
  - New and or temporary facilities coverage.

4. On occasion, the Insurance department, or the organization's "Insurance Policies," may be perceived as the cause of an organization's crisis.

In cases where the department, or its policies, may have caused the crisis, it may be better if the department representatives are not involved in managing the crisis because they can become too defensive. They should recuse themselves during this specific crisis.

Examples of crises in which the Insurance department may be perceived as being the cause, or being too defensive, include those where an insurance company's policy and practices create a company image crisis.

- Refusal to pay claim submitted:
  - *New York City, 2001*. Two European insurance companies, Allianz, of Germany, and AXA, of France, have not paid the insurance money covered by their policy to Deutsche Bank after its New York office tower was badly damaged following the terrorist attack on 9-11. The insurance companies argued that the 41-story building was not so badly damaged in the attack that it could not be repaired. The 29-year-old building at 130 Liberty St. suffered a 15-story gash in its facade when the twin towers collapsed barely 150 feet away. The bank building, exposed to the elements, became infected with mold. Deutsche Bank was forced to file a lawsuit in June 2003 to try to get the insurance companies to pay for the demolition of its badly damaged office tower near ground zero, calling it an "unfortunate remnant of a national tragedy."

The bank said in its lawsuit (filed in state Supreme Court in Manhattan) that tornado-force winds from the fallen 110-story towers distributed asbestos and other contaminants throughout the building, making it impossible to repair safely.

- *Hawthorne, California, 1991.* After a fire burned down a concrete cutting equipment manufacturing business in Hawthorne, California, in 1991, the Maryland Casualty Co. refused to pay owner's insurance claim, saying information provided to the agent was untrue. The owner took Maryland Casualty to court. After three days of deliberations in 1994, jurors awarded the owner $3 million for the loss of his business, and another $58 million in punitive damages after finding that the insurance company "acted in bad faith" by refusing to pay his claim.

- *Riverside, California, 1993.* A Riverside, California, jury ruled back in 1993 that Health Net, California's second-largest health maintenance organization, must pay $89.1 million to the family of cancer patient Nelene Fox, who died after being refused an experimental bone marrow transplant. Fox underwent the transplant after neighbors in Temecula raised more than $200,000. She died four months later. The jury awarded $12.1 million in compensatory damages, and $77 million in punitive damages, for a total of $89.1 million.

- Slow payment of claims:
  - *Arkadelphia, Arkansas, 1997.* The university town of Arkadelphia, Arkansas, experienced a terrible tornado outbreak in 1997. In this town of little more than 10,000 people, a 40-block area was devastated. The storm resulted in five deaths and dozens of injuries. It was reported in *USA Today* (on March 12, 1997) that some people in the Arkadelphia area were having trouble collecting from insurance companies.

Appendix 6G

EXTRA EXPENSE ESTIMATE WORKSHEET

Computer Backup Site Usage Fee

_____

_____

Cold Site/Warm Site Usage Fee

_____

_____

Travel Expenses for personnel

_____

_____

Living Expenses for personnel at backup site (lodging, meals, and transportation)

_____

_____

Transportation expenses for materials moving between the recovery center and the temporary offices

_____

_____

Overtime pay for personnel

_____

_____

Equipment rental costs (equipment for the cold/warm site)

_____

_____

Communication line costs for data transmission

_____

_____

Temporary office expense — facility

_____

_____

Temporary office expense — furnishings and equipment

_____

_____

Appendix 6H

TREASURY/FINANCE: SLA ELEMENTS

Upon notification that a disaster has struck a building housing business units of your organization, the Treasury/Finance department representative, or representatives, will report to the Crisis Management Team Command Center (CMTCC). (See Chapter 9.)

As a member of the Crisis Management Team (CMT), the Treasury/Finance department representative's role will be to use his or her expertise to limit the financial damage caused by the disaster. The representative, or representatives, will act as the coordination point for all financial matters pertaining to the organization's recovery from the disaster.

After the members of the CMT have reported to the CMT Command Center and obtained all known pertinent information regarding the disaster, the Treasury/Finance representative(s) will:

1. Provide recovery team personnel with travel/expense money, if needed.
2. Identify negotiable instruments that may be missing.
3. Implement alternate policies for the business resumption operations.
4. On occasion, the Treasury/Finance department, or the organization's "Treasury/Finance Policies," may be perceived as the cause of an organization's crisis. In those cases, it may be better if the department representative is not involved in managing the crisis because he or she can become too defensive.

Scenario: Disaster

When a disaster has damaged one of the buildings housing one or more of your organization's business units, the Treasury/Finance department will obtain information pertinent to the Finance department.

Examples of information pertinent to the Treasury/Finance department include:

- Using a "fire" as the type of disaster:
  - Were all negotiable instruments accounted for during the damage assessment efforts?
    - If not, what negotiable instruments were unaccounted for?
    - Can we put a stop payment on these instruments?
  - Are there any regulatory or legal issues that will result from the interruption of business operations as a result of the fire?
- Using a "storm" as the type of disaster (e.g., a rainstorm, snowstorm, tornado, hurricane, etc.):
  - Were all negotiable instruments accounted for during the damage assessment efforts?
    - If not, what negotiable instruments were unaccounted for?
    - Can we put a stop payment on these instruments?
  - Are there any regulatory or legal issues that will result from the interruption of business operations as a result of the storm?
- Using a "product problem" as the type of crisis:
  - Was this product expected to produce a significant amount of sales for the year?
  - Will the product problem result in a recall?
  - Will the recall be temporary, or permanent?

1. Provide the recovery team personnel with travel/expense money, if needed.

Following a disaster that affects an organization's business units, organizations often move personnel from one area to another. The organization needs to pre-plan for the expenses involved in moving the personnel.

Is it the employee's responsibility to have the cash available, or credit available on their credit cards, to pay for temporary expenses during the first days of an organization's business resumption operations.

Business Continuity Planning (BCP) professionals have learned over the years that many employees do not carry cash in the amounts needed to travel from one area to another on short-term notice. BCP professionals have also learned that employee's credit cards may not have enough available credit to pay for the temporary expenses incurred during the first couple days of a business resumption operation. For this reason, the organizations need to provide this resource.

Most organizations today have arranged for their offices located near the "alternate operating location" to provide for travel/expense money for employees sent to the alternate site. In cases where an organization does not have offices located near the alternate operating location, organizations have arranged a line of credit with a bank located near the site. As you can see, there are many options to choose from when deciding how to fund the employees who are required to travel during the business resumption operation.

> *City of Hartford, 1992.* During a presentation made by the BCP professional at the City of Hartford, he made an interesting point about the need to provide travel/expense money for the IT people who will be sent to a computer backup site. In 1992, a pipe that supplies water for the computer's chillers ruptured. The water spread throughout the hallway outside the computer room. The Fire Department shut off electric. Then the IT department shut down computers. They activated their Disaster Recovery Plan and they notified their computer hotsite that they would be coming.

> At 9:45 p.m., five cars began traveling to the computer backup site in Philadelphia. As they approached the tolls, one car pulled over to the side of the road. The other four followed the first car. When the Computer Backup Site Team Manager asked what the problem was, the driver said that none of the five people in the car had any money to pay the tolls.

> The lesson learned here was — don't assume. They had assumed that someone would have enough money to pay the tolls through Connecticut, New Jersey, and the bridge between New Jersey and Pennsylvania.

2. Identify negotiable instruments that may be missing.

There have been a number of cases where negotiable instruments (cash, etc.) are unaccounted for following a disaster. This was especially true following the collapse of the World Trade Center buildings in 2001.

At any rate, when an organization is unable to account for negotiable instruments, the Treasury/Finance department representative should be responsible for developing a system that will address this problem. Some of the negotiables may have been destroyed. Some of the negotiables may have been salvaged by the wrong people.

Make arrangements to notify financial institutions and regulatory authorities of the disaster situation. If possible, issue stop payment notices for missing negotiables.

These negotiables may be retrieved a day or two later, or in the case of the World Trade Center collapse, they may be found in a couple months.

> *Bank of America, New York City, September 11, 2001.* Following the collapse of the World Trade Center, the bank was concerned about the U.S. and foreign currency that was stored under the building.

> Then on February 12, 2002, the *Wall Street Journal* reported that a grappler that was being used to excavate compacted material six stories underground at the site came across the money. Police and excavation workers filled about 60 garbage bags with the currency, which they turned over to the city's Processing Clerk Division for handling. This was believed to be part of the U.S. and foreign currency reported missing by Bank of America Corporation.

Another example of a retrieval operation for $10 million in negotiable instruments is:

> *Meridian Bank, 1991.* In an article entitled "Trial by Fire" published in the *Recovery Magazine* (Winter-1992), a Meridian Bank spokesperson shared a story of the retrieval of a sizable amount of negotiable instruments. The spokesperson pointed out that after the fire was contained, they were worried about the vault in the basement of the building.

> Although the vault was airtight, they could not be sure it was watertight. Another concern was the possibility that the entire building, or parts of it, might collapse on top of the vault.

> They needed to get into the vault and retrieve the negotiable instruments. The Meridian Disaster Recovery Director contacted the Mayor of Philadelphia and asked for his assistance in allowing Meridian personnel to get back in the building to remove the securities as quickly as they could. Phone calls were made to the department of licenses and inspections, to the fire commissioner's office, and to the police commissioner's office to coordinate the recovery effort.

"On Monday morning at about 11 a.m., three of our security people went back into that building under the watchful eye of the police department, as well as the fire commissioner's office. They were successful in getting that vault door open, and they were delighted with what they found. There was only about half an inch or so of water on the floor of that vault.

"The question now was, 'How are we going to go back in and remove all those documents?' So they closed up the vault door, came back to the command center, and strategized. The team decided it would go back into the vault that evening at 6:30 p.m. City officials agreed to let them back in to remove the securities, but warned that they would yank them out of there at the first sign of a building collapse, no matter what losses might result.

"The plan was to get the negotiables first, then worry about the non-negotiables. They went in with a handful of workers, and took all the negotiables off the shelves and put them into garbage cans-on-wheels and rolled them out the basement of the building along the concourse underground over to a nearby building (Five Penn Center). There they went up the elevator to the loading dock with eight garbage cans filled with millions of dollars worth of negotiable securities and loaded them into the back of a pickup truck.

"Three corporate security officers sat in the back of that truck with their hands over the lids of the garbage cans so the securities wouldn't bounce out and blow away. The Philadelphia Stakeout Team was on the roofs of buildings all around us, in patrol cars, in vans with semi-automatic weapons strapped to their sides, providing a watchful eye as the Meridian retrieval team moved from that site to another Philadelphia facility, where Meridian had a vault. After they put all of those securities into that backup facility, they went back in and took out all of the non-negotiable securities. They were in the basement until about 2:00 a.m. loading up a tractor-trailer truck with non-negotiables. Then they moved that to the other location and began the process of getting all the non-negotiables out of the tractor-trailer. They finished up around 7:00 a.m."

A different twist to critical documents, not necessarily negotiable instruments, occurred in Ft. Worth following the tornado in 2000.

Ft. Worth, Texas, 2000. In this case, the FBI's Fort Worth office was located in the Cash America International building. "This building was heavily damaged, with computers, documents and glass strewn all around the structure and on the streets below," said Lori Bailey, a spokeswoman for the FBI's Dallas office. At least 20 FBI agents donned jackets and disposable gloves to scour the area surrounding the building, checking if any confidential documents, or sensitive files, might have been blown out of the office.

In an international incident, considerable negotiable instruments had to be secured following a bombing that knocked out windows throughout the building.

City of London, 1993. Following the bombing, there were considerable amounts of money, blank traveler's checks, and other negotiables in the building, and their secure removal was difficult and time-consuming, and interrupted access to the building by all other parties.

3. Implement alternate policies for the business resumption operations.

If there is a need to modify computer applications, approve any modifications to financial controls requested to facilitate backup site processing.

- One of the main concerns is the status of Treasury/Finance applications. How many were completed before the disaster struck?
- When the applications are restored on the computer, or backup computer, how many applications will need data reconstruction?
- Is the data that has been retrieved adequate to reconstruct the Treasury/Finance applications?
- Is the backup data synchronized?
- Verify the status of accounting applications that have been reconstructed during the recovery operation.
- Coordinate the investigation and resolution of any out-of-balance conditions with accounting applications.
- Make arrangements to notify financial institutions and regulatory authorities of the disaster situation. (Regulatory Requirement)
- If your company will be unable to meet the regularly scheduled tax payment schedules, notify the appropriate tax levying agencies.
- Finance/Accounting's role: If the building has been seriously damaged, and needs to be shored up before employees can enter

it to assess damage or make repairs, the organization's Treasury/ Finance department may have to make arrangements to pay the contractors in cash. Many contractors know that there is an insurance claim involved in this work. The insurance carrier may not pay the claim quickly. Contractors will not want to wait for insurance claims to be paid before they are paid for their work Large organizations can make arrangements to obtain the cash needed to pay these contractors (smaller organizations may need to arrange for an extension of their line-of-credit to pay contractors in cash immediately).

4. On occasion, the Treasury/Finance department, or the organization's "Treasury/Finance Policies," may be perceived as the cause of an organization's crisis.

In cases where the department, or its policies, may have caused the crisis, it may be better if the department representatives are not involved in managing the crisis because they can become too defensive. They should recuse themselves during this specific crisis.

In addition to the Enron and WorldCom debacles, some examples in which the Treasury/Finance department may be perceived as being the cause of a financial crisis include:

> *Adelphia Communications, Coudersport, Pennsylvania, 2002.* Adelphia disclosed in 2002 that over the past few years, it funneled millions — often without the board's knowledge — to private businesses controlled by founder John Rigas and his family.

> *America Tissue Co., 2003.* Federal prosecutors announced charges in 2003 against four former top executives of American Tissue Co., accusing them of manipulating financial statements and defrauding banks and investors of $300 million. The charges grew out of an 18-month investigation into American Tissue, which filed for bankruptcy protection from its creditors on September 10, 2001. American Tissue's top executives in July 1999 secured $145 million from a bank by recording $25 million worth of nonexistent sales, according to the indictment. The former CFO (Edward Stein) pleaded guilty to fraud charges, and the former vice president of finance, (John Lorenz) pleaded guilty to a conspiracy charge.

> *Aurora Foods Inc., St. Louis, Missouri, 2001.* In 2001, two former executives of Aurora Foods Inc. of St. Louis, Missouri, pleaded guilty to securities-fraud and related charges. The

former chairman and CEO and the former CFO joined Aurora's former EVP, and a former VP of Finance, who pleaded guilty earlier to related criminal charges and are awaiting sentencing.

Charter Communications, St. Louis, Missouri, 2003. In 2003, the Justice Department charged four former top executives at Charter Communications of St. Louis, Missouri, with inflating revenue and subscriber figures. The effort was allegedly designed to keep investors from realizing how much business the No. 3 cable operator was losing to satellite rivals. The former Chief Operating Officer and the former CFO were charged with 14 counts of mail fraud, wire fraud, and conspiracy to commit wire fraud.

Interspeed Corp., 2003. In 2003, two former executives of defunct Internet equipment maker Interspeed Corp. were charged Thursday with falsely inflating sales figures. The former chief financial officer agreed to plead guilty to falsifying books, records, and accounts at the company, which folded in 2001.

Safety-Kleen Corp., Columbia, South Carolina, 2000. In 2000, the CEO, the COO and the CFO of Safety-Kleen Corp. of Columbia, South Carolina, announced their resignations following an internal investigation into alleged accounting irregularities.

Sunbeam Corp., 2001. In 2001, the SEC filed a civil lawsuit against five former Sunbeam Corp. executives and the Arthur Andersen partner in charge of the company's audit, accusing them of engaging in a massive financial fraud. The SEC said Mr. Albert Dunlap and his executive team concocted a rosy portrait of earnings growth through an assortment of illegal accounting maneuvers. Other defendants named are former CFO, the former controller, and two former VPs.

Royal Ahold NV, 2003. In 2003, Dutch supermarket retailer Royal Ahold NV reported that the chief financial officer and general counsel at its U.S. foodservice unit, which overstated its profits, have resigned. Ahold said last week that an investigation had found that incorrect accounting of vendor rebates at the unit resulted in the overstatement of earnings by $880 million over the last three years.

(**Author Note**: There have been so many examples of "fuzzy accounting" that I did not have room to include all of them in this appendix. I just picked a few to demonstrate the point.)

According to an article published in *USA Today* on June 22, 2001, entitled "Fuzzy Accounting Raises Flags":

"There have been 464 cases of financial statements being restated during the past 3 years, says Financial Executives International (FEI), which studies accounting issues. That's more than all restatements during the previous 7 years. Last year, 53% of all securities lawsuits filed against companies contained some sort of accounting allegations, PricewaterhouseCoopers says. That's up from 45% in 1996. These aren't all frivolous lawsuits: Nearly half of companies sued on allegations of faulty accounting eventually restate their earnings, PricewaterhouseCoopers found. Nearly 40% of earnings restatements from 1995 to 1999 had to do with revenue recognition, says Zoe-Vonna Palmrose, professor of auditing at the University of Southern California. And in half the cases, revenue was completely fabricated, she says."

Chapter 7

THE CRISIS COMMUNICATIONS TEAM

7.1 INTRODUCTION

This chapter discusses the major elements of the Crisis Communications Plan. While other chapters in this book discuss the best methods of managing a crisis, this chapter deals with protecting the reputation of the organization when the crisis has moved into the acute stage.

What is meant by "reputation?" Your reputation is what other people think of you. It is an asset, although it is intangible. There is a value to your organization's reputation (e.g., Johnson & Johnson, Procter & Gamble, etc.). If your organization's reputation is besmirched, (i.e., accused of putting a spin on a situation), it will have a tough time getting anyone to believe what it says.

> *American Red Cross.* A good example of an organization whose "reputation" was in trouble was the American Red Cross. The Red Cross has always had a great reputation. But it only took one incident to threaten that organization's reputation. Remember when the American Red Cross acknowledged that some of the $550 million in donations to the Liberty Fund (special fund established for the victims of the 9-11 terrorist attacks) was going to be used for other Red Cross needs instead? As a result of the brouhaha that plan created, the CEO resigned, and the Interim chief executive officer, Harold Decker, apologized for what he called "a failure in communications between the American Red Cross and the American public." The Red Cross's concern was that people who were future donors might no longer donate to ARC because they could not believe them any longer. Decker righted this perceived wrong when he reversed the original

plan and announced that the Red Cross would use all the money donated for the people affected by the 9-11 attacks.

Once an organization's reputation suffers, bad things happen; that is, in addition to the business suffering, the regulators will begin to investigate the organization, the news media will investigate deeper into the organization's past to see if there were any other negative incidents (and go way back), and its recruitment of employees will be negatively affected. This chapter:

- Identifies the purpose of the Crisis Communications Plan (CCP)
- Identifies the spokesperson and members of the Crisis Communications Team (CCT)
- Provides suggestions on how the spokesperson should work with the news media
- Provides information that will help the team members understand the role and objectives of the news media

When a pre-crisis situation moves into the Acute-Crisis stage (see Chapter 4) and the news media become aware of the crisis, an organization must be in a position to reassure the public that its executives are in control of the situation and that the crisis is being handled properly. At this point in time, the Crisis Management Team (CMT) will activate the Crisis Communications Plan (CCP).

The goal of the CCP is to reassure the public that company representatives are in control of the situation and the crisis will be handled in an organized and timely manner.

It is worrisome to think about how many organizations are still unprepared to respond to a crisis when it occurs. If executives do not recognize the threat to their organization, it is up to the Business Continuity Planning (BCP) professionals to convince their executives that they need to document and implement a viable CCP. To accomplish this, the BCP professional should keep the executives aware of the crises their competitors have experienced. In addition, they should also make executives aware of the crises any organization from another industry has experienced, if that same type of crisis might also strike your organization.

Keep in mind the explanation of why executives may not be prepared:

"Most executives, preoccupied with market pressures of the present quarter, are not inclined to pay much attention to planning for future crises."

—Norman Augustine
Managing the Crisis You Tried to Prevent

When a crisis moves into the acute stage, the executives and the spokesperson for the organization will be expected to answer the following "media-type" questions:

- What happened?
- When did it happen?
- Where did it happen?
- Who was involved?

Based on your existing CCP, how will your organization be perceived during the first hours after the crisis occurs?

- Does your organization have a "viable" Crisis Communications Plan in place to manage the negative effects on the organization's reputation caused by the crisis?
- Can this plan be used to manage those negative effects if the crisis was caused by a disaster (physical damage), by a product problem (failure or tampering), or by an incident that has threatened your organization's reputation?
- Does the plan identify who in your organization will have the responsibility of being the spokesperson during all press conferences?
- Do you have a trained alternate for the spokesperson if the primary is unavailable?
- Have employees been told *not to give statements* to the news media?

7.2   WHAT IS THE CRISIS COMMUNICATIONS PLAN?

The Crisis Communications Plan (CCP) is one of the key elements of the Crisis Management Plan (see Figure 7.1). The main goal of the CCP is to "gather the facts" and "tell your story."

To be effective, a crisis communications plan should:

- Identify strategies to be used in responding to the acute crisis when it occurs (see Section 7.6.1).
- Allow your organization to reach key audiences with your message:

"As the arena of public opinion grows tougher, it's necessary for management to meet the public — the media, employees and their families, customers, vendors, shareholders, the community, activists, and government regulators — head-on, and to be prepared to react effectively to the many possible crises that may occur."

—Bill Patterson, President
Reputation Management Associates
Columbus, Ohio

■ Provide crisis communications spokesperson(s) with the authority to *initiate your crisis communications* strategies as soon as possible when the crisis first moves to the Acute-Crisis stage.

Unfortunately, according to Agnes Huff, Ph.D., President and CEO of Agnes Huff Communications Group LLC (Los Angeles, California), "business continuity planners may find themselves in a headlock when it comes to communicating with the media if they have to wait for upper-level management approval." Organizations need to implement a crisis communications plan "that permits the crisis communications spokesperson to instantly initiate public information and media relations campaigns during an acute-crisis. There's a very narrow window of opportunity to speak out with the facts, and when that passes, there will still be room for eyewitness accounts and activists," Huff explains.

To accomplish this, an organization must first develop a plan that will enable members of the Crisis Communications Team (CCT) to gather the facts and then put forth a spokesperson who will best present the organization's position. The CCP should decide on the "policies" to be followed and decide on the "strategies" that will be used during the acute crisis.

The responsibility for developing, exercising, and maintaining the plan is the CCT.

7.3 WHY DOES AN ORGANIZATION NEED A CRISIS COMMUNICATIONS PLAN?

Executives whose goal for their organization is to grow the image and good reputation of the organization will recognize the necessity of having a state-of-the-art plan — a plan that is ready to respond immediately to protect this image and reputation.

Too often, however, according to Dr. Francis J. Marra, Associate Professor at U.A.E.-based Zayed University, executives and upper management focus only on the technical aspects of crisis management — continuity of operations, personnel and facility safety, data protection, and minimizing legal liability. "It's easy to give communication a low priority during a crisis," says Marra. "Doing so increases the chances a crisis will be managed poorly. Excellent communication can protect and enhance corporate reputation; the absence of communication during a crisis can severely damage the reputation of an organization."

When you have a CCP in place before the crisis strikes — a plan that has been developed, tested, and exercised to prove its "viability" — the plan will help the organization combat rumors and manage the perception of the organization.

On the other hand, to put a plan together on-the-fly after the news of the acute crisis breaks is dangerous. Organizations need to have a CCP in place *before* a crisis becomes acute because the media will want to know the answers to key questions *almost immediately* after the news about the crisis breaks. And if your organization is slow to respond to those questions, the result will likely be that media sources will report stories that are inaccurate. These inaccurate stories — and in some cases rumors — could result in damage to your organization's reputation.

7.3.1   Objective: To Manage the Perception

Everyone has heard the expression "perception is truth." If this is true, executives need to keep in mind that, during a crisis, "the news media will create the perception."

The news media have the resources to report on a crisis rapidly. Your handling of the crisis must be just as rapid. Your window of opportunity is very small.

> As John Paluszak of Ketchum Public Affairs said during the Exxon oil spill crisis, "There is a very narrow window of opportunity for action in a crisis because within several hours public opinion will already have begun to crystallize."
>
> Paluszak also said, "When a company is in trouble, the manner in which its executives manage the release of information, as well as the way they handle themselves in dealing with the media, can be as important as their business decisions."

In addition, the news media also have the resources to continue to report on the crisis throughout the post-crisis stage. The last thing you need is to have your crisis continue to generate stories well after it has been resolved.

Remember that you want to establish a plan that will help you work with the media. The media can and will get your story — with or without your help. By working with the media, you have a much better chance of influencing the perception of your organization.

Keep in mind these words of wisdom:

> "Protect your credibility. With it, you can recover; without it, you are in for lasting damage."

—Gerry Meyers
"When it Hits the Fan"

7.3.2 Objective: To Combat Rumors

During the initial stages of a crisis, rumors often spread about the organization and its crisis. The Crisis Communications Team must combat these rumors, and also stop the further spread of rumors.

Let us look at some instances where rumors were threatening to damage, or did damage to, some organizations.

- AirTran Airlines, 1998:

  According to a story published in the *Plain Dealer of Cleveland* newspaper on January 12, 1998, the FAA has found serious safety-related violations at AirTran. Violations included falsified documents and faulty repairs. The documents, based on a three-week inspection that ended November 7, show the airline had more serious violations than the 1996 report that recommended that ValuJet be grounded. (The airline changed its name from ValuJet after one of its planes plunged into the Everglades in May 1996, killing all 110 people aboard.)

  AirTran officials responded by saying they "understand that the outcome of the probe was excellent."

  Fact: According to a story on January 14, 1998, *USA Today* reported that federal aviation officials say a special inspection found no systemic safety problems at AirTran despite a published report indicating widespread trouble at the discount airline. FAA managers said action already would have been taken against the airline if serious problems had been found.

  Impact: Passengers reading the *Plain Dealer of Cleveland* story could have chosen to fly competitive airlines.

- Kentucky Fried Chicken, 2000:

  In January 2000, a rampant e-mail, supposedly based on a study by the University of New Hampshire that was never actually conducted, claimed that Kentucky Fried Chicken had to change its name to KFC because it was using laboratory-grown "genetically manipulated organisms" instead of real chicken meat. Due to absurd claims of rooms full of tube-fed chicken bodies lacking feathers, feet, or beaks, the phone lines at KFC and the University of New Hampshire became overwhelmed. The public demanded reassurances that KFC was indeed using real chicken in its restaurants.

  Fact: KFC had changed its name almost ten years earlier to emphasize product variety. It continued to use the word "chicken" in its advertising.

  Impact: Despite the fact that KFC's business practices had not precipitated this rumor, the KFC executives still were expected to prove that KFC had done nothing wrong.

"The menacing stuff of rumor and gossip, no matter how unfounded, is damaging enough to corporations, but when your business suffers actual interruptions — a product recall, facility damage, data loss, an employee strike, or a lawsuit — one of your greatest corporate assets, your reputation, hangs in the balance." (From "Keeping Your Name Safe — Effective Corporate Reputation Management," *Contingency Planning & Management*, Sept./Oct. 2001.)

7.4 ESTABLISH A CLEARLY DEFINED CRISIS COMMUNICATIONS POLICY

The executives of an organization must establish the crisis communications policy. The dictionary defines "policy" as a definite course of action selected from among alternatives to guide and determine present and future decisions. The definition used in this chapter is "a policy is a definite course of action the members of the crisis communications team should follow when interfacing with the news media during a crisis."

The overall media policy consists of issues the organization must react to quickly once the news media become aware of the crisis. Some of the issues the executives should consider when developing the crisis communications policy include:

- Who is authorized to speak with the news media?
- When the news media calls the switchboard, how should switchboards handle the incoming phone calls?
- When the news media come to the building, how should the receptionists, or security guards, handle the media representatives?
- When the news media are outside the building, asking questions directly to the employees, how should the employees handle the media representatives?
- Should the organization have only one spokesperson, along with a trained alternate; or should the organization provide multiple spokespersons?
- Who will be the designated spokesperson, or spokespersons?

7.4.1 Only the Spokesperson Speaks to News Media Representatives

Ensure everyone in the organization is aware that all inquiries from the media should be directed to the Crisis Communication Team spokesperson.

Whenever a crisis moves into the acute stage, all employees should be reminded again of the crisis communications policy against speaking directly to members of the news media. They should be told that only the crisis communications spokesperson, or alternate, is authorized to speak with the news media.

- If the news media attempts to phone the organization, switchboard operators should be instructed to refer all incoming phone calls related to the crisis to the crisis communications spokesperson. If they are unavailable, they should put them through to the alternate.
- When a reporter from the news media comes to the building, the security personnel or receptionist should be instructed to escort all reporters to the crisis communications spokesperson's office.
- When the news media are outside the building, asking questions directly to the employees, the employees should have been reminded that all requests for information from the media should be directed to the spokesperson.

7.4.2 Should You Use a Single Spokesperson or Multiple Spokespersons?

Organizations must make a policy decision on whether they want only one person to be their spokesperson or they want multiple people to speak for the organization. The ultimate goal of the Crisis Communications Team is to provide information to the media quickly and accurately. At the same time, the information must be consistent and not vary from interview to interview.

7.4.2.1 Consider a Single Spokesperson

Some crisis management experts suggest that the organization should identify only one spokesperson to represent the organization throughout the crisis. This suggestion is based on the philosophy that the organization must speak with one voice, which is another way of saying one story.

These experts are concerned about the news media obtaining two different stories from two different executives of the organization. When this happens, the credibility of not only both spokespersons, but also the organization is questioned.

An example of a crisis in which multiple spokespeople damaged the image of the organization was the Exxon Valdez oil spill in 1989. Initially, Exxon received good marks in its "crisis communications" for its initial handling of the incident, from Harry W. Clark, managing partner of Clark, Dwight & Associates of Old Greenwick, Connecticut, a crisis management consulting firm. "They have shown an exceptional willingness to accept and disperse the facts rather than try to minimize them."

Exxon selected Dave Parish (one person) to be the official spokesperson. In the first news media briefing, the organization (Exxon) took financial responsibility for the oil spill and told reporters that an uncertified officer piloted the tanker. In that one act, Exxon met the three basic rules of "crisis communication" for handling a disaster that plays out before a global audience. "They moved quickly to gather the facts and were successful at accurately stating what happened so that no other sources contradicted them or blindsided them."

Within a few days, the "crisis communications" strategy began to deteriorate. Why? Many executives were speaking to media representatives, and they were saying the wrong things.

In an article in *Newsweek* magazine, it was alleged that:

- One Exxon executive told consumers that they (the consumers) would pay for the cost of the cleanup with higher gas prices.
- Another Exxon executive reportedly said that as long as people in California continued to drive their Mercedes, they would have to put up with Alaska shipments.
- A third Exxon executive blamed cleanup delays on the Coast Guard and Alaska state officials.

Their comments reversed the entire positive "crisis communications" image that began shortly after the incident took place. Apparently not all of the executives were aware that only the spokesperson assigned by the executives to manage crisis communications was to make statements for the organization regarding the oil spill.

7.4.2.2 Consider Multiple Spokespersons

The other school of thought is that the company should select more than one spokesperson. Some crisis management consultants suggest that the organization select and train a number of key executives to act as a spokesperson during a crisis. Their theory is:

- Depending on the type of crisis, and the expertise needed for meetings with the news media, more than one spokesperson will be needed during the acute-crisis and post-crisis stages.
- They also have clients who have had a need to have a spokesperson located in different places at the same time. A spokesperson might be needed in the Command Center, and also hundreds of miles away at the site of the crisis (or disaster).

These consultants feel that with the right training and good internal communications during the crisis, the organization can use multiple spokespersons and still speak with one voice. A few examples follow where multiple spokespersons were used with excellent results.

British Petroleum (BP) oil spill near Long Beach, California, in 1990. The British Petroleum's oil tanker, American Trader, spilled nearly 400,000 gallons of oil near Long Beach, California, after its hull ruptured. Within hours of the disaster, BP implemented its crisis management and crisis communications plan for dealing with the media.

BP Crisis Communications officials, carrying hand-held cellular telephones, were dispatched to points along the coast wherever reporters were congregating. In addition, BP hired public relations specialists from San Francisco on the night of the disaster to be on hand wherever reporters were located. When a television station wanted underwater footage of the hull of the ship, the BP crisis manager (Chuck Webster) was ready to provide it. When a producer for NBC's *Today Show* corralled a pair of BP executives in Coast Guard headquarters in Long Beach, they agreed to go live on a national television interview being broadcast within the hour. The public affairs command center was located right next to the cleanup command center in BP's Long Beach office. The company's aggressive effort to quickly clean up the mess has won accolades from both oil analysts and the public relations industry.

PepsiCo "Needle in the Can" crisis of 1993. Incident: When PepsiCo was faced with the "needle in the can" crisis in June of 1993, Pepsi's high command mobilized the crisis management team. What had started out as a local incident was threatening to turn into a multi-million-dollar disaster for Pepsi Cola. The team considered a voluntary recall, but the FDA said there was no health threat. Pepsi knew all along that it was not a manufacturing issue. Canning lines are high-speed production lines in which cans are inverted upside down, shot with a blast of air or water, and then turned right side up and filled. The cans are open for 0.9 seconds when being filled. It would be highly unlikely for a needle to find its way into a can during this process. And it would be astronomically improbable to have numerous needles in different cans in different states, produced months apart, and then have them show up in a 48-hour period.

7.4.3 Spokespersons Role — Point Person

Craig Weatherup, PepsiCo's President & CEO, decided he would be the spokesperson for the company. He appeared in person on a dozen network TV news shows. He showed a videotape of the bottling process created by the Crisis Management Team to show, rather than explain, how safe Pepsi's canning process was. He concluded each interview with a statement, "A can is the most tamper-proof packaging in the food supply. We are 99.99 percent certain that this didn't happen in Pepsi's plants."

7.4.3.1 Additional Spokespersons: Telling the Same Story

An open-door crisis communications policy was operative from day one. From Thursday June 10th, when the first syringe complaint was reported, until Monday June 21st, Pepsi spokespersons had conducted more than 2000 interviews with newspaper, magazine, TV and radio reporters. "We had a unique opportunity to talk to our consumers — through the media," said Mr. Weatherup. "We believe, that when presented with the facts, the American public would recognize the truth and their trust in our products would be restored."

Pepsi's strategy was to communicate fast and communicate often. They worked with the media using the tools and time-tables that work best for them. "The hoax story was so visual, videotape news releases distributed by satellite were the key to getting our message out," said crisis communications coordinator Rebecca Madeira.

The policy, "speak with one voice" was followed. But it was pointed out that Pepsi received input on crisis strategies from many camps ... each with valid — but often conflicting agendas. Ultimately, consensus was the key. A divided camp erodes confidence, disrupts the process and breeds skepticism. (This story was excerpted from a brochure produced by Pepsi entitled, "What Pepsi Did Right.")

The key to success of this approach, multiple spokespersons, is that the spokespersons understand that they are responsible for keeping each other up-to-date of any conversations with reporters, focuses of the interviews, and impressions of how they went.

7.5 WHO ARE THE MEMBERS OF THE CRISIS COMMUNICATIONS TEAM?

The Crisis Communications Team (CCT) consists of the spokesperson selected by executives and a support team.

The *spokesperson's role* is to demonstrate that the organization is a responsible organization that deserves the public's trust and support. The spokesperson must be capable of explaining the position of the organization in an effort to safeguard its reputation. The executives must allow the spokesperson to select a group of people who will support them, people who will provide administrative support (i.e., the CCT). In addition, depending on the type of crisis, the spokesperson may need support from technical people who can provide facts regarding the crisis.

The CCT consists of employees who have experience dealing with the news media. They play a vital role in supporting the spokesperson during the crisis by:

- Gathering information about the crisis
- Contacting the media
- Setting up media briefings or conferences
- Providing media kits and press releases

Before a crisis strikes, the CCT should:

- Prepare a media kit for the organization with background on that organization.

7.5.1 Who Should the Spokesperson Be?

The executives of the organization should select a person who will best present, explain, and defend the organization's position. Some attributes executives should seek in selecting the spokesperson include a person who:

- Is articulate
- Will not "freeze up" when talking to the press, or answering questions from the press
- Will remain as calm as possible when talking to the press

The goal of the spokesperson is to provide accurate information on a timely basis. In fact, in most situations today, the spokesperson(s) must be ready to provide the media with information almost immediately. Remember that the media are now 24/7/365. They are ready to report. If the organization is not ready to provide information, the media will get it from someone else — perhaps a competitor.

7.5.2 Role in the Crisis Communications Plan

A key goal of the spokesperson and the CCT is to maintain a good working relationship with the local news media. The spokespersons should know the people behind the pens, note pads, cameras, and microphones. If they do not know the key local reporters, they should find out who they are and get to know them. During a crisis situation, it is much more comfortable to deal with someone you know, and someone who knows you.

During a crisis situation, it is much more comfortable to deal with someone you know, and someone who knows you. Elizabeth Dole pointed this out when she was the president of the American Red Cross, an organization whose very purpose is to deal with crises. According to Norm Augustine, Dole said, "The midst of a disaster is the poorest possible time to establish new relationships and to introduce ourselves to new organizations. ... When you have taken the time to build rapport, then you can make a call at 2 a.m. when the river's rising and expect to launch a well-planned, smoothly conducted response." (Excerpt from "Managing the Crisis You Tried to Prevent," by Norman R. Augustine; in *Crisis Management Magazine.*)

If the spokesperson does not know who the local news media personnel are, have an open house with the reporters:

- Notify the media who the best source of information is for your organization.
- Ask how you can help them to cover any news stories or events concerning your organization.
- Ask them whom your organization should contact in order to provide information.
- Ask them how they can be notified in a crisis. (your organization's crisis, not theirs):
    - Obtain their names and telephone numbers.
- After obtaining this information, develop and document *a News Media Contact Checklist* for your CCP.
- This checklist should contain the names and phone numbers for all the local media, (i.e., newspaper, radio, and television reporters).
- The Crisis Communications Team must maintain and update this News Media Contact Checklist as frequently as needed.

To maintain a relationship with the news media personnel, keep supplying them with news releases.

A crisis was previously defined as a "time of both danger and opportunity." To make it an opportunity, the crisis communications team must maintain good relations with the news media, with the hope that your organization will be treated fairly during a crisis, and you may even receive a favorable story for your organization.

(*Author Note:* In today's environment, receiving a favorable story is more difficult because so many organizations have not communicated honestly in recent times. The reporters, and the people who read the story, have become cynical when it comes to believing the spokespersons experiencing a crisis recently. So they are hesitant to present favorable stories until they know for sure that your organization has been truthful.

In fact, a June 2001 Gallup poll on the American public's confidence in institutions reported that a mere 28 percent of those surveyed had confidence in big business, as opposed to a 66-percent confidence level in the military and a 44-percent confidence level in financial institutions. Only organized labor, Congress, and HMOs ranked lower than big business.)

From now on, organizations need to present themselves to the media, and the public, in a fashion that is credible and believable.

7.5.3   Role of the Crisis Communications Support Team

The Crisis Communications Team should assign a member to document all actions during the Acute-Crisis stage.

■ They should write down your reasons for making decisions. Ask other people to do the same.

Your organization should consider having a photographer or videocamera operator on hand at all times. If you take the time to duly record appropriate comments and events during a crisis, when you respond to the question "why did you do that?" people will give your response more credence.

The use of a camera for Crisis Management Team meeting was effectively shown by the PNC Bank in Philadelphia after the 1989 fire in the Penn Mutual Insurance building. The executives who comprised the Crisis Management Team gathered in the banks CMP command center daily and the meeting was taped by a video camera crew. This allowed them the opportunity to remember the "whats," "whys," and "hows" of their business resumption efforts after the fire. They made a very effective presentation at hot-site company's users meeting in 1990.

7.5.4   Use of an Outside Consultant on the Crisis Communications Team

The decision of whether to hire a consultant to support the Crisis Communications spokesperson depends on internal capabilities and how important the CCP is to your organization. (***Author Note:*** In reviewing information on the many crises that have struck organizations recently, I often read that they have used an outside crisis communications consulting organization or expert.)

7.5.4.1 Why Would a Large Organization with Its Own Internal Staff Use an Outside Consulting Firm?

Large organizations with a large public relations staffs sometimes choose to bring in a Crisis Communications specialist because they want the objectivity of the specialist to reinforce the decisions that are being made by the in-house staff.

> "Often even major corporations with large public relations staffs find they want the objectivity and the expertise they can get from experienced crisis communications consultants. Experience is by far the best teacher in dealing with crises, and gaining that experience on the job can be a costly adventure. Sometimes it just makes sense to go to people who have already gained the experience."

> **—Steven Wilson, President**
> *Wilson Group Communications, Inc.*
> *Columbus, Ohio*

Others have indicated that they have brought in a specialist due to the "type of crisis." They feel that the specialist has the necessary expertise in this type of crisis, which the organization needs at that time.

Some organizations have used Crisis Communications specialists because such specialists are less frightened of upsetting the sensibilities of the senior executives. They will give you an objective opinion and have a willingness to express it. If they are good at what they do, your senior executives will not intimidate them.

The best choice is one who, although he or she is unconnected to your organization, is familiar with your industry — and has faced similar problems with another client.

> More than 60 firms nationwide now counsel corporations involved in product recalls, labor disputes, and environmental disasters, among other issues. In 1999, public-relations revenue grew about 30 percent from the prior year to nearly $3 billion, according to the Council of Public Relations Firms, a trade group. Crisis management accounted for slightly less than 4 percent of the total, or roughly $100 million.

In the past five years, the biggest advertising and marketing corporations, including Omnicom and Interpublic, have bought leading public-relations agencies that boast crisis management units. Omnicom bought Fleishman-Hillard, now the largest public-relations firm in the United States, in 1997. And a year later, Interpublic acquired Shandwick International, which owns the crisis firm Rowan & Blewitt.

7.6 PREPARING THE SPOKESPERSON TO WORK WITH THE NEWS MEDIA?

The spokesperson must be prepared to meet the media. Remember that editors and reporters are accustomed to crises. They report on several every day. They know what they want and how to get it. Your spokesperson, on the other hand, is often unprepared. Before the next crisis strikes your organization, the spokesperson should work with the other members of the Crisis Communications Team to prepare the Crisis Communications Plan.

> (*Author Suggestion:* If your organization already has one, it would be a good idea to read this section, and compare it to your existing preparations to determine if it needs to be enhanced.)

7.6.1 Strategies

There are a number of strategies the spokesperson should consider during the crisis:

- *Use the crisis communications plan.* When a crisis moves to the acute stage, the spokesperson should use the Crisis Communications Plan to work with the news media. Remember that when the Crisis Communications Plan was developed, it was a time when there was minimal, if any, stress. The people involved in the planning tried to think through the appropriate actions that would fit the various crises they thought the organization would face. The probability is that those actions will best serve the crisis communications efforts during the immediate crisis.

  Stay flexible. Also, stay flexible so you can adjust to changing events. When the Crisis Communications Plan identifies actions to be taken in a situation, and the spokesperson recognizes that they are not appropriate, they should adjust. Oftentimes, as evaluations are made throughout the crisis, the story that was given earlier needs adjusting. This can be accomplished during one of the daily news media briefings.

Example — USS Cole. The Navy revised its account of the terrorist attack on the Cole the following week. Initially, the Navy statement said the destroyer had tied up at a fuel station in the port of Aden nearly two hours before the bombing. An Admiral (Vern Clark, Chief of Naval Operations) told reporters that the Cole crew's "ability to deal with this kind of attack" had been "limited" by the mooring operation that was under way. This account had been based on unconfirmed reports from the stricken ship. A week later, the Navy said it now had obtained additional information from the Cole's records that changed at least three points of fact in the official timeline:

1. The explosion occurred at 11:18 a.m. local time, or about an hour earlier than originally reported;
2. Refueling began at 10:30 a.m. and was going on at the time of the attack. Before, the Navy said refueling had not yet begun; and
3. The Cole was completely tied up at the fueling dock in Aden harbor at 9:30 a.m., nearly two hours before the attack. The Navy had said the mooring operation was completed just minutes before.

As the Navy explained, "As is often the case, these initial relayed reports contained some errors and in some cases were misunderstood." ("Questions are raised on Cole's security," *Philadelphia Inquirer,* October 21, 2000.)

When a crisis moves to the acute stage, the spokesperson(s) should be prepared to:

- *Get and give facts as early as possible.* When your organization is the victim of a disaster, or of an acute crisis, your organization is in the spotlight. When the news media start reporting on the crisis, everyone will be looking at your organization and, in turn, your executives.
  - *Get the facts.* Obviously, the spokesperson cannot be out gathering facts and also be responding to all media calls at the same time. The Crisis Communications Team needs to assign people to go to specific areas that are being affected by the crisis. When they get to the assigned areas, they should report back to the Crisis Communications Team. This will provide up-to-date information.
  - *Give the facts.* The organization must give facts as early as possible, and it needs to continue to give facts as changes occur.

■ *Deal only with verified information; avoid engaging in conjecture.* The spokesperson(s) must verify the information before actually giving it to executives or media. Because the crisis manager for the specific crisis your organization is dealing with will be the Crisis Management Team member with the most expertise in the situation (see Chapter 6), everything should be verified for accuracy through that person.

They should release only the confirmed facts. (There will be time enough to add to the facts as they become apparent.) Every speculation, accurate or not, will be reported by the media. If you do not want to see it in print, or broadcast on radio or TV, do not say it.

■ *Recognize times when emotions are high and cold facts are inappropriate.* It is important to project a sensitive and humane concern. In many instances there have been injuries to employees, and even fatalities. This situation requires the spokesperson(s) to cushion the message with the appropriate amount of compassion.

Example — World Trade Center Terrorist Attacks on 9-11. As the smoke cleared from the remains of the World Trade Center, the tragedy for many companies became clearer. Organizations such as Keefe Bruyette & Woods, Fred Alger Management, Morgan Stanley, Marsh & McLennan, Aon, and Cantor Fitzgerald were responding to media requests on the injuries and loss of life. The organizations mentioned above all handled this situation with a high regard for presenting information in an appropriate manner.

■ *Issue positive steps.* Issue a statement on any positive steps the organization plans to take to lessen the effects of the crisis.
■ *Accept responsibility.* As mentioned elsewhere in this book, when PECO suffered an explosion that killed two people and injured a third person back in 1995, PECO shouldered the blame. "PECO Energy takes full responsibility" for failing to respond to reports of a leak in time to avert the tragedy, CEO Corbin McNeill said in a prepared statement. He called PECO's delay in dispatching a technician "unacceptable and regrettable."
■ *Do not blame others.* In firing public salvos at each other, Ford and Firestone turned their damage control efforts into a mudslinging feud. It is difficult to say which company, if any, came out on top; both suffered in 2001.

Example — Central Sprinkler (March 27, 1998). Santa Clara County filed a lawsuit alleging that one of the nation's leading manufacturers of automatic fire sprinklers is putting out a defective product. Santa Clara County's suit, filed on behalf of any public agency in the nation that may have faulty Central sprinklers, is believed to be the first case brought by the public sector, Acting County Counsel Ann Ravel said. According to the lawsuit, the allegations against Central focus on the company's line of Omega sprinklers made before June 1996. The lawsuit maintains that the sprinklers have failed in at least six instances across the country in the last two years. This includes one fire at a Florida marina that enveloped 150 boats, and another, at a Marriott Hotel in Michigan that prompted the chain to replace 200,000 Omega sprinklers in 220 hotels. It also alleges that Central has known of the faulty systems since early 1995, but failed to notify customers. The lawsuit attempts to force Central to replace the sprinklers and pay installation costs. Court papers show that Underwriters Laboratories Inc., a product safety group, found the Omega sprinklers to be defective. The Fairfax, Virginia, Fire Department reached a similar conclusion in its own tests.

Central Sprinkler's CEO George G. Meyer blamed others, not the sprinkler design or manufacture. He tried to blame (1) sloppy work by installers; and (2) the use of illegal leak-stopping products by maintenance workers not employed by his company. The result of this problem — the company was sold to Tyco International in 1999.

When a crisis moves to the "post-crisis" stage, the spokesperson(s) should be prepared to:

- *Keep up communications even after the crisis subsides.* The initial press briefing does not end an organization's communication requirements. It is just the beginning, and you should be prepared to give the facts even after the crisis is under control. To reestablish the good will the organization had developed with the local community and with the customers before the crisis occurred, it would be a good public relations practice to continue communications even after the crisis subsides.
- *Express appreciation to appropriate parties* who assisted the organization during the crisis — for example, fire and police departments, emergency crews, community leaders — and do not forget to also include the employees.

  How many times have you noticed an advertisement placed in the local newspaper thanking the police, firefighters, emergency response crews, and community leaders for their assistance during the crisis, or disaster? Some bigger companies can afford to place these advertisements in papers throughout the country. This strategy provides the organization with an opportunity to thank the people who served the organization during its crisis, and allows the organization to continue positive communications after the crisis is over.

(*Author Note:* I have purchased papers in which there were full-page ads thanking everyone who helped during a crisis; for example the Olin Company after its fire in the 1970s, the Norwest Bank after its fire in 1982, the First Interstate Bank after its fire in 1988 [to the city of Los Angeles and the civil service personnel].

■ *Reestablish credibility.* One of the goals during the Post-Crisis stage is to reestablish the credibility and reputation of the organization. Some examples of organizations that changed their operations to correct the problems that led to the crisis include:

■ *Argenbright Security, 2001.* Under fire from the government, the nation's largest airport security company announced a management shake-up and policies to improve security. Argenbright, which screened passengers on two of the flights that were hijacked on Sept. 11, named David Beaton, a former lieutenant colonel in the British Army, its chief executive officer. The company also announced that its founder, Frank Argenbright Jr., will retire from its board of directors. Argenbright has boosted the wages of most employees in an attempt to reduce the turnover rate, which has been at least 100 percent annually. The company also says it will upgrade its training program, fingerprint new employees, and fire any employee who doesn't follow procedures or FAA regulations. (From *USA Today*, November 19, 2001.)

■ *ConAgra, 2001.* ConAgra said that it would restate three years of financial results. The problems occurred within one of ConAgra's subsidiaries, United Agri Products Cos., which sells seed, fertilizer and chemicals to farmers. The unit accounts for about 9 percent of the company's operating profit. ConAgra said revisions would reduce pretax earnings for fiscal 1998, 1999 and 2000 by a total of about $123 million. ConAgra, maker of Butterball turkeys, Hunt's ketchup and Wesson oil, said it began investigating its subsidiary last year, and the SEC subsequently launched an informal inquiry of its own. The Greeley, CO. subsidiary recorded fictitious sales and improperly recorded revenue on deferred sales. The company had been recording revenue at the time of the sale rather than at the time of the delivery. But some farmers never took delivery and never paid. The subsidiary also recognized rebate payments as income in the fiscal year they were received rather than in the year in which they were earned. In addition, United Agri Products accrued insufficient bad-debt reserves and increased write-offs in 2001 that should have been taken in previous years. Bruce Rohde, ConAgra's chairman and CEO, said that accounting controls would be strengthened; that personnel at the subsidiary would be changed; and that the major financial problems at the subsidiary already had been identified and addressed. Mr. Rohde said the irregularities "circumvented generally accepted accounting practices and violated ConAgra Foods' corporate policy." He added, "Those actions will not be tolerated." (From *Wall Street Journal,* May 29, 2001.)

■ *Ford Motor Company, 2001.* Ford defended its Explorer model and blamed the tires. The recall cost Ford about $500 million in the third quarter. Ford says it will offer tire pressure monitors and other safety improvements on all its Ford-branded SUVs by 2005. The changes come as the company is dealing with the aftermath of defective Firestone tires on Ford trucks that have been linked to about 140 deaths. (From *USA Today,* January 9, 2001.)

■ *Coca-Cola, 2004.* On April 11, Gen. Counsel Deval Patrick resigned, the eighth top executive to leave during the tenure of Chief Executive Douglas Daft. Patrick had been feeling the heat or his handling of a whistleblower lawsuit that led to government probes of the company's accounting. More departures are likely as Coke's board moves to bring in a successor to Daft, who plans to retire by year-end after five years at the helm. (From *Business Week,* April 26, 2004).

7.6.2 Importance of Training the Spokesperson

The role of the spokesperson is critical to the perception of how your organization is managing the crisis. In fact, their actions reflect on the organization's perception as a whole. Therefore, the executives of an organization should approve of the budget and resources needed to properly prepare and train the spokesperson or spokespersons.

The most common mistake organizations have made is to not have a trained person prepared to act as the spokesperson when a crisis strikes. They assume that the head of the Public Relations department or the Chief Executive Officer will be the spokesperson and therefore have not trained a person to act as the spokesperson when a crisis strikes.

"Many people think they do their best work in the midst of a crisis or controversy, when the adrenaline is flowing and we make vital decisions in a split second. But when the wrong decision can cost a company millions in negative publicity, not being prepared isn't worth the risk."

Steven Wilson, President
Wilson Group Communications, Inc.
Columbus, Ohio

Some of the type issues on which they will be trained are to:

- *Be prepared.* Spokespersons should know the facts. They should not overreact or exaggerate.
- *Be candid.* Spokespersons should tell the news media what they know, as of the time of the news briefing. The reporters should be assured that the spokesperson will continue to inform them of the facts, as more of them become known.
- *Respond to every media question.* Spokespersons should attempt to answer all questions. If they do not know the answer, they should not answer with "no comment." They should tell the reporters that they will find out the answer, and then notify the reporter. They should return every call from a reporter within a reasonable period of time.
- *Do not begin talking before beginning to think.*
- *Do not continue talking after the question has been answered.*
- *Never lie* — not even one "little white lie." Once you lie to one reporter, you have destroyed your reputation with all of them.
- *Never go off the record.* If you do not want to see it in print, or broadcast on radio or television, do not say it.
- *Do not use business jargon.* Do not use inside business acronyms. Keep your words basic. While it is tempting with all those reporters hanging on your every word, do not try to intellectualize. Remember that it is the general public you want to impress, not peers or college professors. (See Appendix 7A: Iron Mountain, New Jersey.)
- *Remain as calm as possible when talking to the press.* Do not *debate the subject* with reporters. Try to answer the reporter's questions calmly, authoritatively. Do not argue with a reporter, even when provoked. You will inevitably end up making yourself look bad in print. On the other hand, *do not let a reporter state an inaccuracy without correcting it*, but be sure to correct it by stating the accurate information, in a positive manner — and do not repeat back to the reporter the incorrect statement.

- *Be positive.* Do not discuss negatives.
  - *Not repeat negative questions or inflammatory words used by a reporter.* If you repeat them in your response, they may end up as part of your quote.
  - *Do not try to blame another organization for the incident.* The press may jump on this as an example of "big business" attempting to shift the blame elsewhere. Instead, focus on providing positive, thoughtful responses explaining how you are moving ahead and correcting any problem raised.
  - *Never volunteer negative information.* The news reports will be negative enough. Look for opportunities to say something positive about the situation.
- In the event of injuries:
  - Direct company's attention toward injured people, employees (or contractors), or customers.
  - Do not release specific personal information about employees. Respect their right to privacy.
- Not look for sympathy:
  - Do not talk to the news media about how much this is costing your organization. Nobody cares.

Do not talk to the news media about all the problems this is causing your executives. (Ken Lay's wife's sad story.) Nobody cares.

7.6.2.1 Special Training for Television Interviews

The spokesperson should be trained also for television interviews. Some of the issues about being on television will deal with "eye movement." Too much eye movement indicates that the spokesperson is uncomfortable with the questions. Other suggestions include:

- Do not look too stern.
- Do not be too quick to defend your organization.
- Do not show anger.

7.6.3 Initial News Media Briefings

After a crisis has struck the organization, and after the Crisis Communication Team has gathered the preliminary facts that are known up to that time, the spokesperson should schedule the initial news briefing. The spokesperson should determine the best location for the briefing (e.g., the headquarters building or the site of the crisis).

In preparation for the briefing, the spokesperson should prepare the statement that will be given during the briefing. This statement should be general but have enough information to satisfy the media initially. It should also be technically correct.

7.6.3.1 Scheduling the Initial News Briefing

1. *Set up a media briefing area* at, or near, the Crisis Communications Command Center, for example.
2. *Establish security procedures to be used in the briefing area.* Reporters should sign in. The Crisis Communications Team should provide a sign-in sheet that all reporters should complete when attending a briefing. (The minimum information required would be the Attendee's Name, the Organization's Name, and the telephone number.)
3. *Provide news media personnel with information on the background of your organization.*
4. *During the briefing, attempt to simplify technical information.* Do not use inside business acronyms. Keep your words basic. Remember that it is the general public you want to impress, not the news media reporters.
5. *Give all media equal access to information.*
6. *Provide press releases.*
7. *Keep a record of officially released media information.* Make a note of the reporter's name and the name of the media when the caller first offers identification. This serves two purposes: you have an accurate record so you can follow up to see how the story appears, and you can use the reporter's name during the interview, to help you build rapport with the reporter.
8. *Monitor the news coverage of the event and make an effort to bring inaccuracies to the media's attention.* This is a good reason for keeping a TV, VCR, and radio in the command center.

7.6.3.2 Need to Be Technically Correct

The Crisis Communications spokesperson should answer the questions asked by the media, but should not over-commit. The spokesperson needs to be technically correct. For example, if a disaster has struck the organization and a building is damaged, or employees have been injured, the response to questions could be:

■ When asked a question about the cause of the disaster or crisis, one option would be to say that "The cause is under investigation."

- When asked a question about the financial losses caused by the disaster or crisis, one option would be to say that "The financial impact is being determined."
- When asked a question about a possible safety problem, one option would be to say that "The company strictly adheres to all safety regulations."
- When asked a question about injuries to personnel, one option would be to say that "Injuries are being determined. This information will be released after notification to the next of kin."
- When asked a question about viewing the site under question, one option would be to say that "For safety reasons, we prefer that you stay clear of the affected areas."

7.6.3.3   Follow-Up News Media Briefings

For future briefings with the news media, the spokesperson should be prepared to answer the following questions with updated information on the following questions:

- What happened?
- When did it happen?
- Where did it happen?
- Who was involved?
- Why or how did it happen?

The spokesperson should have been trained on how to answer tough questions and how to maintain control of a possible hostile interview. The spokesperson can expect that during the follow-up briefings, the investigative journalists will be asking the tough questions.

> (*Author Note:* Do not hold a meeting if there is nothing new to report. The media will feel that you are wasting their time.)

7.6.4   Suggestion: Use a Tape Recorder

I suggest that the Crisis Communications Team support the spokesperson by tape-recording all news media briefings with the news media. Try to get the reporters to identify themselves and their organization when they ask the question because this gives you the opportunity to check their stories and make sure they quoted the spokesperson accurately.

Another value to the tape recordings during the crisis, when you respond to the question "why," people will give your response more credence because you have taped sessions and can add this information to your written information to better answer upcoming questions.

(*Author Note:* Back in the early 1980s, the Director of Public Relations for a telephone company with headquarters in Georgia indicated that she wanted to ensure that she would have a tape recorder available when she provided a news media briefing. When I asked her what she would use the tape recorder for, she explained that this was a resource she used to help control the media. When she had been a reporter earlier in her career, she used a tape recorder when interviewing people. She explained that this was her way of ensuring that quotes she attributed to the person were accurate; and that if there was any repercussions or denials, she had the tape as proof. She went on to explain that she incorporated the same process now that she was the one being interviewed. She found that many reporters tried to report the story from written notes. As she said, the notes were often faulty. These incorrect notes, if not corrected, would present the story inaccurately.

From that point on, my consulting firm, Devlin Associates Inc., always recommended that a tape recorder and tapes be included as one of the items needed by the Public Relations department during news media briefings.)

7.6.4.1 Meeting with News Media One-on-One

When meeting with the news media, even if it is only one representative, tape-record the meeting. This will come in handy when there is a discrepancy between a story reported by the media person and your recollection of the meeting or interview.

Remember that reporters are not always accurate. If they have reported inaccurately, and it produces a negative impact on your organization, you will be able to ask for a retraction. If the story makes it look as though your spokesperson does not even understand your organization's business (or service), and you want a retraction, you may want to ask for a retraction.

Your only option is to have a recording of the interview to set the facts straight.

When a reporter does make an error, the news media will usually file a correction. Unfortunately, misstatements or misinterpretations that are part of a front-page story do not usually get corrected on the front page (they are often buried deep in the next issue of the newspaper or magazine).

7.6.4.2 All Crisis Management Sessions

The tape recorder should be used to tape-record all planning sessions, all crisis management team meetings, all fact-gathering meetings, etc. Because you may be asked time and again to recount your actions and decisions, you will be able to call on more than your memory to respond. Ergo, the tape-recorded or video-recorded tapes will provide an accurate account of what went on — particularly if you are being asked a year later.

When you are in the Post-Crisis stage and you are performing the post mortem, the tape-recorded sessions will make it easier to recall the situations you faced during the Acute-Crisis stage.

Now, let's move on to Chapter 8, "Developing the Crisis Management Plan." This chapter will discuss a methodology for developing and documenting the Crisis Management Plan.

Appendix 7A

IRON MOUNTAIN, NEW JERSEY

A suspicious fire destroyed a warehouse full of corporate documents on March 10, 1997. The fire, which began just before 10:30 a.m., just off the New Jersey Turnpike at Exit 8, came two days after a smaller blaze damaged another warehouse several hundred feet away (March 8, 1997). That same building had also been the scene of a fire on March 7. Firefighters were still battling the second blaze in the smaller building, on Wednesday morning, when the third fire broke out down the street.

Both buildings are owned by Iron Mountain Inc., a company that stores government and corporate records at 117 sites around the country. The two warehouses contain nearly 1.25 million cartons of records belonging to 200 companies.

Ms. Judith Brackley, a spokeswoman for Iron Mountain, supposedly said the following, which was reported by *The New York Times*:

> Roughly 250,000 cardboard cartons full of records were stored in the warehouse where the first two fires broke out. Most of those boxes were retrieved from the fire, and Iron Mountain will try to salvage them. But the most recent fire gutted a much larger warehouse, where 850,000 cartons full of records were stored. Those records, which belonged to more than 100 customers, were probably all incinerated.

> ***Typically, the records stored at Iron Mountain warehouses are old administrative records that companies do not need to keep close at hand. Since they are legally required to keep administrative records for up to seven years, many rent space in warehouses. The records stored in the two fire-damaged warehouses are mundane.***

They might include accounts payable files or bank statements. Vital records, which were much more important, are usually stored in underground storage facilities that are more secure and more expensive. Such records might include secret formulas, patents or master recordings.

I spoke with Ms. Brackley after reading *The New York Times* article to find out if she was quoted directly. I explained that I was writing an article for the *Disaster Recovery Journal,* and wanted to discuss the fire in the Iron Mountain facility. When I asked if the quotes in the *Times* article were accurate, she explained she was misquoted. I asked her to explain what she told the reporter so that I could put it in my article. She told me what she said. I understood what she meant by the interview material. We both came to the conclusion that *The New York Times* reporter didn't take very accurate notes, and somehow jumbled them up into a "story." Needless to say, Ms. Brackley was happy that someone who understood our business jargon was going to set the story straight.

Chapter 8

DEVELOPING THE CRISIS MANAGEMENT PLAN

8.1 INTRODUCTION

This chapter addresses developing and documenting the Crisis Management Plan (CMP). As seen earlier in the book, the CMP consists of two groups of executives: (1) the Executive Management Team (see Chapter 5) and (2) the Crisis Management Team (see Chapter 6).

The Crisis Management Team (CMT) comprises executives with the specific expertise needed to support business units and executive management during a crisis. The members of the CMT would include the heads of, or designated representatives of, the following departments:

- Public Relations
- Human Resources
- Facilities
- Security
- Treasury, Finance
- Insurance
- Procurement, Purchasing
- Transportation

The Public Relations team will have developed the Crisis Communications Plan (CCP). The CCP, which is a key element of the CMT, is a little more complex than the other members of the CMT and has therefore been given its own chapter in this book. (For more information on the CCP, see Chapter 7.)

As discussed in Chapter 5, when the crisis moves to the acute stage (i.e., it is being reported by the news media, customers, or vendors), the

Executive Management Team (EMT) needs to activate the Crisis Management Plan (CMP). Once the CMT is activated, the members will assemble at the CMT Command Center (see Chapter 9). Once assembled, their goals will be to:

1. Take charge quickly.
2. Establish the facts.
3. Tell your story.
4. Fix the problem.

For more details on the steps in managing a crisis, see Chapter 4.

8.2 ROLE OF THE BUSINESS CONTINUITY PROFESSIONAL

After CMT members have "taken charge quickly" and "gathered the facts," they will meet with the members of the Executive Management Team (EMT), who will have a number of questions to ask about the status of the crisis/disaster (EMT Agenda). As discussed in Chapter 5, questions have been documented for a disaster (or a crisis) and can be found in the EMT agenda. Members of the CMT will be expected to have the answers.

8.2.1 Initial Meeting

Chapter 5 explained that many of these questions to be asked of the members of the CMT because the answers will be used when the members of the EMT are asked the same questions by shareholders or government agencies later on in the Acute-Crisis stage. As a review, the questions the EMT will want answers to include:

- What happened?
- Why did it happen?
- When did we know about it?
- How could we have prevented it?
- Where in the building did this happen?
- Who is located on that floor (those floors)?

8.2.2 The Executive Management Team Agenda

When the two groups of executives get together (i.e., the CMT and the EMT), they will review the status of the crisis using the questions from the EMT agenda.

There will be several agendas in existence, for physical disasters, i.e., fire, flood, explosion, etc., or for nonphysical crises, i.e., product problems, company image problems, financial problems, etc. Some questions will differ, depending on the "type" of disaster or crisis.

In Chapter 5, the scenario used to select the agenda questions was that of a fire. The basic questions the EMT would ask of the members of the CMT would be:

- Were there any injuries to personnel?
- What was the cause of the fire?
- Have security precautions been implemented?
- What is the damage to the organization's assets?
- Is there a potential for adverse publicity?
- Do we have any contractual concerns?
- Does our insurance policy cover our losses?
- What is the status of the affected business functions?
- Where are the business functions located? Is this a temporary situation?
- How did the employees get to the temporary sites? Transportation support? Monies?
- How is the network operating? Do we have communications with the key organization and people?

EMT agendas differ from one organization to another — different organizations will add some specific questions based on the way they operate or their culture. Some organizations might remove some of the questions for the same reasons.

8.2.3   Crisis Scenario: Customer Service

Let us look at a crisis scenario, not a disaster scenario. It seems as if "customer service" has frequently been ignored by organizations. It is as if they can overcome a "customer service" crisis because the crisis is the customer's crisis. And many times, the crisis is affecting only one person, not a large group of people. When it affects a large group, organizations approach the resolution with a sincere desire to resolve it.

So let us look at a "customer service" crisis using the Sears Roebuck organization. Sears has always been a top-notch organization. In fact, at the current time, Sears has done a great job at positive marketing in its partnering with ABC on the television show "Extreme Makeover — Home Edition."

That is why it is difficult to believe that they did not make a customer service adjustment to avoid the publishing of the following negative article.

Sears began dunning an 81-year-old sick widow who lives in West Philadelphia. Sears was dunning the woman for a $4,000 home improvement loan for which she had already paid.

The woman has a letter from a finance company indicating the loan was paid in full. On May 9, 2000, the Associates Consumer Discount Company notified the woman that the home improvement loan was paid in full. (The problem is that the finance company has since been absorbed b another finance company in texas, which can't locate Brown's record.)

In an effort to resolve the issue, the woman, who has no offspring of her own, turned to one of six children of an affluent Main Line family that she helped raise as a housekeeper. (This family founded the Royal Bank in Pennsylvania.) The eldest of those six children agreed to try to resolve the problem for the woman, who was there for him every day from the time he was a baby. The former president, and now director of his family's bank, who also teaches classes at Philadelphia University, couldn't get answers for the woman.

But, in reviewing the woman's records, he discovered something else. I've talked about an "Opens the Door" crisis before — one that opens the door to other problems. This is another example of "open the door."

> The gentleman reviewing the woman's records found that Sears billed nearly $2,000 over a four-year period for a service contract on four appliances she bought from Sears **more than a decade ago.** the woman apparently never signed an agreement extending the contracts. They were simply renewed over the phone every two years, he said. (The contracts probably cost more than the appliances are worth.)

The man assisting the woman has sent 11 letters to resolve the situation, including on to the company president, and has had no substantive response from Sears.

(This information comes from a story entitled, "This is hardly the softer side of Sears" that was printed in the *Philadelphia Daily News* on February 21, 2002.)

This story reminds me of the situation I found myself in with United Airlines.

> I was flying from Chicago to Cleveland on Flight 1746 on January 30, 2002. I checked in at the ticket counter, checked my bag, and received my seat assignment. I then went to clear security. I placed my articles on the metal detection machine: a computer travel case and a small bag carrying business items and computer backup files. I placed my laptop computer in one of the plastic boxes United provides. (I use my computer to make my presentations. As such, it is the most important piece of luggage that I carry on my business trips.)

After passing through the metal detector, I was told I was to be "wanded." Before being wanded, I attempted to pick up my computer and place it inside my computer travel case, both of which had already passed through the metal detector. The security person was very adamant: leave everything at the metal detector and get wanded immediately. I assumed my belongings would be watched while I was being wanded, especially since I had no view of my belongings while I was being wanded.

After being wanded and shoed, I went over to the metal detector to claim my belongings. The computer was not there! Someone accidentally had picked up my computer and left theirs behind. This incident, the loss of my computer, would not have happened if the security person would have allowed me the courtesy of returning my computer to my computer carrying bag.

The person who accidentally picked up my computer left their computer. I told the United representative and the Argenbright representative about the situation, the missing computer. They took all my information in case the person returned to the security point to return the computer. I gave them the "unclaimed" computer that apparently belonged to the other individual. They told me that when the person returned my computer, United would send it to me.

When I arrived in Cleveland, I went to United's Lost & Found office and made a "lost-luggage" claim. They assured me that if the computer was found, it would be sent to me.

On Saturday, Feb. 2nd, while I was out, a United Airlines representative from "Lost & Found" called me at home and left a message on my answering machine. The United representative explained that my computer had been returned. The message said that they were going to send the computer to my house via Federal Express. The United representative gave me the FedEx tracking number and indicated that it would be delivered in two days.

On Wednesday, February 6th, upon arriving home from my trip, I was elated to find the box had arrived. But after seeing the FedEx box that was used, I became alarmed. The box was a standard FedEx box. It would be ideal to send a pair or two of pants or a couple golf shirts, but not a computer.

The box measurements were 17-1/2 inches long, 12-1/2 inches wide, and 3 inches high.

My computer is 12 inches long, 10 inches wide, and 2 inches high.

When I opened the box, I found the computer inside a white plastic bag, which in turn was inside a yellow manila envelope. The manila envelope had a thin layer of bubble wrap that was part of the envelope. There was no packing inside the box to prevent the computer from sliding back and forth inside the box. When I turned the computer on, I found the laptop's screen was cracked — in two different spots.

I immediately phoned the United Airlines Lost & Found department. I spoke with a representative in Lost & Found and explained my tale of woe. The representative said she was sorry but there was nothing she could do. I asked her what I should do. She said that United is only responsible to send the "found" item back to the owner. She felt it was a Federal Express responsibility. She said that I could call United's "Customer Relations" and she gave me the phone number.

I called Customer Relations and, after waiting for quite a while, I spoke with a United representative. I explained the whole story and that I needed a computer for presentations that were scheduled for the upcoming week. He said there was nothing he could do. He said it was a Federal Express problem. I explained that if United had either insured the $1500 computer, or had put "fragile" on the box, I could go to Federal Express and complain. But United's Lost & Found representative did not package the computer properly, did not insure the package, or even identify the contents as fragile. The customer service representative still said that it was not United's responsibility, but rather that it was Federal Express' fault.

I asked the Customer Relations representative if I could speak to his supervisor, and he said he could not do that. I then asked for the name of the Manager of Customer Relations. He told me he could not give me the name. I then asked for the name of the Director of Public Relations. He said he could not give me the name. I then asked him for the name of the President of United Airlines. He said he could not give me the name. So much for "Customer Services."

I was a little surprised that he was trying to "blame" someone else for United's responsibility. In my BCP presentations, I teach the basics of managing a crisis. One of the recommendations crisis management experts recommend executives follow is "don't shift blame to others." When faced with a "Pre-Crisis" situation, where your Customer Relations representative could have attempted to help resolve the problem, or turn it over to someone with more authority that could help resolve the problem, he chose to "blame someone else." This was a missed opportunity to keep the crisis from becoming acute.

I then called Baggage Claim and explained my story. She said there was nothing she could do. I asked to speak to a supervisor or manager, and she gave me a phone number. When I called, I was connected to a Customer Relations representative. I finally gave up. I was very angry and frustrated.

I have read United's "Customer Commitment" from the director of Customer Relations on their Web site. "United employees around the world are committed to ensuring you and your loved ones enjoy safe, seamless travel and superior customer service every time you fly with us."

It appears that some of United's employees have a different opinion of "superior customer service" than I do. On the other hand, if United's "customer relations policy" is to ignore the problems of their passengers, United is achieving their goal. While United's representatives were polite, they did not help me at all. The three groups I spoke with (namely, "Lost & Found," "Baggage Claim," and "Customer Relations") took the same position — that United Airlines is not responsible for the damaged laptop computer. It must be someone else that is responsible, but not United.

I am totally frustrated. I am the customer. I follow the United Airline instructions. I leave my belongings behind in order to get "wanded and shoed." Their security contractor's (Argen-bright) employees do nothing to protect my belongings. They are very courteous with me while they are deciding what to do about my missing computer. I give them my name and address. I make a claim in Baggage Claim in Cleveland. I wait to hear the news that my computer has been found. When I receive that news, I am thrilled. I wait for the computer to be delivered. When it arrives, it is broken. What have I done wrong?

My concern is that I am now afraid to fly on United again. Even with 200,000+ frequent flyer miles, I am afraid what the airline and its representatives will do to my belongings, because it appears that United is not responsible for their actions.

My faith in United has been shattered. What steps will United take to restore my faith and confidence in United and their stated "superior customer service" policy?

On April 19, 2002, I sent a letter to the CEO (Jack Creighton) explaining my frustration and disappointment with United's effort to resolve this issue (see Appendix 8A).

One part of my irritation was feeling that after all the loyalty I had shown United Airlines over the years, they were not interested in resolving a problem they caused. I could handle this irritation by not ever flying on United Airlines again.

In fact, I was able to gain solace by sharing my story during my Crisis Management presentations throughout the country. I was able to use this experience to show attendees "how not to handle a crisis." I wanted the attendees to think about what could be facing them should they choose to fly on United Airlines rather than another carrier.

The other part of my irritation was when I was told that the person I was trying to resolve my problem was located in another country. This person told me that he was certain that United had outsourced some of this work, if not all of this work. This, in my mind, explained the feeling of complete helplessness in trying to solve a problem with a person located in another country. To me the idea of putting a customer's problems or complaints in the hands of people in other countries does not make much sense.

I have often been told that when traveling in other countries to avoid being the proverbial "ugly American." People have told me that Americans fail to understand the customs in other countries, and that our behavior often is looked at as ugly.

Well I guess I felt the same about the man I was trying to deal with. I felt he did not understand our customs, and that it was he who was "ugly." I then wondered why a major organization in the United States would hire people with a different culture and different customs to resolve "customer service" problems. The person I dealt with never offered to resolve my service problem.

In America, I have found that most American organizations want to resolve customer problems to everyone's satisfaction. But I did not feel that there was any room for resolving anything with that particular United person. After being frustrated by this person, I took my case to the executives of United Airlines. The answer I received showed me that United Airlines had no interest in resolving my problem. They knew they were dealing with one person. What can one person do to hurt United Airlines? The letter from United appears in Appendix 8B.

On the other hand, to make my point about customer service for one person, versus for many people, compare United Airlines' response when they had customers upset during the large number of flight cancellations during the summer of 2000. United spent big money producing a television advertisement featuring Jim Goodwin, United's chairperson, who apologized to customers for the disruptions.

When United Airlines CEO Goodwin stepped up to the camera in a TV spot, he apologized for United's summer of disruptions. In shirtsleeves, straight face, and solemn tone, the chief of the world's largest airline tried to reach out to thousands of angry United customers. United's decision to go on the air with the apology followed weeks of dizzying cancellation numbers and traveler horror stories (see *Newsweek,* September 9, 2000).

8.2.4   Identifying Members of the Crisis Management Team

Something not discussed in Chapter 5 was that rather than sending the document to the CEO for approval, it was preferable to ask for a one-on-one "short" meeting. The purpose of the meeting is to have the CEO identify "who" the he or she expects will provide, or should provide, the answers to each of the questions on the "agenda." That is, have the CEO select the members of the Crisis Management Team.

This one-on-one meeting with the CEO saves a huge amount of time for BCP professionals later when they are trying to get the senior executives to "volunteer" that they are the persons who should be assigned that role on the Crisis Management Team.

Permit me share an experience I had with one of my clients.

Devlin Associates had been contracted to develop and document an IT Disaster Recovery Plan with an organization in Connecticut.

During the project, I was scheduled to make a presentation to the senior executives on the role of the executives in supporting the IT department's recovery from disaster.

This organization was one of the leaders in implementing a Disaster Recovery Plan. In fact, it was the priority of the CEO. To stress the point that the project was a priority of the CEO, the Director of IT scheduled the CEO to introduce the presentation. Before he introduced me, the CEO explained that there was another meeting he had to attend and that he would only spend ten minutes in our presentation.

The CEO kicked off the meeting by identifying the priority of the project, and then introduced me.

In those days, the mid-1980s, I used overhead transparencies for my presentations. (I had a couple transparencies with all of the "agenda" questions written on them, and I also had a group of transparencies with actual disasters that had occurred in the United States.

I explained the purpose of the meeting and then asked the first question on the transparency (the one that had the questions written on it). I then showed an example of a disaster where that question specifically applied. I gave a brief explanation of the disaster and explained how the question applied to this disaster. I then asked which senior executive would have that crisis support role, and which department. After receiving an answer from the executive, I wrote that person's name and the department name on the overhead transparency with the questions on them.

Understand that I had given these presentations at client locations throughout the United States many times during the years I was an active consultant. On occasion, when I asked the question, the executives in attendance were not very quick to volunteer. (I think many of them had served in our military, and learned to never volunteer.) When this happened, I would rephrase the question with the hope that it was now clearer than the original question. This of course elongated the length of the presentation, usually scheduled for 1 to 1.5 hours.

This pause in volunteering did occur on the second question at this particular client. When there was the short delay, the CEO (who was still sitting in the back of the room) spoke up and said, "Raise your hand, Jerry." Jerry raised his hand. I wrote it on the overhead transparency and moved on to the next question.

When I asked the fourth question and showed the disaster that applied to the question, I again did not get a volunteer. I was surprised when I heard from the back of the room, "Raise your hand, Jim." (The reason I was surprised was that we were 20 minutes into the presentation and I thought the CEO had left for his other meeting.)

To make a long story short, the CEO stayed through the entire presentation. His presence made it very easy to obtain the names and departments that would have the crisis support roles. (By the way, these "support roles" were the basis for the Crisis Management Team's plan. Obviously, there have been a great number of additions, but it all started here.)

At the conclusion of my presentation, the CEO thanked me. He said he found it very interesting. I thanked the CEO, John Emery, for his assistance in getting the right parties assigned to the roles. That is right; it was John Emery of Emery Airfreight.

8.2.5   Ongoing Meetings

After the initial meeting, the CMT will set up a schedule for future meetings. Depending on the severity of the crisis, there could be a meeting each day the crisis remains in the "acute" stage.

> (*Author Note:* There have been numerous conference presentations made by BCP professionals who have experienced a disaster or crisis and explained in their presentation that during the "acute" stage of the crisis, daily meetings took place between the EMT members and the CMT members. The topics obviously dealt with a recap of what had gone "right" and what had not since the last meeting.)

One of the conference presentations I attended was made by the BCP professional for the CoreStates Bank. The bank had employees located on four floors of the Penn Mutual Insurance Company building in downtown Philadelphia.

> In April 1989, the Penn Mutual building suffered an extensive fire. The fire started in a records storage room on the 9th floor of the 20-story building. The room contained thousands of boxes of computer printouts and historical files.

> The room was a windowless 172,000-square-foot room. (About a third the size of a football field.) Because the room was windowless, it trapped the intense heat and smoke inside the room. The fire fed on the paper records stored there.

> It took 54 hours to finally extinguish the fire. At times, the temperature hit 2000 degrees as the fire spread quickly among

the largely paper contents. Firefighters used jackhammers to break holes into the ceiling so they could send water into the area. An estimated four million gallons of water was used to put out the fire.

During the fire, there were no lights or elevators working. The effect of the fire on Penn Mutual employees and other tenants in the building could be summed up in two words: inconvenience and disruption.

The CoreStates BCP professional explained that the bank had employees located on four floors of the building. There were a total of 15 departments and 500 people housed in the building, including the Trust, Consumer Loan, Community Banking departments. The BCP professional explained that they activated their business resumption plans in order to resume the operations of the affected departments.

He explained the daily meetings they held every evening with the members of the Crisis Management Team. He also showed a series of pictures depicting the activities of the participants attending those meetings.

This was not the first example I found of daily meetings being scheduled to exchange information about the management of a crisis or disaster. The first example I found was where the CMT of the New York Telephone Co. suffered a fire in its switching center on Second Ave. in New York City. The CMT met daily throughout the crisis. This daily event was written up in an article that discussed the successful recovery from a fire at the New York Telephone Co. in February 1975. The article, published in an AT&T publication entitled "Disaster on Second Avenue," described the effectiveness of the executive meetings that were held daily throughout the "acute" stage.

8.3 METHODOLOGY TO ASSIST CMT MEMBERS IN DEVELOPING AND DOCUMENTING THE CMP

Now that we know the Executive Management Team will have questions to ask, and we know who the CEO and members of the EMT expect will provide the answers, the BCP professional can concentrate on assisting the CMT members in preparing their CMP.

There is no standard methodology being used by all organizations for assisting the executives in developing and documenting their CMP.

Let me share with you two, of the many, methods people use to develop and document plans.

8.3.1 Method 1: BCP Professionals Develop and Document the CMT by Themselves

The first method involves the BCP professionals developing and documenting the CMP by themselves. The concern I have with this method is that the BCP professional needs buy-in and input from the executives to develop a "viable" plan (viable = capable of working or functioning).

BCP professionals can assist with the scope of the CMP, and can assist with some of the questions that must be answered during a crisis. But there usually will be additional questions that members of the CMT will want to add, and there are usually a few that they want removed. When BCP professionals need an explanation of specific details, or information on "who," "when," or "how" the team would carry out the responsibilities, they need direct input from the executives involved. Unfortunately, with this methodology, BCP professionals may find that none of the executives have any time to help them.

If the BCP professional does complete the documenting of the CMT Crisis Management Plan, as well as the distribution of the plan to the appropriate executives, he may find out that the plan has been placed on a shelf somewhere, and that it was never read.

The plan just sits on a shelf, waiting for the crisis to occur. Then when the crisis does occur, the executives begin reading it — for the first time. In reality, at this point in time what the members of the CMT should be doing is "taking charge" and "gathering the facts."

To make matters worse, some of the members of the CMT could even be disagreeing with the content of the plan. They should have done that when the plan was being developed and documented.

Needless to say, organizations that use this method do not fare well in managing a crisis.

When organizations do not fare well, the Executive Management Team will want to know why. Members of the CMT will begin looking to point the finger at someone. (Being the fine upstanding executives that they have shown themselves to be during the development of the plan, they immediately point the finger at the BCP professional. It was the mistakes of the BCP professional — not the different members of the Crisis Management Team — that caused this situation.)

BCP professionals may find they made a career-path-ending decision when they decided to develop and document the CMT Plan by themselves. They may need to begin looking for another career at another organization.

What would make this even a more difficult pill to swallow would be if the organization decides it does not want the outside world to know that they performed poorly. To demonstrate that the organization really did an excellent job of responding to the situation, the same executives who were too busy to help develop the plan, or read the plan before the crisis struck, are praised publicly by the CEO of the organization. (Worse yet, they may receive a promotion or a bonus.)

As you can tell by the previous few paragraphs, this is not a method I would recommend.

8.3.2 Method 2: CMT Members Develop Their Parts of the CMP by Themselves

The second method discussed is the one I always used when I was consulting. This method went something like this:

1. Establish the list of departments and business areas identified by the CEO as the executives the CEO expects will answer the questions in the EMT "agenda."
2. Invite them to a presentation. (Ask the CEO if he could introduce the presentation and the importance of formalizing the role of the CMT during an acute crisis or disaster.) During the presentation, explain the goals of the plan and the members selected by the CEO for the CMT. Preparations needed before the actual presentation is made consist of:
   a. Prepare two scenarios for the presentation. One scenario will deal with a physical disaster; the second will deal with a non-physical crisis that could harm the reputation of the organization if not dealt with immediately.
   b. Prepare examples of the two scenarios for the presentation.
   c. Prepare a working checklist to record the information identified during the presentation.
3. Upon completion of the presentation, schedule a one-hour meeting with each department (business area) to further discuss their unique part of CMP.
   a. Document each team's crisis management role based on the discussions and findings of the one-hour meeting.
   b. Identify the resources they will need to carry out their role and responsibilities.
   c. Send a "draft" copy of the team's crisis management role to the person interviewed for corrections or additions.
4. After receiving the corrected version, document the "final" copy of the team's role for inclusion into the Crisis Management Team's Plan.
5. Schedule a 1-1/2 hour training presentation in which each member of the crisis management team will attend. The presenter will use a disaster scenario that incorporates at least one responsibility for each member of the CMT.

      a. Use the EMT "agenda" to ensure that the agenda questions are assigned to a team within the CMT.

      b. Show a copy of each team's role to the other members of the CMT to identify any interfaces that must be addressed. (e.g., we need to move employees to a temporary location; Facilities will make arrangements for the location; Security will make provisions for a secure environment; IT communications will ensure that the network is tied in to the temporary location; etc.)

6. At the conclusion of this presentation, ask the members of the CMT how they will handle their CMT role if their department, their equipment, their computers, their hard-copy records are destroyed by the disaster. Use this as a "food for thought" closing. You are not asking them to respond just then. Your main purpose is to strengthen your point on the need for all business units, and the functions within those units, to have a "business resumption plan."

7. The BCP professional should then offer his or her assistance to help them think through the elements needed in their department's plan.

8.3.3 Level of Detail

A question that always arises when developing and documenting the CMP is: How detailed should it be? Answer: It should be more than an overview. It should be less than minutia.

First of all, determine the level of detail you want in the plan. How much key information, and how much minutia? How much of an overview? Remember the pro–con thoughts for each concept.

8.3.3.1 Should It Be More of an Overview?

The value of "less" detail, and "more of an overview," is that it allows for quick development and documentation.

The problem is that the "less" detailed overview only tells "what" must be done by a member of the CMT. It does not tell "how" to do it.

This philosophy can result in a completely ineffectual plan.

8.3.3.2 Should It Be "Detailed"?

On the other hand, the more detail level plan tells the team member "what" must be done and explains how to do it.

The concern here is that it can cramp the style of the CMT member who can carry out the responsibilities and make good decisions that are not presently documented in the plan. So there needs to be a compromise here.

The level of detail for the CMP is more than an overview and less than the level of detail identified in some of the technological areas of the organization. Keep in mind that "overviews" are fine, as long as a person does not require it to carry out the actions that have been identified.

I have often referred to overviews during my seminars as "a plan-to-plan." The overview tells "who" is responsible for "what," but not "how" to do it. Because the plans are being developed to assist executives in successfully managing a crisis, it might be necessary to include "how" they can accomplish their mission. I believe that most senior executives in organizations know "what" is expected of them during a crisis based on their expertise, but may not know exactly "how" they would accomplish it.

On the other hand, the level of detail should not require a three-ring binder for each member (team) of the CMT. That is, if a member of the CMT has four major responsibilities to carry out during a crisis, four three-ring binders are not necessary.

The best way to determine if you have the right level of "detail" in the plan is to exercise that part of the plan. Present the key members of the CMT with an exercise scenario that allows them to practice "what" they would do in a real crisis, and "how" they would do it. Do not be surprised if some members of the CMT want more "details" in their plan.

I know first hand, during exercises I participated in with some of my clients, that at the conclusion of the exercise, executives approached the CMP professional sand asked how they could add material to the plan.

8.3.4   Think the Unthinkable

Executives must be able to "think the unthinkable." This is not generally their focus. Their day-to-day job is to produce results. Executives sometimes feel that the CMP is an interruption to their more-important role in the organization.

Face it — in today's business environment, executives often focus mainly on the financial picture of the organization's next quarter. Taking time to think about something that probably will never happen causes them to be somewhat disinterested and, on occasion, abrasive. They cannot think long-term. For many of the executives, long-term is two quarters from now, rather than two years from now. This situation puts those organizations in a position where they will not fare well when the crisis strikes.

8.3.5   Some Executive's Exhibit a Limited Focus

Many executives feel that if they spend a lot of money on "prevention," there is no need to spend money or time on Business Resumption or Crisis Management Plans — they will never be needed. Executives might believe that devoting time to low-probability events is a waste of their time. Most executives feel that their skills are better spent running the day-to-day activities of the organization. Their attention is directed toward the financials for the quarter, not into the future.

I do not know how many times I have heard executives say to me, "That will never happen in our organization." On one occasion when I was helping to develop and document a CMP for a manufacturing organization that had plants in multiple locations throughout the United States, the vice president in charge of manufacturing said that these crisis plans were a waste of time and money. "This will never happen in our organization." He went on to point out, "We have prevention and emergency response plans in all locations. We take care in our manufacturing process to ensure that it couldn't happen."

Less than two months later, an explosion destroyed one of those plants. Their prevention plan did not work. As a matter of fact, an investigation after the explosion identified the cause as poor safety procedures. This vice president thought that by having documented procedures, nothing could happen. The explosion killed a number of employees and devastated the plant. It took more than a year to resume operations at the restored plant.

Fortunately, the CEO realized that the main reason for spending the time, and the money, was to have a plan to refer to when something did happen. The CEO realized that although the probability was small, the impact could be significant. When the event that could never happen did happen, the organization was able to activate its CMP to manage the effects of the fire.

8.4 DOES A DOCUMENTED PLAN GUARANTEE SUCCESS?

True or false? Having a documented prevention plan, or even a documented recovery plan, does not mean that when you have to use it, it will work. One reason is that if the scope of the plan is not sound — that is, the plan was built for a best-case scenario, rather than a worst case — then the plan probably will not work when needed.

Using the Exxon Valdez example again, they had a 1700-page "Contingency Plan." The plan was required to be developed in order for the oil companies to gain the support of the politicians to drill in Alaska. But by the time the oil spill occurred, the plan had grown old; it was out of date.

Here are some excerpts from various newspapers during the investigation of why the Alyeska Pipeline Co. contingency plan was not honest, and why it failed.

> During hearings conducted by the House Interior Subcommittee on Water, Power and Offshore Energy Resources, a part of the

House Interior Committee, Rep. Richard Durbin, (D-Illinois) suggested the contingency plan was a sham. He went on to say Alyeska violated the public's trust by its ineffectual response to the spill. The plan was Alyeska's assurance "to the nation at large" that the oil companies were prepared to handle a disaster.

"But do you think that had you put in this document...what actually happened when the Exxon Valdez ran into Bligh Reef... that any agency of government, state or federal, would have given you permission to pump oil through the pipeline?" Durbin asked.

Durbin noted that the plan estimates Alyeska would be able to recover 50 percent of a 200,000 barrel spill. The Exxon Valdez spilled more than 240,000 barrels yet Alyeska and Exxon have captured less than 20 percent of the oil spilled six weeks ago, according to Exxon's optimistic numbers.

Theo Polasek, vice president of operations for the pipeline company, insisted assumptions made in the contingency plan — including oil recovery projections and response times — applied only to the scenario set out in the plan and not any spill in the Sound. However, a diagram in the back of the 1987 contingency plan does set out general response times for spills in all parts of the Sound.

In that diagram, Alyeska projected it could be at the Bligh Reef area within four hours. "Well, Sir let me tell you something, you made a promise to a lot of people with this document," Durbin said, waving the red-and-white covered contingency plan at Polasek.

"And without that promise I don't think you'd have been in business. And quite honestly, I believe you abused the basic trust, which was given to the company. You can make all the excuses you want," he added, "but the fact is a lot of damage has been done when a lot of people think it could have been avoided." (Excerpts from "Congressmen bear down on Alyeska's role in spill," *Anchorage Daily News,* May 8, 1989.)

Another excerpt on the same subject — the scenario was not for the worst situation, but rather the best.

ANCHORAGE, Alaska – An oil-industry official, in a major public concession, said yesterday that his company's frequently cited contingency plan for a quick response to a major Alaskan oil spill could not be applied to a real-world situation.

The admission by Lawrence D. Shier, marine manager for the Alyeska Pipeline Service Co., came as oil-company executives and Alaska government officials clashed in the first full-scale public confrontation between the estranged partners in the exploitation of Alaska's North Slope petroleum.

Questioned repeatedly by state officials at a National Transportation Safety Board hearing in Anchorage about their slow response to the nation's worst oil-tanker spill, Alyeska officials said that conditions when the tanker Exxon Valdez ran aground March 24 did not conform with their plan for handling a 200,000-barrel, or 8.4-million-gallon, spill in Prince William Sound.

Alyeska is the consortium of oil companies that owns the Trans-Alaska pipeline and Valdez terminal, from which the crude is shipped to the West Coast.

Although industry officials had cited the plan before the spill as evidence of their preparedness for a catastrophe, Shier and Alyeska engineering manager William Howitt said the 8.4-million-gallon "scenario" assumed daylight conditions and better weather than existed when the tanker dumped 10.9 million gallons into the sound.

Shier said that, despite the plan's promise that oil-containment and cleanup equipment would be on the scene within five hours, it took more than 13 hours to reach the ship.

Howitt noted that an equipment barge crucial to the quick response had not been loaded at the time and revealed that there had been no requirement that Alyeska keep the barge loaded at all times.

Pressed by Robert E. LeResche, spill coordinator for the Alaska governor's office, on the differences between the planned and actual response to the spill, Shier said: "The 200,000-barrel scenario is a set of conditions that cannot really be extrapolated to a real-world situation."

Apparently taken aback, LeResche paused, then said softly, "Very interesting."

Shier said fear for the safety of company crews on rough, dark seas slowed the cleanup. He said the plan for a quick cleanup also assumed that crews could use chemical dispersants, controlled burning and mechanical skimming but that weather conditions and red tape intervened.

The two sides sparred over the meaning of various directives and often signaled contempt for each other's contentions. LeResche has taken every opportunity to blame oil executives, rather than the tanker's allegedly intoxicated captain, for the spill and had to pry answers out of his industry adversaries.

"Was the barge ready for response at midnight March 24?" LeResche asked. "Yes, the barge was ready for response," Howitt replied.

"Was it loaded?" "No, the barge was not loaded."

Late Thursday, Alyeska and the tanker's owner, Exxon Shipping Co., had their turn to challenge state officials on the handling of the spill, which has fouled hundreds of miles of Alaska's shoreline and killed thousands of birds and sea animals.

Exxon officials have said the spill was too large for anyone to control.

Capt. William J. Deppe, a tanker expert representing Exxon Shipping, asked Dennis Kelso, commissioner of the Alaska Department of Environmental Conservation, whether "there was any power on earth that could have completely cleaned up that spill." "There would have been a different situation if we had been running it," Kelso replied.

When Deppe pressed the point, noting that one former official of Kelso's department had said the spill was beyond human control, Kelso replied, "It was the industry's responsibility to deliver on its promises." (Excerpts from "Oil firm says plan is flawed," *Washington Post,* May 20, 1989.)

The final excerpt shows how changes that were made in the day-to-day operations at Alyeska were not changed in the contingency plan:

While it will be almost a year before the National Transportation Safety Board releases its conclusions on the grounding of the tanker Exxon Valdez, some points are apparent after a week of federal hearings into the cause of the nation's worst oil spill.

One is that success can breed complacency, and complacency can give birth to disaster.

The approximately 50 hours of testimony that ended Saturday portrayed an oil-tanker safety system in Prince William Sound that deteriorated over the last 12 years.

The cockiness of the industry was expressed in 1986 by Alyeska Pipeline Co., the consortium of oil companies that owns the Alaska oil pipeline and Valdez terminal, when it assured the state that statistically, a spill of more than 200M barrels should happen once every 241 years.

Accordingly, local pilots who are more experienced on the waterway in 1977, rode tankers 75 miles to the entrance of Prince William Sound, but by last March 24 they were riding only a dozen miles through Valdez Narrows.

On that day the Exxon Valdez spilled 265,000 barrels, or nearly 11 million gallons.

Also in the last 12 years, tanker crews shrank.

Radar became weaker, unable to detect ice or to track ships passing Bligh Reef except in good weather.

A full-time Alyeska oil-spill response team was disbanded. Another point is that policies died regulations mean little unless they are emphasized and enforced.

(Excerpts from "After hearings into Exxon spill, some clear lessons," *Seattle Times*, May 22, 1989.)

Now, let's look at Chapter 9, "The Crisis Management Team Command Center." This chapter will address various options that can be used by the CMT for a command center during a crisis.

Appendix 8A

LETTER TO CEO AT UNITED AIRLINES

April 19, 2002

Mr. Jack Creighton
CEO
United World Headquarters
1200 E. Algonquin Rd.
Elk Grove Village, IL 60007

Dear Mr. Creighton:

I'm writing to you directly to share with you my "frustration" and "disappointment" with United Airlines and some of your employees. I have a story to share with you that concerns me. As a long-time customer of United, I feel that the airline has changed, and not for the good.

First, let me clarify that I don't only send letters of complaint. When the occasion warrants, I will send a complimentary letter. I have, in fact, sent complimentary letters to the United Airlines CEO a number of years ago. Before my retirement, I spent quite a bit of time on the road with my consulting business. On two different occasions, I had serious problems with my back. On both occasions, United and its employees helped me travel from the West Coast back home to Philadelphia and into the hospital. From the time I arrived at the airport I was taken care of by United's finest. I felt a sincere concern and compassion for me on the part of the United employees. I wrote to the CEO to let him how much I appreciated the attention I had received from United and its employees. As a CEO of a small consulting company at that time, I appreciated it when a client would write me, or phone me, with a comment on my employee's actions. I knew that the way they handled situations with my clients could make or break my company.

> *Even before these incidents, United had been my airline of choice when traveling while I was working as a consultant. I traveled hundreds of thousands of miles on United before I retired in 1992. While my retirement plans in 1992 called for me traveling only for fun, I soon discovered that many organizations and associations in my industry wanted me provide speeches in various locations throughout the world. (I am in the Disaster Recovery/Business Continuity Planning industry.) I did return to limited business travel during the 1990s, again choosing United as my preferred airline. Since the "9-11" incident, I've have been contracted by a large telecommunications company to provide "Business Continuity Planning" presentations at luncheons for executives of their customers and prospects.*

> *This is the crux of my problem, and why I am writing to you. As part of a trip to speak to their customers on Jan. 30 and 31, the telecom company chose United to fly me from Philadelphia to Chicago, and then Chicago to Cleveland the next day. This would have been great, because it allowed me to add to my frequent flyer miles that I am accumulating for a future vacation.*

Unfortunately, it was not a great experience. On this trip, my computer was accidentally picked up by someone else while going through United's security control point at the Chicago airport. The computer was returned a couple days later. United's Lost & Found department shipped the computer back to me via Federal Express. The screen on the computer is cracked in two places. It cannot be used. I've spoken to your representatives in Baggage Claim, in Lost and Found, and in Customer Relations. While they understand my frustration over the damaged computer, they feel that United is not responsible for the damage. One group blamed Argenbright, your subcontractor.

> *The other two groups blamed Federal Express. I find the explanations of each area unbelievable, and certainly not like responses I've had in past dealings with United.*

> *None of them felt that the fact the United's Lost & Found department sent a laptop computer in a large Federal Express box, without placing protective packing around it, without insuring*

it, without even identifying it as fragile, was cause for United to be responsible for the damage.

Then when I asked to speak with someone else, a supervisor or manager, who would have more authority to handle this problem, I was told that they could not give me the supervisor/manager's name or phone number.

Mr. Creighton, I was so infuriated, I could not communicate with you right away. I sat down to write this letter time and time again, but could not send it to you. Why? It was not a business-like letter. There was so much anger, caused by a disbelief that this company that I held in such high esteem, would respond so poorly. I have to admit, my letter contained so much venom, and it was unreadable. I had to wait until I was calm so I could write a letter devoid of emotion, or devoid of most emotion. I felt betrayed by a company that I was loyal to. Granted it was a loyalty earned many years ago, by another generation of employees.

I have attached a detailed story of the incident with this letter. I don't expect that you will have time to read it, but I would appreciate it if you would have someone in your organization read it.

In closing, I ask you to have someone from United explain to me why I must suffer a financial loss.

Edward S. Devlin

Appendix 8B

LETTER FROM UNITED AIRLINES, 2002

✈ U N I T E D

May 15, 2002

Dear Mr. Devlin

The letter that you sent Mr. Creigthon was forwarded to me in our baggage service office for reply.

The process of lost articles, or in your case switched items is an ongoing challenge. We are putting our best efforts into reuniting these items with their owners. Since this is done as a courtesy to our customers, we have elected to return the items using Federal Express.

The item belonging to you was received from another customer that inadvertently took the item from one of the checkpoints, the item was shipped to you as it was received.

I truly regret the loss you have incurred. United Airlines does not assume responsibility for lost or damage items that were not checked.

John E Cervantes
Baggage Services Supervisor
O'Hare International Airport
Chicago, IL 60666

Chapter 9

THE CRISIS MANAGEMENT TEAM COMMAND CENTER

9.1 INTRODUCTION

This chapter addresses the Crisis Management Team's options for a Command Center. It deals with strategies to consider, such as using multiple rooms for the members of the CMT versus using one large room; different options for a location, such as the headquarters building, another nearby building, a nearby hotel or motel, etc.; the different resources needed in the command center; and finally, the need to take into consideration the crisis management plans of federal, state, and local organizations to ensure that there are no conflicts.

9.2 WHAT IS THE COMMAND CENTER?

Sometimes there is confusion when a person uses the term "command center." This is because the term, or a variation thereof, will be found in a number of locations throughout the Business Continuity Plan (BCP).

A command center's function is to provide a central control point for operations involved during the crisis. As such, each element of the BCP will have a "command center" in it, namely, in the Prevention element, in the Emergency Response element, and in the Business Resumption element.

Keep in mind that these command centers are not the same center. They are in separate locations, they have different people assigned to them, and they have different objectives associated with them.

People with key responsibilities in the Prevention, Emergency Response, and Business Resumption elements want to have a central control point where they can go, to give and get, any and all, information available on the status of the crisis.

Within in the Business Resumption element of the BCP, there will be a "command center" for the Information Technology department (ITCC); and there will be a command center identified for each of the various revenue-generating or business units in the organization.

(**Author Note:** A few years back, the ITCC was known in the book entitled *Business Resumption Planning* as the Disaster Recovery Plan Command Center, or DRPCC. For this reason [i.e., the potential confusion about the different command centers], I try to make it clear when I am using the term in this book to identify the specific command center to which I am referring. For example, because this book focuses on the Crisis Management Team, the command center is identified as the Crisis Management Team Command Center [CMTCC]. There is also a mention of the Executive Management Team's command center as the Executive Management Team Command Center [EMTCC].)

The command center for the Executive Management Team is a separate location from the command center for the Crisis Management Team. The Executive Management Team usually will meet in the organization's boardroom during a crisis. (This will change if the building housing the boardroom has been damaged and is not usable.)

While the Crisis Management Team will also select a location in the headquarters building as their primary command center, it will not be the boardroom. (It will be used by the EMT.) If the building housing the site selected as the CMT command center has been damaged and is not usable, an alternate site will be used.

When Crisis Management Team members arrive at the command center, they will:

- Take charge of the situation quickly.
- Gather the facts.
- Tell your story.
- Fix the problem.

9.2.1 An Example Organization That Used a Command Center during a Crisis

Meridian Bank; Philadelphia, Pennsylvania, 1991. A major fire destroyed eight floors of a 38-story building in downtown Philadelphia, Pennsylvania, in February 1991. The fire started when oily rags, left by a wood refinisher during renovations on the 22nd floor, triggered spontaneous combustion. It burned out of control for nearly 19 hours, gutting eight floors of a 38-story high-rise office building.

Meridian Bank was a tenant in the building. Ken Maher, Meridian Bancorp's Vice President for Corporate Risk and Insurance Management, headed Meridian's Crisis Management Team. The team at Meridian is comprised of key officers from property management, security, risk management, human resources, legal, purchasing, media and internal communications, voice and data equipment, data processing, PC support, and a few other groups.

Command Center: Initially, the Meridian Bank Business Continuity Officer met the divisional security manager and the property manager at a command post they established outside the fire department's van. "The three of us were in downtown Philadelphia on cellular phones communicating with members of the CMT at Meridian's headquarters in Reading, PA. Philip Toll, the president of our facilities company, headed this group of CMT members."

Based on the information that they had received from the fire department officials around 11:00 p.m., they decided to wait to assemble the members of the Crisis Management Team until 10:00 a.m. on Sunday morning. At that point they would have more information on the status of the business units located inside the building.

When the CMT met on Sunday morning, they had a better picture of the problems they were faced with in the downtown Philadelphia building.

First they identified their priorities and put those plans in action. Then they laid out the plans for the less time-sensitive activities that they would address later on Sunday. By opening time on Monday morning, they had the critical customer services back in operation. (From *Recovery Magazine*, Winter 1992.)

9.3 KEY FUNCTIONS PERFORMED IN THE COMMAND CENTER

A key function performed in the command center is to maintain a status on all activities throughout the crisis. As an example:

Merrill Lynch: Merrill Lynch was affected by the terrorist attacks on 9-11. Merrill Lynch headquarters was located in the World Financial Center, directly across from where the

World Trade Center towers once stood. In addition to the company's headquarters, several other Merrill Lynch office buildings were affected by the terrorist attacks.

According to a story published in the *Disaster Recovery Journal* (Fall 2001 edition), Paul Honey, Director of Global Contingency Planning, said "Within a few minutes of the evacuation Merrill Lynch was able to switch its critical management functions to their command center in New Jersey."

Since the CMT command center had been predesignated in corporatewide contingency plans, all personnel immediately knew where to dial into and transfer information.

Another key function is to establish and maintain communications to various elements within your organization. Some of these communications would be with senior executives, employees and shareholders informed. Some of these communications would be with external organizations, such as the media, the general public, customers, other business relationships, and the government authorities informed.

A third key function would be to coordinate media activity and manage rumors. Sometimes, bad information about your organization and the crisis at hand starts to passing around. As an example:

AirTran Airlines: According to the *Plain Dealer of Cleveland* (see *USA Today,* January 12, 1998), the FAA has found serious safety-related violations at the AirTran airline. The violations included falsified documents and faulty repairs. According to the newspaper, the documents were based on a 3-week inspection that ended Nov. 7, 1997. Allegedly the documents show the airline had more serious violations than the 1996 report that recommended that ValuJet be grounded. (The airline changed its name from ValuJet after one of its planes plunged into the Everglades in May 1996, killing all 110 people aboard.)

AirTran officials said they "understand that the outcome (of the probe) was excellent." They demanded a retraction from the newspaper, calling it "grossly inaccurate." AirTran President D. Joseph Corr said his airline is safe (*USA Today,* January 13, 1998).

Confirmed as Rumors: Federal aviation officials say a special inspection found no systemic safety problems at AirTran despite a published report indicating widespread trouble at the discount airline. FAA managers said action already would have been taken against the airline if serious problems had been found. (*USA Today,* January 14, 1998.)

After the crisis is "under control," and the crisis has moved to the Post-Crisis stage, the command center can remain useful in:

■ Reconstructing the events that occurred
■ Establishing a new early warning system (better evaluations of pre-crisis warnings)
■ Developing new strategies for dealing with a similar crisis (based on the lessons learned)

(***Author Note:*** I like the definition given by Colonel Ed Badolato, U.S. Marine Corps (Retired) in his article entitled "Learning from the Exxon Valdez," in which he described the purpose for the command center as "to establish and maintain communications, to provide control, to coordinate media activity, and to focus outside liaison. Most contingency plans rely on the availability of an emergency operations center facility with supporting infrastructure.")

9.4   CMT COMMAND CENTER: CONSIDERATIONS

One of the first questions people have asked me is, which options do organizations choose for their Crisis Management Team Command Center: a single room for each member or department, or one large room for all members of the CMT? They are interested in what other organizations are doing with their command centers.

I have worked with an organization that has tried both options. Initially, they could not decide on which option would work best for them. They decided to use the multiple room option for their first exercise. Using the multiple room option, they found:

■ *Value of the multiple room option:* They found that the value of the multiple room option for each member or department was that it was quieter. There was less commotion going on during the crisis, allowing the CMT members to concentrate on the issues relating to the crisis.
■ *Problem with the multiple room option:* The problem with this option is that when the CMT members need to communicate quickly with other members of the team, they may find it more difficult when they have to get up from their location and walk to the other room(s).

The plan was for each team to have the phone numbers of the other CMT members and use the phone for rapid communications.

The plan broke down because when a CMT member tried using the phone, the phone line at the other end was busy. Most of the members of the CMT use the telephone extensively during the time they are carrying out their CMT responsibilities.

For their second exercise, the client decided to locate the CMT command center in one, large conference room in the headquarters building i.e., single room option). This option worked well.

- *Value of the single room strategy:* All members were able to interact quickly and efficiently. When the team reviewed its own performance, it chose to use this option for all future activations of the command center.
- *Problem with the single room strategy:* The only disadvantage found was that the single room was noisy.

9.4.1   How Large a Space Is Needed for the CMT Command Center?

Another consideration is how large a space is needed if the single room option is chosen. If the strategy is to use one large room as the command center, it should be large enough to comfortably house the number of people, or representatives, who will be operating from the facility. Generally, the CMT consists of the following departments, or their representatives:

- Security
- Facilities, Building Engineering
- Human Resources
- Public Relations
- Legal
- Risk Management, Insurance
- Treasury, Finance
- Procurement, Purchasing
- Information Technology, Communication
- Medical Department (if there is one)
- Transportation or Administrative Services
- Internal Auditing

How large an area is needed for this Crisis Management Team? This has been discussed extensively. There is no real answer, but a good rule of thumb for the space requirements to accommodate a group of this size would be somewhere between 1000 and 1500 square feet of space. As an example:

A financial organization in Florida, 1982: Following Hurricane Andrew, a financial organization in Florida activated its command center. In addition to the conference room, it employed a couple functional rooms where it set up status boards.

The first contained the current status of recovery operations and was updated every hour. The second contained a status board for telecom operations; it showed the locations of all the cellular phones and pagers being used during the Acute-Crisis stage.

The CMT held a status meeting every day at 4:00 p.m.

Lesson: During the postmortem at the conclusion of the crisis, this organization decided to make a change to its Business Continuity Plan based on experiences during the acute crisis. During the crisis, many of the people they had to communicate with did not speak English, so they added a number of bilingual employees to their teams.

Now let us consider the location of the Command Center.

9.5 LOCATION OF CRISIS MANAGEMENT TEAM COMMAND CENTER

When members of the CMT are notified that the Crisis Management Team has been activated, how will they know where to assemble? If your organization has a documented Crisis Management Plan (CMP), CMT members will know because the location is identified in that plan. During the development of the CMP, potential locations were identified. A decision was made as to where the primary command center will be located. That location should be clearly identified in the CMP.

The purpose of preidentifying the "command center" is twofold: (1) to provide CMT members with a specific location where they are to report during any activation of a plan, and (2) to allow the prepositioning of any resources that must be available to properly support the CMT's activities. This prepositioning will eliminate the confusion caused by missing resources the team needs (see Section 9.7).

Most of the companies I have worked with that have documented CMPs, also have preidentified CMT Command Center location(s). (CMTCC). So when a crisis or disaster does strike, and the members of the CMT are activated, they will already know where they are to report in order to begin managing the effects of the crisis.

9.5.1 Selecting a Primary Site for the Command Center

The logical first choice for the primary command center location would be the "headquarters" building. In most organizations' headquarters buildings, there is usually a room large enough to be used by members of the CMT. Remember: do not select the "board room" for the CMT Command Center, as the board room will be used by the Executive Management Team (EMT) for its command center.

9.5.2 Optional Locations for Command Center Site(s)

In the event the crisis or disaster strikes the building chosen as the primary CMT Command Center, there should be an alternate site identified in the CMP. This alternate location should be located in another building, other than the headquarters building.

9.5.2.1 Option 1

A good choice for an alternate or secondary command center location would be another building already housing business units of the organization. This affords the ability to pre-position resources needed by the CMT members inside the other building before the crisis strikes. As an example,

> *The Port Authority of New York and New Jersey.* The Port Authority of New York and New Jersey was affected by the terrorist attacks on 9-11. It lost its headquarters. Executives assembled in the command center. Shortly after assembling, the command center collapsed. After digging out, bleeding and dust-covered employees moved to an alternate command center in Jersey City, New Jersey, across the river from New York City. Later on in the recovery process, it shifted many of its 2000 World Trade Center staffers to a third temporary headquarters.

This option (another building already housing business units of the organization) presents some considerations that must be included in the planning process. For example, let us assume the crisis is a disaster, and the disaster occurs in the headquarters building at 10:00 p.m. Because the location in the headquarters building will not be usable immediately, the CMT should plan on using the alternate command center.

Consideration: Will there be any security provisions that must be adhered to to gain access to the building (the other building already housing business units of the organization)? Does your organization own the building that will be used as the alternate or secondary command center?

If your organization owns the building, who will notify your Facilities/Buildings people to gain access to the building for the members of the Crisis Management Team after 10:00 p.m. at night? If your organization leases space in the building, who will notify the building owner's Facilities/Buildings manager to gain access to the building for the members of the Crisis Management Team after 10:00 p.m. at night?

Does your organization own the building that will be used as the alternate or secondary command center? This becomes more critical if the cause of the disaster that has occurred is believed to be intentional. If your organization owns the building, now all the security policies will go into effect that your organization has established to minimize the potential for another attack, or minimize the potential for additional damage to occur.

- Will you require the employees entering the building to follow a security procedure?

Consideration: If your organization leases space in the building, and the cause of the disaster that has occurred is believed to be intentional, now all the security policies the owner of the building has put in place to protect their building will go into effect. The owner may refuse to admit anyone into the building due to security or insurance liability issues.

9.5.2.2 Option 2: Hotel Location

If your organization does not have business units operating from another building close to your headquarters building, a third option is to rent facilities at a hotel near the headquarters building, or near the site of the disaster or crisis.

From a planning point of view, this option is cost effective. Why? It does not cost any money until it is needed. On the other hand, from an operational point of view, it is not as efficient as the primary and alternate options.

This option forces the CMT members to bring with them the resources they will need (e.g., laptop computers with key information regarding their expertise and responsibilities). There is no ability to stage these critical resources at the hotel beforehand. The remainder of the resources will have to be gathered quickly and moved into this type of command center. Examples include:

IBM Program Information Department, fire in 1972. In 1972 when an IBM computer center (the Program Information Department installation) was destroyed by fire, a nearby hotel/motel was used as a command center/alternate operating location.

A more recent example of the use of a hotel as a command center/alternate operating location occurred after the 9-11 attacks on the World Trade Center.

Lehman Bros. Holdings Inc. Lehman Bros., the fourth largest securities firm, owned most of its space in the World Financial Center, and also had about 600 employees across the street in the World Trade Center's North Tower. The Financial Center building is unusable because of damage sustained when the Trade Center's towers collapsed.

Alternate work location: So Lehman leased temporary office space in Jersey City for its stock traders and top executives, and shoe-horned about 50 employees into the law offices of Simpson Thacher & Bartlett.

The brokerage firm rented the entire 650-room, 22-story Sheraton Manhattan Hotel in midtown Manhattan and replaced beds with desks for 1300 employees in its investment banking and stock research departments. This extraordinary move underlines the lengths Wall Street firms went to in the wake of terrorism.

Lesson: After Lehman Brothers Inc. took over a Sheraton hotel in Midtown, its bankers quickly discovered that the phone system, engineered for tourist traffic, could only handle about 75 outgoing calls at a time.

9.5.2.3 Option 3: Mobile Location

A third option is to provide a *mobile location* for the command center. Some organizations have a preequipped trailer with key equipment already installed. This could be moved from the headquarters building to a site near the crisis location. (Government agencies often use a mobile command center during a crisis.) It could also be used as an on-site command center when the problem has occurred near the location where the mobile trailer is housed. As an example,

An Insurance Company in Wisconsin. This organization has identified three different command centers it will use if and when it experiences a disaster or crisis:

Primary Command Center — a central control point for all activities involving the crisis

Site Command Center — located near the crisis site, to complete the incident assessment

Mobile Command Center — on location, the focal point of the crisis

9.5.2.4 Creative Option 1: Parking Lot Location

Finally, if all else fails, be creative. Use whatever option is available. As an example,

> *Banking organization in Southern California.* This organization used just such an option when the building that housed the IT department and computer facility was severely damaged by the Whittier Narrows earthquake in October 1987.
>
> Because the building was severely damaged, and it was deemed too dangerous to enter, the head of IT operations decided to use temporarily an automobile in the parking lot, equipped with a car phone, as the on-site IT Command Center.
>
> For about 24 hours, all activities involving the IT Business Resumption activities were controlled from that car and its car phone. After 24 hours, a tent was constructed in the parking lot. Resources such as phone lines and handsets were installed in the tent.
>
> Fortunately, the organization's headquarters building was located approximately 15 miles from the IT building. The Crisis Management Team used the CMT Command Center located in the headquarters building.

9.5.2.5 Creative Option 2: Competitor's Location

Would a competitor allow you to use its facilities temporarily? You will not know unless you ask. As an example,

> *Duane Morris LLP law firm, Philadelphia, Pennsylvania.* John Sroka, Chief Technology Officer for the Duane Morris LLP law firm, awakened to face the big challenge of a power outage. The main computers for all 19 branches of this large, national law firm are in One Liberty Place (in Philadelphia) and were disabled by the power outage.

By midday, Sroka had shifted work usually handled by Philadelphia computers to the Chicago office, where a backup system had been recently installed. Although Philadelphia computers remained down, the other 18 offices could access the Internet and set up Hotmail e-mail accounts to communicate with clients and colleagues. The power failure came while Duane Morris was installing a new e-mail system. Its disaster recovery component had not yet been installed, so the firm's global e-mail system would remain down until the power was restored at One Liberty.

Command Center: A rival law firm, Hecker Brown, Sherry & Johnson at Two Logan Square (where Sroka's wife works) "was kind enough to let us set up a command center at their office." (From *Philadelphia Inquirer,* July 8, 2003.)

9.6   A DEDICATED COMMAND CENTER IS "A SORE THUMB"

Why do organizations *not* have a permanent location for use as a command center? They could have one in their headquarters building; and for contingency reasons, they could have another in a different building that already houses business units. That question has been asked many times during the development of Crisis Management Plans, and it remains a legitimate question.

Some of my former clients have chosen to do this — establish a permanent command center somewhere in the headquarters building and another command center in a different building. Most others have not chosen to do this; they have taken the cost-effective approach to this conundrum. The cost can be significant, especially if it is only going to be used during the Acute-Crisis stage of an incident. This dedicated space, especially if it were to sit unused throughout the year, stands out like a "sore thumb."

We know that the command center will be active around the clock throughout the duration of the crisis. The majority of activity will be during the Acute-Crisis stage. The problem is that during the remainder of the year, the facility goes unused. Executives end up asking themselves, "Isn't it a waste of money and resources to have a room set aside for managing a crisis that might occur once a year?" The answer is usually, yes.

How then do organizations choose to have dedicated facilities as part of their Crisis Management Plan? In those organizations that do have facilities set aside as the command center(s), they counter this objection of the cost by using that facility throughout the year.

In addition to using the dedicated command center during the acute stage of the crisis, the Business Continuity Plan officer can schedule the use of the command center at various times throughout the year for other activities, including:

- *During a pre-crisis situation.* When the EMT is dealing with a "potential crisis," the members of the CMT can meet in the command center to:
  - Assess the situation and determine the steps to take if it moves to the acute stage.
  - Gather information that will be used if it moves to the Acute-Crisis stage.
  - Assist the EMT in assessing the potential threat from the impending crisis.
- *During the post-crisis period.* The command center can be used to:
  - Reconstruct the events that occurred.
  - Establish a new early warning system.
  - Develop new strategies for dealing with a similar crisis based on lessons learned
- *For training classes for CMT members.* This is especially helpful when a crisis has taken place within another organization in the same industry. The BCP officer can use a similar scenario as the other organizations have faced. Based on the results from the other organizations' management of their crises, the BCP officer can strengthen their plan.
- *For the semiannual exercises that the crisis management team will perform.* In addition to full-blown exercises, the BCP officer can set up individual exercises for a member of the CMT, or for two or more members at various times throughout the year.

Once the command center location is identified during the development of the CMP, the various resources the team will need during a crisis can be prepositioned there.

9.7 RESOURCES NEEDED IN A COMMAND CENTER AT SOME STAGE DURING THE CRISIS

This list of resources may not be all-inclusive. Those identified here were the resources some of my clients chose to have in their command center as part of the planning done in the Y2K crisis project.

- *Furniture:* desk and chairs for each team; conference table(s) and chairs; lockable filing cabinets; white boards with markers; flipcharts with easel; pull-down/projection screen.

- *Communications equipment:* televisions (one for local news, one for international news), radios (AM/FM, battery operated), telephone on each desk, cell phones, pagers. Some command centers even have a ham radio.
- *Computer equipment:* one workstation per member of the CMT; one laptop per team; Internet access; a couple of printers.
- *Office and other equipment:* photocopier; paper shredder, facsimile machine, digital camera, video camera, VCR, portable voice recorders, and an LCD for computer projection.
- *Supplies:* notepads, notebooks, pens, pencils, staplers and staples, tape and dispensers, hole punch, special forms (e.g., corporate, overnight shipping, other), check stock, pack and shipping materials, postage (or machine).
- *Administrative and medical supplies:* first aid kit, emergency food and water supplies.
- *Informational resources:* the following informational resources should be located in the primary CMT Command Center:
  - Most current version of the Business Continuity Plan
  - Emergency Response Plan
  - Business Resumption Plan elements (the Business Resumption element contains all the business units' [departments'] resumption plans, the IT Disaster Recovery Plan, and the Crisis Management Plan)
  - Employee personnel directory, and a telephone directory for shareholders, customers, vendors, etc.
  - Many organizations keep building plans and maps of surrounding areas in the command center

To rapidly review the information located in the plans, the informational resources should be stored on computers as well as on paper.

Are resources located in the Crisis Management Team's Command Center now? If not, how long will it take to get them?

- Other considerations:
  - *Some type of controlled access procedure.* Either an automatic access control system or security guards allows security personnel to identify employees wanting to enter the command center to be checked to determine if they are authorized personnel.
  - *Some type of assured power (i.e., backup power).* Most organizations have generators installed. They should ensure they have an adequate supply of fuel on hand.

If we look back a couple of years, most BCP professionals will find that their organization had a CMT Command Center in place for the Y2K rollover. Unfortunately, most of these facilities have been disassembled. If they were still in existence, they would be a perfect solution for the primary command center location. Let us now review the planning activities for the Y2K impending crisis.

9.8 THE Y2K CRISIS MANAGEMENT COMMAND CENTER

9.8.1 Prepositioned Command Center: Year 2000

Because Y2K was a very real threat, companies allocated the necessary time and resources to make sure they would be able to resume business operations on a timely basis.

Many Fortune 1000 companies indicated that they had Y2K Crisis Management Command Centers in-place and "hardened." At the end of 1998, there were an estimated 40 percent of the Fortune 1000 companies that had hardened command centers. By December of 1999, 85 percent of Fortune 1000 companies had "hardened" Y2K Command Centers. Most companies had hardened a second location as a contingency site, in case the primary site had problems.

The sites were "hardened" by providing contingency resources — in case the infrastructure was affected Y2K. The sites ensured that power, heat, air conditioning, water, telephone, etc., resources would be available.

> (***Author Note:*** I worked with two large organizations to assist them to prepare their CMT to respond to problems that might develop on January 1, 2000. As part of their Y2K preparations, they identified a command center location and placed all resources they felt they would need if problems occurred.)

The prepositioned resources included:

- Large-screen televisions, one for local news, one for international news; a VCR for each television to tape any information that may need to be reviewed; personal computers, servers, and other peripherals; FAX machines; copy machines; power strips; dual-powered radios; status boards; alternate phone capability; backup generators (with prepositioned arrangements for additional fuel); dual phone feeds for the switchboard.
- Support resources, such as courier services, overnight delivery services, and food service provisions were made for the duration.

How did they ensure they would work if needed? They exercised the command center a couple times prior to January 1, 2000, using some of the different scenarios they believed they would face on January 1, 2000.

9.8.2 Y2K: This Author's Perspective

It is very frustrating to hear people throughout the country laugh about the Y2K issue and suggest that it was much ado about nothing.

The Y2K threat was indeed valid. Companies spent a great deal of time and resources testing their facilities to see if older equipment would succumb to the outages that were being predicted. Many of these organizations went on record with their findings that indicated that there would have been interruptions to the equipment if they had not made the necessary changes.

As a result of the concerns, companies throughout the world spent many billions of dollars to correct the problems they anticipated. They replaced a large amount of equipment that was not Y2K compatible. This eliminated potential Y2K problems.

The people who worked on the Y2K projects around the world did a great job in minimizing the potential effects of Y2K. Make no bones about it: if they had not worked so well, and if the companies had not spent the money, there would have been problems on January 1, 2000.

Interestingly, what was not really discussed by the economists was the financial impact of Y2K. Companies spent huge amounts of money to replace equipment they did not think was Y2K compatible. These monies were not in the companies' business plans or budgets for 1998 and 1999.

Therefore, there was a great deal of business transacted in 1998 and 1999 that gave a false picture of the economy. Companies that benefited from these expenditures — hardware and software companies — had grown rapidly in 1998 and 1999. They were expected to continue to grow at this rate in 2000, 2001, and 2002. Not only was it unlikely, it was impossible. The companies that bought large amounts of equipment to ensure they were Y2K compatible had no need to buy any of this equipment for another four to five years.

9.9 PLANNING EXTENSION

This section is designed to emphasize that the Business Continuity professional needs to think "outside the box."

For example, take the plan from the "best-case scenario" to the "worst-case scenario." Crisis Management Plans that are built using a "best case" will be overwhelmed when the crisis exceeds the scenario for which it was built.

As previously discussed, many of the people who have written articles, or given presentations, regarding their experiences with managing a crisis have said, "I never expected to talk about this," "I never thought it would be this complex," "I never thought we would run into so many things we didn't plan for."

Think of the outcry you could face if one of your executives had to respond with a statement such as the one Alyeska responded to after the Exxon Valdez oil spill.

> An oil-industry official, in a major public concession, said that his company's frequently cited contingency plan for a quick response to a major Alaskan oil spill "could not be applied to a real-world situation."

> The admission by Lawrence D. Shier, marine manager for the Alyeska Pipeline Service Co., came as oil-company executives and Alaska government officials clashed in the first full-scale public confrontation between the estranged partners in the exploitation of Alaska's North Slope petroleum.

> Questioned repeatedly by state officials at a National Transportation Safety Board hearing in Anchorage about their slow response to the nation's worst oil-tanker spill, Alyeska officials said that conditions when the tanker Exxon Valdez ran aground March 24 did not conform to their plan for handling a 200,000-barrel, or 8.4-million-gallon, spill in Prince William Sound.

Alyeska is the consortium of oil companies that owns the Trans-Alaska pipeline and Valdez terminal, from which the crude is shipped to the West Coast.

> Although industry officials had cited the plan before the spill as evidence of their preparedness for a catastrophe Shier and Alyeska engineering manager William Howitt said the 8.4-million-gallon "scenario" assumed daylight conditions and better weather than existed when the tanker dumped 10.9 million gallons into the sound.

Shier said that, despite the plan's promise that oil-containment and cleanup equipment would be on the scene within five hours, it took more than 13 hours to reach the ship.

Howitt noted that an equipment barge crucial to the quick response had not been loaded at the time and revealed that there had been no requirement that Alyeska keep the barge loaded at all times.

Pressed by Robert E. LeResche, spill coordinator for the Alaska governor's office, on the differences between the planned and actual response to the spill, Shier said: "The 200,000-barrel scenario is a set of conditions that cannot really be extrapolated to a real-world situation."

Shier said fear for the safety of company crews on rough, dark seas slowed the cleanup. He said the plan for a quick cleanup also assumed that crews could use chemical dispersants, controlled burning, and mechanical skimming but that weather conditions and red tape intervened. (From "Oil firm says plan is flawed," *Washington Post*, May 20, 1989.)

This executive has admitted that the plan was not based on a "worst-case" scenario, but that it was really built on a "best-case" scenario. When things did not go as planned in the "best case," Alyeska was unable to perform according to the contingency plan.

Another lesson learned was the need for dual Crisis Management Command Centers. Stop limiting the scenario to a crisis in your hometown. Think about some of the remote areas in which your organization operates. Are you prepared to set up command centers there?

When an organization is thrust into an acute crisis, where the location of the crisis is hundreds of miles away from the headquarters location, it is a good idea to activate both the command center in the headquarters building and to set up an on-site command center at the crisis location. The command center at the site of the crisis can handle on-site issues such as life safety issues as well as the damage assessment issues. Some examples of this include:

Exxon Valdez Oil Spill, 1989. The on-site CMT command center was located in the remote town of Valdez, Alaska. Exxon began command center operations in a hotel in Valdez. They had to bring in additional resources, such as microwave transmitters for the increased communications requirements.

Other command centers were established by the public sector. The State of Alaska set up its command center in the courthouse building in Valdez. The Coast Guard had the best facilities, with its port headquarters and maritime safety office in Valdez.

Lesson Learned: Because the three organizations had to work together on the clean up, the dispersal of the three groups caused some of the principal officials and response-team members to spend considerable time moving from meeting site to meeting site.

Southwest Airlines, 2000. A Southwest Airlines Boeing 737 jetliner skidded off the end of a runway at Burbank Airport (Southern California) and crashed through a barrier, then hit two cars on a street before coming to rest a few feet from a gas station located across the street from the airport. The flight from Las Vegas to Burbank carried 137 passengers and a crew of five. Six people were injured; the most seriously injured was the pilot, who suffered cuts to his scalp. The injured people were transported to a nearby hospital.

Command Centers: At headquarters in Dallas, senior executives set up a command center for the Crisis Management Team.

> One hundred calls came in the first hour.
> About 3 hours after the accident, CEO Herb Kelleher held a press conference.

On-Site Command Center. At the same time, about 50 employees were flown to Burbank to set up an on-site command center. (From "Southwest manages a crisis," *USA Today,* March 20, 2000.) For more information on Southwest's Crisis Management Plan in action, see Appendix 9A.

Think outside the box when it comes to working with the public sector. How many organizations will you have to interface with during a crisis? Who will interface with these public-sector organizations? Has your organization reviewed the public sector's plans to identify if there needs to be better coordination between your organization and the public sector organizations? Interestingly enough, you may find out that their plans do not provide coordination between plans. For example, when there was an oil spill in Alaska, Exxon had to interface with five organizations.

Each of the major players in the shipment of Alaskan oil had its own contingency plan:

- The Alyeska (the pipeline company that runs oil the 800 miles from Prudhoe to Valdez and onto the ships) plan
- The captain of the port's plan
- The national contingency plans
- The regional contingency plans
- The Alaska Regional Response Program

The problem was that, in general, each of the plans ignored the plans of the other organizations.

The lesson BCP professionals should take from this example is that "the middle of a crisis is not the time to try to interface your plans with five other organizations." Rather than calling this "a time for coordination," it would be more accurate to refer to it as "a time of chaos."

Think outside the box when it comes to where your CMT might be working. Have you taken into account that in a "worst-case" scenario, the supporting infrastructure may be limited? As an example,

> ***Exxon:*** While Crisis Management professionals for Exxon may have considered that they would be operating in a region with limited supporting infrastructure, they apparently did not take into account that they would be forced to deal with a high-profile oil spill out of a remote town such as Valdez.

The port terminal town of Valdez had a population of 3500, was fairly remote by transportation standards, and was not equipped with a highly developed contingency support infrastructure.

> *Hotel accommodations.* No one really considered the requirements if the town's population doubled practically overnight. With thousands flooding into a small fishing town, hotel rooms vanished and people slept on floors and in cars.
> *Travel.* The airport, which usually accommodated eight to ten flights a day, suddenly had to cope with 1000 flights daily at the peak of the crisis. Air traffic control was overloaded. A Coast Guard cutter's air search radar assisted with the air-control overload.
> *Cargo planes.* Because the C-130 Hercules was the largest aircraft that could be handled, all large cargoes had to be flown to Anchorage, then shipped six hours over a mountain road through the Thompson Pass. At that time of the year, Thompson Pass could experience avalanches and heavy snows.
> *Surface transportation.* From Valdez to the Prince William Sound area took hours by boat.
> *Telephones, working space, and transportation.* All were major headaches.

> (***Author Note:*** I remember hearing Gerry Meyers, an acknowledged crisis management expert, speak at a Computer Security Institute conference years ago. He said organizations must "Protect your credibility. With it, you can recover; without it, you are in for lasting damage." Later on, I read the same statement in Meyers' book entitled *When It Hits the Fan.*)

The Crisis Management Plan should be built to protect the credibility of the organization. If it cannot protect the organization's image, or credibility, one can expect that regulators will criticize the organization, as did Rep. Richard Durbin after the Exxon oil spill. Look at this excerpt from an article entitled "Congressmen bear down on Alyeska's role in spill," published in the *Anchorage Daily News* (May 8, 1989), and you can see what I mean.

Durbin suggested the contingency plan was a sham. He said Alyeska violated the public's trust by its ineffectual response to the spill. The plan was Alyeska's assurance "to the nation at large" that the oil companies were prepared to handle a disaster.

"But do you think that had you put in this document ...what actually happened when the Exxon Valdez ran into Bligh Reef, that any agency of government, state or federal, would have given you permission to pump oil through the pipeline?" Durbin asked Theo Polasek, vice president of operations for the pipeline company.

Durbin noted that the plan estimates Alyeska would be able to recover 50 percent of a 200,000 barrel spill — the Exxon Valdez spilled more than 240,000 barrels — yet Alyeska and Exxon have captured less than 20 percent of the oil spilled six weeks ago, according to Exxon's optimistic numbers.

Polasek insisted assumptions made in the contingency plan — including oil recovery projections and response times — applied only to the scenario set out in the plan and not any spill in the Sound.

However, a diagram in the back of the 1987 contingency plan did set out general response times for spills in all parts of the Sound. In that diagram, Alyeska projected it could be at the Bligh Reef area within four hours.

"Well, Sir, let me tell you something, you made a promise to a lot of people with this document," Durbin said, waving the red-and-white covered contingency plan at Polasek. "And without that promise I don't think you'd have been in business. And quite honestly, I believe you abused the basic trust which was given to the company. You can make all the excuses you want," he added, "but the fact is a lot of damage has been done when a lot of people think it could have been avoided."

I believe that organizations have enough trouble keeping regulators satisfied without creating a situation where they can no longer be trusted. And furthermore, this lack of trust may linger for a long time. Organizations have spent years establishing a reputation and gaining their market share. It only takes minutes for the same organization to lose both. So when you, the Business Continuity professional, are looking at the depth of your BCP, check out the basis for your scenario. Is it "real-world" (the term used by the Alyeska executive)?

Now, let's look at Chapter 10, "Exercising the Crisis Management Plan." This chapter will discuss the importance of exercising the CMP. It also discusses the role of the CMP Administrator.

Appendix 9A

"SOUTHWEST MANAGES A CRISIS"

A Southwest Airlines Boeing 737 jetliner skidded off the end of a runway at Burbank Airport and crashed through a barrier, then hit two cars on a street before coming to rest a few feet from a gas station located across the street from the airport.

The flight from Las Vegas to Burbank carried 137 passengers and a crew of five. Six people were injured; the most seriously injured was the pilot, who suffered cuts to his scalp. The injured people were transported to a nearby hospital.

The plane was towed back through the broken fence onto airport property the next morning.

When Southwest Airlines spokesman Ed Stewart picked up his home phone that Sunday, he heard five words every airline employee dreads: "This is not a drill." Stewart and other managers were told a Southwest Boeing 737 had overshot a runway in Burbank, Calif.

No one was seriously hurt, but Southwest executives didn't know that at first.

When the executives landed in Burbank later that night, the sight of the orange-and-red jet straddling a highway was "surreal," Stewart says.

So began Southwest's first crisis response in its 29-year history, a history with no fatal accidents.

After training handpicked teams and studying how other companies had handled disasters, Southwest was thrust into the real thing. How its crisis plan worked is a lesson for any company that someday might get the same call. "All we'd ever done before was role play," says Ginger Hardage, the airline's head of communications.

At the accident scene, flight attendants hustled passengers off the crippled jet. The forward exit was blocked by a faulty escape slide. "The flight attendants jumped into action," says passenger Kevin McCoy of Pasadena, Calif. Shouting through a bullhorn, one flight attendant ordered passengers to forget their luggage and go out the rear door.

Once outside, passengers were relieved — and cold, because the temperature had dropped sharply ahead of a storm front.

"They left all of us standing in the middle of the road on Hollywood Way for an hour," says passenger Lawson Brown, 78, of Van Nuys, Calif.

Southwest says rescue officials wanted to make sure passengers were OK before putting them on buses. Police said it took time to round up shuttle buses and thread them through the emergency vehicles.

(Command Center) At headquarters in Dallas, five senior executives set up a command center. One hundred calls came in the first hour.

(CMT-PR) (EMT) About three hours after the accident, CEO Herb Kelleher held a press conference.

Meanwhile, about 50 employees were on a plane to Burbank. One was Mark Clayton, the flight safety manager, who had been in bed with bronchitis. He and many others would not sleep that night.

(CMT) People whose day-to-day jobs were handling ad campaigns and employee benefits would be responsible for helping passengers in the aftermath. "Job descriptions went out the window," Hardage says.

Family assistance team members had been picked and trained in advance. "We look for people who are mobile," says Joyce Rogge, the marketing vice president who ran the assistance effort. And team members must pass a "wellness" test that screens for medical, emotional or family problems. "If you're under stress of your own, you can't help someone else."

(CMT-Training) In training, employees had studied how TWA and Swissair had responded to crashes. Family assistance team members heard a presentation from the widow of a passenger who died in the 1994 US Airways crash near Pittsburgh. "She talked about how she was notified, how she had to call her son in college," Rogge says. "It's important for team members to understand what these people experience."

(Command Center — 2) In Burbank, Southwest's assistance team members set up a command center at the Airport Hilton. The morning after the accident they began calling passengers, offering medical care, counseling, even groceries.

One passenger, a pizza shop owner, had been ordered to rest by his doctor and was fretting about his business. After talking with Southwest he hired a couple of friends to deliver pies, and the airline paid them.

Passengers received letters of apology, ticket refunds and travel vouchers.

(Glitch) Passenger McCoy got one of those family assistance calls but thought he was OK. The following day, however, "it really hit me," he

says. He couldn't sleep or concentrate and broke down without warning. When he called the airline's main 800-number, the agent had no idea where to send his call. "I was left on hold and finally hung up," he says. After calling Southwest's headquarters, McCoy was referred to the Red Cross. Southwest put a help number in a letter to passengers after the accident, but McCoy missed it. He thinks reservations agents should have been more helpful.

(Post-Crisis) The whole experience will prompt a review of Southwest's crisis plan soon. "In a strange way, we couldn't have had a better drill," Rogge says.

But no drill could have foretold some things. One caller who had not been on the flight demanded cash, saying the accident was giving him nightmares. A tabloid TV show offered Southwest $30,000 to interview the pilots. The airline declined. "In a situation like this, all bets are off," Stewart says. "You learn an awful lot very quickly about how life really works." (From *USA Today,* March 20, 2000.)

Chapter 10

EXERCISING THE CRISIS MANAGEMENT PLAN

10.1 INTRODUCTION

This chapter discusses the role of the Crisis Management Plan (CMP) administrator. It identifies the CMP administrator's responsibility to exercise the CMP, the objectives of an exercise, and the steps used in performing a CMP exercise.

The steps one should take to pre-plan the exercise to ensure it is successful include:

1. Decide on the "type" of exercise.
2. Prepare the scenario.
3. Complete the "Exercise Planning Form."
4. Schedule the exercise (date, day, time).
5. Evaluate the results.
6. Prepare a written report.
7. Ensure changes are made.
8. Maintain the "Exercise Scheduler Matrix."

The chapter identifies some organizations that have experienced a disaster or crisis and have commented on the value of the exercises. These examples are not limited to Crisis Management Plan exercises; they also include any exercise related to the Business Continuity Plan that was shown to be a value to the organization.

The chapter also presents some examples of crises and disasters where, had the organization performed an exercise, it would have found problems with its plan. These "Lessons Learned" from the exercise would have eliminated, or minimized, the problems experienced during the crisis or disaster.

10.2 CLARIFICATION OF TERMS

Before delving into this chapter, let us clarify terms. Business Continuity professionals often use the terms "testing" or "exercising" interchangeably when referring to running a simulation for the members of the Crisis Management Team. While some Business Continuity Plan professionals use the terms interchangeably, many others have a distinct different meaning for the two terms. Is there a difference?

- The dictionary definition of "test" is an examination, a trial, or proof.
- The dictionary definition of an "exercise" is an act of employing or putting into use.

My thoughts on the two words as they relate to the Business Continuity Plan (BCP), and that includes the Crisis Management Plan (CMT) section, is that there is a difference, even if it is just a subtle difference.

- *Testing* verifies that the plan procedures "work." *Exercising* verifies that the plan procedures are "current."
- *Testing* verifies that the plan checklists are "accurate." *Exercising* verifies that the plan checklists are "current."
- *Testing* identifies any omissions. *Exercising* identifies that the plan strategies "still meet the business objectives."
- *Testing* verifies that CMT members are prepared. *Exercising* serves as a training resource for CMT members.

(***Author's Note:*** See Appendix 10.01.)

For years, Devlin Associates Inc. consultants were trained to use the term "exercise" when referring to the simulations or practices of the plans. This was the result of having numerous Devlin clients report on their Data Processing (Information Technology) "tests" in the 1980s. We always asked clients to present information on their plans, especially on "tests" at the Annual User Meeting.There was a common thread in all of the presentations from different clients. Each client seemed to have the same objective. The objective of their test was to pass, not necessarily to find out if their plan actually worked. They were more interested in showing management that the test was a success.

As an example, when they presented their "tests," they explained the planning steps they took before going to their computer backup site. Their preplanning efforts were designed to ensure that the test was successful. When I asked them why they did this, they said they did not want to fail. Most clients expressed the position that they felt that the executives of their organization would not understand, or accept, a test that failed.

This "pass-fail" concern reminded me of when I was a child going to elementary school. At breakfast, my parents would ask me if I was scheduled to have any tests that day. Then at dinner that evening, my parents would always follow up the morning question with, "How did you do in your test?" The meaning of the question was: did I pass or fail? Before I finished elementary school, I was well aware that "failing" was not acceptable.

This mindset (i.e., failing was not acceptable) seemed to be the goal my clients had for planning their tests. (In fact, I often said to them that they not have to run the test because they were absolutely certain is would "work as planned.")

When I spoke to this subject in my seminars in the 1980s and even the early 1990s, I found that most Data Processing/Information Technology attendees admitted that in preplanning for the test, they *identified* the backup tapes they would need for the exercise. They rotated those tapes to the off-premises storage location weeks before the test was scheduled. (In fact, to ensure they were not accidentally returned, they locked the boxes that held the "test" tapes.)

Then when the test took place, they retrieved the "preidentified" tapes and moved them to the computer backup site. They loaded the tapes from the box and ran a day's processing to verify they could recover and balance their applications. In fact, what they verified was that if you took all the data you used in running a day's processing on your computer, and loaded it onto a piece of iron that was similar to the iron in your computer center, then the backup site iron would come up with the same results as the iron in your computer center.

I asked why they took copies of the backup tapes they would need to bring to the backup computer center weeks before the test.

I asked why they did not use the procedure documented in the Disaster Recovery Plan, which usually was to:

■ Identify the most current generation of backup tapes from the tape library listing. (Leave all older-generation backup tapes in the off-premises storage location for protection.)
■ Retrieve those tapes and send them to the computer backup site.
■ Load system software backup tapes. Bring up systems software at backup site.
■ Load application backup tapes. Balance to a specific point in time.
■ Request all transactions be resubmitted to be able to balance to a point in time just before the crisis or disaster occurred.

The answers were always the same, that is, one of the following:

- They saved time by having the tapes prepared to travel.
- They could not be sure that the backup tapes they needed would be in the off-premises storage location. They had often found that the some of the tapes they needed were not even scheduled to be rotated to the off-premises location.
- They were also concerned that the tapes they needed might not be in synchronization with each other. The synchronization of backup tapes has always been a problem. That is why image coping has reduced the problems with data recovery.
- Another experience factor they would mention was that sometimes the tapes had been recalled in an effort to recover an application before the test and had not been returned to the off-premises location.

And in some cases, the answer was all of these.

With this stigma for the concept of the word "testing," we at Devlin made a concerted effort to get our clients to change the word to "exercising." We even suggested "to practice" or "to rehearse." We used the analogy that professional actors rehearse every day they have time, even though they are professionals. We also used the analogy that professional athletic teams practice every day during the season, even though they are professionals. (This became a joke with our clients because I was born and raised in Philadelphia. My clients asked me if the professional teams in Philadelphia ever took my advice and practiced, because it did not show on the field.)

We finally decided on the term "exercise." We used it with our clients. I used it at my seminars. Any one from Devlin who spoke at conferences around the world used "exercise." We still used the word "test" but it was clearly limited to validating a role, a procedure, a checklist. We did not want the stigma of "pass-fail" to cause our clients to limit the scope of their exercises out of fear that a major glitch would not be found by the limited "test."

Appendix 10A provides a comparison of the differences between "testing" and "exercising."

10.3 EXERCISE RESPONSIBILITIES OF THE CRISIS MANAGEMENT ADMINISTRATOR

Crisis Management Plan Administrators are responsible for developing, documenting, and testing the organization's CMP. They are also responsible for exercising and maintaining the CMP.

As part of the responsibility to exercise and maintain the plan, they are responsible for the scheduling, monitoring, and evaluating the CMP exercises.

10.3.1 Objectives of the Exercise

The exercise is designed to rehearse the members of the CMT, with the purpose of familiarizing the CMT members with the content and organization of the plan. It is designed to evaluate the clarity of the plan by having the members perform their assigned responsibilities. Most importantly, it will identify changes that are needed in the plan. Thus, an exercise is designed to:

- Rehearse the Crisis Management Team's plan
- Familiarize the CMT members with the content and organization of the plan
- Evaluate the clarity of the plan in defining how teams are to act
- Identify changes needed

10.3.2 Frequency of CMP Exercise

Organizations should plan to exercise the members of the CMT with a simulation exercise at least once a year, and preferably twice a year. If they can schedule two exercises a year, the CMP Administrator could use a disaster scenario in one exercise, and a nonphysical damage crisis in the other (i.e., a product or service crisis).

In addition to exercising the CMP team, they should conduct an exercise once a year for the Executive Management Team (EMT). After a couple exercises have been conducted and the members of the CMT feel comfortable with the process, it would be ideal to incorporate the EMT exercise into one of the exercises conducted for CMT members.

10.3.3 Other Responsibilities of the Crisis Management Plan Administrator

CMP administrators are also responsible for assisting the organization's business unit Business Resumption planners in performing their exercises. They can help by reviewing the results of the business unit's exercise. They can work with the business unit's planner to evaluate the exercise they performed. If they have the time, they can even participate in a couple business unit exercises each year.

A key responsibility is to serve as the "scorekeeper." Someone must ensure that each business unit in the organization is keeping its plan current. Also, to keep the business unit maintaining the plan, they need to exercise it a couple of times each year. The business unit, or the crisis management plan exercise requires preplanning. As part of the preplanning efforts, an Exercise Planning Form should be completed.

The Exercise Planning Form contains sections used to describe information involved in completing the exercise that include the type of exercise, the objectives of the exercise, the sections of the plan to be exercised, the scenario that will be used, and the criteria on which the exercise will be measured. A sample of the Exercise Planning Form can be found on Page 12.

10.4 STEPS USED IN PLANNING THE EXERCISE

There are a number of steps that should be taken before performing an exercise. The preplanning before you actually exercise the Crisis Management Team will allow you to manage the exercise and answer any questions raised by CMT members.

And why is this an issue? The simple answer is that when you have the senior management tied up performing an operation that they think will never be needed, and it is evident when they ask you questions that you have not thought through all aspects of the exercise, you are going to lose their attention and participation.

This results in a couple bad things. First, this exercise will not be valid because you lost their support and enthusiasm. Second, when you try to schedule your next exercise, most of the team members who participated in the first bad exercise will find some reason why they will not waste their time with this exercise. It could take the Crisis Management Team Administrator years to regain their support. Or it could mean that you will have to be replaced in order to regain their support.

The eight steps I recommend people use when planning the Crisis Management Team exercise are:

1. Decide on the *type of exercise* you will conduct.
2. Prepare the exercise scenario. Decide on the type of disaster or crisis will be used during the exercise. It could be "physical damage" (disaster) or nonphysical damage (crisis).
3. Complete the "Exercise Planning Form."
4. Schedule the exercise (date and time).
5. Evaluate the results of the exercise.
6. Prepare a written report of results.
7. Ensure the changes are made.
8. Maintain the "Exercise Matrix Schedule."

10.4.1 Decide on the Type of Disaster or Crisis

The first step is to determine whether the exercise will be a "Walk-Through" type exercise, a Simulation type exercise, or a Desk Check type exercise.

10.4.1.1 The Walk-Through Exercise

In this exercise, the CMP Administrator provides the participants with a scenario of the disaster from which they are to respond. The participants should be given time to read their section of the CMP, converse among themselves, plan their crisis management activities, and then present how they will respond.

The participants describe what they will do and how they will do it to the CMT Administrator and any other members of the Crisis Management Team who may be involved in the exercise.

10.4.1.2 The Simulation Exercise

In this exercise, the CMP Administrator provides the participants with a scenario of the disaster from which they are to respond. The participants should be given time to read their section of the CMP, converse among themselves, plan their crisis management activities, and then actually perform the activities in the CMP that pertain to the type of crisis presented in the scenario.

The participants travel to the CMT Command Center. There, they perform the crisis management activities using the procedures, checklists, and forms that have been documented in their section of the CMP.

During simulation exercises, CMT members are usually not permitted to return to their offices to retrieve copies of their CMP or other CMT resources.

This is the most effective of all the exercises because it verifies that the CMT members can perform their assigned responsibilities.

10.4.1.3 The Desk Check Validation Exercise

In this exercise, the CMP Administrator selects one or more elements of the CMP and confirms that they are still current and accurate. For example, the CMP Administrator might validate the CMT member personnel notification checklist by phoning members one evening to verify their non-business phone numbers (home or cell).

The CMP Administrator can perform this exercise with little or no participation on the part of CMT members.

10.4.2 Prepare the Scenario

Decide on which type of crisis you will exercise, that is, a physical disaster or a nonphysical crisis. Once the administrator has selected if it will be a disaster or a nonphysical crisis, he needs to develop the scenario.

As discussed in Chapter 1, nonphysical crises include:

■ A product issue, where a product does not work as promised (credibility), is injuring people (safety), has been tampered with); a market-shift (sudden change, or over a long period of time)
■ A negative public perception of your organization (your organization has a problem, and it appears it does not care about the problem)

- A financial problem (cash problem, fraud, or fuzzy accounting)
- An industrial relations problem (worker strike problem, employee lawsuits)
- An adverse international event (disaster at their location has jeopardized your product or service)
- Workplace violence (employees have been violently attacked while working on your organization's property)
- Executive succession problem (senior executive has died or been killed)

Chapter 1 also identified the following as disasters that the CMT should be prepared to manage:

- Acts of nature (e.g., earthquake, tornado, flood, etc.)
- Accidents (e.g., fire, leak, lengthy power outage, etc.)
- Intentional acts (e.g., bomb or arson)

Developing a strong scenario may be the most important part of a Crisis Management Plan exercise. When the members come together for the exercise, they will expect that the crisis they are being presented is something that could happen. In fact, I never presented a scenario that was not accompanied by a number of case studies. (In other words — provable.) If the scenario is weak, incomplete, or not specific, the members of the CMT may be confused and misinterpret elements of the exercise.

Was I ever challenged by an executive who felt the scenario was not realistic? The answer is yes. After it was done the first time, I never again entered into an exercise without a couple of case study examples that would justify the scenario.

For example, if the scenario I used was that of a fire, I always had the most recent example of a fire to an organization in the same industry, or an example of the most recent fire of an organization geographically located nearby your organization. If I failed to find any examples that fit those categories, I would use an example of the most recent fire somewhere in the country.

One of the worst things a CMP Administrator can do is to develop a scenario that cannot be justified. That is when you will likely have a member of the CMT team challenge it.

During many of my seminars, I have asked participants to develop a disaster scenario for an exercise of the CMP. Many of these scenarios were "far-out." When I would ask them to give me an example of an organization in which this scenario occurred, they would not have one.

Now "far-out, unusual scenarios" are fine — as long as you can provide an example of where this did happen to someone else.

A second major consideration when developing a scenario is to make it complete. The CMP Administrator must ensure there is at least one statement that requires each member of the CMT to use their section of the CMP. If you develop a scenario in which someone, or more than one member of the team, has nothing to do, you are going to receive some major criticism. They will want to know why they were there. Why did they waste a couple of hours that they could have used for something really important? They may even ask the CMP Administrator if they are not important enough in the CMP to receive, from the scenario, something to do.

10.4.2.1 Sample Exercise Scenario for a Disaster: Fire

A fire has occurred at 4:00 p.m., on Wednesday, December 14, at the XYZ Building. This is a nine-story building, with three floors of sub-basements:

- Sprinklers are located throughout the building, with the exception of the electrical rooms.
- The building is protected by an access control system, as well as by security guards.
- The building houses key business units of the organization.

Representatives from the Buildings department, the Security department, and executives from the affected business units have been at the scene and have set up an Emergency Operations Center (EOC) next to the fire department's command center.

Initial information obtained from the fire department personnel includes:

- The fire is "under control."
- The second and third floors have been gutted.
- The fire was "knocked down" on the fourth floor, which has been seriously damaged by flames and heat.
- The fifth through ninth floors have suffered smoke and soot damage.
- The first floor (B1) and B2 have suffered water damage from the fire-fighting water.
- It was mutually agreed by the Buildings department and the fire department that the building is not safe to perform a formal damage assessment.
- Although it was believed that all employees safely evacuated the building, there have apparently been a couple of injuries, because there have been reports of a couple of ambulances taking people to hospitals.
- Radio, television, and newspaper reporters are outside the building. They appear to be taking pictures and interviewing people.
- It appears the cause was arson, because a preliminary investigation suspects that fires were started in more than one location.

- In addition, the sprinklers failed.
  - An investigation will take place on the cause of the sprinkler failure.
- The EPA is sending a representative to check for hazardous substances.
- Received the following new information from fire department personnel:
  - Very little salvageable on the second, third, and fourth floors.
  - Equipment and records on the other floors are damaged, but may be salvageable after being cleaned.
  - The telephone system is not working.
  - Fire department personnel have indicated that less than 1 percent of the contents on the second and third floors are salvageable
  - Damage is extensive. It appears that there is a good possibility that it will require five to six months to repair.
- The affected business unit representatives, consulting with the Buildings department, have indicated that of the six business units located in the building, three are key business units and must be in operation immediately.
  - Key financial records were located in some of the business units damaged by the fire. These records are needed for the financial continuity of the organization.
  - One business unit contained blank officers checks to be used by the vice president in that department in case of emergency. These checks are usually locked up when not being used. One vice president indicated that a couple checks were given out today, and he is not sure if the file was relocked before the evacuation took place.

10.4.2.2 Use Checklist to Verify That the Scenario Is Complete

Crisis Management Team Member	Scenario Statement
Security	It appears the cause was arson because preliminary investigation suspects that fires were started in more than one location.
	In addition, the sprinklers failed. An investigation will take place on the cause of the sprinkler failure. (Were they tampered with?)
Facilities/Buildings	The second and third floors have been gutted. The fire was knocked down on the fourth floor, but it has been seriously damaged by flames and heat. The fifth through the ninth floors have suffered smoke and soot damage. The first floor, B1, B2, and B3 have suffered water damage from the fire-fighting water.

Crisis Management Team Member	Scenario Statement
Public Relations	Radio, television, and newspaper reporters are outside the building. They appear to be taking pictures and interviewing people.
Human Resources	Although it was believed that all employees safely evacuated the building, there have apparently been a couple of injuries, because there have been reports of a couple of ambulances taking people to hospitals.
Finance/Treasury	Key financial records were located in some of the business units damaged by the fire. These records are needed for the financial continuity of the organization. One business unit contained blank officers checks to be used by the Vice President in that department in case of emergency. These checks are usually locked up when not being used. One Vice President indicated that a couple of checks were given out today, and he is not sure if the file was relocked before the evacuation took place.
Procurement/ Purchasing	Very little salvageable on the second, third, and fourth floors. Equipment and records on the other floors are damaged, but may be salvageable after being cleaned.
Insurance/ Risk Management	Equipment on the other floors is damaged, but may be salvageable after being cleaned. Fire department personnel have indicated that less than 1 percent of the contents on the second and third floors is salvageable. Damage is extensive. It appears that there is a good possibility that it will require five to six months to repair. What is covered?
Legal Transportation/ Administration	
Information Technology/ Communications	The telephone system is not working.

It appears that all CMT members have something to work on, except the Legal department and the Transportation/Administration department:

■ By the very fact that the scenario covers the fact that key business units have been affected, and that their operations may have been interrupted, the Legal department must determine if there are contractual situations that should be addressed. In addition, because the scenario mentions damage to the equipment, the Legal department may need to review vendor contracts to resolve any conflicts.

■ The same situation exists with the Transportation/Administrative member of the CMT. Because the scenario points out that key business units have been affected, and that their operations may have been interrupted, what support will be required to transport people, equipment, supplies, etc., to alternate operating locations?

10.4.3 Complete the "Exercise Planning Form"

The "Exercise Planning Form" contains sections that are used to describe information involved in completed that include the type of exercise, the objectives of the exercise, the sections of the plan to be exercised, the scenario that will be used, and the criteria on which the exercise will be measured. For example:

Type of Exercise

Walk-Through Exercise _____

Simulation Exercise_____

Desk Check Validation Exercise_____

Objectives of the Exercise: (Identify the purpose for the exercise)

_____

_____

_____

_____

_____

Exercise Scenario: (Describe the type of incident that has occurred. Also provide an initial assessment of damage)

_____

_____

_____

_____

_____

Measurement Criteria: (Identify the measurement criteria that will be used to evaluate the exercise results)

_____

_____

_____

_____

_____

Results of the Exercise: (Document the results of the exercise)

_____

_____

_____

_____

_____

10.4.4 Schedule the Exercise

When dealing with senior executives of the organization, it is important to recognize that the time of year could make it difficult for someone to participate. Even the day of the week, or the time of day, enters into the equation. The CMP Administrator must take this into consideration when planning the day, week, and month for the exercise.

10.4.4.1 Time of Year

You will probably hear that there is really no good time to schedule a two- to three-hour block of time for the executives to participate in an exercise. While that is generally true, there are windows where they can break free and participate.

The end of year is *not* a good time. The month immediately following your end of year is usually busy, and *not* a good time. (When referring to end of year, I am referring to your organization's end of year, not necessarily the calendar end of year.)

When is it considered a good time? I have found that the executives who are members of the CMT find more time available in November and December. Perhaps the time around the holidays is slower; perhaps they are in a better mood. At any rate, many of my experiences assisting clients with their CMT exercises have occurred in the November, early December timeframe.

10.4.4.2 Day of the Week

I have found that a Monday or a Friday is best. I have found that very few organizations that I have helped conduct an exercise choose Tuesday, Wednesday, or Thursday.

Depending on the time of year (as I mentioned above, November or early December), Fridays have always resulted in more members participating. (It seems that Mondays are less well attended because there were incidents that occurred over the weekend that require the executives' immediate attention on Monday morning.)

10.4.4.3 Time of Day

I have found that early in the morning is the best time to schedule the CMT exercise. If you wait until the afternoon, many unexpected events might have occurred during the morning that will prevent some CMT members from participating. In addition, some of the members who can attend may be too preoccupied with problems that occurred earlier in the day to be effective, or even interested.

10.4.4.4 Schedule: Preannounced or Unannounced

Should you plan the exercise based on the member's availability, or schedule an unannounced exercise? I have often been asked this question. I believe the question comes from the fact that I suggest unannounced exercises for the IT department and for the business units.

I always suggest that all CMT exercises be scheduled for the first three years, and I do this for a number of reasons:

- You want to be assured that as many members as possible participate. One of the main objectives of the exercise is to familiarize the executives with their part of the CMT, and familiarize them with the other members' roles.
- Because you are planning on conducting two exercises each year, the first using a disaster scenario and the second using a nonphysical crisis, you would like the members to obtain as much information on the challenges the team will experience and "how" the members will handle those challenges during the exercise.

If limited to only one exercise each year, I would suggest that you wait for at least five years before attempting an unannounced CMT exercise (Year 1, a disaster exercise; Year 2, a nonphysical crisis exercise; Year 3, a disaster exercise; Year 4, a nonphysical crisis exercise; and Year 5, either a disaster exercise or a nonphysical crisis exercise). At this point you may want to try an unscheduled, unannounced exercise.

What will you learn from an unannounced exercise? You certainly will learn who can participate and who cannot. Also, you will learn that some of the alternates will have to be used because the primary is not available. Finally, you will learn that some of the alternates cannot perform all of the actions required of the CMT.

10.4.5 Evaluate the Results

After the exercise is finished, evaluate the results. Were the objectives measurable?

One objective is to find out if the members of the team know what to do. This can be measured by watching the participants during the exercise. If a participant is not participating, the administrator can ask if they can help.

> In one exercise I participated in, I found there was one participant who appeared confused. In checking with that person, I found out that he had not participated in the earlier exercise. He was promoted and moved into this position recently. This person did not really understand what was expected of him.
>
> This gave us the chance first to train the individual on what is expected of them during the exercise. Basically, it was on-the-job training.
>
> Then we looked at the probability that by the next exercise, there would be more participants who were new to the process. So, in anticipation of this, we set up a plan to train them on their role — while the exercise was taking place.

Objective: Evaluate the clarity of the plan in defining how teams are to act.

- Did they know what to do?
- Did they know how to do it?
- Were the plan procedures available?
- Were they correct, or accurate?
- Were they current, not old and out-of-date?

Objective: Which CMP procedures, which checklists, and which forms *did work*? Which CMP procedures, which checklists, and which forms *did not work*?

- Was it a people problem?
- Was it a strategy problem?
- Was it a plan documentation problem?

10.4.6 Prepare a Written Report of Results

The Exercise Planning Form provides a section for measuring the performance of the CMT Team. This will be the basis for the report that will be prepared at the conclusion of the exercise. The report will identify "what" went right and "what" went wrong.

The written report will contain information determined by the members of the CMT themselves during their self-critique.

10.4.7 Ensure the Changes Are Made

During the exercise, the CMT members will learn that the CMP, as written, does not contain all the information, or resources, they would need to carry out their CMT responsibilities.

During the critique of the exercise, they should identify any information, or resources, they will want added to their section of the CMP.

The BCP Administrator should make notes on the need to get back to the CMT members who want additions or changes. Once the CMT member gathers the information needed to change the CMP, the Administrator should either make the changes or ensure that the CMT members have made the changes. The responsibility of *who* makes the changes depends on who has access to the CMP. Is it documented electronically in a software package? If the answer is yes to the software package, does everyone on the CMT have access to make changes to the CMP?

Who has responsibility to "ensure the changes are made"? The ultimate responsibility should rest with the Crisis Management Plan Administrator.

10.4.8 Update the Exercise Performance Matrix

The "Exercise Performance Matrix" is an excellent scheduler for future exercises, and also a scorecard of past exercises. (Appendix 10.02 is an example of a blank Exercise Performance Matrix.)

The Exercise Performance Matrix identifies when exercises are scheduled and the date the exercise was performed. It identifies each CMT member. The matrix provides a tool that quickly identifies which members of the CMT have been participating in the exercises (and are ready to perform their responsibilities) and which members of the CMT have not been participating in the exercises (and may not be ready to perform their responsibilities.) As you can see in Appendix 10.02, the sample matrix allows two exercises per page.

In planning the exercises for the year, complete the "Scheduled Date" for the exercise. When working with my clients, I would assist them in selecting two dates for the next year. I recommend that the CMT be exercises two times each year. This provides the CMT administrator with an opportunity to:

Use the training exercise to ensure the CMT members know what to do when a crisis strikes. (Remember: the IT people usually perform some type of exercise four times per year.)

Use the training exercise to train new members (recently promoted individuals) of the CMT that have not participating in any prior exercises.

Based on information learned from the members of the CMT, we might avoid certain times of the year because they created a problem for some CMT members. Appendix 10C contains completed information on the scheduled dates for Exercise 1 and Exercise 2 for the year 2004. And Appendix 10D contains completed information for the scheduled dates for Exercise 1 and Exercise 2 for the next year — 2005.

Can you develop your own matrix rather than using the sample? The obvious answer is yes. The example used here goes back several years yet I remain very comfortable with it. I will use it to explain the value of using a matrix. But should you determine that there is a better format, by all means, use your own.

Following an exercise, the "Date Performed" section of the matrix should be completed with information as to which team members participated (use date of exercise) and which team members were unable to participate (use "Didn't Participate"). Appendix 10.05 shows that Legal and Procurement/ Purchasing were unable to participate in the first exercise of 2004.

When sending a memo to all CMT members announcing the date of the next exercise, it would be a good idea to attach a copy of the most recent matrix (same as Appendix 10.05).

Following the second exercise of the year, the matrix should be completed with information as to which team members participated (use date of exercise) and which team members were unable to participate (use "Didn't Participate"). Appendix 10.08 shows that Human Resources and Legal were unable to participate in the second exercise of 2004.

After completing the matrix with information from the second exercise, you are now in a position to determine who has, and who has not been participating in the scheduled exercises:

- If the team members *are participating*, there is some evidence to conclude that they would be able to perform adequately during an actual crisis.
- On the other hand, if some team members *are not participating* in every exercise, there is a gap in their training.

Now what do you do with this "Exercise Matrix"? First of all, it is your "scorecard." With just a quick glance at a couple of pages (which could total four exercises), you can tell if any of the team members are lax in their role on the CMT. It is a precrisis warning for the CMT. A member of the team, or possibly more than one member, has failed to participate in some, or all, of the four exercises. (Check Appendices 10.06 and 10.07, and identify the members of the CMT who did not participate in the three scheduled exercises.)

What can you quickly tell from looking at these two appendices? The answer is that the Legal member of the CMT has not participated in any of the exercises.

In fact, if you want to look at Appendix 10.08, you will see that the Legal member of the CMT did not participate in the two exercises in 2003. That totals to the last five exercises that the Legal member was not present.

Then the question that pops up is: What happens when a disaster or nonphysical crisis occurs? Will this CMT member, or members, know what to do and how to do it?

If you have conducted four exercises (I will assume at least two years to conduct them, possibly four years), and this member, or members, has not participated in some, or all, of the exercises, there is a good possibility that their documented section of the CMP has not changed during that period of time. Based on an organization in which I assisted in the exercise of their CMP every other year, I found that there were a number of changes that had taken place between the exercises.

It should be updated and included with the report of results of each exercise. This will enable members who are not participating to realize that a record of nonparticipation is being made and distributed to:

- All members of the Crisis Management Team
- All members of the Executive Management Team (see Chapter 5)
- Any auditors (internal or external), or regulatory agency officials who are auditing the Crisis Management Plan

10.5 PERFORMING AN EXERCISE

When the CMT members assemble, the CMP Administrator should explain the purpose for the exercise and the procedures to be followed during the exercise.

10.5.1 Give Instructions to Exercise Participants

- Read the scenario. Are there any questions regarding the scenario?
- Use your plan to carry out your CMT responsibilities.
- Please call contacts. Verify that:
  - The phone numbers are correct.
  - The contact called would be able to provide your organization with the support or resources needed.
  - You are supposed to interface with regulatory authorities.
- Carry out your team's assigned responsibilities:
  - If you are supposed to interface with local or regulatory authorities, contact them to verify how you would interface in this scenario.
  - Note any areas of the plan that are incorrect or incomplete.
  - Log all discrepancies in the plan.
  - Record the success or failure of steps taken from the documentation in the plan.
- At the conclusion of the exercise, ask yourselves:
  - Is your plan documentation adequate?
  - Do the procedures and checklists provide sufficient information to carry out your responsibilities?
  - What needs to be changed?
  - What needs to be added?
- We will fix them following the exercise.
- At a given time, we will review the actions taken by the members of the CMT. Each team will be given five minutes to present its activities to the rest of the CMT members.

10.6 VALUE OF EXERCISE

Exercising a plan can pay significant dividends for an organization. The following provides examples of organizations that have benefited from their organization's exercises prior to experiencing the disaster.

The First Interstate Bank, Los Angeles, California (May 4, 1988). The First Interstate Bank's headquarters building, located in Los Angeles, suffered a serious fire in 1988. Five floors were destroyed by the fire. As pointed out in *a Los Angeles Times* article just after the fire, 18 months before the fire occurred, the bank developed a sophisticated company-wide Business Resumption Plan. After implementing the various elements of the plan, the BRP professionals responsible for the plan first tested and then exercised the various elements of the plan.

In fact, less than a month before the fire occurred (April 14), the bank went through a practice drill. While the scenario used in the exercise was an earthquake, the actions taken were similar to the actions taken during the fire. This lead William E.B. Siart, the bank's CEO to comment during a news briefing, "That was the best $15 million we ever spent."

Penn Mutual Life Ins., Philadelphia, Pennsylvania (May 30, 1989). The Penn Mutual Insurance building located in Philadelphia suffered a serious fire in April 1989. The fire started in a records storage room on the ninth floor of the 20-story building containing reams of computer printouts and files. The room was "one-third the size of a football field," (a 172,000-square-foot room). Because the room was windowless, it trapped the intense heat and smoke inside the room. Firefighters could not enter the door to the room (only one door) due to the intense heat generated by the thousands of boxes of records stored there. To extinguish the fire, firefighters used jackhammers to break holes into the ceiling (floor of the tenth floor) so they could send water into the area. An estimated four million gallons of water was used to put out the fire.

The lesson learned from this serious fire incident was that the Penn Mutual Information Systems department had documented a Disaster Recovery Plan. They also had contracted for a computer backup site (to resume processing critical applications). The third lesson was that they tested *and* exercised their plan. Penn Mutual's policy was to exercise its plan regularly, at least twice a year.

In fact, two weeks before the fire, Penn Mutual exercised its Disaster Recovery Plan by moving to their computer "hotsite."

This drill was credited with the successful recovery of the critical applications in less than 12 hours. (From "Testing Pays Off For Penn Mutual," *Disaster Recovery Journal,* July/Aug./Sept. 1989.)

Meridian Bank, Philadelphia, Pennsylvania (February 23, 1991). Meridian Bank, of Reading, had an excellent Business Continuity Plan. Part of the BCP was the Crisis Management Plan. Meridian preferred to call this crisis management team their Business Resumption Support Team (BRST). The BRST included actions to be activated by Meridian Properties, Security, Risk Management, Media Relations, Human Resources, Legal, Communications, Purchasing, Controllers, Data Processing (Coordinator), PC Support Services, and Hardware Support Services.

In November 1990, as part of their annual training, they scheduled an exercise of their crisis management executive team, the BRST. They used a fire as the scenario for the exercise. It gave the team a chance to review the current status of the elements of the CMP/BRST.

Three months after the exercise, they had the real thing. On February 23, 1991, a fire started in a 38-story office building in downtown Philadelphia. The fire was reported shortly after 8:00 p.m. and burned out of control for nearly 19 hours, gutting eight floors of the high-rise building. The fire was declared "under control" at 3:01 p.m. on Sunday. Meridian Bank leased space on six of the 38 floors. The bank had around 300 employees that work in the building.

Fortunately, the fire occurred on a Saturday, and no bank employees were killed or injured. (Unfortunately, three firefighters were killed when they ran out of air while checking the upper floors for people who might have been trapped in the building. There were some cleaning people working in the building.)

"They mobilized their BRST, which had fortuitously gone through … (an exercise)… of a mock blaze only a few months earlier. We figured that if we had an exposure, it would be a fire," said Ken Maher, Vice President, Corporate Risk Management & Insurance. So when Maher declared a disaster, the 25-member team … knew exactly what to do.

Another quote was from the EVP of Meridian Properties, "Meridian Bank's business resumption plan is an on-going plan the company initiated two years ago. It outlines how to get back in operation when an emergency strikes. The team smoothly dispersed 300 employees to Meridian Bancorp facilities throughout Philadelphia."

By Tuesday, most of the employees were on-line again.

"Because we had a team and a tested plan in place, it was a relatively smooth transition to a workable environment."

"The question is not whether you can afford to plan, the question is whether you can afford not to plan. The fire proved that planning has to be part of every organization. It's far easier to respond to a loss if you've done some planning than try to handle a crisis in crisis situation," Maher said. (From *Disaster Contingency Journal*, July/August 1991.)

Kemper Financial, Chicago, Illinois (April 13, 1992). In April 1992, river water poured through an aging tunnel system beneath a 12-square-block area of Chicago's Loop, paralyzing the downtown area. According to *Chicago Resource* magazine, 229 buildings and 7671 business tenants were affected. The hole developed in a branch of the tunnel beneath the Chicago River. A large whirlpool formed. An estimated 250 million gallons of river water rushed through car-size hole flooding basements in the Loop at a rate of two feet per hour. Power was cut off to the area at 10:48 a.m. CDT and as much as 30 feet of water flowed into skyscraper basements.

Kemper Financial, one of the largest asset managers in the U.S., was obliged to shut down its computer processors and evacuate its data center that Monday morning. Fortunately, Kemper confronted the flood with a comprehensive and fully tested and exercised disaster recovery plan. As part of the plan, Kemper's data center in Kansas City had been designated to be the computer backup site in case operations in Chicago were disrupted.

To ensure that Kansas City would work, the staffs in facilities management, technical support, operations and programming had tested and exercised the plans and therefore were prepared for the measures needed to quickly bring up production in Kansas City. As a result of their preparations for a crisis, Kemper was back in business by the start of the trading day on Wednesday, less than 48 hours after its main DP facilities were closed.

(From "Subterranean Swirl Scrambles Chicago Data Centers," *Enterprise Systems Journal,* September 1992.)

According to the *Network World* newspaper (April 20, 1992), eighteen (18) companies went to Comdisco's hotsite. Seven (7) companies went to other "hotsites"

Business units moved LAN equipment to temporary locations. One month after a service-tunnel flood interrupted business in the downtown area, some establishments remained closed, and officials said some will never reopen. (From *USA Today,* May 13, 1992.)

Meridian Bank's Regional location in the Corporate Plaza, Allentown, Pennsylvania (February 23, 1994). A sinkhole, 20 feet deep and 40 feet wide, developed overnight. By 5:00 a.m., water was shooting from the street near the sinkhole, and authorities were rushing to evacuate the area. Over the next few hours, as the Corporate Plaza building, a seven-story building, listed into the hole, glass and debris tumbled to the street, the upper floors on the northwest corner partially collapsed. Meridian Bank's regional location was located across the street from the Corporate Plaza. The building was temporarily closed because there was a danger the sinkhole was moving toward the Meridian building.

The bank activated its BRP and resumed operations in other locations preidentified in the Business Resumption Plan. The BRP worked extremely well. Executives attribute their success to the fact that the Crisis Management Team had exercised its plan on November 14, 1993, about three months before the crisis. The scenario for the exercise was that of a bomb, similar to the bombing of the World Trade Center. The executives simulated the actions they would take to get the bank's critical operations back in business quickly, based on the scenario for the exercise.

One interesting lesson we learned from this exercise was that two of the members of the crisis management/BRST team were new. They had not been involved in any prior exercises. So again it provided us another opportunity to help train key executives in what they are expected to do when their BRST is activated. They obviously benefited from the exercise because they had no problems handling their responsibilities during the sinkhole crisis.

10.7 LESSONS FROM OTHER ORGANIZATIONS' EXPERIENCES

There have been instances where, in attempting to exercise a plan, an organization has ended up "creating a disaster," or made the exercise scenario "too threatening." The person responsible for developing the exercise scenario should avoid creating a disaster.

10.7.1 Avoid Creating a Disaster

The Federal Reserve Bank of San Francisco, California. An article in the *Information Weekly* newspaper on April 9, 1992, pointed out that an exercise could result in a disaster, rather than recover from one. The article indicated the Federal Reserve Bank in San Francisco wanted to exercise its computer Disaster Recovery Plan.

"They planned on using the Federal Reserve's computer in Los Angeles for the exercise. Unfortunately, this exercise resulted in the computer in Los Angeles being knocked off-line for 12 hours, leaving thousands of consumers in California and Arizona stranded without automatic payroll deposits.

"There were no specific figures regarding the funds affected, but according to the Information Weekly newspaper, about $2 billion was processed per day through its LA office. Customers were assured by the banks affected that they would be covered for any over draft charges. About 15 banking institutions were affected. The Federal Reserve blamed human error."

City of Ventura, California. An article in the *Philadelphia Inquirer* on January 31, 2000, reported that the City of Ventura (California) wanted to test a siren system that would warn residents of a failure at a dam near Ventura in January 2000.

"To prepare residents for the exercise, radio and newspaper announcements of the exercise were placed in local newspapers for a week prior to the test.

"When the test started, a loudspeaker was used in the area to warn the residents. The loudspeaker warning was prefaced with the statement 'This is a test,' and followed with 'This is an emergency. Head for high ground. You have one hour.'

Despite the radio and newspaper announcements of the exercise placed in local newspapers for a week prior to the test, and the 'This is a test' announcement from the loudspeaker, some residents panicked, rushing for higher ground, trampling fences and jamming streets. Emergency telephone lines were jammed with anxious callers, and police and sheriffs deputies were called out to help calm the panic."

10.7.2 Do Not Make the Scenario Too Threatening

Memorial Hospital, Martinsville, Virginia. The hospital apparently wanted to test elements of their Security section of the Business Continuity Plan. They decided to use an unannounced exercise.

An article in *USA Today's* March 23, 1996, edition said, "Five masked men burst into the emergency room waving guns and demanding drugs. Real, but unloaded, guns were pointed at the nurses during the 5-minute drill, which was arranged by the hospital's security staff. Several emergency room nurses and patients badly shaken. One emergency room physician said at least two patients were put in danger — a boy suffering an asthma attack and an elderly patient whose heart started racing. The exercise resulted in a lawyer being hired by three of the nurses. The lawyer said, 'I don't think you can point a gun at someone's head and get away with it.'"

TCI Cablevision; Tulsa, Oklahoma: Similar to the Memorial Hospital test of their Security element of the Business Continuity Plan, this cable company decided to use an unannounced exercise. *The New York Times* reported in the February 17, 1997, edition, "During an after-hours meeting on security, two strangers burst into the cable company's lobby, aiming guns at terrified employees and demanding money. Some of the 25 workers were shaken and physically ill as the robbers fled with the cash.

"Managers then revealed the break-in was a fake; the robbers were actors. The purpose, according to a memo three days after, was 'to prepare the possible victims to be alert and to take action to help make them a less desirable target should a real robbery occur.'

"The unfortunate result of the exercise was that five women at the simulated robbery quit their jobs and sued the company, saying the faked event amounted to a vicious assault and outrageous conduct. In depositions among the 6 volumes of documents in the case: one woman said she couldn't sleep and her hair fell out. Another said she cried a lot and was depressed, and a third said she began vomiting the day she returned to work. Each seeks in excess of $10,000 in damages from the Englewood, CO-based Tele-Communications Inc.; its Tulsa subsidiary, and Elite Protective and Security Services Inc., contracted to run the seminar."

10.7.3 Determine if Your Plan Will Work or Be in Conflict with Public Sector Plans

There is a need to coordinate public and private sector plans. If there is no coordination before the crisis strikes, organizations oftentimes find that these plans will conflict with one another. How can we determine if the plans conflict?

1. Contact public officials to find out how your plans will work together.
2. Run a joint exercise with the private and public sector participating together. That is when you will find where the plans will conflict.

Pennzoil Products Co., Rouseville, Pennsylvania. Pennzoil experienced an explosion at its oil refinery in Rouseville, Pennsylvania, in April 1995. Seventeen storage tanks, including four new ones not yet in service, were destroyed or severely damaged.

Pennzoil implemented the incident command system (ICS) at its Emergency Operations Center, with police and fire department and emergency management personnel. They accounted for all workers in the refinery and removed the injured to the Northwest Medical Center in Oil City, Pennsylvania. Five employees were killed.

Fortunately, the day before, area fire departments had participated in the refinery's annual fire drill, which included an LPG gas fire simulation. (From *USA Today,* April 16, 1995.)

Three Mile Island — Nuclear Drill, Harrisburg, Pennsylvania. The owner of the Three Mile Island nuclear plant agreed to pay $210,000 in fines proposed by the NRC for weaknesses in operations and management oversights that need attention. One of the problems uncovered could hamper water pumps used to cool the reactor in the event of an emergency. Workers erred by trying to economize on safety costs by not properly evaluating equipment. During a safety drill, plant managers performed so poorly at recognizing serious danger signs that the exercise had to be repeated. (From *Philadelphia Inquirer*, October 10, 1997.)

Seton Hall University, South Orange, New Jersey (2000). The state fire code governing dormitories requires a multitude of fire-safety devices, including twice-yearly drills and various alert systems.

"After a fire in the University's dormitory (Boland Hall) that killed 3 and injured 62, Seton Hall University officials acknowledged they have not held any fire drills at Boland year since September, 2000. Why? Because false alarms provided enough practice, said a Seton Hall spokeswoman. "There were no called fire drills because we were evacuating students at a rate of more than two times a week with false alarms," she said.

But because students experienced 18 false alarms since September of 1999 — most simply rolled over and went back to sleep. The students had become accustomed to ignoring the alarms." (From *Newark Star Ledger*, January 20, 2000; *USA Today*, January 20, 2000.)

The Exxon Valdez, Alaska (March 1989). One crisis that provides many lessons that we can learn from is the Exxon Valdez oil spill of 1989.

Exxon developed and documented a contingency plan. When the original contingency plan was documented, the worst-case premise was that a 140,000-barrel tanker would have an oil spill. Reviews of the plan did not revise the potential size of the spill, even though tankers in the late 1980s carried 1 million barrels, not 140,000 barrels. Exxon's Contingency Plan's worst-case scenario was no longer viable.

Lesson: The important lesson here is that an event can occur that far exceeds the planning horizons of those individuals who create the response plan.

Test/Exercise: Emergency drills were held periodically by the principal organizations involved in the Alaska oil spill; but according to the reports from the State of Alaska, the industry exercises were not considered successful.

Training was sometimes not realistic; drills were held in the Valdez harbor area and operational supervisors were not exercised.

Equipment and emergency response groups were not adequately prepared for large-scale oil spills. When dealing with emergency preparedness for large-scale oil spill accidents, tough, skeptical, continuous exercises are required.

Coordinating the Plan Actions: According to Colonel Ed Badolato, U.S. Marine Corps (Retired), each of the major players in the shipment of Alaskan oil had its own contingency plan. There were at least five organizations that had plans to deal with the oil spill:

> Alyeska (the pipeline company that runs oil the 800 miles from Prudhoe to Valdez and onto the ships) plan
> The captain of the port's plan
> The national contingency plan
> The regional contingency plans
> The Alaska Regional Response Program.

According to Colonel Badolato, "In general, each of the plans ignored those of the other players."

"This situation is not unique. It reinforces the importance of having a strong relationship in place before a crisis strikes between the Private and Public Sectors. If we expect them to work together on resolving the crisis, they have to on the same page when it comes to identifying whose responsibility is it. Had the Alyeska people, the Captain of the Port's people, the National contingency plan people, the Regional contingency plan people, and the Alaska Regional Response people come together during an exercise or test of the plans, the communications and control problems that led to this situation might have been uncovered.

A sudden crisis causes ad hoc responses and a costly shakedown period to develop working relationships. Experts, people who have already been in a serious crisis, recommend that roles should be worked out through training exercises ahead of time. Crisis management teams must not be groups of individuals working at cross purposes. In a crisis situation, operational need, politics, and egos are difficult to balance; the Alaskan situation has been a prime example." (From *Learning from the Exxon Valdez*, Colonel Ed Badolato, U.S. Marine Corps [Retired].)

Appendix 10

Comparison of Terms
Testing – Versus - Exercising

● Testing

- ◆ Verifies that the recovery procedures "work"

- ◆ Verifies that the checklists are "accurate"

- ◆ Identifies any omissions

- ◆ Identifies if personnel are prepared

● Exercising

- ◆ Verifies that the recovery procedures are "current"

- ◆ Verifies that the checklists are "current"

- ◆ Identifies that the strategies "still meet the business objectives"

- ◆ Serves as a training resource

Appendix – 10.01

© Copyright Edward S. Devlin & Associates. 2005. All Rights Reserved. (610) 429-9029. esjdevlin@aol.com

Crisis Management Team

Exercise Matrix

Exercise Schedule & Performance Matrix Form

Section #	Team Responsibilities, Procedures, Checklists	Annual Exercises Scheduled	Exercise 1 Scheduled Date	Date Performed	Exercise 2 Scheduled Date	Date Performed

Appendix – 10.02

Crisis Management Team

Exercise Matrix - 2004

Exercise Schedule & Performance Matrix Form

Section #	Team Responsibilities, Procedures, Checklists	Annual Exercises Scheduled	Exercise 1 Scheduled Date	Date Performed	Exercise 2 Scheduled Date	Date Performed
300.01	Crisis Management Team Alert	2	03/09/04		11/19/04	
300.05	Executive Management Team Alert	1	03/09/04		No Schedule	
300	C. M.T. Command Center Activation	2	06/04/04		12/03/04	
310.10	Human Resources	2	06/04/04		12/03/04	
310.15	Buildings/Facilities Management	2	06/04/04		12/03/04	
310.20	Security	2	06/04/04		12/03/04	
310.25	Legal	2	06/04/04		12/03/04	
310.30	Communications	2	06/04/04		12/03/04	
310.35	P. R./Corporate Communications	2	06/04/04		12/03/04	
310.40	Transportation/Administration	2	06/04/04		12/03/04	
310.45	Procurement/Purchasing	2	06/04/04		12/03/04	
310.50	Finance	2	06/04/04		12/03/04	
310.55	Audit	2	06/04/04		12/03/04	
310.60	Risk Management/Insurance	2	06/04/04		12/03/04	

Appendix – 10.03

Crisis Management Team

Exercise Matrix - 2005

Exercise Schedule & Performance Matrix Form

Section #	Team Responsibilities, Procedures, Checklists	Annual Exercises Scheduled	Exercise 1 Scheduled Date	Date Performed	Exercise 2 Scheduled Date	Date Performed
300.01	Crisis Management Team Alert	2	03/09/05		11/15/05	
300.05	Executive Management Team Alert	1	03/09/05		No Schedule	
300	C. M.T. Command Center Activation	2	06/04/05		12/09/05	
310.10	Human Resources	2	06/10/05		12/09/05	
310.15	Buildings/Facilities Management	2	06/10/05		12/09/05	
310.20	Security	2	06/10/05		12/09/05	
310.25	Legal	2	06/10/05		12/09/05	
310.30	Communications	2	06/10/05		12/09/05	
310.35	P. R./Corporate Communications	2	06/10/05		12/09/05	
310.40	Transportation/Administration	2	06/10/05		12/09/05	
310.45	Procurement/Purchasing	2	06/10/05		12/09/05	
310.50	Finance	2	06/10/05		12/09/05	
310.55	Audit	2	06/10/05		12/09/05	
310.60	Risk Management/Insurance	2	06/10/05		12/09/05	

Appendix – 10.04

Crisis Management Team

Exercise Matrix - 2004

Exercise Schedule & Performance Matrix Form

Section #	Team Responsibilities, Procedures, Checklists	Annual Exercises Scheduled	Exercise 1 Scheduled Date	Date Performed	Exercise 2 Scheduled Date	Date Performed
300.01	Crisis Management Team Alert	2	03/09/04	03/09/04	11/19/04	
300.05	Executive Management Team Alert	1	03/09/04	03-09-04	No Schedule	
300	C. M.T. Command Center Activation	2	06/04/04	06/04/04	12/03/04	
310.10	Human Resources	2	06/04/04	06/04/04	12/03/04	
310.15	Buildings/Facilities Management	2	06/04/04	06/04/04	12/03/04	
310.20	Security	2	06/04/04	06/04/04	12/03/04	
310.25	Legal	2	06/04/04	Didn't Participate	12/03/04	
310.30	Communications	2	06/04/04	06/04/04	12/03/04	
310.35	P. R./Corporate Communications	2	06/04/04	06/04/04	12/03/04	
310.40	Transportation/Administration	2	06/04/04	06/04/04	12/03/04	
310.45	Procurement/Purchasing	2	06/04/04	Didn't Participate	12/03/04	
310.50	Finance	2	06/04/04	06/04/04	12/03/04	
310.55	Audit	2	06/04/04	06/04/04	12/03/04	
310.60	Risk Management/Insurance	2	06/04/04	06/04/04	12/03/04	

Appendix – 10.05

Crisis Management Team

Exercise Matrix - 2004

			Exercise Schedule & Performance Matrix Form			
Section #	Team Responsibilities, Procedures, Checklists	Annual Exercises Scheduled	Exercise 1 Scheduled Date	Date Performed	Exercise 2 Scheduled Date	Date Performed
300.01	Crisis Management Team Alert	2	03/09/04	03/09/04	11/19/04	11/19/04
300.05	Executive Management Team Alert	1	03/09/04	03-09-04	No Schedule	No Schedule
300	C. M.T. Command Center Activation	2	06/04/04	06/04/04	12/03/04	12/03/04
310.10	Human Resources	2	06/04/04	06/04/04	12/03/04	Didn't Participate
310.15	Buildings/Facilities Management	2	06/04/04	06/04/04	12/03/04	12/03/04
310.20	Security	2	06/04/04	06/04/04	12/03/04	12/03/04
310.25	Legal	2	06/04/04	Didn't Participate	12/03/04	Didn't Participate
310.30	Communications	2	06/04/04	06/04/04	12/03/04	12/03/04
310.35	P. R./Corporate Communications	2	06/04/04	06/04/04	12/03/04	12/03/04
310.40	Transportation/Administration	2	06/04/04	06/04/04	12/03/04	12/03/04
310.45	Procurement/Purchasing	2	06/04/04	Didn't Participate	12/03/04	12/03/04
310.50	Finance	2	06/04/04	06/04/04	12/03/04	12/03/04
310.55	Audit	2	06/04/04	06/04/04	12/03/04	12/03/04
310.60	Risk Management/Insurance	2	06/04/04	06/04/04	12/03/04	12/03/04

Crisis Management Team
Exercise Matrix - 2005

Exercise Schedule & Performance Matrix Form

Section #	Team Responsibilities, Procedures, Checklists	Annual Exercises Scheduled	Exercise 1 Scheduled Date	Date Performed	Exercise 2 Scheduled Date	Date Performed
300.01	Crisis Management Team Alert	2	03/09/05	03/09/05	11/15/05	
300.05	Executive Management Team Alert	1	03/09/05	03-09-05	No Schedule	
300	C. M.T. Command Center Activation	2	06/04/05	06/04/05	12/09/05	
310.10	Human Resources	2	06/10/05	06/10/05	12/09/05	
310.15	Buildings/Facilities Management	2	06/10/05	06/10/05	12/09/05	
310.20	Security	2	06/10/05	06/10/05	12/09/05	
310.25	Legal	2	06/10/05	Didn't Participate	12/09/05	
310.30	Communications	2	06/10/05	06/10/05	12/09/05	
310.35	P. R./Corporate Communications	2	06/10/05	06/10/05	12/09/05	
310.40	Transportation/Administration	2	06/10/05	Didn't Participate	12/09/05	
310.45	Procurement/Purchasing	2	06/10/05	Didn't Participate	12/09/05	
310.50	Finance	2	06/10/05	06/10/05	12/09/05	
310.55	Audit	2	06/10/05	Didn't Participate	12/09/05	
310.60	Risk Management/Insurance	2	06/10/05	06/10/05	12/09/05	

Appendix – 10.07

Crisis Management Team

Exercise Matrix - 2003

			Exercise Schedule & Performance Matrix Form			
Section #	Team Responsibilities, Procedures, Checklists	Annual Exercises Scheduled	Exercise 1 Scheduled Date	Date Performed	Exercise 2 Scheduled Date	Date Performed
300.01	Crisis Management Team Alert	2	01/09/03	01/09/03	07/17/03	07/17/03
300.05	Executive Management Team Alert	1	02/21/03	02/21/03	No Schedule	
300	C. M.T. Command Center Activation	2	01/09/03	01/09/03	07/17/03	07/17/03
310.10	Human Resources	2	03/14/03	03/14/03	09/19/03	Didn't Participate
310.15	Buildings/Facilities Management	2	03/14/03	03/14/03	09/19/03	09/26/03
310.20	Security	2	03/14/03	031/14/03	09/19/03	09/26/03
310.25	Legal	2	03/14/03	Didn't Participate	09/19/03	Didn't Participate
310.30	Communications	2	03/14/03	03/14/03	09/19/03	09/26/03
310.35	P. R./Corporate Communications	2	03/14/03	03/14/03	09/19/03	09/26/03
310.40	Transportation/Administration	2	03/14/03	03/14/03	09/19/03	09/26/03
310.45	Procurement/Purchasing	2	03/14/03	Didn't Participate	09/19/03	09/26/03
310.50	Finance	2	03/14/03	03/14/03	09/19/03	09/26/03
310.55	Audit	2	03/14/03	03/14/03	09/19/03	09/26/03
310.60	Risk Management/Insurance	2	03/14/03	03/14/03	09/19/03	09/26/03

Appendix – 10.08

SUMMARY

In summary, I hope I have provided a new thought or two on how a reader's organization can improve their Business Continuity Plan (BCP).

As I said in the Preface, I have found that the best Business Continuity Programs were those in which the organization's executive management has an active role to play. This "active" role, when documented, is what I call the Crisis Management Plan.

I have attempted to share with other BCP professionals how to work with their senior management by sharing how I have worked with the senior management of different organizations to get them to participate in the BCP (see Documenting).

I have attempted to stress the need to include the nonphysical crises during the project. They provide additional opportunities for the CP professional to deal with executives who comprise the Crisis Management Team. Most executives feel the organization can prevent disasters from occurring, but most executives have experienced a product (service) crisis or a public relations crisis.

I attempted to point out that the CEO, and other executives that comprise the Executive Management Team (EMT), play an important role during the Pre-Crisis Stage and the Post-Crisis State.

The focus of Chapters 4 through 10 Is on the members of the Crisis Management Team (CMT).

Throughout the book, I have used a number of examples I accumulated over the 30 plus years I have been in the business. My purpose was to make this book real, rather than a "blue sky" concept book. Hopefully, I have been able to accomplish this.

In conclusion, I believe this book will provide most BCP professionals numerous ideas that will assist them in incorporating the Crisis Management Plan into their organization's "Business Continuity Plan."

INDEX